Congress Overwhelmed

Congress Overwhelmed

The Decline in Congressional Capacity and Prospects for Reform

EDITED BY TIMOTHY M. LAPIRA,
LEE DRUTMAN, AND KEVIN R. KOSAR

The University of Chicago Press
Chicago and London

The University of Chicago Press, Chicago 60637
The University of Chicago Press, Ltd., London
© 2020 by The University of Chicago
Published 2020
Printed in the United States of America

29 28 27 26 25 24 23 22 21 20   1 2 3 4 5

ISBN-13: 978-0-226-70243-8 (cloth)
ISBN-13: 978-0-226-70257-5 (paper)
ISBN-13: 978-0-226-70260-5 (e-book)
DOI: https://doi.org/10.7208/chicago/9780226702605.001.0001

Library of Congress Cataloging-in-Publication Data

Names: LaPira, Timothy M., editor. | Drutman, Lee, 1976– editor. | Kosar, Kevin R., 1970– editor. | New America Foundation, host institution.
Title: Congress overwhelmed : the decline in congressional capacity and prospects for reform / edited by Timothy M. LaPira, Lee Drutman, and Kevin R. Kosar.
Description: Chicago ; London : University of Chicago Press, 2020. | Papers based on presentations at the State of Congressional Capacity conference, held at New America, March 1–2, 2018. | Includes bibliographical references and index.
Identifiers: LCCN 2020006467 | ISBN 9780226702438 (cloth) | ISBN 9780226702575 (paperback) | ISBN 9780226702605 (ebook)
Subjects: LCSH: United States. Congress—Congresses. | United States. Congress—Officials and employees—Congresses. | United States—Politics and government—Congresses. | LCGFT: Conference papers and proceedings.
Classification: LCC JK1021 .C5574 2020 | DDC 328.73—dc23
LC record available at https://lccn.loc.gov/2020006467

♾ This paper meets the requirements of ANSI/NISO Z39.48-1992 (Permanence of Paper).

Contents

Online appendixes are available
at https://dataverse.harvard.edu/dataverse/congressionalcapacity/.

Overwhelmed: An Introduction to Congress's Capacity Problem

TIMOTHY M. LAPIRA, LEE DRUTMAN,
AND KEVIN R. KOSAR

Congress is overwhelmed.

In this volume, leading scholars make the case that the United States Congress is overwhelmed because it has allowed its own capacity to atrophy. By *congressional capacity*, we mean the organizational resources, knowledge, expertise, time, space, and technology that are necessary for Congress to perform its constitutional role. Capacity is the human and physical infrastructure Congress needs to resolve public problems through legislating, budgeting, holding hearings, and conducting oversight. Without sufficient capacity, Congress can't properly lay and collect taxes, regulate commerce, raise an army and navy, or make all laws necessary and proper. And it certainly can't check and balance an executive branch to which it has delegated so much power. Whatever outcomes members of Congress wish to achieve, be they liberal or conservative, they can't achieve them without adequate capacity.

By all accounts, the capacity of Congress is in sorry shape. By whatever metric we use—days in session, hearings held, bills passed, budgets adopted, reauthorization of even the most popular and noncontroversial statutes—the Congress of today is grossly underperforming.

The typical critique is that Congress is paralyzed by the gridlock and polarization stemming from the mismatch between two-party majoritarian electoral politics and consensus-requiring supermajoritarian governing institutions (Krehbiel 1998; Binder 2003; Brady and Volden 2006; Mann and Ornstein 2012).

Indeed, partisan polarization deserves significant blame for Congress's dysfunction. But not all of Congress's problems stem inexorably from ideological differences. Since 1980, Congress as an institution has been steadily divesting itself of its own resources. Overall legislative staffing levels have declined.

Turnover has increased. Member and staff tenures have shrunk. Days in session have dropped. And in the increasingly rare days when members are actually in Washington, legislators must spend valuable time dialing for dollars rather than overseeing agencies, assessing program performance, investigating market failures, uncovering social problems, or studying the issues of the day that they were elected to resolve.

Demands on Congress have increased markedly as the scope of government has expanded. The complexity of policy has grown exponentially (B. Jones, Theriault, and Whyman 2019). The number of lobbyists and interest groups making demands on Congress has grown steadily (Schlozman, Verba, and Brady 2012). The constituent demands on Congress have grown dramatically (Neblo, Esterling, and Lazer 2018). Put simply, Congress is expected to do more and more, with less and less. Though the decline in resources is no doubt related to the centralization of congressional leadership that goes alongside polarization, it is not synonymous with either centralization or polarization.

The objective of this volume is to understand the causes and consequences of the changes in legislative capacity as they have coincided with other macro-level forces in American politics. To better think through how to make Congress less overwhelmed, we have to understand the intersection between organizational resources and institutional structure. Put another way, everything that Congress does is the work product of individual humans. Members and staff try to make sense of a complex world, but they are limited by their own knowledge and cognitive capabilities, the number of waking hours in a day, the demands placed on them, and the boundaries of the art of the possible.

The Legislative Branch Capacity Working Group and the Congressional Capacity Survey

This volume can trace its origins to a coffee meeting that two of its editors, Lee Drutman and Kevin Kosar, had in early 2016. Both were working in Washington, DC, think tanks; Drutman at the left-of-center New America, Kosar at the right-of-center R Street Institute. They were deeply concerned that Congress was a struggling institution, and they shared a similar diagnosis: its failures were self-imposed. By shortchanging its own internal resources for decades, Congress had effectively outsourced policymaking to the executive branch and to the thousands of lobbyists who have become the true keepers of expertise and policy know-how in Washington.

In May 2016, after a few months of planning, Drutman and Kosar launched the Legislative Branch Capacity Working Group, a joint, bipartisan project that has become the central forum for the many folks around Washington who care about our national legislature and want to improve it. The problem of a dysfunctional Congress is not a new one. But very few scholars were making an affirmative case for Congress to invest in itself, and even fewer were thinking about how it ought to do so even if the will was there. The third coeditor, Timothy LaPira—associate professor of political science at James Madison University—came to an early meeting. What if, he asked, we brought together the scholarly threads on questions of capacity into one big conversation? Thus was born the idea for the State of Congressional Capacity Conference, held at New America March 1–2, 2018. This volume is the result of the generous contributions and stimulating discussions from that meeting.

To encourage participation and improve our collective understanding of congressional capacity, the volume editors—along with Alexander Furnas from the University of Michigan and Alexander Hertel-Fernandez from Columbia University—designed and fielded the original 2017 Congressional Capacity Survey (CCS) and made the data available for contributors.[1] The study uses a mixed-methods approach to learn about the current state of legislative capacity. In the first stage, from February through June 2017, LaPira conducted semistructured interviews with more than fifty current senior staffers in Congress, plus about a dozen additional interviews with former members of Congress and senior staffers. These conversations were designed to uncover fresh insight into the daily work in Congress. The transcripts serve as original qualitative data to illuminate how Congress goes about its legislative business, but they also informed the subsequent questionnaire design. In the second stage of the study, the CCS team surveyed a random sample of more than four hundred current staff to find out more about their backgrounds, career paths and future plans, policy views, technical knowledge, substantive expertise, and job experiences. Nearly half the chapters in the volume use these original data.

Toward a Theory of Congressional Capacity

Going into the project, the version 1.0 theory of solving the congressional capacity problem had a just-add-water feel. If Congress would just beef up its own staff as it had prior to 1980, it could build expertise that would allow it to go toe-to-toe with the executive branch and K Street. Surely, if Congress could invest in robust policy shops—particularly in the committees, but also at the individual member level—it would stop letting the lobbyists write the bills and the bureaucrats dictate the budgets.

But this theory encountered two problems. First, few legislators in Congress wanted to pay for the water. And second, it soon became apparent not all parts of Congress would bloom even if watered.

Congress is a rare institution in that it can effectively decide its own budget. But the legislative branch appropriations subcommittee has long been a sleepy backwater in Congress. Few members are eager to take up the cause of trying to fix the least loved branch of government. It is not the place where ambitious lawmakers go to make their mark. It's a hard sell to convince colleagues to invest precious tax dollars in themselves. Single-minded seekers of reelection are understandably wary that constituents will accuse them of enriching themselves and wasting taxpayers' hard-earned money, especially in an increasingly anti-incumbent environment.

Long gone are the days of the die-hard institutionalists such as Mike Mansfield, Robert Byrd, Lee Hamilton, Robert LaFollette, and Bob Michel. Speakers Joseph Cannon and Thomas Reed are often thought to have been opportunistic power seekers and partisans, but they were also ardent protectors of institutional prerogatives. Few members of Congress today behave as *institutionalists*—individuals dedicated to upholding the rules, norms, and standard operating procedures for the sake of maintaining the organization. Unlike appointed bureaucrats or judges, Congress does not have an oversight committee to report to, so its priorities lie elsewhere. Members of Congress have reelections to pursue, funds to raise, party leaders to go-along-to-get-along with, and social media followers to court (Goldschmidt 2017). Give legislators more staff and they may well put those people to tasks other than policymaking and oversight, and rationally so.

Congress has delegated large portions of lawmaking to the executive branch through vague regulatory guidance with little oversight. It has all but capitulated its constitutional responsibility to declare war. It has been unable to enact budget resolutions and spending bills in accordance with the processes it created. At odds with the US constitutional separation-of-powers system, the national legislature too often behaves in a quasi-parliamentary fashion, ignoring executive branch excesses during periods of one-party government and treating the president as an illegitimate usurper during times of divided control. And it has divested in itself.

In January 2019, in an exceedingly rare moment of institutional introspection, the House of Representatives voted 418–12 to create the Select Committee on the Modernization of Congress (H. Res. 6). Split equally between majority Democrats and minority Republicans, the twelve-member committee, led by Chair Derek Kilmer (D-WA) and Vice Chair Tom Graves (R-GA), is charged with investigating congressional capacity, including staffing and compensation, information technology, and other administrative efficiencies. As this volume goes into production, the select committee is diligently investigating these problems, including soliciting advice and testimony from many of its contributors. Though we have every reason to expect the select committee to move the ball on congressional capacity, its extremely limited charge and original one-year authorization makes it unlikely to be able to solve the capacity decay that has been generations in the making.

In researching this project, we have talked to current and former members from both sides of the aisle who privately agree with our assessment but who also acknowledge the quixotic effort to sell it to constituents. We have met with dozens of congressional staffers whose enthusiasm for public service is boundless. And we have uncovered many creative ideas on how to improve a variety of basic functions in congressional offices that promise to be more productive than just adding water.

Members of Congress are frustrated with the status quo. They are retiring in record numbers, and not just because of the challenges of reelection. Too often the job is thankless and tiresome, and it offers few rewards after the initial status bump wears off. Many elected officials come in with great enthusiasm; most leave with intense frustration. They're trapped in an increasingly obsolete institution that doesn't work. And the one thing they could do to improve the situation—call a bipartisan truce and invest in the people's house—strikes such a fear of a primary challenge they're not even willing to contemplate it. So they remain trapped.

The challenge of reform is understanding this trap, both inside and outside Washington. We hope this volume is a first step in that direction.

Plan of the Book

The chapters that follow offer a guide to thinking about congressional capacity and the opportunities and challenges for such renewal. *Capacity* has different meanings in different contexts, just as the expectations for a "healthy" Congress are many. We expect lawmakers to have a variety of objectives and a legislature to be many things. To accomplish these objectives, Congress needs many kinds of capacity, as found in its human capital, in its internal organization (e.g., committee and leadership structures), in the rules it has for prioritizing and carrying out certain tasks and for binding itself from engaging in other tasks, in the legislative branch support agencies it uses to understand complex problems, and in the decisions members collectively make to allocate their time and attention.

The chapters ahead offer particular ways of assessing Congress's capacity in these particular areas. Some chapters provide historical context. Others assess the current decay and the ways in which the institution is managing (or failing) to cope. Collectively, they offer the most comprehensive, sophisticated appraisal of congressional capacity to date. But we hope they represent just the start of what may be a long-term, serious, and genuinely bipartisan effort to improve the first branch of US government. Ultimately, we look to the future, explore the prospects for reform, and suggest some practical recommendations on what it would take to get there.

The sixteen chapters that follow are organized into four parts. In part 1, contributors explore fundamental features of congressional capacity. Lee Drutman and Timothy LaPira (chapter 2) pose the abstract question "Capacity for what?" to juxtapose congressional capacity with other well-established features of legislative organization. Molly Reynolds (chapter 3) uses the well-known and recently expanded Vital Statistics on Congress to show general trends in how Congress has shifted its resources away from its legislative functions in Washington, and Philip Wallach (chapter 4) documents how Congress has failed to keep up with the growth of the administrative state.

In part 2, contributors dive into various aspects of political knowledge and policy expertise. The CCS collaborators (chapter 5) offer an overview of who staff are, their work, and their career paths. Kristina Miler (chapter 6) follows with an analysis of staff policy knowledge. Casey Burgat and Charles Hunt (chapter 7) reveal how committee staffers' experience systematically improves their legislative and oversight operations. Kevin Kosar (chapter 8) shows how legislative branch agencies have suffered from long-term cuts in their own capacity, yet still remain incredibly trusted sources of information on Capitol Hill.

Part 3 offers a more critical assessment of whether, or when, staff experience and knowledge have an impact on legislative performance. Peter Hanson (chapter 9) shows that despite the intense politicization of the appropriations process in the late twentieth and early twenty-first centuries, staff expertise is still key to making progress in Congress. James Wallner (chapter 10) offers a critical assessment of senators who fail to take advantage of the procedural tools they have available to them. Jonathan Lewallen, Sean Theriault, and Bryan Jones (chapter 11) show how information-processing capacity varies across committees, with some issues suffering from a decline in useful information and others not, suggesting that capacity decline is not uniform across the agenda. Using new data on legislative reauthorizations, Scott Adler, Stefani Langehennig, and Ryan Bell (chapter 12) suggest that the breakdown in congressional capacity may explain why Congress is failing to follow through on prior commitments to revisit program functions. Jess Crosson, Geoffrey Lorenz, Craig Volden, and Alan Wiseman (chapter 13) connect the legislative staff experience with members' lawmaking effectiveness, suggesting that experienced staff are most useful early in members' careers. James Curry and

Frances Lee (chapter 14) take seriously what congressional capacity means in an era of centralized, partisan legislative management, suggesting that simply going back to the way it was in previous generations would be counterproductive. To conclude part 3, Laurel Harbridge-Yong (chapter 15) investigates how institutional structures shape bipartisan relationships and, potentially, the institution's ability to achieve legislative success.

Part 4, comprising the final two chapters, takes a step back to consider prospects for reforming legislative capacity. Ruth Bloch Rubin (chapter 16) revisits earlier reform attempts to caution that the same partisan conflict that leads to policy gridlock may well lead to gridlock for reform efforts. But history suggests that optimists indeed have reason to hope that today's capacity problems set the stage for similar cross-partisan efforts we have witnessed in the past. Anthony Madonna and Ian Ostrander (chapter 17) offer a final assessment: that the electoral fears that cause members to flinch at spending more money on staff may be unfounded, as such minutiae as office budgets and compensation packages may not be salient enough to trigger a backlash.

For those inside Washington, who live and breathe the daily routines of Congress, we hope these chapters will add a broader perspective that moves beyond the reactive presentism that vacuums up all the attention in Washington. For fellow scholars, we hope this discussion can open up a new and fruitful line of research in the legislative studies field. Just as the study of congressional parties and ideological polarization has matured and flourished since the 1990s, we hope the contributions collected here will stimulate a rigorous, collective research agenda on legislative capacity that goes well beyond the version 1.0 just-add-water theory. For those who follow politics more casually, we hope this volume adds some nuance to the superficial "Congress is broken" diagnosis. All told, the theoretical and empirical breadth and scope these chapters collectively bring to bear on questions about congressional capacity represent the most comprehensive and diverse evidence-based analyses to date.

PART I

The Foundations of Congressional Capacity

Capacity for What? Legislative Capacity Regimes in Congress and the Possibilities for Reform

LEE DRUTMAN AND TIMOTHY M. LAPIRA

The United States Congress is widely derided as broken, dysfunctional, and failing to fulfill its constitutional role. Though Congress has never been an exceptionally popular institution in the American political tradition, its current standing, both by popular and by expert judgment, is abysmal.

Observers tend to offer two explanations for the current crisis of Congress.

The first, and primary, explanation blames the divisiveness and polarization of Congress. In this era of record-high partisan polarization, the Democratic and Republican Parties' voting records no longer overlap as they did before (Rohde 1991; Sinclair 1995; Poole and Rosenthal 1997; Theriault 2008, 2013; Lee 2009, 2016; Koger and Lebo 2017). A Congress organized into two disciplined partisan teams that refuse to compromise is a Congress that will produce very little meaningful legislation and very high rancor in a political system set up to make majority rule difficult.

The second, and less widely discussed, explanation focuses on knowledge and competence. The claim is that Congress lacks the basic knowledge resources to perform its legislative and oversight duties well. Individual members and their staff simply don't have the time and expertise to adequately understand the public problems they are attempting to resolve (Adler and Wilkerson 2012; Baumgartner and Jones 2015). As a result, Congress is left to rely on external sources of expertise, especially from executive branch staff whom they are supposed to check and balance (Aberbach 1990; Kiewiet and McCubbins 1991) and outside lobbyists who represent narrow, predominantly business, interests (Drutman 2015; LaPira and Thomas 2017). This dependence undermines the effective functioning and independent judgment of Congress and leads to policies that respond mostly to narrow and well-resourced interests, to the extent that Congress responds at all.

While it seems clear that Congress has moved too far in the direction of overly divided parties and inadequate internal resources, we note that earlier critiques of Congress claimed the opposite problems.

At the height of bipartisanship in the 1950s and 1960s, when the two parties were loose overlapping coalitions with little centralized direction, political scientists and reformers alike called for party leadership to exercise more centralized authority. They believed that clear and coherent majorities would bring much-needed order, and much-needed democratic accountability would follow (APSA 1950; Bolling 1965; Zelizer 2006).

In the late 1970s, when Congress was at the height of its expert-driven policy development, scholars and reformers began to complain that Congress had too much staffing. Staffers were operating as "unelected representatives," creating a deluge of information and proposals that were overwhelming Congress (Malbin 1980), or they were leading to member "enterprises" that were fracturing the coherence of Congress by allowing members to enjoy perpetual reelection through casework and pork-barrel politics (Salisbury and Shepsle 1981b; Cain, Ferejohn, and Fiorina 1987).

In other words, there has never been a truly golden era of congressional government. In every era, political scientists and reformers have looked at Congress as an institution and found it deficient in some respect or another. Every Congress has been dysfunctional in its own way.

In this chapter, our goal is to provide a new analytical framework to better assess normative claims about legislative politics across historical periods. Our analytical framework argues that although organizational structure is fundamental, resource allocation adds an important, orthogonal dimension. Together, it is the interaction of these two factors that determines the nature of congressional capacity.

To construct this framework, we start with the more well-known dimension: *the organizational structure dimension*. Broadly, congressional scholars have focused on a single dimension of organizational structure, centralized versus decentralized, most commonly operationalized as party-centered or committee-centered. Various theories explain why Congress has alternated between a centralized, party-based structure and a decentralized, committee-based structure (Polsby 1968, 2004; Cooper and Brady 1981; Brady and Volden 2006)—an understandable focus since different organizational structures lead to fundamentally different agendas, procedures, and outcomes.

Our contribution here is to add a second dimension: *the resource allocation dimension*. The basic intuition here is that people and their experiences matter because it is people, not organizational structures, that ultimately make decisions. Decision making depends not only on anticipated rewards and punishments but also on knowledge, experience, cognitive information-processing constraints, and norms. The range of possible solutions will depend on what people writing the laws know and what they have the resources to pursue. Accordingly, we classify resources as either *simple* or *complex*.

Rather than measure capacity in terms of more of "more" or "less," our approach creates a framework for examining specific types of capacities. Different interactions of structure and resource allocation will yield different legislative capacity *regimes*.

When we describe Congress as broken or dysfunctional, we often fail to provide a baseline standard. What is it that we expect Congress to do? To answer that question, we offer a normative framework.

We tend to measure things like legislative productivity and bipartisanship, as if these outputs were ends in themselves. In reality, they are means to broader ends. Analysts and pundits focus on them because, by historical standards, both of these outputs seem low. But what is the optimal amount of bipartisanship or legislative productivity for a legislature? Can there be too much? Too little? And what would we think of a bipartisan legislature that had record productivity in removing every health, safety, and labor protection statute on the books? Would we be satisfied with a Congress that was highly productive in undoing every anticorruption law?

Thus, as a way of evaluating Congress, we offer four criteria that we believe resonate broadly with both democratic theory in general and American republican tradition: *representativeness*, *responsiveness*, *deliberativeness*, and *oversight*.

The remainder of this chapter will proceed as follows. First, we will elaborate on these four evaluative criteria. Second, we will describe our two analytical dimensions of Congress—organizational structure and resource allocation—and explain how their interaction defines what we call *legislative capacity regimes*. Third, we will describe the regime types in greater detail, using historical examples, and evaluate how they perform on our four evaluative criteria. Finally, we will examine the prospects for change. Given that each of these regimes creates trade-offs and produces tensions, no regime is ever stable for the long term. Each regime highlights some criteria over others, and they all benefit some members of Congress and some societal interests at the expense of others. Thus, we'll conclude by examining the ways in which the current regime might fall apart and, based on our reading of the underlying historical cycles and trade-offs, what might follow (Cooper and Brady 1981; Schickler 2001; Pierson 2004).

Criteria for Evaluation

What should a legislature do? In a classic essay on legislatures, Nelson Polsby (1975) described them as "official, accountable, deliberative assemblies" (262) and argued that a "melange of characteristics—officiality, a claim of legitimacy based on links with the people, multi-memberedness, formal equality, collective decision making, deliberativeness—typifies and distinguishes legislatures in a wide variety of settings" (260).

The US Congress is one particular legislature among thousands of legislatures, operating at the local, national, and supranational levels. It sits within an unusual political system, distinguished by the unique combination of the separation of powers, federalism, and a two-party system. Compared with most political systems, American political parties have few formal powers, and individual members have more autonomy (Taylor et al. 2014). Thus any normative framework of the American legislature must combine broader normative goals of legislatures in general alongside the idiosyncratic conditions of the US Congress.

Here we judge the US Congress on the four following criteria, drawing from various normative theories of democracy:

> *Representativeness*: How well does Congress represent the diversity of interests in society and ensure their equal opportunities to influence in the policy process?
> *Responsiveness*: How congruent are congressional agenda priorities and the priorities of the public at large?
> *Deliberativeness*: Does Congress seek out and incorporate the best available information and reason through the causes and consequences of public problems?
> *Oversight*: How well does Congress monitor and evaluate the executive branch?

Our aim with these questions is not to reinvent the wheel but rather to catalog the many benchmarks political scientists and reformers use to evaluate how well or poorly a legislature is functioning. Let us now go through each of these criteria, in turn.

REPRESENTATIVENESS

Representation is an admittedly complicated concept, and there are many types of representation (see, e.g., Pitkin 1967; Mansbridge 2003, 2009; Urbinati 2006). We do not wish to get bogged down in a measure of perfect representation. The United States is a diverse country with a diverse economy, a diverse population, and a sprawling geography. As the country has grown, the diversity has only expanded.

Scholars from the late twentieth century onward have examined how well these diverse perspectives get represented in the legislative process (Mayhew 1974; Fenno 1978; Miler 2010). Do individual members come from diverse backgrounds? Do they make space for diverse perspectives even if they themselves do not personally represent those perspectives? Are they open-minded enough to recognize competing or underrepresented perspectives? Members can either represent perspective diversity themselves as direct advocates for differing positions or give voice to a diversity of perspectives through their actions.

When there is broader ideological and perspective diversity among individual members, when more diverse perspectives can participate through hearings and other mechanisms, we would describe Congress as more broadly representative. One challenge here is how much to weight descriptive representation. On its face, a Congress that looks more like the American people in terms of gender, race, class, or other social identities should result in a broader diversity of perspectives in the policy process. But if the policy process is narrowly controlled by a small clique of leaders and influential well-resourced interests, then descriptive representation may merely put a representative face on an unrepresentative policy process.

RESPONSIVENESS

A second feature of a legislature is its ability to prioritize and call attention to public problems. We call this *responsiveness*. A legislature should respond to public problems. In theory, a responsive legislature calls forth and attends to the most important public problems, prioritizing in a way that reflects the significance and urgency of the issues at hand (Kingdon 1984; Arnold 1990; Baumgartner and Jones 1993; Powell 2000).

Agenda setting has both a positive and a negative dimension (Bachrach and Baratz 1962; Cox and McCubbins 1993, 2005). It involves not only putting issues on the agenda but also keeping issues off the agenda. Agenda control involves both formal and informal powers, formal and informal resources. Members and interests are always competing to have their issues atop the agenda, while keeping the issues they oppose off the agenda.

Again, there is no single measure of agenda-setting quality, and as with representation, there is no expectation of perfect correspondence with the public at large. And as with representation, we can ask a similar question: Does the agenda of Congress broadly respond to the most urgent and pressing public problems that Congress has the authority and potential to resolve? Or does the agenda broadly represent the narrow concerns of a small and unrepresentative share of the population whose members happen to control certain levers of power?

DELIBERATIVENESS

A third expectation for a legislature is deliberation. A legislature should provide a space for reasoned deliberation about the merits of public policies. High-quality deliberation is informed and realistic, driven by the best available expertise, and open to alternatives. Low-quality deliberation is purposely ignorant, with predetermined positions that are immune to the force of the better argument and new information (Mansbridge 1980; Stone 1997; Guttman and Thompson 1998; Mucciaroni and Quirk 2006).

High-quality deliberation involves claims that are persuasive and credible and, more important, legislators who are at least receptive to being persuaded by credible claims. Genuine deliberation demands being willing to hear out the other side, to see the world from other perspectives, and to seek outcomes that will be as widely supported as possible.

Low-quality deliberation involves arguments where nobody is persuaded because persuasion is not the intent. Information is presented not to convince the other side but to justify and bolster the motivated reasoning of one's own side. Low-quality deliberation involves erroneous and debatable claims as well as high tolerance for specious analysis. In low-quality deliberation, both sides have not only their own opinions but also their own facts.

In Polsby's (1975) classic typology, a *transformative* legislature has the "independent capacity . . . to mold and transform proposals" (277), as opposed to being a mere *arena* in which the legislative outputs are perfectly predictable given the external policy inputs and some basic vote counting. Our evaluation of deliberation also needs to account for obstruction and other sources of friction that undermine it. Deliberation is important, but endless deliberation is crippling. Public problems demand a response, and if the legislature does not respond, other actors will, either in the private sector or in the executive branch.

However, Congress is the only institution in society that is set up to reconcile diverse perspectives and achieve a legitimating compromise solution. Thus, a key aspect of deliberation is building legitimacy for an outcome—if a wide range of groups are represented, and if there is a genuine deliberative process, we should expect a broad public to feel that the outcome is more legitimate. The outcome will also likely reflect a broader and thus more lasting agreement. Legislation that is enacted quickly without broad support is less stable, since its opponents may wish to undo it should they get into power again in the near future.

OVERSIGHT

Congress is not only a lawmaking institution. It also checks the power of the executive, which is a central function in the unusual separated-powers system of the United States. Moreover, even making laws is not a linear process. It requires reflection, careful monitoring, institutionalized feedback mechanisms, and the potential to recognize ineffective policy commitments as a matter of routine lawmaking. Under the US separated-powers system with an independent president, this typically means that Congress bears oversight responsibility for policy implementation (Arnold 1979; McCubbins and Schwartz 1984; Aberbach 1990; Carpenter 2001).

Congress accomplishes both forms of oversight through episodic, sometimes inquisitorial oversight hearings and through the more continuous budgetary and authorization process. The power of the purse over executive programs means that Congress can shut down dysfunctional or corrupt programs and boost effective programs. Congress also institutes automatic mechanisms such as sunset provisions to credibly commit future Congresses to evaluate program effectiveness.

We need to be careful here. Again, more doesn't automatically mean better. Programs and executive agencies that are functioning well may face undue interference in the guise of oversight, and politically motivated oversight and budget cutting may abuse the power of the purse more than it is constitutionally intended to check and balance the execution of law.

As with deliberation, the right balance is challenging. We may recognize legendarily good congressional investigations, which involved detailed, careful efforts (Watergate, Church Committee), as well as the legendarily bad investigations, which were sloppy and hyperpolitical (McCarthy's anticommunism hearings, Benghazi). But much lies in between. Ultimately, objective judgments about oversight have to be qualitative as well.

AN EVALUATIVE FRAMEWORK

All of these criteria can suffer from excess as well as absence. A legislature that was perfectly representative would have too much diversity to function. A legislature that deliberated too carefully would never get anything done, just as a legislature that was extremely efficient would almost certainly make mistakes in its haste. Too much oversight can be just as bad as too little oversight, since the executive branch needs some amount of bureaucratic autonomy to function well. Too much responsiveness to the whims of public problems runs the risk of excessive overcorrection and policy whiplash. A certain degree of policy stability is valuable as well.

Still, though these criteria create trade-offs, some capacity regimes strike a better balance than others. Certainly, Congress will never be everything we want it to be. But it can be more or less of what we want it to be, depending on organization structure and internal resources. But understanding even the best that Congress can be is not perfect, we aim to calibrate expectations in a way that produces more realistic judgments of the institution.

The Two Dimensions of Congressional Organization: Structure and Resources

Let us now turn to the two dimensions of congressional capacity—organizational structure and resource allocation—in a little more detail. For simplicity, we break both concepts into binary conditions, though we recognize that they exist on a continuum.

ORGANIZATIONAL STRUCTURE

The simple binary dimension here is centralized versus decentralized. This dimension has been thoroughly explored by political scientists.

In the *centralized* condition, a small group of party leaders controls the agenda of Congress. They determine when, how, and which bills come to the floor (Sinclair 1983, 1998; Cox and McCubbins 1993). They determine the content of the bills, with minimal input from rank-and-file members (Curry 2015; Lee 2015, 2016; see also chapter 14 in this volume). Voting tends to follow predictable patterns, primarily along a single (party) dimension (Poole and Rosenthal 1997; Theriault 2008). Coalitions are stable and tend to be rigid.

In the *decentralized* condition, leadership is much more ad hoc, and it varies on an issue-by-issue basis. Bargaining can happen along multiple dimensions, rendering party labels less useful in predicting votes. As a result, voting is less predictable, and coalitions are fluid and flexible. Party leaders have fewer formal and informal powers, while committee or even subcommittee chairs have more opportunities to develop leadership and power in narrow but frequently overlapping issue fiefdoms (Cooper and Brady 1981; Schickler 2000, 2001; Krehbiel 1991). Individual members play a much more important role as policy entrepreneurs who shape and drive their own voting coalitions for specific issues (R. Hall 1996; Wawro 2000; Adler and Wilkerson 2012; Bernhard and Sulkin 2018).

ORGANIZATIONAL RESOURCE ALLOCATION

The binary dimension here is simple versus complex. This concept represents more than mere counts of personnel and the size of office budget line items for information technology. It reflects the level of specialized knowledge and the ability of Congress to tackle complex problems. Certainly, we may expect that complex staff cost more, so budgets and head counts may be our best quantifiable measure of how Congress reveals its collective preferences for simplicity or complexity.

The concept here builds on Baumgartner and Jones's The *Politics of Information*, in which they describe "the tension between the desire for clarity and clear organizational rules and procedures and that of finding the proper fit with the environment and the problems the organization seeks to resolve" (Baumgartner and Jones 2015, 20). Organizing for simplicity is organizing for clarity and predictability; organizing for clarity narrows the range of considerations, but it does improve efficiency. Organizing for complexity means giving up some control to search for new solutions, wherever they may lead. It means being open to a wider range of alternatives, forsaking predictability, and trading off efficiency for adaptability.

To illustrate, consider two hypothetical congressional member offices.

In Office One, the primary objective of the member is predictability. The main task of staffers is to take party leadership talking points and turn them into press releases and constituent response letters for the individual member. The secondary task of staffers is to take legislative suggestions from campaign donors and introduce them as bills, then let the donors' lobbyists recruit cosponsors. The tasks are simple, easily learned on the job. The roles require minimal legislative process knowledge, virtually no substantive policy knowledge, few long-term relationship-building or personal connections in established peer networks. The ideal staffer avoids risk and defers to the status quo. Just about any fresh-out-of-college staffer could accomplish these tasks with minimal training. Even supervisors such as chiefs of staff and legislative directors' roles are straightforward—one does not need deep, institutional memory to achieve the member's goals.

In Office Two, the member of Congress is less concerned with following simple rules. The role of staff is to seek out unresolved public problems and to discover innovative new solutions. This requires considerable work, not only in identifying the problems and assembling the solutions but also in building the unusual coalitions necessary to carry bills through the legislative sausage-making machine. Staffing roles in this office are complex and redundant. There is differentiation in primary responsibilities, but there are few clear and discrete tasks. The work demands experience, ingenuity, and a high tolerance for risk seeking. Staffers in this office must have experience with the political process, know the jargon and historical minutiae of the specific policy, and have well-established, wide-ranging relationships in and out of the institution that are necessary to build supportive coalitions.

In Office One, the goal is to provide certainty and predictability. The tasks are clear, actionable, and categorical. There are few open questions because everyone knows what to do ahead of time. In Office Two, members recognize that the world is complex and relinquish expectations of predictability and certainty. They are comfortable delegating details, leaving much to broad, general goals. The tasks on any given day are more variable.

Legislative Capacity Regimes

Taken together, we can envision four ideal-type legislative capacity regimes under varying organization and resource allocation interactions. As illustrated in table 2.1, these types are *parochial patronage, adversarial clientelism, pluralist adhocracy*, and *consensual coalition*.

These are obviously ideal types. Both dimensions exist along a continuum, and most historical periods fall somewhere in between these ideal types or combine the elements of more than one in varying proportions. These ideal types are thus not meant as pure descriptors but rather as a way to help us consider the broader trade-offs of various institutional arrangements and the impossibility of ever "solving" Congress.

We also expect that these regime types will be reflected more purely in the House of Representatives than in the Senate because the simple majoritarian structure of the House allows for more wide-ranging rules changes over time. As a supermajoritarian institution, the Senate tends toward less dramatic changes, even though its internal organization also reflects the broader political currents.

TABLE 2.1. The legislative capacity regime schema

	Resource allocation	
Organizational structure	*Simple*	*Complex*
Decentralization	Parochial patronage	Pluralist adhocracy
Centralization	Adversarial clientelism	Consensual coalition

PAROCHIAL PATRONAGE

In a decentralized legislature with little ambition for solving big problems, we expect individual members or small minorities—such as state delegations, common-interest caucuses, identity groups, factions—to be relatively autonomous, each looking out for their own sustainers (e.g., constituents, donors). In such an arrangement, parties are weak. Members delegate relatively little authority to party leaders, preferring to control their own fiefdoms, often proliferated through autonomous committees, temporary commissions, or one-off task forces. They are happy to cooperate across party lines to achieve the efficiencies of logrolling, but only to the extent that doing so benefits local constituencies, particular industrial interests, or some other faction in society or the economy.

Under these conditions, members of Congress prioritize individualism, independence, and parochialism. To do so, they will employ personnel who are exclusively loyal to the member's individual legislative enterprise. Little expertise is required beyond knowing what the member's parochial constituencies' and political patrons' needs are. The overarching objective of the legislative enterprise is analogous to retailers' traditional customer relationship management mantra: the customer is always right (even when they're wrong). One does not need to know much more than to follow the analog political maxim: The donor or constituent group is always right.

The result will be a legislative body that is disorderly and unpredictable. But with high reelection rates, individual members have little reason to fix a system that isn't broken to them. At the extreme, these conditions will also implicitly encourage outright corruption, where highly independent members have incentives to personally obtain private benefits for themselves and their allied benefactors, often through private bills, highly specific earmarks, and other nonlegislative constituent favors. The legislator's enterprise is geared toward securing largesse for rent-seeking special interests.

Representativeness. Well-organized parochial interests can do quite well, but benefits are distributed unequally, usually to those who have the connections, resources, and political know-how to get what they want. Larger-scale public-minded interests or party-loyal—as opposed to *member*-loyal—groups fare poorly.

Responsiveness. Congress suffers from free riders, and the institution has little ability to agenda set. Congress does not act as a genuine national legislature.

Deliberativeness. There is no forum or reason for open discussion and debate, since individual members know their idiosyncratic patronage needs more than any of their colleagues, who themselves are their own best experts. There are few opportunities for introducing impartial expertise on general consequences of the legislature's actions, especially if the expertise reveals the ills of the system.

Oversight. Oversight is sporadic and done only to justify the extraction of rents for parochial interests. On issues where particular industries or constituents have a concern with a government agency, individual members can jump to respond, but lacking such demands, otherwise have no incentive to monitor and evaluate government programs.

In short, this is a Congress that performs poorly and fails on all objective evaluative metrics.

This ideal type is found in the disordered, corrupt Congresses of the 1880s that Woodrow Wilson railed against in *Congressional Government*—and for good reason. Some elements of this Congress reappeared in the late New Deal period as well, creating conditions for the Legislative Reorganization Act of 1946.

Of the four regime types, only one—parochial patronage—reflects a non- or deinstitutionalized arrangement, in which the institution is porous and unbounded by rigid, formal institutions and structures. The other three conditions all reflect particular versions of "institutionalization," each with their own set of bounded, complex organizational features. A full "deinstitutionalization" would reflect a return to the parochial patronage condition.

ADVERSARIAL CLIENTELISM

When party leaders prioritize resolving collective action problems by centralizing power yet still allocate resources for simple predictable purposes, Congress winds up in this second legislative capacity regime, adversarial clientelism. The hallmarks of such an arrangement are highly polarized parties with intense partisan teamsmanship. Each party represents a distinct coalition of interests, with minimal ideological overlap and little expectation of winning over the other side's groups.

We describe it as *adversarial clientelism* because we believe that this term captures the two primary elements of this arrangement. It is adversarial because it involves contested two-party competition. And it is clientelistic because both parties represent coalitions of groups that benefit exclusively from one or the other party in power. The parties collaborate with these groups to control both the agenda and policy outcomes, in exchange for electoral resources.

Under these conditions, Congress has limited need for its own independent expert staff. Party leaders delegate considerable authority to organized groups, which gladly subsidize lawmaker-allies (R. Hall and Deardorff 2006). Committees exist primarily to deliver the client groups' and partisan priorities, and they lack the genuine independence to produce compromises. Party leaders instead work out compromises among coalition groups and party donors. There is no need to develop new ideas. Under the sway of a clear and predictable ideological catechisms that define the membership of the coalition, the world appears as a much simpler place, with a clear "us" and a clear "them" (Bawn 1999).

Members outside of leadership have little ability to carve out their own individual brands and instead depend on national party brands. While their personal ambitions may be to do something grander than being a rank-and-file member, the realities of day-to-day lawmaking and campaigning don't allow for it. They staff their offices accordingly. Elections are referenda on the party in power, rather than individual members, leading to more wave elections and higher turnover.

Representativeness. Given the majoritarian nature of the two-party system, such a regime is only capable of collectively representing the groups who ex ante belong to the governing coalition. Individual legislators restrict their dyadic representation only to those who neatly fit party-aligned voter coalitions. Parties are simply coalitions' organized interests and ideological identities that commit to representing only the most active interest groups (Bawn et al. 2012; Krimmel 2017), especially if they underwrite their primary objective of winning the next election. And there's always a next election, so seeking out legislative solutions to social and economic problems is always secondary.

Responsiveness. Majority parties have a strong incentive to respond to broad public issues. However, because centralized leadership creates a bottleneck as it tries to limit the agenda to only issues that unify and benefit its side, many public problems never get a hearing.

Deliberativeness. When a few party leaders are making decisions based on prejustified conclusions, there is little space for deliberation. Moreover, without significant investment in complex resources, they have little access to information that might change their mind.

Oversight. If government is unified, there is little oversight. If government is divided, oversight is primarily intended to expose or manufacture scandal in the opposing party. The purpose is not to reflectively inquire about policy implementation but to reflexively undermine the opposing party's brand. Oversight is not objective inquiry. It's a performative spectacle.

While this regime often has strong appeal to individual members in its early stages, when individual members crave the order and predictability it promises, this regime quickly leads to a weakened Congress. When all policy most go through the bottleneck of leadership, Congress is limited in the range of public problems it can address that also gives the party a collective advantage in the next election contest.

The most notable episodes that approach the ideal type of the adversarial clientelism regime include the Gilded Age Congresses of 1890–1910 and the era from 1995 to the present.

PLURALIST ADHOCRACY

When authority is widely diffused and individual members and committees have access to considerable expertise, we have pluralist adhocracy. In this third legislative capacity regime, coalitions assemble issue by issue. Entrepreneurial members will be well positioned to achieve ambitious legislative outcomes, so they and their staff are motivated to put in the grueling work to develop ideas into successful, enduring government programs.

In this regime, party leadership is weak. Instead, committees and subcommittees balkanize into substantive policy domains, which include interested legislators, bureaucrats, external stakeholders, and other interested committees (Heclo 1978; Lowi 1979; Laumann and Knoke 1987; Browne 1990; Hansen 1991; Heaney 2004; Heinz et al. 1993). Because these areas are specialized, active participation will require some claim on expertise. Accordingly, members of Congress require expert staffs, who build relationships and develop, pass, and oversee policy over a long time frame.

Pluralist adhocracy creates an unpredictable environment, in which individual members must each carve out their own way. As a result, members create durable, flexible enterprises to support them. In such a Congress, individual member turnover will be relatively low because individual members can create unique personal brands that help with reelection. Electoral success depends less on party identity and more on the development of a personal vote. Low member turnover allows for more long-term policy thinking, though critics complain that consistently high incumbency reelection rates undermine accountability. In this more open policy environment, competing interests have opportunities to compete in a rough-and-tumble contest of ideas and interests, reflecting the group-based nature of American politics that mid-twentieth-century pluralist theorists favored (Truman 1951; Dahl 1961; Polsby 1963).

Representativeness. Broadly, this is the most substantively representative that Congress gets. In pluralist adhocracy, there is space for a wide variety of groups and interests to gain access and participate in the policymaking process, and enough staffing capacity and time for hearings so that many groups can present their perspectives on an equal footing.

Responsiveness. Pluralist adhocracy gives Congress the greatest capacity to deal with many issues at the same time, since there is no hierarchical partisan bottleneck. And assuming overlapping jurisdictions and active subcommittees, it is harder for any one committee to bottle up legislation.

Deliberativeness. This regime produces high-quality deliberation. Highly specialized experts are able to debate and discuss issues with multiple stakeholders. And since many issue domains operate outside of partisan constraints, individual members are more open to a range of perspectives and willing to consider alternative outcomes.

Oversight. Oversight under this regime is generally strong, for two reasons. First, members and staff who carefully craft laws are likely to have a strong interest in their implementation. Second, entrepreneurial members have space to pursue their ambitions in this regime, and oversight is one avenue for ambition.

From the outside, this regime often looks chaotic and disordered, and critics might complain that it often doesn't do much, simply "muddling through" by maintaining a status quo series of compromises among competing interests (Lindblom 1965). Over an extended period, individual members may feel frustrated by the lack of leadership and by the ways in which partisan majorities can be thwarted by semi-invisible interest groups (Bolling 1965; Zelizer 2006).

Historically, the closest Congress came to this ideal type was the 1970s, an era in which well-resourced committees and subcommittees dominated, and voting coalitions were at their most fluid. What may have appeared to be "all politics is local" was actually "all politics is ad hoc," which marginally benefited local and parochial interests as it produced broader public goods such as clean air and water, automobile safety regulations, and improved education resulting from free and reduced-cost lunches for hungry kids.

CONSENSUAL COALITION

When authority is centralized and resource allocation is complex, Congress will make decisions in a top-down manner, utilizing internal human resources that are oriented toward complex problem solving.

This capacity regime is the most unlikely. The most fitting episodes are those that appear during major threats, such as depression or war, in which unity emerges from the rally-around-the-flag effect when disparate interests share a common enemy. Congress will marshal its internal assets toward experts seeking to find consensus to resolve the problem. It will temporarily put aside other unrelated policy conflicts that differentiate the parties and factions. This capacity regime will prioritize interparty consensus, develop effective policies and programs, and justify their policies as responsive to common good principles. Concerns about party-affiliated interests or parochial constituent interests will matter much less. Because of the nature of these complex problems, Congress will prioritize investing specialized resources into understanding them. And the scale and importance of these problems will attract top talent.

Representativeness. In a strict sense, this regime represents the concerns of the American people well, since in moments of national crisis, the public orients around a single, shared concern: solving the crisis at hand. However, in a more literal sense, the centralized decision making is unlikely to be broadly representative.

Responsiveness. This regime is highly responsive to public problems, almost by definition. It exists only when there is broad public agreement over the most important problems, which it then prioritizes.

Deliberativeness. This regime is not deliberative, since by the very nature of the problem, it is oriented to move with speed. Under this regime, the perfect is seen as the enemy of the good. Congress under these circumstances prioritizes a rapid, unified response—perhaps simply rubber-stamping presidential demands—even if it is sure to result in unintended consequences and negative externalities.

Oversight. Oversight is mixed. On the one hand, the urgency and importance of the problems demand high oversight and create many opportunities
for ambitious politicians for career-making oversight (see, e.g., the Truman
Committee, aka the Senate Special Committee to Investigate the National
Defense Program, to investigate military waste and mismanagement). However, because of the scope and speed of national problems, Congress may give
considerable deference to the executive branch.

Since this regime depends on common-threat problems, it is highly unstable
(once the threat is resolved, the regime dissolves). And while it is responsive
to large-scale problems, it responds in a way that marginalizes other concerns
and limits dissent.

Congress during the Civil War was for all practical purposes a one-party
state, with one goal: reconstituting the Union. The same can be said for Congress during World War II. In the immediate aftermath of the 1941 Japanese
attack on Pearl Harbor, both parties were in lockstep—at least in public—
about presidential wartime authority, and they swiftly and dramatically increased defense spending and set into place strict economic regulations ra-
tioning the distribution of critical products. This consensus on nationalizing
economic activities is inconceivable outside the context of war, where parties
and ideologues will conflict the most on fundamental questions such as the
government's role in regulating markets. Of course, consensus policies are
not necessarily good policies. The internment of citizens of Japanese descent
was a wartime consensus that was ultimately rejected by a Supreme Court
that was not party to the capacity regime.

And, though this regime may be temporary, many of the programs developed under this consensus may endure as legacy projects. For example,
though the parties returned to their respective domestic policy corners after
World War II, the perpetual Cold War priorities compelled Congress to create ambitious programs such as "putting a man on the moon" or proliferating
nuclear power plants across the country.

OVERALL SCORECARD

At different times or depending on ideological commitments, the public may
assign different weights to these different criteria. Moreover, when in the
midst of any regime, it is always easier to see the shortcomings instead of the
advantages. The "focusing effect" cognitive bias suggests that members will
always see the grass as greener in some other, bygone era of congressional

TABLE 2.2. The legislative capacity regime scorecard

	Parochial patronage	Adversarial clientelism	Pluralist adhocracy	Consensual coalition
Representativeness	Narrow	Narrow	Broad	Broad
Responsiveness	Incongruent	Mixed	Congruent	Congruent
Deliberativeness	Weak	Weak	Strong	Weak
Oversight	Sporadic	Weak	Strong	Mixed
Historical examples	1880s, late New Deal period	Gilded Age, now	1970s	Civil War, World War II

capacity. As a result, reformers eye the deficiencies without understanding the ways in which they represent trade-offs. The most dangerous outcome would be if political reform advocates were so blind to their own preferred regime's deficiencies that they adopted institutions without fully anticipating the consequences of doing so. Our legislative capacity regime framework, summarized in the scorecard presented in table 2.2, offers a guide to identifying potential pitfalls in shifting from one regime to the other or to being so blind to existing faults that advocacy for reform is dismissed without merit.

To be sure, maximizing any one value at the extent of all others is ultimately destructive. To borrow from Bertrand Russell, "all movements go too far." As a result there is always some compelling reason to "reform Congress," to correct for some hypertrophy or other. Like navigating a car with a poorly responsive steering wheel, it's almost impossible to stay in the middle of the lane for long.

How Congressional Capacity Regimes Change

No magic wand will create a legislature capable of achieving the perfect mix of oversight and representativeness, deliberation and responsiveness. Congressional institutional arrangements often lumber along despite widespread criticism because individual members cannot agree on a better alternative or because upending "the way it is" feels too risky. Members' interests are complex and often themselves involve trade-offs among competing goals (Schickler 2001). But typically, when one goal is undermined over a long period of time, that becomes the most pressing problem to solve. And often, when member turnover is high (as it is, from time to time), new members less familiar with the existing order will be more attuned to its shortcomings and less likely to have mastered its ways to their own advantage (Dodd 1986).

As a result, no regime is stable over the long term. Each regime sows the seeds of its own destruction because the longer each regime goes on, the more its excesses and shortfalls become apparent, provoking widespread criticism. Moreover, as with any organizational regime that goes on for too long, winners and losers eventually emerge, and eventually the losers outnumber the winners and demand change. The process unfolds as an endogenous cycle of reform, with identifiable episodes in "political time" akin to business cycles in the economy that share common elements despite being separated by generations (Truman 1951; Skowronek 1982; Pierson 2004).

This story is a familiar one in the study of legislative organization. Broadly, however, our analysis suggests there are two independent cycles, one for each of the two dimensions.

THE CYCLE OF ORGANIZATIONAL STRUCTURE

Throughout history, Congress—and its respective chambers—has waxed and waned between periods predominantly structured by centralized party leaders (Polsby 1968; Dodd 1977, 1986; Aldrich 1995; Jenkins and Stewart 2018) or by relatively decentralized committees (Cooper 1970; Cooper and Brady 1981; Jenkins 1998; Adler 2002). After relatively long, stable periods under a centralized (decentralized) organization, election-minded and opportunistic members seek individual autonomy (efficient collective action; Polsby 2004). Figure 2.1 summarizes the periodic centrifugal and centripetal pressures members use to gain autonomy under more flattened power structures or the efficiencies of more hierarchical organization.

Congress first centralized in the 1890s, during a period of strong party leadership, which responded to member frustrations with the incoherence

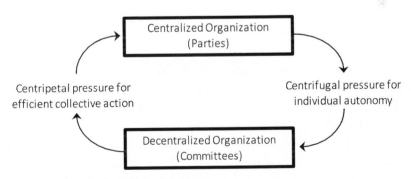

FIGURE 2.1. The cycle of organizational structure

and chaos of the existing arrangements. By 1910, members were chafing under the strong party leadership, and divisions within the majority Republican Party opened up to topple the centralized leadership, moving Congress back toward decentralized committee government. This period of committee government lasted until a sufficient mass of Democratic members of Congress empowered the party caucus and leadership in the 1970s to depose or circumvent conservative Southern committee leaders out of step with the party. Since then, Congress has moved toward a more partisan, leadership-driven, centralized institution, ushering a reinforcing cycle of increasing polarization.

At some point, it's possible that individual member demands for more independent authority will override concerns for party power. Still, one complication is that unlike the 1910s, when the dissident "progressives" united Democrats and Republicans against their established leadership, the dissenting factions of today are on the extreme ends of each party, sharing little in common with their cross-partisan rivals other than a shared dislike of centralized power. This situation suggests that for congressional reform to happen, extremists in one party would have to take control of the party in a way that allows a more moderate faction to unite with the other side.

THE CYCLE OF RESOURCE ALLOCATION

So just as Congress experiences periodic organizational cycles, so too will it undergo endogenous cycles of resource simplicity and resource complexity. Sometimes members have certainty and seek predictability on behalf of identified issues and groups. Other times, they recognize complexity and are willing to embrace it as part of the ambitious quest for transformative legislation. Figure 2.2 illustrates the cycle of competing pressures for ambition and certainty.

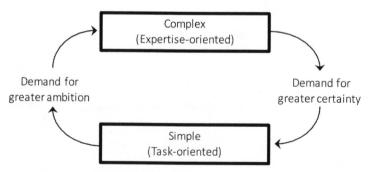

FIGURE 2.2. The cycle of resource allocation

The rise and decline of legislative resource allocation is captured well by what Baumgartner and Jones (2015) call the "Great Issue Expansion" from the early 1960s through the late 1970s. But the bubble burst, and since the 1980s, Congress has contracted its agenda, decreased the amount of time and energy it collectively dedicates to legislative operations, reduced the number and the scope of its investigations, and passed fewer bills (Lewallen, Theriault, and Jones 2016; Lewallen 2018). Scholars often point to the 1995 Gingrich era as the start of some new episode in American politics, but it is probably better understood as the codification and institutionalization of a decades-long trend toward prioritizing "message bills" over complex problem solving (Lee 2016).

Taken to its extreme, complex resource allocation leads individual members of Congress to be captives of their staffs, overwhelmed by the complex details worked out by enterprising networks of ambitious wonks. For example, in a recent memoir, Michael Pertschuk recalls his time as a staff director for the Commerce Committee in the 1970s, at the height of pluralist adhocracy. Committee chair Warren Magnuson was increasingly checked out, and drinking heavily, but if Pertschuk could get to him in the morning before the vodka took over, Magnuson would usually give him the thumbs-up on whatever consumer protection project he was pursuing (Pertschuk 2017).

When Newt Gingrich assumed the House speakership in 1995, he understood not only that long-standing expert committee staffers had their own long-standing agendas but also that they gave individual members of Congress independent power bases. Accordingly, he slashed committee staffing levels and weakened nonpartisan legislative support agencies. Congress has not yet recovered from the institutional brain drain.

Historically, Congress has increased its own internal resources to expand expertise at moments in which members collectively saw their prestige and power diminishing in comparison to the executive branch (1940s, 1970s) or felt overwhelmed by the crushing workload that they were ill equipped to manage (1940s).

CONSIDERING LINEAR AS WELL AS CIRCULAR TIME

Just as the criticisms of Congress have changed over time, the environment that Congress operates has changed over time considerably. Prior to the New Deal, the federal government had much less responsibility, and the president was therefore considerably less powerful. Since the New Deal, the presidency has taken on a more and more central role in American politics, as a source of both real and symbolic power. This change has obviously altered the role of Congress in the larger political system. Prior to the New Deal, if Congress didn't act, the states would. Now, if Congress doesn't act, the president does. To some extent, votes for Congress have always been a referendum on the popularity of the president. But now, that calculation weighs much larger, which has significant implications for how individual members of Congress operate—largely in the shadow of the presidency.

The increased centrality of presidential power has happened alongside the increased nationalization of everything else about American politics, which has also contributed to the polarization of politics, as both parties have shifted from federated networks of state and local parties to national messaging machines (Hopkins 2018). This shift has happened alongside a unique period in American political history, in which both parties are almost equally balanced at the national level, creating a hypercompetitive partisanship in which the balance of power is always up in the air, a condition that creates strong political incentives for negative partisanship (Lee 2015).

Additionally, as public policy has become more complex, not just the presidency but also the lobbying and interest group environment in Washington have become much thicker, representing the increased differentiation of interests in society, the increased stakes of public policy, and self-perpetuation of interests as the business of lobbying continues to supply its own demand (Drutman 2015).

All of these developments have fundamentally changed the environment in which Congress operates, leading some critics to wonder whether an institution like Congress is now but a "relic" (Howell and Moe 2016). But, again, criticisms of a dysfunctional Congress are as old as Congress itself. In every era, our national legislature struggles to muddle through. The world changes, and Congress adapts. In every era, the distinct legislative regimes manifest themselves in distinct ways.

By historical standards, party leadership has never been more centralized, and complaints from rank-and-file members are high. Simultaneously, complaints about Congress's failures and overwhelming office workload resemble (in volume and quality) those that the 1945 Joint Committee on the Organization of Congress unearthed during its investigations, which led to the Legislative Reorganization Act of 1946 (Galloway 1946; Stid 2017). Members of Congress run for office at great personal expense, only to land in a role where there's little meaningful work to do other than kowtow to party leaders' admonitions to go along and dial for dollars. Their frustration has the potential to create a groundswell for change.

But while individual members might naturally demand more autonomy, they also need to recognize that without added capacity, decentralization could turn Congress into a very parochial institution. Thus, the biggest danger is that if there is a revolt against party leadership and the organizational structure shifts from centralized to decentralized, Congress would wind up in the parochial patronage regime, given the current pattern of resource allocation. This would be the worst of all conditions and could undermine Congress's role in the constitutional system altogether.

Conclusion: Capacity for What?

When we ask questions about congressional capacity, we frequently speak of Congress's capacity to solve public problems or fulfill its constitutional duties. In this chapter, we've pushed beyond this broad definition and attempted to be more specific about what it is, exactly, that we want Congress to accomplish as an institution. In short, we ask: "Capacity for what?"

We have argued that congressional capacity involves the interaction of congressional organizational structure and resource allocation. Congressional authority can be either centralized or decentralized. Resource allocation can be either simple (task-oriented) or complex (goal-oriented). The combinations of these collective choices yield particular legislative capacity regimes. Our analysis does not prescribe the solution for designing the perfect institutions, but it does offer a road map for thinking through the costs and benefits of adopting some arrangements over others. We can never have a Congress that "does it all"—no wonder the public is always dissatisfied with congressional performance. There is always a legitimate critique out there.

Ultimately, the institutional arrangements of Congress are what members collectively want them to be, though institutional leadership obviously plays a role in recognizing deficiencies and offering solutions. The majority of the time, few members give much thought to the functioning of the institution as a whole. Mostly they complain about the problems that seem most salient to them and then worry about pursuing their own immediate goals of getting reelected and advancing their policy and career ambitions. But at certain moments, enough members' personal goals line up with congressional regime change. In these moments, reforms happen.

Every regime is unstable in the long range. Congressional reform is inevitable, but which reforms are adopted and when is unpredictable. We hope that by recognizing trade-offs, future reformers both inside and outside the institution can be more intentional. As they make decisions that affect congressional capacity, we hope that they will also ask, "Capacity for what?"

The Decline in Congressional Capacity

MOLLY E. REYNOLDS

The business of Congress has become huge, complicated, and technical.

The information available to Congress today is overwhelming. Less certain is whether Congress can readily access the information it needs, when it needs it, and in the form that will expedite and abet meeting its policy making and oversight responsibilities.[1]

Nearly forty years separate these two quotations. More than twenty-five have passed since the latter was included as part of a set of proposals for the United States Congress to consider during a major reorganization effort in 1992–93. The House of Representatives has recently turned its attention to institutional reform once again, creating special committees to look at reforming the budget and appropriations process (in 2018) and modernizing the House more generally (in 2019). This work follows in the footsteps of several significant twentieth-century internal efforts at reforming Congress; each of these reform attempts examined whether Congress has sufficient capacity to meet the nation's challenges. In 1945, the first Joint Committee on the Organization of Congress (JCOC) was formed; it produced the Legislative Reorganization Act of 1946, which reduced the number of committees and laid the groundwork for increasing staff levels. A subsequent JCOC in 1965–66 provided the foundation for the Legislative Reorganization Act of 1970, which increased the transparency of the committee process and permitted recorded roll call votes in the Committee of the Whole House. Other efforts continued throughout the 1970s, including the Congressional Budget Act of 1974; the Bolling Committee (1973–74), the Obey Commission (1976–77), and the Patterson Committee (1979–80) in the House; and the Culver Commission (1975–76) and Stevenson Committee (1976–77) in the Senate (Brudnick 2014; Deering and Smith 1997; Schickler 2001; Zelizer 2004).[2]

The specific concerns that gave rise to each of these efforts, and of congressional observers at the time of their work, have varied. In 1941, one scholar—who would surely be shocked to watch a modern-day hearing featuring an administration witness—noted, "Congressional staffing might well be more expert than it is, but to make it too expert might create difficulty. If, for example, the Committee on Banking and Currency had an economic adviser who would brief committee members to criticize proposals coming from the Treasury and frame cross examination for the Treasury's witnesses, experts would be pitted against experts" (Rogers 1941, 21–22).

Attempts to increase Congress's capacity, moreover, have generated their own challenges. After a period of significant growth in staff levels, for example, several scholars in the late 1970s and early 1980s highlighted the increased role of staff in the policymaking process and its potential consequences, both positive and negative, for the quality of legislative deliberation (H. Fox and Hammond 1977; Malbin 1980).

In asking questions, then, about the resources the current Congress has to fulfill its responsibilities, we join nearly a century of voices. In one sense, capacity is difficult to measure. We cannot know for certain, for example, whether a given member of Congress has all of the knowledge necessary to make the "right" decision on a vote, or even whether that information was knowable at the time, without asking him. Even if we were to ask him, moreover, he might be apt to report sufficient expertise, even if an outside observer would disagree. To document the decline in capacity, then, I will rely on a set of *correlates of capacity*—that is, observable features of the institution that should be associated with its ability to function well. We can never be sure that a House member has internalized the contents of a Congressional Budget Office (CBO) score, for example, but we do know that an understaffed Congressional Budget Office is likely to have more difficulty producing that estimate.

Here, I will highlight three correlates of capacity, all of which are primarily concerned with the second dimension of capacity (organizational resource allocation) identified by Lee Drutman and Timothy LaPira in chapter 2: personnel, financial resources, and expertise and information. Together, they provide the foundation necessary for Congress to carry out its varied responsibilities, including, but not limited to, solving policy problems through legislation, exercising the power of the purse, and engaging in meaningful oversight of the executive branch. Concern about Congress's ability to carry out these duties may not be new, but as we will see in this chapter, recent trends should heighten our interest.

Much of the focus on capacity and its decline in this volume and elsewhere rightly emphasizes nonpartisan sources of information and expertise. But, as Drutman and LaPira note in their discussion of the first dimension of capacity (organizational structure), the underlying form of congressional organization matters for its institutional capacity. Here, I will argue that because the contemporary Congress is organized in a centralized, partisan way, and because the importance of those parties has shown no signs of receding, we would be naive to ignore changes over time in the party-based institutions that can provide members with the resources they need to do the work of the nation—and have done so. In addition, the trends over time in these correlates of capacity cannot be considered in isolation from broader changes in Congress's underlying atmosphere. To understand the effect of declining capacity, we must also examine the workload that Congress is being expected to tackle with the resources it has. Within the institution, legislative support agencies are being asked to do more, while outside the institution, the overall policymaking environment has become more complex.

Personnel

There are several ways to track congressional staff levels over time, but they send a similar message: there are fewer people serving on congressional staffs than in the late 1970s.[3] In the House, this decline has been more dramatic. In 1979, there were between approximately 8,500 and 9,000 total staff working in House personal and committee offices. Staff levels grew by roughly 5 to 8 percent in the House, peaking in the late 1980s and early 1990s. Since then, the total number of staff has generally fallen, and by 2015, had declined to between approximately 7,200 and 7,900. Throughout this period, the ratio of personal staff to committee staff has been skewed consistently in favor of the former, but that relationship has also changed over time. In 1979, there were roughly 3.5 times as many personal staffers as committee personnel in the House; in 2015, it stood at approximately five personal office staff members for every committee employee. (At its peak during the first few years of the twenty-first century, the ratio came closer to 6:1).[4]

Staff levels in the Senate, meanwhile, have been more consistent. According to *Vital Statistics on Congress*, total Senate committee and personal office employment was roughly the same in 1979 and 2015 (roughly 5,000 versus approximately 4,900). The number of individuals working in personal offices was actually greater (approximately 3,900) in 2015 than in 1979 (roughly 3,600), but is down from its peak at about 4,400 in 1997 (Brookings Institution 2019, Table 5-1). Committee staff levels, meanwhile, have also declined over the last several decades; this includes a decline between 2011 and 2015, during which total Senate committee employment declined by roughly 10 percent.[5]

An important exception to this trend is the growth over the same period in leadership office staff. The number of staff working in House leadership offices grew approximately 285 percent between 1977 and 2016. The Senate saw a similar change, with leadership staff increasing by 263 percent over the same period

(Chausow, Petersen, and Wilhelm 2016a, 2016b).[6] This growth has not been monotonic—leadership staff levels peaked in the House in 2011 and in the Senate in 2012—but the overall trend reflects an increasingly centralized legislative process that is coordinated out of leadership offices (Rohde 1991; Sinclair 2016).

While dramatic, we should not automatically associate this precipitous growth in leadership staff levels as a signal that Congress in underinvesting in capacity. When analysts at the Congressional Research Service (CRS), at the request of the four cochairs of the 1992 JCOC, prepared a briefing book on congressional organization, one option they discussed was "creat[ing] a policy corps for party leaders" that would provide the necessary information to pursue a coordinated policy agenda.[7] As analysis by Frances Lee makes clear, however, the growth in leadership staff levels has been accompanied by a significant increase in the share of those staff doing communications work. Prior to 1977, none of the employees in Senate leadership offices were primarily responsible for public relations. By 2015, nearly half of the Senate's leadership staffers were doing communications work. Similarly, in the House, the share of staff in leadership offices handling public relations grew from less than 10 percent in the late 1970s to approximately 30 percent by 2015 (Lee 2016). Congressional leaders have clearly chosen to invest increased resources not in the kind of expertise that helps *make* policy but in the kind that helps sell it to the public.

A shift in the distribution of staff members away from policy- and legislative-focused functions has also happened among rank-and-file members. Legislators in both chambers allocate a greater share of their staff to their state and district offices now than in the late 1970s; in the House, the proportion of district-based staff grew to approximately 47 percent in 2016 from roughly 35 percent in 1979; the share of House staff outside of Washington, DC, peaked at just over 50 percent in 2004 and 2005 (Brookings Institution 2019, Table 5-3). The Senate saw a similar change. About 24 percent Senate staff worked in state offices in 1979, but by 2016, that figure had grown to approximately 43 percent (Brookings Institution 2019, Table 5-4). These non-DC-based staff tend to be caseworkers, constituent service representatives, grants coordinators, field representatives, and community outreach specialists. While assisting constituents with an increasingly complex federal bureaucracy is an important part of a representative's job, we would not generally consider these functions as enhancing Congress's capacity to legislate.

Financial Resources

The number and types of staff employed by members of Congress is not just a function of their individual choices about how to invest their resources.

Developing capacity in personal offices is constrained by the budgets allocated to each office for staff pay and benefits. In the House, each member receives a Members' Representational Allowance (MRA) that can be used to
pay for personnel, official office expenses, and official mail. The Senate's analogous mechanism for allocating funds to individual members is the Senators'
Official Personnel and Office Expense Account (SOPOEA). These current
approaches—which date to fiscal year 1996 in the House and fiscal year 1989
in the Senate—were the culmination of efforts in both chambers to provide
increased flexibility for members in how they expended their resources (for
House, see Committee on House Administration 2012; for Senate, see Brudnick 2016c).

The overall value of these allocations, however, has fluctuated over time.
Figure 3.1 displays the total appropriation for the MRA and the SOPOEA (and
their approximately analogous predecessor accounts in the House) for each
year since 1991 in constant 2016 dollars.[8] In the House, we see that the MRA
stagnated beginning in the early 1990s before growing again in real terms
throughout the first decade of the twenty-first century. An especially large
increase—approximately 15 percent when using the constant dollar figures
reflected in figure 3.1—came between 2001 and 2002. According to reports
at the time, the increase was meant to address "what appear[ed] to be a disproportionately high turnover rate among House staffers . . . [and] concerns
about losing employees to the executive branch" (Wallison 2001) at the start
of the George W. Bush administration. MRA levels then peaked in real terms
fiscal year 2010, before suffering a roughly 10 percent cut in fiscal year 2011,
and have continued to decline in real terms since then. In the Senate, meanwhile, individual office allocations experienced approximately steady growth
through fiscal year 2010 and have generally declined in constant dollar terms
since fiscal year 2011 as well.

Not only has this overall level of spending fallen in real terms, but Congress also has made conscious choices that restrict the ability of representatives and senators to build capacity with the resources they are given. In the
House, the number of permanent employees that a House office can employ
with its MRA has been fixed at eighteen since 1975; four additional "other than
permanent" employees have been permitted since 1979 (Brudnick 2016a). The
budget constraint imposed by the MRA can also limit offices' ability to carry
the maximum number of permissible staff at competitive pay rates; as one
senior House committee staffer described it when asked why he or she was
filling only about two-thirds of the potential positions, "it's literally budget, it
really is" (Drutman et al. 2017a, Interview 15). As policy problems have gotten more complex, therefore, House members have not been able to enlarge

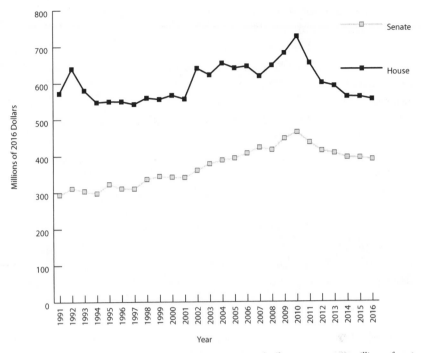

FIGURE 3.1. Total appropriations for House and Senate personal offices, 1991–2016, in millions of 2016 dollars

Note: For the House, all data are from Justification of the Budget Estimates submitted to the House Legislative Branch Appropriations Subcommittee. Data prior to 1996 include the line items for Clerk Hire, Official Expenses, and Mail. For the Senate, data for 1991–2003 and 2011–2016 are from the reports accompanying the Legislative Branch Appropriations bill; data for 2004–2010 are from annual Congressional Research Service (CRS) reports on the Legislative Branch Appropriations bill. Generally, figures include subsequent rescissions if reported by CRS.

their staffs in response. In both chambers, meanwhile, the maximum staff salary in members' personal offices has declined in real terms over time. In the House, the maximum allowable salary for a personal staff member (measured in 2016 dollars) was roughly $190,400 in fiscal year 2001, but only $168,400 in fiscal year 2016—a 12 percent decline. The Senate saw a similar change, from $190,500 in fiscal year 2001 in real terms to $169,500 in fiscal year 2016.[9]

Analyses suggest that this decline (in inflation-adjusted terms) in overall resources is reflected in the salaries of individual congressional staffers. In fiscal year 2001, for example, the average chief of staff in a House office earned approximately $134,000 in 2016 dollars, but by fiscal year 2015, that figure had fallen to roughly $97,000. The same holds true for staffers lower down the office hierarchy, with the average staff assistant earning, on average, $32,000 in 2016 dollars in 2001 versus $25,000 in fiscal year 2015 (*CQ Magazine* 2017).

Similar trends have been on display in the Senate. The average salary for a Senate chief of staff declined by roughly $12,500 in real 2016 dollars between fiscal year 2001 and 2015; for staff assistants, the average salary fell from approximately $42,000 to roughly $39,000 over the same time period (Petersen and Chausow 2016b). When congressional staffers have credible outside options from lobbying shops, law firms, corporations, and other well-resourced interest groups, it becomes difficult to retain them and their expertise in Capitol Hill offices (Blanes i Vidal, Draca, and Fons-Rosen 2012; LaPira and Thomas 2017; McCrain 2018).

While members have an interest in offering competitive salaries in order to keep high-quality staff on their payrolls, some legislators choose to leave some of their office allocations unspent. Tracking the share of members who do not spend all of the funds allocated to them over time is difficult, in part because the underlying data from the House of Representatives has only been available in machine-readable digital form since fiscal year 2016 and remains unavailable from the Senate.[10] From the CRS information displayed in table 3.1, we can see that, while most members use nearly all of the funds allocated to them, some share do not; in 2011, for example, an estimated 21 percent of members spent less than 90 percent of the funds allocated to them, while in 2013, approximately 7 percent did. This practice is not new. Prior to the transition to the MRA, one 1992 analysis by *USA Today* identified a number of members spending under their full allotment—including one legislator, Rep. Andrew Jacobs (D-IN), who spent only 49 percent of his allocation (Schwin 1992). Members of both parties regularly issue press releases touting the fact that, in the words of Rep. Betsy Markey (D-CO), "they are doing more with less" (*Fort Collins Coloradan* 2010) or that, to quote Rep. Mike Turner (R-OH), they are "tightening their belts" (Turner 2012). Media reports also document this behavior. One *Politico* report indicates, for example, that, in 2009 and 2010, Senator Daniel Akaka (D-HI) returned a full 34 percent of his office

TABLE 3.1. Distribution of spending as a percentage of authorization (by percentage of members)

Year	< 60	60–65	65–70	70–75	75–80	80–85	85–90	90–95	95–100
2005	0.2	0.0	0.0	0.7	1.6	3.9	9.7	21.4	62.4
2011	0.0	0.0	0.7	0.2	2.1	5.6	12.8	24.0	54.7
2012	0.0	0.0	0.2	0.7	1.6	3.1	11.3	21.6	61.5
2013	0.0	0.0	0.2	0.0	0.7	1.4	4.4	17.5	75.7
2014	0.0	0.2	0.2	0.2	0.0	3.5	7.0	21.9	66.9
2015	0.0	0.0	0.5	0.0	0.2	0.5	6.5	17.6	74.7

Note: Data for 2005 from Brudnick 2009, Table 4. Data for 2011–2015 from [Brudnick] 2017, Table 3.

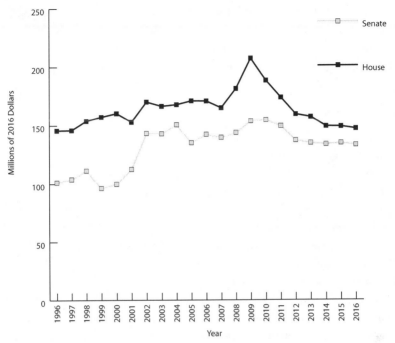

FIGURE 3.2. House and Senate committee funding levels, 1996–2016
Note: For the House, all data are from Justification of the Budget Estimates submitted to the House Legislative Branch Appropriations Subcommittee. For the Senate, all data for 1996–2003 and 2011–2016 are
from the reports accompanying the Legislative Branch Appropriations bill. Senate data for 2004–2010 are
from annual Congressional Research Service reports on the Legislative Branch Appropriations bill. Data
for the House include the House Appropriations Committee; data for the Senate exclude the Senate Appropriations Committee.

allocation, while Senator Jim Risch (R-ID) sent back approximately 25 percent (Wong 2012). Congressional staff are also aware of this phenomenon
and the incentives it creates. As one senior House personal office staffer explained, "it's actually now a talking point for members when they go home . . .
we have Democrats who do that religiously" (Drutman et al. 2017a, Interview
18). Together with the data in table 3.1, this information suggests that as long a
contingent of representatives perceive the return of available funds to the US
Treasury as something for which credit can be claimed, the notion of increasing office budgets as a way to build capacity may meet significant resistance.

Data on the allocation of resources to committees in both chambers also
suggest that resources have become scarcer. Figure 3.2 contains information
on funding for staff provided to all House and Senate committees from fiscal year 1996 to 2016.[11] In the House, we see moderate growth between fiscal

year 1996 and 2007, a significant increase between fiscal year 2007 and 2009, and a period of decline and stagnation in real terms since then. In the Senate, meanwhile, we saw a more dramatic increase between fiscal year 1996 and 2004, followed by slow growth through fiscal year 2010, and an approximately 14 percent decline between fiscal year 2010 and 2016.

Expertise and Information

Congressional capacity does not only reside in member-controlled settings; support agencies within the legislative branch also provide representatives and senators with information and expertise that aid in the policymaking process in important ways. Currently, there are three principal legislative support agencies. The CBO, created in 1974, provides nonpartisan, objective analysis of budgetary and economic issues, including cost estimates of individual pieces of legislation under consideration. The CRS, whose history dates to the creation of a special reference unit within the Library of Congress in 1914, supplies members with research material on a wide range of issues on Congress's agenda throughout the legislative process. The Government Accountability Office (GAO), founded in 1921, assists Congress in fulfilling its oversight responsibilities through investigations and reports on the implementation of federal programs.

When we examine trends over time in the staff and funding levels of each of these agencies, we see evidence that each has, to varying degrees, suffered a decline in its capacity. Figure 3.3 depicts the staff and budget levels at the CBO between fiscal year 1980 and 2016. Total employment is slightly higher in fiscal year 2016 than in fiscal year 1980 but is below both a 1980s high-water mark and a more recent maximum level of 250 in fiscal year 2010. The agency's funding, meanwhile, generally grew in real terms through fiscal year 2011 but saw a roughly 8 percent cut between fiscal year 2011 and 2012 from which it has not fully recovered.

Examining CRS and GAO, however, makes clear that CBO fared the best of the three support agencies in the period from 1980 to 2016. Figure 3.4 displays the same data for CRS, which has seen a relatively consistent decline in staff levels since the 1980s. The agency's budget generally grew in real terms through the middle of the first decade of the twenty-first century, though it did see occasional cuts in inflation-adjusted terms, including a 2.5 percent reduction after Republicans took control of the House in 1994. Like CBO, however, CRS has seen a decline in funding in real terms from a peak in fiscal year 2010. GAO, for which data appear in figure 3.5, has suffered the most significantly. Unlike the other two agencies, it has experienced few extended

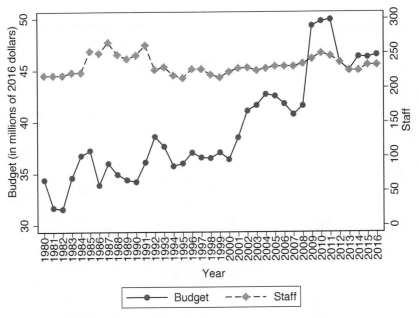

FIGURE 3.3. CBO staff and funding levels, 1980–2016

Note: Congressional Budget Office (CBO) staff levels are from the annual Justification of the Budget Estimates submitted to the House Legislative Branch Appropriations Subcommittee. Budget data for 1980–1996 are from Dwyer et al. 1996, Table 3. Budget data for years since 1996 are from annual Congressional Research Service reports accompanying the Legislative Branch Appropriations bill.

periods of consistent growth in either staff or funding levels since the early 1990s, including an approximately 18 percent reduction (in real terms) in its budget after Republicans took control of Congress in 1994.

Not displayed graphically is the Office of Technology Assessment (OTA), which, in a particularly notable choice to undermine expert capacity on Capitol Hill, was defunded entirely in 1995. Eliminating the OTA, which provided Congress with analysis of emerging science and technology issues, allowed the new Republican congressional majority to claim credit for eliminating an entire agency that it saw as too slow and duplicative (Keiper 2004–5). Notably, some Democrats, including Senator Harry Reid (D-NV), also favored eliminating the OTA, calling it a "luxury" whose work "can be done by other agencies" ("Congress Cuts Legislative Funds" 1996).

Beyond these changes in legislative support agencies, we have seen important changes to party organizations in Congress that have affected members' access to expertise and information. Take, for example, the decline of the Democratic Study Group (DSG), which had formed in the late 1950s

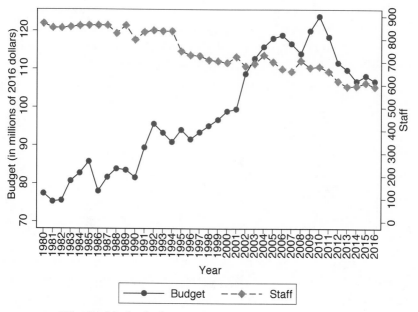

FIGURE 3.4. CRS staff and funding levels, 1980–2016

Note: Congressional Research Service (CRS) staff levels are from Brookings Institution 2019, Table 5-8, except for 2016 staff figures, which are from the 2017 Justification of the Budget Estimates submitted to the House Legislative Branch Appropriations Subcommittee. Budget data for 1980–1996 are from Dwyer et al. 1996, Table 3. Budget data for years since 1996 are from annual CRS reports accompanying the Legislative Branch Appropriations bill.

to represent the interests of liberal members of the House Democratic Caucus. By the early 1980s, however, the group had transformed from a policy-oriented group into a legislative services organization. This transition was driven in part by the fact that liberal members had accomplished many of the legislative goals that brought them together originally. Legislators' needs, then, had shifted to focus more on "'better information on legislation and proposed amendments'" (Bloch Rubin 2017, 257). The DSG was largely successful in transitioning to a primarily research-focused organization, providing information such as fact sheets and summaries of the views of interest groups and federal agencies on key legislation. By 1988, all but six Democratic House members—and twenty-four of their Republican colleagues—were DSG subscribers (Zelizer 2015). Following the Republican takeover of the House, however, Speaker Newt Gingrich eliminated congressional funding for all legislative service organizations—of which the DSG was one—leaving the group without the financial resources to continue (Bloch Rubin 2017; Zelizer 2015). Although the DSG's underlying orientation was partisan, its ability to provide high-quality research to members was significant, and its demise is consistent with the broader undermining of information resources in the chamber.

The DSG's closest Republican analog—the Republican Study Committee (RSC)—has also evolved over time, though in a somewhat different way. The RSC was founded in 1973 with a staff structure explicitly modeled after that of the DSG, with eleven researchers and subject matter experts whose job was to provide information to conservative House members that would help them coordinate both policy and procedural strategy. Although it still provides legislative analyses to its members, the fact that its membership comprises approximately two-thirds of the House Republican conference means that it is less of an "ideological rallying point" for the party's conservative wing (Wallner 2017, 270). Staffers recognize its potential value as a source of information, but mainly in an ideological context. As one senior House Republican staffer described it, "I would love it if there were more staffers [with] say [the] RSC, or [a] similar organization[,] to share our ideological, philosophical view of things and can really dive deep on" (Drutman et al. 2017a, Interview 29) certain policy issues. This description illustrates a key challenge of developing internal institutions that provide expertise in the contemporary Congress, as the demand for information is often filtered through an ideological lens.

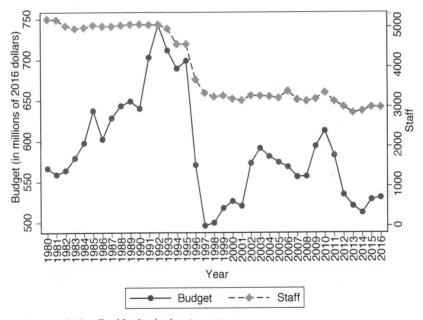

FIGURE 3.5. GAO staff and funding levels, 1980–2016

Note: Government Accounting Office (GAO) staff levels are from Brookings Institution 2019, Table 5-8, except for 2016 staff figures, which are from the 2017 Justification of the Budget Estimates submitted to the House Legislative Branch Appropriations Subcommittee. Budget data for 1980–1996 are from Dwyer et al. 1996, Table 3. Budget data for years since 1996 are from annual Congressional Research Service reports accompanying the Legislative Branch Appropriations bill.

Changes in the informational environment outside Congress also have implications for the provision of expertise. Since the 1970s, the number of think tanks operating in the United States has grown significantly, with many of the new players taking on ideological orientations (Rich 2005). The difficulty, driven in part by the pay dynamics described earlier, in retaining staff for long tenures has, in the words of one senior House staffer, "given outside experts, probably a larger voice than they've had in the past, because we just don't have the bandwidth to handle it . . . I think it has also expanded the role of think tanks" (Drutman et al. 2017a, Interview 1). In addition, staff also seek out these outside organizations to help advance particular goals, including to counter other sources of expertise; one senior House Republican staffer, for example, described how "we need those outside guys as well to come and critique the CBO scores" (Drutman et al. 2017a, Interview 29). The growth of the think tank sector, then, has likely ameliorated some of the challenges created by the decline in internal expertise, but not without creating new issues of its own.

Relative to What? The Changing Congressional Environment

The trends in personnel, funding, and expertise presented in this chapter all tell a consistent story. That account becomes even starker, however, when we put them in context by considering the changes in the broader congressional environment over the same period. Consider, for example, changes in Congress's workload. As Sarah Binder has documented, the number of salient legislative issues on the congressional agenda has generally increased since the 1980s, and markedly so in the twenty-first century. This change is likely driven, in part, by increasing gridlock: when an issue is not addressed in one Congress, it remains on the docket the following year (Binder 2016).

If Congress has more work to do, we would expect it to rely more heavily on congressional support agencies. Many such offices do not release systematic data over time on their workload, but even snapshots indicate that that changes in staffing may not be keeping up with the demand from congressional offices. In the 97th Congress (1981–82), the Office of the Senate Legislative Counsel—the entity responsible for providing committees and individual members with drafting services—received 9,221 requests for legislative drafts. By the 113th Congress (2013–14), the office prepared 50,698 requests—an increase of approximately 450 percent. Over roughly the same period, the staff of the office grew, but by a much smaller magnitude (from twenty-one employees in 1981 to forty-three in 2012—an increase of only about 100 percent to handle the 450 percent increase in work volume).[12]

Congress has also occasionally given legislative support entities new responsibilities, but it has not necessarily provided all of the resources needed to meet those demands in a timely fashion. Take, for example, the passage of the Unfunded Mandates Reform Act in 1995. Among the law's requirements was that the CBO would provide analyses indicating whether pending legislation would impose mandates on state, local, and tribal governments and, if they did, what those requirements would cost. In the first year the law was in effect, CBO provided roughly 1,400 mandate cost statements, which took an estimated twenty-four work-years of staff time. Existing resources, however, only allowed for thirteen additional staff positions. As CBO director June O'Neill explained in 1997, "The number of analytic studies we provided to the Congress last year was sharply reduced. Part of the slowdown in the production of programmatic analyses was the result of diverting analysts from doing in-depth analysis of various budget issues to the more immediate requirements of work on unfunded mandates."[13]

Even when Congress has successfully responded to new capacity challenges, it does not necessarily take the steps necessary to maintain that capacity. Another example from the CBO is illustrative. In 2008, as the development of what would eventually become the Affordable Care Act began in earnest, CBO "became concerned that it did not have sufficient resources to analyze policy changes regarding health care delivery and financing that were emerging as a critical issue in the Congress" (Committee on Appropriations 2010, 329; see also Starr 2011). Congress approved an increase in CBO's authorized staff levels of approximately twenty positions over two years, but following overall cuts in discretionary spending beginning in 2011, CBO's staff levels fell (K. Hall 2016). The agency's workload, however, did not. Figure 3.6 tracks the ratio of cost estimates produced to full-time CBO employees (the bottom line) and to Budget Analysis division staff (those most responsible for producing cost estimates) from fiscal year 1990 to 2016, and although that ratio fluctuated over time, it has generally increased under both measures since 2011.

There is also evidence of increasing workloads in member offices, especially in terms of responding to constituent communication; between 2002 and 2011, House offices reported a 158 percent increase in mail volume, while Senate offices indicated a 548 percent increase (Congressional Management Foundation 2011). In addition to evidence of increasing workloads, there are also indications that the task of policymaking has become more complex over time. Some of this increased complexity is due to changes in the external environment, including technological and economic change. As Drutman and Teles have put it, if one would consider "almost any subject matter—finance, medicine, any technology—and think what it would take to have an informed opinion about it now, as opposed to in 1980. . . . To legislate intelligently on any

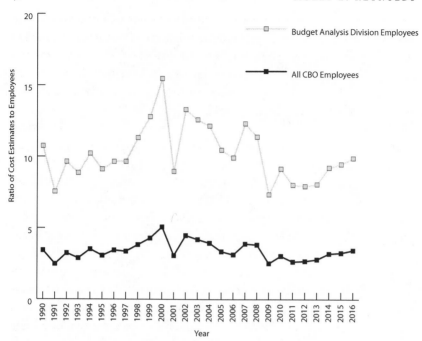

FIGURE 3.6. Ratio of CBO cost estimates produced to CBO employees, 1990–2016

Note: Data for Congressional Budget Office (CBO) cost estimates and numbers of employees are from the annual Justification of the Budget Estimates submitted to the House Legislative Branch Appropriations Subcommittee and include full-time and other than full-time permanent staff. For 1990–1992, cost estimates include federal bill cost estimates. For 1993–2010, cost estimates include appropriations bills and other federal bill cost estimates. For 2011–2016, cost estimates include formal cost estimates and score-keeping tabulations.

subject—or even to intelligently consume policy analysis—requires considerably more information and conceptual sophistication than it did at the dawn of the Reagan administration" (Drutman and Teles 2015a). Congress has also taken to writing longer, more complicated laws, in part because building the support of a sufficient majority to pass them has become difficult in increasingly polarized times (Drutman 2015). As one previously quoted senior House staffer pointed out, "the U.S. Code has gotten incredibly complex itself, it's really tough reading bills and comparing it" (Drutman et al. 2017a, Interview 29). Adding complexity to the underlying policy environment increases members' need for staff and informational capacity, making its decline more notable.

Conclusion

Other chapters in this volume will address in greater detail the causes, consequences, and potential remedies for the decline in congressional capacity. But a brief overview of some major explanations that emerge from the discussion of the major trends outlined in this chapter is useful. First, it is worth noting that, while the overall trend displayed here is one of decline in the correlates of capacity, particularly in the 2010s, there are notable exceptions. The example of CBO's successful efforts to enhance its health-specific capacity after 2008 in anticipation of greater attention to health care issues—borne out by the development and passage of the Affordable Care Act in 2010—illustrates this dynamic well. With the right alignment of political incentives, then, capacity can be not only dismantled but also built up.

Indeed, political incentives and motivations have driven much of the change in congressional capacity in recent decades. In some cases, these are intraparty politics. The changing ideological alignment among House Democrats, for example, helped drive the growth of the DSG as a source of information within—and beyond—the party caucus. More generally, as power became centralized in the hands of leaders of more homogeneous parties, especially in the House, staff capacity logically followed. The choice by members to allocate more of their staff resources to their state and district offices is also a rational outgrowth of a policymaking process in which party leaders have centralized more power.

In other instances, the political drivers of capacity change involve conflicts between the parties within Congress. Efforts to reduce legislative support agency staff in the mid-1990s were driven, in part, by Republicans' partisan goal of reducing the size of government after they retook control of Congress following the 1994 elections. Trends in funding levels—decline in some cases and stagnation in others—can be attributed, in part, to the more restrictive budget environment that has represented a major source of conflict between the parties since the 2010 elections and the passage of the Budget Control Act in 2011. Still other explanations rest with political dynamics between the branches of government. In another example of political incentives driving a potential increase in capacity, the decision to increase significantly House MRA levels in 2001 was motivated partially by a desire to keep staff members on the congressional payroll when they might otherwise leave for jobs in a new Republican administration. Finally, in other circumstances, broader changes in the political environment have led to changes in capacity. The growth of communications positions among leadership staff, for example, follows from an increasing emphasis on messaging over legislating as part of an effort to maintain or regain majority status in an increasingly competitive political environment.

As we (and, increasingly, interested members on Capitol Hill) consider remedies for the decline of congressional capacity—whether they be targeted at member offices, committees, party leaders, legislative support agencies, or elsewhere—it is important to keep these political dynamics in mind. As many legislative scholars have argued in reference to legislative procedures, choices about what happens with Congress's rules are rarely questions of principle but rather of politics. The same likely holds true for questions of capacity.

How Congress Fell Behind the Executive Branch

PHILIP A. WALLACH

Grover Norquist once famously declared that he hoped to shrink government to the point where he could "drown it in the bathtub." When one looks out across the vast expanse of the federal government's activities today, one wonders what kind of canyon-sized bathtub he had in mind. Not counting the Postal Service, the central government of the United States has more than two million civilian employees and currently spends roughly $4 trillion every year—that's four million *million*, or roughly one-fifth of the product of the world's largest economy (Carter et al. 2006; Chantrill, n.d.; Norquist quoted in Liasson 2001). It is difficult to even contemplate the sprawling and complex reality underlying such figures, let alone fully master it.

And yet, the US Constitution charges the nation's first branch of government, Congress, with the tasks of structuring, directing, overseeing, and paying for the work of the federal government. Just 535 members of Congress, with about 20,000 staff working to support them, must contend with their counterparts in the executive branch, whose numbers are several orders of magnitude greater than their own and whose permanence and institutional memories tend to be far superior.

Things were not always thus. When the First Congress convened in New York City in 1789, the executive departments carried over from the government under the Articles of Confederation could indeed be squeezed into, if not a bathtub, at least a medium-sized swimming pool. John Jay ran the office of foreign affairs out of his law office, and Henry Knox ran the War Department out of "rented rooms at a Water Street tavern" (Bordewich 2016, 29). Not surprisingly, the representatives of the new government quickly set about expanding the executive branch, including creating the first three executive departments (State, War, and Treasury) and establishing a system of customs collectors and port officials capable of enforcing a revenue-raising tariff. Still, in the early years of the republic, members of Congress probably felt that understanding and overseeing the work of the small executive branch was among the least of their challenges.

This chapter offers a brief account of how the executive branch of those humble beginnings grew so expansive relative to the legislature. Executive empowerment has, predominantly, been driven by decisions made by Congress itself, though a grasping presidency arrogating new powers to the executive, especially in wartime, has also made lasting contributions. The divergence in capacity has been unevenly paced and not entirely unidirectional; at times, Congress has treated its own relative institutional diminishment as a problem to be reckoned with and recovered some ground. I offer a chronological descriptive account of executive branch growth relative to the legislature in three parts: (1) the Constitution's first century, during which time the federal government grew steadily but remained small and geographically decentralized by modern standards, such that Congress could fairly reckon itself coequal; (2) the period encompassing the Progressive Era and the two world wars, during which Congress caused the central government to grow exponentially, especially in terms of personnel, while seeing to its own development considerably less; and (3) the post–World War II record of a federal government that has developed increasingly complex ways of expanding its reach without expanding its workforce, overseen by a Congress that at first seemed determined to master the executive branch but that since the late twentieth century has allowed itself to stagnate.

Throughout, I employ some fairly crude metrics to quantify the relationship between the legislative and executive branches, such as the ratio of the number of employees in the two branches. I do not mean to suggest that these metrics can, in themselves, fairly summarize the entirety of what passes between Congress and our scores of executive branch agencies. But I do mean to put the arithmetic of congressional-executive relations front and center because doing so throws into stark relief the basic challenges confronting a generalist legislature attempting to oversee a vast, shape-shifting network of specialized executive organs. Since the early twentieth century, critics of Congress have argued that it is, by its nature, a premodern body ill-suited to the complexities of modern life. I reject this view as misunderstanding Congress's basic constitutional role, which is deliberative and political rather than managerial. Still, it is important to understand just how much more difficult a task Congress (to say nothing of the citizenry at large) faces today when it seeks to survey and understand the federal government's activities, and the crude metrics forcefully communicate this difficulty.

Steady Executive Branch Growth, 1800–1880

Alexander Hamilton famously worked to build an energetic executive branch during his tenure as Treasury secretary in New York, establishing a pattern of elite staffing for core departments that would last for decades (Carpenter 2005a). By the end of John Adams's administration, the federal government had moved to Washington and its executive branch had grown considerably. The federal government comprised roughly 3,000 officers in 1801 (including a newly created Department of the Navy), although just 150 were located in the new capital (Mashaw 2012, 55). Although President Thomas Jefferson famously espoused a minimal role for the federal government, in practice he made choices that necessitated building executive branch capacity, including fighting the Barbary pirates and consummating the Louisiana Purchase. Most ambitiously, he also successfully pushed Congress to pass the Embargo Act of 1807, which required a sprawling administrative system to suppress foreign trade. Under President James Madison, the necessity of fighting a major war led to a major expansion of the federal government, the budget of which quadrupled between 1811 and 1815. Peace brought a decrease in spending, but total expenditures remained at levels significantly higher than those that prevailed before the war (Carter et al. 2006, Series Ea585). This ratchet effect of wars is a major theme in the history of executive branch expansion: wartime buildups are somewhat reduced after the conflict has ended, but never all the way back down to their previous levels (Higgs 1987).

Throughout this period, members of Congress remained largely without professional staff. There was, however, one built-in mechanism for expanding legislative capacity that we sometimes forget about today, which is that the House of Representatives automatically grew with the nation's population. From 65 representatives in 1789, the House grew to 141 members by 1803 and to 213 by 1821. The Senate, meanwhile, grew from its original 26 members to 48 in 1821, reflecting the admission of eleven new states during that time. (Such automatic growth continued all the way into the twentieth century, until the Apportionment Act of 1911 capped the members of the House at 435.)

This growing Congress was charged with overseeing a very different kind of federal workforce than the one we are used to thinking of today. As illustrated in figure 4.1, the US Post Office was far and away the largest part of the federal establishment; with upward of three-quarters of all federal government workers in its employ during the first part of the nineteenth century, it was instrumental to early nation-building (John 1998). (It would not be until World War I that nonpostal federal employees outnumbered postal employees.) Monitoring the activities of federal officers throughout the nation,

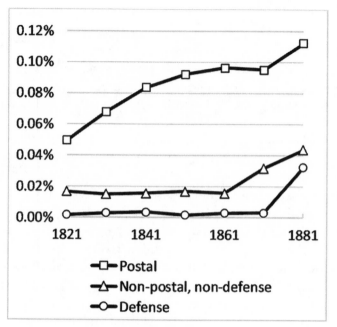

FIGURE 4.1. Percentage of Americans employed in federal executive branch, 1821–1881
Sources: Carter et al. 2006, Series Ea894, Ea898, Ea899, Ea900; decennial US Census.

including postal workers as well as land agents, federal marshals, and excise
tax collectors, was considerably complicated by limitations of communications
and transportation technologies, which required some creativity in creating
proper incentives. Congress responded in several ways: by creating administrative hierarchies, by requiring officials to post bonds that would be forfeited if
they neglected their duties or face criminal fines, or by conditioning compensation on a system of commissions (Mashaw 2012, 55–62; Parrillo 2013).

By modern standards, then, the federal government in the early nineteenth century was a loose and improvisational affair. Lines of responsibility
were not well established, and the sheer logistical challenge of creating nationwide networks capable of extending the federal government's reach was
immense. Congress could and did pick its spots to intervene in this development, encouraging experimentation with some accountability mechanisms
(including a great many congressional reporting requirements) and steering
away from others.

One decisive step Congress took to ensure that bureaucratic positions
would not become the private fiefdoms of gentlemen officeholders was the
Tenure of Office Act of 1820, which limited many officers' terms to four years,

at which point they would need to be reappointed. That legislation was meant to ensure that Congress had a periodic say, but it even more empowered the president, who would have the responsibility to fill vacancies. President Andrew Jackson seized on this opportunity to institute the infamous spoils system, in which presidential supporters would be given federal offices as a matter of course and would be expected to donate some of their salaries to the political party that brought them into government. This arrangement made parties the center of government power and stood against extensive specialization of the bureaucracy. If "jobs" were to be mastered by normal party regulars, they would need to stay relatively simple, and by nature that made them more legible to the generalists in Congress. Through the age of Jackson up until the Civil War, Congress molded a growing administrative apparatus more varied and active than is often remembered, including a sub-Treasury system that shaped American banking, an extensive regulatory system for steamboats, and an expanded patent system (Mashaw 2012, 147–226). These developments notwithstanding, the organization of the executive branch remained relatively simple until the proliferation of new bodies late in the nineteenth century, generally facilitating easy congressional oversight.

The onset of the Civil War accelerated the growth of the federal government in a way no previous challenge had done. Federal spending in 1861 was $63 million; in 1862 it jumped to $475 million; and by 1865 had soared all the way to $1.3 billion. Most of this added expenditure (a good part of which was certainly attributable to wartime inflation) went toward the massive war effort, and, naturally, much of it ceased after the war. But once again there was a ratchet effect, with spending levels never returning all the way to their antebellum levels. The central government's importance was also irreversibly increased; while there were just 2,199 federal employees in the Washington area in 1861, in 1871 that figure had jumped to 6,222 (Carter et al. 2006, Series Ea896). Among nonpostal executive branch employees, the workforce as a whole skyrocketed from fewer than 10,000 before the war to nearly 40,000 by 1876 (see figure 4.2). A good part of this workforce was devoted to serving Union veterans and their families after the war; as Theda Skocpol famously argued, Civil War pensions maintained throughout the second half of the nineteenth century were a pathbreaking first chapter in building the nation's federal welfare programs (Skocpol 1995).

Reconstruction is generally regarded as a period of strong congressional government and weak presidents, and this balance of power was the result of a struggle in the wake of President Abraham Lincoln's assassination between his Republican allies in Congress and his Democratic successor, President Andrew Johnson. Johnson envisioned a restoration of Jacksonian-style

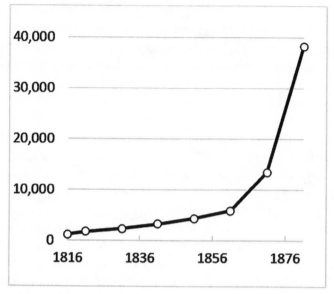

FIGURE 4.2. Nonpostal executive branch employees, 1816–1881
Source: Carter et al. 2006, Series Ea894, Ea900.

government, but Congress bridled at this idea and instead acted to ensure its own primacy. Most important, it passed a new Tenure of Office Act in 1867 that claimed for the Senate the effective right to override the president's decision to fire officials. This disagreement, which led to Johnson's impeachment by the House and near conviction in the Senate, was, at bottom, about which branch could expect to control the growing bureaucracy. Although neither side scored a decisive victory, Congress succeeded in establishing the principle that the president was not to treat the executive branch as a playground for patronage, as well as in largely establishing the legislature as "the only legitimate representative of the people" (Whittington 1999, 132). In addressing the Republican convention in 1868, soon-to-be president Ulysses Grant assured his listeners that he saw the president as "a purely administrative officer" (Whittington 1999, 139). In terms of staff capacity, Congress kept pace with the executive branch in the decades following the war, beginning to supply its members with paid staff (see figure 4.3).

Rapid Buildup of Administrative Capacity, 1880s–1945

Though Congress may have mostly painted the presidency into a corner for the last decades of the nineteenth century, it also took actions during this period to build the administrative state we are familiar with today, or at least to make a start. It did so in response to a period of rapid economic and technological change, and with a self-conscious sense that it needed to rely on professionalized expertise it could not build internally. First Theodore Roosevelt and then even more Woodrow Wilson and Franklin Roosevelt would build on these foundations to forever transform the federal government. They did so with willing partners in Congress, but eventually the executive branch's accumulation of power sparked a significant backlash from a legislative branch that feared it had gone too far in its own marginalization.

A necessary condition for the transformation of the federal government was the professionalization of the American bureaucracy, against the wishes of some members of Congress who were happy to see patronage continue as long as it was controlled by them. Flowing out of the clash between President Johnson and his Republican adversaries, a movement advocating removal of federal offices from the vagaries of political electioneering gained strength in the 1870s. It was galvanized by the assassination of President James Garfield by Charles Guiteau, a frustrated (and deranged) would-be patronage recipient, and it culminated in the Pendleton Act of 1883, which created a merit-based

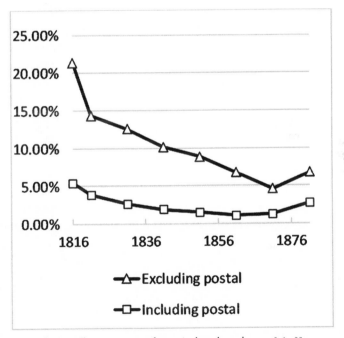

FIGURE 4.3. Legislative staff as a percentage of executive branch employees, 1816–1881
Source: Carter et al. 2006, Series Ea894, Ea900, Ea902.

Civil Service Commission. Over time, federal employees under the merit system would develop a reputation for nonpartisan policy expertise; they would
also develop their own professional interests and even unions—explicitly authorized by Congress in the Lloyd-LaFollette Act of 1912, which additionally
ensured that bureaucrats could communicate directly with Congress rather
than only through their superiors in the executive branch (Skowronek 1982).

By cultivating an explicitly nonpolitical bureaucracy, progressives in Congress set the pattern of relations between the legislative and executive branches
with which we are familiar today, in which Congress empowers bureaucrats
who command technical expertise and professional credibility to pursue
policy goals. Overwhelmingly, the rationale for this delegation is efficiency:
agencies are thought better capable of pursuing optimal policy in a complex
and dynamic economy. At the same time, Congress never simply gives agencies carte blanche to pursue optimal policy but rather holds them accountable
to (politically fluid) standards reflecting the values of the public and stands
ready to act against agencies if they misuse their authority or fail in their
charges.[1]

As Daniel Carpenter describes it, this process, while complex, produced
fairly rational results. The Department of Agriculture and the Post Office demonstrated their competence in practice—as well as developing networks of
elite support that included key members of Congress—and were rewarded by
Congress with enlarged mandates. The Department of the Interior showed
itself to be an irresponsible steward of money and power transferred to it
in the Reclamation Act of 1902 and subsequently found itself penned in and
subjected to congressional appropriations by the Reclamation Extension Act
of 1914 (Carpenter 2005b).

Carpenter is undoubtedly correct that Congress generally acted for coherent reasons when it decided where to empower and where to constrain
the federal governments' growing bureaucracies. Nevertheless, when we survey the full range of government expansion from the late nineteenth century
through World War II, the sheer volume of activity should make us wonder
just how carefully Congress was able to calibrate its choices as time went by.
In other words, we should see Congress as acting intentionally and often even
attentively as it grew the executive branch—but we should wonder (as later
Congresses did) whether the cumulative result of these choices was a government that Congress found itself incapable of holding accountable.

Expansion came in several distinct forms. First, as Carpenter highlights,
much expansion involved building up the work of bureaus within existing
cabinet agencies, such as the Bureau of Chemistry (later renamed the Food and
Drug Administration) in the US Department of Agriculture. Second, Congress

chose to set up independent bodies, often of a quasi-judicial nature, to decide thorny economic questions, beginning with the Interstate Commerce Commission (1887) and continuing with the Federal Reserve System (1913), Federal Trade Commission (1914), Federal Power Commission (1920), Federal Radio Commission (1926) and its successor Federal Communications Commission (1934), Securities and Exchange Commission (1934), and National Labor Relations Board (1937), among others. These featured independent boards (whose members, once appointed, could only be removed for cause) with representation of both political parties, in hopes of elevating regulatory choices above politics. Third, Congress also experimented with a variety of semigovernmental "public authorities," which often had some characteristics of private corporations and some of governmental entities. These included everything from the Isthmian Canal Commission (which oversaw the Panama Canal; 1899) to the Federal Land Banks (1916), War Finance Corporation (1918), Reconstruction Finance Corporation (1932), Tennessee Valley Authority (1933), Federal Deposit Insurance Corporation (1933), and Rural Electrification Administration (1936), among many others.

As the dates in the previous paragraph indicate, many of these new boards and corporations were wartime innovations—or they were products of the Great Depression, which President Franklin Roosevelt said, in his first inaugural address, needed be confronted "as we would treat the emergency of a war" (Roosevelt 1933). American involvement in World War I permanently changed the nation's understanding of its federal government's potential. Unsurprisingly, there was a massive ramp-up of spending: federal expenditures in 1916 were roughly $713 million but shot up precipitously, hitting nearly $2 billion in 1917 and some $18.5 billion in 1919. This expansion was paid for by instituting an income tax, as authorized by the Sixteenth Amendment, which had been ratified in 1913. Many of the new agencies were conceived of and structured by the Wilson (and later Roosevelt) administrations with relatively little input from Congress, thereby realizing Wilson-the-political-science-professor's vision of a more Westminster-style operation for the federal government, in which Congress supported the program of a prime-minister-like president. Certainly, Congress saw its staff capacity relative to the executive branch decline steeply during the 1910s and 1930s (see figure 4.4).

As historian Gail Radford recounts, many of the governmental and quasi-governmental bodies Congress agreed to set up existed outside the normal civil service system because of a widespread sense that public authorities could "get things done" more efficiently, but without any grand vision of how these structures ought to hang together or ensure public accountability. She argues that "the miscellaneous and obscure character of these agencies did raise legitimate

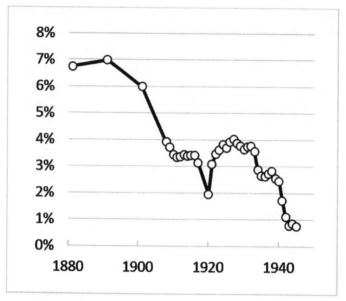

FIGURE 4.4. Legislative staff as a percentage of executive branch employees, excluding postal, 1881–1945
Source: Carter et al. 2006, Series Ea894, Ea900, Ea902.

worries, making them easy targets for those who wanted to couch their critique of activist government in legal and constitutional terms" (Radford 2013, 105). Congress did some thinking about how these boards might be kept accountable, but it left quite a lot of legal murkiness about such issues as whether state corporation laws applied or whether bodies would automatically shut down after their authorizing terms expired.

With Republicans securely in control of Congress after the election of 1920, Congress sought to bring some order to the growing federal government (see figure 4.5) by enhancing the White House's ability to act as manager, most notably with the Budget and Accounting Act of 1921. That law also strengthened congressional capacity by creating the General Accounting Office (GAO, renamed the Government Accountability Office in 2004) as an independent agency capable of conducting in-depth investigations and audits of executive branch activities. Though the story is neglected in scholarly literature, the 1920s were a time of modest rebalancing toward Congress. While there was something of a pause in the creation of new executive branch programs (owing in large part to the unusually cautious mind-set of President Calvin Coolidge), Congress significantly increased its staff levels, going from about eight thousand staff at the end of Wilson's presidency to about eleven thousand by the beginning of Roosevelt's (Carter et al. 2006, Series Ea902).

The history of Congress as an institution during the long presidency of Franklin Roosevelt is a complicated one. The Seventy-Third Congress, elected with Roosevelt in 1932, was overwhelmingly Democratic, with the party holding 70 of 96 Senate seats and 322 House seats, but those numbers mask some of the profound divisions in a party that included all of the South as well as northern progressives. As Ira Katznelson recounts, in a time of global political and economic upheaval, this Congress was often eager to accept Roosevelt's leadership, including in pushing executive branch capacity to never-before-seen levels in order to fight the economic effects of the Great Depression and, eventually, to prepare for and fight World War II. But Congress was hardly a passive partner in doing so, and its Southern wing decisively shaped the new regime (Katznelson 2014). By the end of Roosevelt's tenure, Congress was itching to reassert itself institutionally (as the next section discusses).

In partnership with Roosevelt, Congress reshaped American government during the 1930s and 1940s. It gave its wholehearted assent to Roosevelt's initial volley of emergency economic measures, helping him establish the famous alphabet soup of New Deal agencies (albeit sometimes with important alterations to allay legislators' concerns). Many of these had independent policymaking authority that meant they could take new directions as needed without any further input from the legislature. At the far extreme

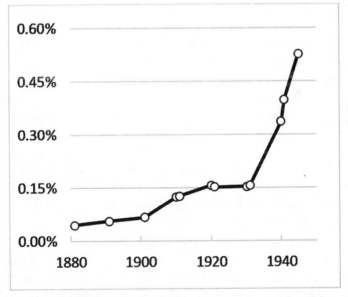

FIGURE 4.5. Percentage of Americans employed by federal government, nonpostal, nondefense, 1881–1945
Sources: Carter et al. 2006, Series Ea894, Ea898, Ea899, Ea900; decennial US Census.

was the National Recovery Administration, which gave industry leaders the power to plan, create codes of "fair practices," and fix prices as they deemed necessary—and which the Supreme Court unanimously struck down as unconstitutional in 1935, with Justice Benjamin Cardozo in his concurrence warning of "delegation running riot."[2] Such concerns would remain for the surviving agencies. After Roosevelt's unsuccessful attempt to purge his opponents in the 1938 midterm elections, Congress became a significantly more reluctant partner and took steps to limit what legislators saw as an executive branch growing powerful enough to control politics. Perceiving that Roosevelt was transforming the federal government into a giant political machine, they passed the Hatch Act in 1939, prohibiting any federal employees from using public resources for political purposes.

It is also worth noting that, during the New Deal, Washington became forever after the dominant source of government funds in the country (see figure 4.6), supplanting state and local governments.

As war broke out in Europe, Roosevelt often led Congress into new empowerments of the executive branch. In September 1939, Roosevelt invented and proclaimed a "limited" state of emergency to ensure the United States' neutrality and strengthen its national defense (Roosevelt 1939). Late in 1940, he entered into a deal to convey destroyers to Great Britain without first going to Congress, forcing legislators to play catch-up in authorizing his decision in the Lend-Lease Act of March 1941. In May 1941, he proclaimed that the scope of the emergency had become unlimited, requiring all citizens to "place the Nation's needs first in mind and action" (Roosevelt 1941). After the Japanese attack on Pearl Harbor, Congress proved willing to endow the commander in chief with vast organizational powers—and he demanded no less. Indeed, Roosevelt at one point demanded that Congress give the executive branch power to control agricultural prices, threatening, "In the event that the Congress should fail to act, and act adequately, I shall accept the responsibility, and I will act. . . . I cannot tell what powers may have to be exercised in order to win this war" (Roosevelt 1942). Congress soon acceded to his demands, though it did take care to include provisions that would allow congressional supermajorities to claw back powers. In terms of sheer numbers, Congress responded to total war by expanding the federal government to previously unthinkable levels. Some 3.7 million Americans (2.7 percent of the population) were *civilian* employees of the federal government in 1945, including a huge increase in nondefense roles (in addition to 12.2 million members of the military). Congress provided enough funds to create an atomic weapons program as large as the automobile industry that then existed—while knowing hardly anything about it (Rhodes 1987, loc. 13012).

FIGURE 4.6. Federal government expenditures as a percentage of all government expenditures, 1900–2017
Source: Chantrill, n.d.

During World War II, Congress also established new, insulated bureaucratic structures. In creating the Office of Price Administration, it gave the presidentially appointed administrator the hugely consequential discretionary power of determining prices, with only general guidance about controlling principles. This action led to an underappreciated but crucial Supreme Court decision, *Yakus v. United States* (1944), in which the justices affirmed Congress's right to set up administrative agencies that lacked formal legal constraints (including judicial review) as long as it took *some* substantive steps to secure accountability (Conde and Greve 2015).

To summarize, Congress and the president together took steps to vastly expand and complicate the US executive branch during the Progressive Era, the two world wars, and the New Deal. They did so in response to massive social, economic, and military challenges, and, although this transformation has been subjected to varied critiques over the years, there has never been a politically potent movement actually committed to restoring the much smaller and simpler federal government of the nineteenth century. Instead, the live questions have been about how this edifice ought to be altered in response to new challenges and how it might be adequately controlled.

Expansion in New Guises and the Struggle for
Meaningful Control, 1945–Present

In the wake of victory, that search for legislative control motivated a serious episode of congressional self-reflection and reform, which self-consciously centered on the ways in which Congress had lost the ability to effectively control the executive branch. Speaking in 1946, leading reformer Representative A. S. Mike Monroney (D-OK) said:

> We are sitting before this country today serving as the board of directors of the world's largest enterprise. It is a hundred times larger than General Motors, Ford Motor Co., A.T. & T., the Pennsylvania Railroad System, and General Electric all rolled into one. Yet we are trying to do this work sitting on an old-fashioned high bookkeeper's stoop with a slant-top desk, a Civil War ledger, and a quill pen. Unless we get new techniques, the tools, the organization, we simply cannot handle the work load that the country expects us to carry.

Concluding his speech, Monroney spoke of the need to preserve and renew Congress:

> The representative system is the best guardian of the people's liberty in the world. It can only be able to guard liberty where it is strong enough and well organized enough to carry the load that present day problems place upon them. (Reproduced in Rosenbloom 2000, 9, 16–17)

Such sentiments ultimately led to a number of sweeping institutional changes. Taking aim at the welter of government corporations accumulated since the turn of the twentieth century, Congress passed the Government Corporation Control Act of 1945, which required GAO audits and sunsets for all state-chartered entities without congressional approval by 1948 (Radford 2013, 108). More significant, a years-long process of debate and bargaining culminated in two major reform statutes in 1946, the Legislative Reorganization Act and the Administrative Procedure Act (APA). In the words of David H. Rosenbloom, in taking these actions, the legislature "self-consciously framed a comprehensive role for itself in federal administration" in response to a sense that it had created too much unaccountable power in the executive branch in the 1930s and early 1940s (Rosenbloom 2000, ix). The APA and a long string of later reforms conceived of executive branch agencies as adjuncts of Congress, which therefore should have their operating procedures dictated by Congress. In this way, legislators could ensure their own continuing relevance and the primacy of their values even as they routinely relied on delegation to specialized bureaucrats.

The Legislative Reorganization Act, meanwhile, would structure Congress so that its standing committees would be capable of exercising "systematic, continuous oversight" of the complex executive branch (Rosenbloom 2000, 60). A sense that members were overextended on too many committees that ended up doing little work led to the establishment of a smaller number of committees that better corresponded to executive branch functions and could be "continuously watchful" of agency decisions. When an agency deviated from Congress's desired course, its committees would be ready to correct it through informal means of intervention or, when necessary, through legislation. Congress in 1946 also sought to improve its effective capacity vis-à-vis the executive by off-loading certain decision-making burdens onto the executive branch or courts, most important among them approving bridge construction and addressing harms done by the government in the course of its routine operations (Rosenbloom 2000, 110–14).[3] In this vein, we can also note that over the course of the two world wars, Congress moved away from its previous practice of voting for every single bond issuance and instead moved to simply agreeing on an aggregate debt limit. Certainly, in Congress's own conception, not every grant of power to the executive branch is a diminution of the legislature's power; rather, by freeing up Congress to direct its attention to more important matters, some kinds of delegation could potentially increase congressional capacity.

One can think of the relationship between Congress and the executive branch established after 1946 as existing in a kind of balance, with some observers judging that it was Congress which had the upper hand in spite of its often reactive manner. In this view, as Congress proliferated executive branch agencies to build the modern American welfare and regulatory state, legislators retained all the political control they cared to have.[4] Legislators built a variety of devices to effectively monitor and keep agencies in line that supplemented the APA, including the Freedom of Information Act of 1966, Federal Advisory Committee Act of 1972, Government in the Sunshine Act of 1976, Regulatory Flexibility Act of 1980, Paperwork Reduction Acts of 1980 and 1995, and Government Performance and Results Act of 1993, among others. The organizational correspondence that the 1946 Reorganization Act had aspired to would be recalibrated with the Legislative Reorganization Act of 1970, Congressional Budget Act of 1974, Inspector General Act of 1978, and Chief Financial Officers Act of 1990 (Rosenbloom 2000, 60–103).

The story of Congress reasserting itself against an executive branch getting out of hand played out especially prominently in the 1970s. With the extensive use of budgetary impoundment by President Lyndon Johnson and

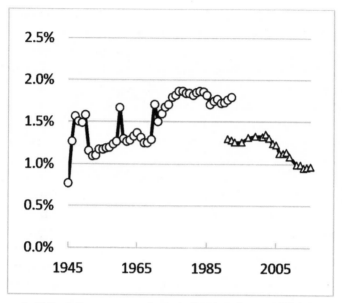

FIGURE 4.7. Legislative staff as a percentage of executive branch employees, excluding postal, 1945–2017
Sources: Carter et al. 2006, Series Ea894, Ea900, Ea902, for 1945–1992; Brookings Institution 2019, Table 5-1; Office of Management and Budget 2019b, for 1991–2017; author's calculations.

especially President Richard Nixon, Congress felt its power of the purse slipping away; it responded with the Congressional Budget Act of 1974. When it felt the national security state growing impervious to its gaze, it responded with a series of impactful investigations, such as the Pike and Church Committees, as well as with targeted reorganization, such as by creating the Senate Select Committee on Intelligence in 1976. Responding to the accumulation of emergency-facilitated powers in the executive, it passed the War Powers Resolution of 1973, the National Emergencies Act of 1976, and the International Emergency Economic Powers Act of 1977. It also beefed up the legislature's staff relative to the executive branch (see figure 4.7). If the nation had an "imperial presidency" under Nixon, it also had a resurgent legislature in the wake of his precipitous fall.

If we might judge that rebalancing as favoring Congress (which is far from self-evident, given the decidedly uneven success of many of the reforms just mentioned), it has become harder to justify the metaphor of an enduring balance after the 1970s and especially since the 1990s. In many ways, the Republicans who retook control of Congress in the election of 1994 rejected the idea that the previous arrangements represented an acceptable balance; to their eyes, the relationships between the Democratic Congress and the executive branch agencies it had spawned were cozy and corrupt, rather than reflective of any appropriate level of congressional control. Whatever one thinks of that assessment, it is certain that the idea of Congress-as-principal and executive-as-agent has lost much of its luster in the twenty-first century (Carpenter and Whittington 2003).

Reforms in the 1990s did not mostly end up paralleling the dynamics of the 1970s; a reorganization attempt fizzled in 1993 and, after Republicans took control, they set about dismantling many of the congressional resources that had been built up over the previous decades in the name of plain-republican frugality and Cincinnatus-like citizen-legislators. They also pushed for the privatization of many government functions, arguing that it could deliver equivalent service for citizen-customers with greater efficiency. This push for privatization led to a boom in federal dollars spent through contracts with private entities, which has meant that even as federal expenditures have risen considerably since 1994 (around 50 percent on an inflation-adjusted per capita basis; see figure 4.8), federal employment has remained flat or even negative (see figure 4.9). Federal government spending per government employee has

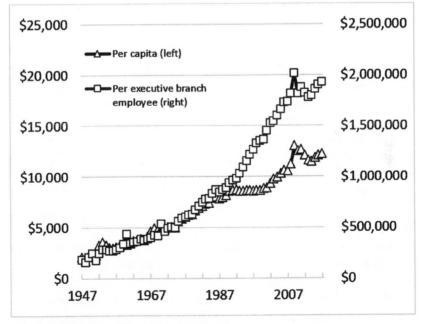

FIGURE 4.8. Federal expenditures in constant 2017 dollars, 1945–2017
Sources: OMB Historical Series 1.1 and 16.1; Carter et al. 2006, Series Ea898, Ea900; US Bureau of Economic Analysis 2019a, 2019b; author's calculations.

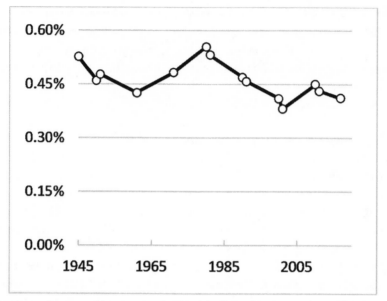

FIGURE 4.9. Percentage of Americans employed by federal government, excluding postal, defense, and census, 1945–present
Sources: Carter et al. 2006, Series Ea894, Ea898, Ea899, Ea900; decennial US Census.

consequently almost doubled. As of 2012, there were nearly 74,000 federal acquisition workers, supervising contracts valued at about $500 billion annually, which works out to roughly $6.8 million per acquisition worker (Federal Acquisition Institute 2013, 5). The biggest five contractors (defense firms Lockheed Martin, Boeing, General Dynamics, Raytheon, and Northrop Grumman) all receive more annual spending than the entire federal government did before World War I (Federal Procurement Data System 2017).

Also consistent with the desires of Republicans in 1994, the federal government has increasingly come to act as a collector and conduit of funds ultimately spent by state and local governments, in a pattern political scientists dubbed "marble cake" federalism (Grodzins 1966, 8). In 1945, the federal government made grants amounting to 0.5 percent of gross domestic product to state and local governments; in 1965, 1.5 percent; in 1985, 2.5 percent; in 2005, 3.3 percent; and in 2017, 3.5 percent (Office of Management and Budget 2019a).[5]

These developments mean that the federal government's organization chart is more complicated today than it has ever been before in the nation's history. There are learned observers who dismiss the importance of this complexification, saying that "the general relationship of the political to the administrative—the degree to which elected officials make and control national policy and its implementation—has changed much less than we conventionally imagine" (Mashaw 2012, 25). But others convincingly argue that today's densely layered pattern of "government by proxy" poses special problems of accountability and leaves Congress effectively shut out of bureaucratic worlds opaque to outsiders (DiIulio 2014).

Concerns about an overweening executive branch have been a consistent theme of twenty-first-century American politics, in no small part because all three of its presidents thus far—George W. Bush, Barack Obama, and Donald Trump—have inspired fervent enmity, both partisan and principled. There are plenty of signs of a movement for Congress-promoting reform mounting again, although to date it has not resulted in much important legislation. To give just one example, throughout the 2010s congressional Republicans sought to pass some version of the Regulations from the Executive in Need of Scrutiny (REINS) Act, which would have required all of the most important regulations to be put before Congress for an expedited vote before becoming law. While the House passed several versions of this act, it never received serious attention in the Senate.

At the same time, Congress has remained an enthusiastic user of expanded delegations to the executive as a way of addressing pressing problems. To confront the terrorist threat in the wake of 9/11, Congress built up the national security state still further. To confront the financial crisis of 2008, Congress conferred extraordinary powers upon the Treasury secretary and was willing to rely on insulated policymakers at the Federal Reserve. The most important new agency created in the wake of that crisis, the Consumer Financial Protection Bureau, is perhaps more insulated from congressional influence than any other. And, to counter the ferment of activity in support of rebuilding Congress's institutional capacity to check the executive, there is also a growing intellectual chorus that sees congressional dysfunction as a national calamity and calls for reforms that decisively move Congress from "the driver's seat" to "the backseat" of American policymaking (Howell and Moe 2016, xv). With these conflicting forces in play, it is uncertain how Congress's capacity vis-à-vis the executive branch will develop in the years to come.

Why Has Congress Fallen Behind the Executive?

This chapter has offered a necessarily cursory look at how Congress itself has facilitated the disproportionate building of capacity in the executive branch; it can scarcely skim the surface of why it has done so. Still, in closing, I offer the reader a brief acquaintance with some of the competing explanatory stories.

First, one can take several paths to arrive at the postulate that the eclipse of representative legislatures is rendered inevitable in late modernity. The mechanism may be social: as we evolve more complex and intricately interconnected networks, a centralized giver of broad rules becomes outmoded (E. Rubin 2005). Or technological: it may be that as the cost of communication has fallen, the specialists in the executive branch have become better able to hear and respond to citizen demands, such that the whole ritual of political representation has less to offer (DeMuth 2016). Or expertise-based: the increasingly specialized nature of knowledge has left legislative generalists with the correct sense that they really do not know very much and should therefore get out of the way (Posner and Vermeule 2010). In each of these stories, Congress simply becomes less able to effectively hold the executive branch to account, and society has less and less need for it to do so.

Alternatively, one might see the key variable as Congress's willingness to take front-end responsibility for the exercise of federal authority. In this story, members of Congress evolved a technique for successfully recasting themselves as ombudsmen of a federal administration over which they disclaim any thoroughgoing power. When constituents feel wronged by the federal bureaucracy, their legislators (i.e., their offices) then perform back-end damage control and wind up with grateful constituents. This mode of relating to citizens effectively ensconces incumbents, and, after all, that is what matters to members most of all (Fiorina 1989).

Each of these stories is powerful—perhaps too powerful. None of them really has the resources to explain major course corrections, such as the ones that Congress undertook in 1946 or the 1970s. If Congress was becoming progressively less able to compete with the executive branch because of the onward march of social or technological progress, or if members of Congress were gradually and eagerly discovering their ability to off-load responsibility for the acts of the federal government, why should there have been any major reversals at all?

My own view is that most of these stories are making category errors in their expectations of what Congress's engagement with the administrative state should or could look like. Indeed, this very chapter may sometimes do the same because it is so easy to characterize the relationship between the two political branches as a simple struggle for political primacy. But in the end, the legislative and executive functions are quite distinct; they are not simply two different means of "setting policy," as so much of the principal-agent-based political science literature formally assumes.

If we spend any time contemplating the scale and scope of the contemporary executive branch and the contemporary Congress, we ought to be thoroughly deterred from thinking of Congress as a managerial body attempting to exercise control over a vast corporate empire of federal agencies. Instead, we ought to recognize the fundamental disunity of Congress—which is in fact its greatest and most distinctive institutional asset. Congress's strength is not in acting as a manager: it is in doing representative politics.

That said, Congress must attempt to know something of the government's activities before it can legislate sensibly, and clearing that bar is no mean feat. It must provide itself with the wherewithal to deliberate systematically and thoroughly, lest the politics it provides degenerate into pure theater disconnected from mundane governing realities. If it aspired to build itself up as a bureaucratic manager, it would cease to be a deliberative body, but if it fails to be strategic about the way it engages with the executive, it will cease to have any relevance. This last concern seems to be especially pressing today (Wallach 2018).

The foundational Madisonian insight of ambition counteracting ambition ought to push toward some kind of rebalancing today as much as ever, however. The assumption that members of Congress want nothing more than to be elected is a useful one in many contexts, but it is not literally true; if members feel as though they are participating in a farce while the executive branch becomes the center of all significant political decisions (whether treated as such or masked in the technocratic language of optimality), they are likely to bitterly resent it. Ambitious members are likely to push their institution to become what it has successfully been many times in the past: an irreplaceable provider of political accountability. This is not the same as providing managerial accountability; if we think of Congress as just having failed in the latter, we are likely to overlook the importance of the former.

PART 2

Knowledge and Expertise in Congress

The Congressional Capacity Survey: Who Staff Are, How They Got There, What They Do, and Where They May Go

ALEXANDER C. FURNAS, LEE DRUTMAN,
ALEXANDER HERTEL-FERNANDEZ,
TIMOTHY M. LAPIRA, AND KEVIN R. KOSAR

Congressional staff play many roles in supporting the work of the United States Congress, from opening constituent mail to drafting laws to conducting oversight.[1] Few if any legislators or congressional committees could function long without them (Price 1971; H. Fox and Hammond 1977; DeGregorio 1995). As a result, they are an essential component of congressional capacity.

Scholarly examinations of legislative staff—who are they? what are their roles and responsibilities? how do they see their work?—have ebbed and flowed over the years, usually in response to congressional action. After Congress increased the number of personal and committee staff it employed in the mid-1940s, these analyses were "primarily descriptive, reporting data on demographic characteristics and tenure, recruitment and turnover, and partisanship" but did take up normative matters, such as the value of nonpartisan staff (Hammond 1977, 272–73).

As congressional staff continued to grow in the 1960s and 1970s, studies became more empirical and more rigorously probed the effects and influence of staff on policymaking and oversight and their role in the "small business" and "enterprises" that are the congressional member office and committee (Bibby 1966; Loomis 1979; Malbin 1980; Salisbury and Shepsle 1981a).

Thereafter, scholarship on legislative staff waned. Some studies examined staff gender and racial composition, while other small-n reports considered the functioning and well-being of congressional staff. The last broad surveys of congressional staff demographics, pay levels, and tenures were conducted in at the beginning of the twenty-first century (Friedman and Nakamura 1991; Grose, Mangum, and Martin 2007; Congressional Management Foundation 2004, 2005, n.d.).

Why scholarly attention to congressional staffing waned is unclear. Whether the significant decline in the number of congressional staff and legislative support agency personnel since the turn of the twenty-first century is debatable (LaPira and Thomas 2017). Regardless, staff do remain a significant feature on Capitol Hill through whom much of the work of governance passes. Hence, a close look at congressional staff is overdue.

In 2017, we conducted an online survey of staff regarding the legislative branch's capacity.[2] The survey sought to find out more about the backgrounds, career paths, policy views, technical knowledge, substantive expertise, and job experiences of congressional staffers, as well as the procedures and organizational structures that allow them to assist members of Congress to do their work in the most effective and democratically responsive ways.

What follows in this chapter are top-line results that focus on who congressional staff are, how they get there (i.e., their career paths), what they do for Congress, and where they see their careers leading.

How Did They Get Their Job?
Education, Internships, and Pre–Capitol Hill Jobs

Our first set of questions asked how congressional staffers arrived at their current positions, including their education, pre-Hill employment, and any internships they may have used to secure their present job. Table 5.1 summarizes the educational backgrounds of our survey respondents using matched data from LegiStorm. Some 22.8 percent of staffers surveyed did not report their highest degree. Of the staffers for whom we can identify their highest degree, bachelor's degrees were the most common degree held by staffers, at around 50 percent. About 16 percent held law degrees, and 30 percent held master's degrees. PhDs were the least common degree. In general, higher-ranking staffers tended to have more postgraduate education.

Like other employers, Congress depends heavily on internships to screen and select its potential full-time staff. "Thinking back to how you got your start working in Congress, was your first position an internship (either paid or unpaid)?" we asked. Nearly two-thirds of staff responding to our survey described some sort of internship experience (see table 5.2). The most common internship experience for Hill staffers involved working in the DC office of a member of Congress. About 40 percent of all Hill staffers worked as either paid or unpaid interns on Capitol Hill. Fellowships and unpaid district office internships were the next most common experiences, at 9 percent and 8 percent, respectively. It was rarest for staffers to come from paid or unpaid campaign internships (at a combined total of only 4 percent of Hill staffers).

TABLE 5.1. Congressional staff education

Highest degree attained	%
Bachelor's	39
JD	13
Master's	23
PhD	2

Note: Calculated by authors. Percentages rounded.

TABLE 5.2. Internship experience in (and around) Congress

Staffer's previous internship experience	%
Unpaid DC	31
Paid DC	10
Fellow	9
Unpaid district	8
Unpaid campaign	3
Paid campaign	1
Paid district	0
No previous internship	38

Note: "DC" refers to working in a member of Congress's office in Washington, DC. Calculated by authors. Percentages rounded.

Unpaid internships received significant attention from the media in the late 2010s. Prominent outlets such as the *New York Times*, the *Washington Post*, and *Washington Monthly* have all reported on how such experiences are vital for career advancement—yet are often out of reach for low-income and minority young people (Shepherd 2016; Vera 2017; Desai 2018). Such positions not only require forgone wages but can often involve temporarily relocating to very expensive cities (such as Washington, DC) for a summer. Although no government surveys ask about the use of internships, private-sector polling suggests that perhaps half of all internships are unpaid (Desai 2018). Compared with that benchmark, Congress is even more reliant on unpaid internships, with 67 percent of Hill staffers who were previously interns saying that their internships were unpaid on our survey.

Longer-serving staffers were, however, much more likely to report having paid internships. More than half of staffers serving ten or more years in Congress reported having a paid internship, compared to less than a fifth of staffers who had just arrived on the Hill. However, in 2019, Congress approved a stipend of $1,800 a month for all interns. Though the pay is low, it is better than nothing.

Who Are Congressional Staffers?

The modal staffer on Capitol Hill is a white, non-Hispanic male between the ages of twenty-five and twenty-nine with a bachelor's degree. That said, there is more variation in the demographic composition of legislative staff than there is among members of Congress, but it is relatively homogeneous compared to the population at large. Table 5.3 reports the nonweighted demographics of respondents' self-reported ethnic and racial identities and age, and LegiStorm-reported data on gender and level of education.

In the 115th Congress (serving from January 3, 2017, through January 2, 2019), members of the House and Senate, respectively, were about 78 percent and 92 percent white, about 80 percent and 78 percent male, and most likely between the ages of fifty and fifty-nine (Manning 2018). The difference in age between the typical staffer and the typical member is not surprising, but the overrepresentation of whites and underrepresentation of women among staff is notable.

Compared with all employees in Congress—as reported in summary by LegiStorm[3]—the political appointees targeted by this survey are more likely to be white men (LegiStorm, n.d.). The population of all House and Senate employees, respectively—including those excluded from our sampling frame—is roughly 81 percent and 84 percent white and about 51 percent and 50 percent male, suggesting that politically sensitive positions are more likely to be those filled by people who look like members themselves. Table 5.4 categorizes respondents by their employing chamber, party, and type of office.[4]

The average staffer has worked in a single congressional office for three or fewer years and holds a midlevel position primarily assigned to legislative operations. Table 5.5 summarizes staff tenure, employment patterns, and salary.

The mean number of years of experience is about six, with more than 60 percent of the sample having worked six or fewer years. The general pattern is clear: most staffers stay on Capitol Hill for a few years and move on, whereas a select few commit their professional lives to congressional service. Ideally, more of the latter type would improve congressional capacity. Notably, about 16 percent of staffers had a tenure of "more than 15 years," though the concentration of those who have spent a significant portion of their careers working as congressional staff is partially artifactual.[5]

The median salary among respondents is $62,723 (mean = $75,498; standard deviation = $48,587), which is about 9 percent higher than the national median income in 2016.[6] However, congressional staffers' incomes are 35 percent lower than the $96,000 median income in the Washington metropolitan area in 2016.[7]

TABLE 5.3. Congressional staff demographics

Variable	Categories	Frequency	%
Ethnicity	White	276	91
	Asian	14	5
	Black or African American	12	4
	American Indian or Alaska Native	4	1
	Other	8	1
	Middle Eastern or North African	2	1
	Native Hawaiian / Pacific Islander	1	0
Spanish, Hispanic, Latinx	No	294	94
	Yes	18	6
Age	Under 25	43	14
	25–29	72	24
	30–34	56	19
	35–39	43	14
	40–44	30	10
	45–49	18	6
	50–54	16	5
	55 and over	23	8
Gender	Male	283	64
	Female	158	36

Note: Calculated by authors. Percentages rounded.

TABLE 5.4. Congressional staff employing offices

Variable	Categories	Frequency	%
Party	Democratic	210	48
	Republican	229	52
	Other/nonpartisan	2	1
Chamber	House	268	61
	Senate	173	39
Employing office type	Personal	298	68
	Committee	126	29
	Party	11	3
	Other/institutional	6	1

Note: Calculated by authors. Percentages rounded.

The hierarchical organization of congressional offices reveals a great deal of variation in staffer salary. Based on staffers' job title and employing office, we categorize staff into six substantive categories describing their primary function and seniority. Based on this classification, we find the median salary for a staffer with a job title of staff assistant in a member's personal office (a junior office management role) is roughly $23,000, whereas the median

TABLE 5.5. Congressional staff employment status, 2017

Variable	Categories	Frequency	%
Tenure	Fewer than 4 years	193	44
	4–6 years	77	18
	7–9 years	43	10
	10–12 years	32	7
	13–15 years	25	6
	More than 15 years	71	16
Number of employers	1	201	49
	2	108	26
	3	47	12
	4	32	8
	5 or more	12	5
Staffer function	Legislative	256	59
	Office management	81	19
	Political management	52	12
	Communications	31	7
	Institutional	11	3
	Constituent service	1	0
Staffer seniority	Junior	83	19
	Midlevel	255	59
	Senior	94	22
Staffer salary	Less than $30K	69	17
	$30–59K	129	31
	$60–89K	80	20
	$90–119K	41	10
	$120–149K	42	10
	$150K or more	50	12

Note: Calculated by authors. Percentages rounded.

committee staff director or chief of staff (both senior political management positions) salary is about six times that at $138,000.

Finally, we asked respondents a series of questions to self-report their partisan identities and ideologies. Modeled after the standard two-part conditional questions from the American National Election Studies, we measure staffers' self-reported party identification on a seven-point scale in table 5.6, by the party of their employing office.

Not surprisingly, staffers' party identification typically matches that of their employers, with some minor variation. Respondents in Democratic offices were much more likely to identify as strong partisans than their Republican office counterparts—77 percent of Democratic staffers identified as "Strong Democrats," while only 53 percent of Republican staffers identified as "Strong Republicans." And roughly 9 percent of respondents in Republican offices identified as Democrats, while only 3 percent of respondents in Democratic offices identified as Republicans. However, close inspection of the data suggests that several of these people serve in nonpartisan institutional offices, meaning these are artifacts of the current majority parties in the House and Senate.

To calculate ideology, we adapted five substantive policy questions from a study by Heinz and colleagues (Heinz et al. 1993; see also Esterling 2018). Respondents self-report their preferences on a five-point Likert agree-disagree scale. These items have an interitem covariance of 0.93 and a Cronbach's α of 0.86. To calculate a latent variable measure of ideology, we use a Rasch partial credit model (Masters 1982), a type of item response theory model that works for categorical and ordinal variables as implemented in the eRm R package (Mair and Hatzinger 2007). Figure 5.1 is a box-and-whisker plot describing staffers' ideology by their party affiliation.

The average respondent is slightly left of center (mean = −0.17, standard deviation = 0.52). As expected, staffers' ideological responses are more conservative as they self-identify more with the Republican Party. The median staffer in a Democratic office is 0.85 points more liberal than the median Republican staffer, suggesting that staff are as polarized as members themselves.

What Do Staff Do When They Are on the Hill?

Consistent with widespread reporting, staff work long hours. More than two-thirds reported working at least fifty hours: almost half—46 percent—of legislative staffers reported working between fifty and fifty-nine hours per week, and roughly 20 percent reported working more than sixty hours per week.[8] Long work hours are particularly pronounced among legislative staffers (e.g., legislative assistant, legislative director, policy advisor), and political

TABLE 5.6. Congressional staff party self-identification, by party of employer

	Democratic		Republican	
	Frequency	%	Frequency	%
Strong Democrat	118	77	2	1
Democrat	15	10	4	2
Lean Democrat	15	10	10	6
Independent	1	1	2	1
Lean Republican	0	0	22	13
Republican	2	1	42	24
Strong Republican	3	2	93	53
Total	154	100	175	100

Note: Calculated by authors. Percentages rounded.

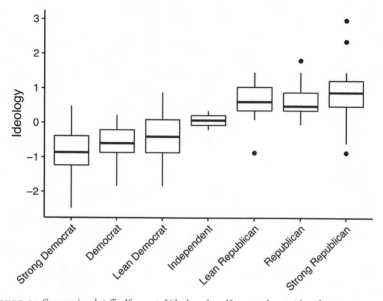

FIGURE 5.1. Congressional staff self-reported ideology, by self-reported party identification
Note: $N = 419$.

management staffers (e.g., chief of staff, staff director). A complete break-down of reported hours worked by staffer title category is shown in table 5.7.

An individual congressional staffer almost inevitably works on a wide variety of issues. There are more policy issues than there are staffers in an individual member's office, so staffers are pressed into generalist duties as a matter of course.[9] As shown in table 5.8, budget and appropriations, government operations, health, and defense have the most respondents reporting daily work on those topics, with about 29 percent, 25 percent, 23 percent, and 19 percent, respectively. Table 5.8 also shows that, conversely, only about 23 percent of staffers reported never working on budget and appropriations policy. The issue on which the fewest respondents reported working by far is the topic of culture: about 67 percent of staff reported never working on cultural policy, and merely 6 percent reported working on it on a daily basis. About 10 percent of respondents reported working daily on the issues of domestic commerce and banking and of civil rights and civil liberties.[10]

Table 5.9 illustrates the percentage of respondents in each party that reported working on an issue daily. The rightmost column reports the difference between the share of Republicans reporting daily work on an issue and the share of Democrats reporting daily work on an issue. Staffers of both parties were most likely to report working daily on budget and appropriations,

TABLE 5.7. Staffer hours worked per week

Primary responsibility	40–49 hours	50–59 hours	60–69 hours	70+ hours
Legislative	75	110	34	14
	32%	46%	14%	6%
Office management	23	38	9	5
	30%	49%	12%	6%
Political management	12	20	14	7
	23%	38%	26%	13%
Communications	15	13	1	1
	50%	43%	3%	3%
Constituent service	0	1	0	0
	0%	100%	0%	0%
Institutional	2	10	3	0
	13%	63%	19%	0%
Uncategorized	3	3	2	0
	33%	33%	22%	0%
Total	130	195	63	27
	31%	46%	15%	6%

Note: Calculated by authors. Percentages rounded and truncated. Staffers who reported working fewer than 40 hours per week were excluded from the table.

TABLE 5.8. Congressional staff focus, frequency by policy topic (percent)

	Never	Occasionally	Daily
Budget and Appropriations	23	48	29
Government Operations	29	46	25
Health	48	30	23
Defense	47	34	19
International Affairs	43	39	18
Transportation and Infrastructure	48	34	18
Macroeconomics	50	33	17
Energy	48	36	16
Environment	52	33	15
Foreign Trade	49	37	14
Space, Science, and Technology	46	41	13
Immigration	52	35	13
Law, Crime, and Judiciary	53	34	13
Public Lands	62	25	13
Social Welfare	55	33	12
Education	60	29	11
Agriculture	62	27	11
Labor	53	37	11
Civil Rights and Civil Liberties	53	37	10
Domestic Commerce and Banking	58	32	10
Housing	63	29	8
Culture	67	27	6

Note: Calculated by authors. Percentages rounded. Policy topics include all major categories, plus the Budget and Appropriations subtopic no. 0105, National Budget, encompassing "issues related to public debt, budgeting, and efforts to reduce deficits" (see Comparative Agendas Project n.d.).

TABLE 5.9. Daily attention to policy topics, by party

Policy topic	Daily, Democratic (%)	Daily, Republican (%)	Difference (%)
Social Welfare	16	9	7
Civil Rights and Civil Liberties	14	7	7
International Affairs	21	16	5
Space, Science, and Technology	16	11	5
Environment	18	14	4
Defense	21	17	4
Public Lands	15	12	3
Labor	12	10	2
Housing	9	8	1
Average	15	15	0
Immigration	12	13	−1
Foreign Trade	13	14	−1
Education	11	12	−1
Macroeconomics	17	18	−1
Transportation and Infrastructure	17	18	−1
Culture	5	6	−1
Law, Crime, and Judiciary	12	14	−2
Budget and Appropriations	28	30	−2
Health	21	24	−3
Domestic Commerce and Banking	8	12	−4
Agriculture	9	13	−4
Energy	13	18	−5
Government Operations	22	27	−5

Note: Calculated by authors. Percentages rounded.

government operations, and health. However, we also observe some attentional differences across party. Considerably more Democratic staffers reported working on civil rights and civil liberties (7.0 percentage points difference [ppd]), social welfare (7.6 ppd), international affairs (5.8 ppd), space, science, and technology (4.9 ppd), and the environment (4.1 ppd) on a daily basis than Republican staffers. Meanwhile, considerably more Republican staffers reported working on government operations (4.6 ppd), energy (4.4 ppd), and agriculture (4.3 ppd). The average issue receives the daily attention of about 15 percent of respondents from both parties.

As noted earlier, staffers typically are pressed into service on multiple issues, rather than focusing on the details of single policy domain. Figure 5.2 illustrates the number of issues on which respondents reported working on a daily basis. The median legislative staffer reported working on three issues on a daily basis (mean = 3.5), while the median nonlegislative staffer reported a single issue as requiring their attention every day. About 28 percent of legislative staffers reported at least five major issue areas that require their daily attention.

Figure 5.3 reveals large and statistically significant differences in knowledge scores between staffers who work on budget or health issues on a daily basis and their counterparts who don't.[11] However, we do not find a similar difference across activity levels for defense or foreign affairs. These findings suggest that staffers who work more on an issue tend to know more about it than those who do not. This is hardly surprising, but it is good validation of our knowledge battery, which is investigated in greater detail in chapter 6.

Staffers frequently work outside of their job descriptions. Legislative staffers in members' personal offices often assist with constituent service and communications.[12] As one of our interview respondents noted, "Our [legislative correspondent] also does some communications work. [. . .] Let's say we want to give our subscribers an update on health care. She's going to put together the text and push that out to our subscribers, or she's doing out social media, which is more direct to constituent." As table 5.10 shows, about 30 percent of legislative staffers in members' personal offices reported managing constituent mail turnaround "a great deal," and roughly 28 percent reported drafting constituent response communications "a great deal."

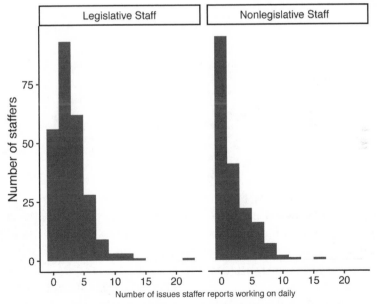

FIGURE 5.2. Distribution of major policy topics, by congressional staff primary responsibility
Note: $N = 419$.

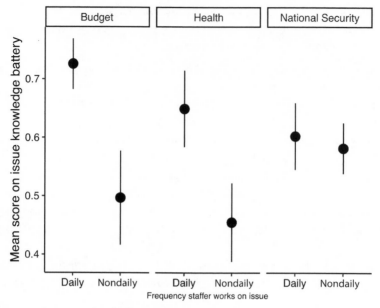

FIGURE 5.3. Congressional staff policy knowledge
Note: N = 419.

TABLE 5.10. Congressional staff daily attention, by activity (percent)

Activity	Never	Occasionally	A great deal
Managing constituent mail turnaround	35	36	30
Drafting constituent response communications	18	54	28
Writing press releases or similar public relations copy	35	50	16
Handling constituent casework	65	29	7
Communicating with the press	65	29	6

Note: Calculated by authors. Percentages rounded.

How Long Do Staffers Plan to Stay? Where Are They Headed?

Turnover is a widespread problem in Congress. Consistent with past work documenting a high degree of staff turnover, table 5.11 shows that about 10 percent of staffers indicated that they planned on leaving Congress within a year, and 25 percent expected to serve between one and two years.[13] Adding in the 33 percent who expected to serve between three and five years means that looking five years into the future, about two-thirds of staffers reported that they planned to leave the Hill. Our findings suggest that party makes little difference. Self-identified Democrats were more likely than Republicans to indicate that they would leave within a year. But other than that, longer-term

TABLE 5.11. Anticipated duration of Capitol Hill service

Length of service	Staffers' estimates (%)
Less than 12 months	10
1–2 years	25
3–5 years	33
6–10 years	19
More than 10 years	11
Don't know/missing	5

Note: Calculated by authors. Percentages rounded.

ambitions did not vary by party. There were similarly only small gaps when it came to staffers' job ranks. In general, midlevel staffers were more likely than either junior or senior staffers to report wanting to leave sooner rather than later, but differences were small.

Where do the staffers who want to leave Congress plan to go? To tap into this question, we asked respondents, "What would be the ideal next step in your career?" and found that 41 percent of respondents said that they would like to stay in government. A nearly equal proportion (38 percent) reported wanting to move to the private sector, 6 percent said they would like retire, and 14 percent didn't yet know. Democrats and Republicans differed slightly on these future paths. Republicans were more likely than Democrats to want to go into the private sector, while Democrats were more likely to say that they didn't know what they wanted to do or that they would like to retire. Staffers from both parties were about equally likely to say they would like to stay in government.

Many observers consider the "revolving door" to be a widespread problem in Washington, DC. When staffers move from Congress to other organizations, including lobbying firms, business associations, and other government agencies, they carry with them the connections and deep knowledge of congressional policy and procedure that they have built up during their time on the Hill. Past research suggests that personal connections to members of Congress in particular can be a valuable commodity for staffers to exchange for jobs in the lobbying and governmental affairs sectors (Blanes i Vidal, Draca, and Fons-Rosen 2012; LaPira and Thomas 2017; McCrain 2018).[14]

Table 5.12 summarizes the responses for staffers who said that their ideal next step would involve continuing to work in government. Most of these staffers (about two-thirds) said that they would like to stay in Congress, and they were divided nearly equally between staying in their current office (31 percent) and moving to another office (33 percent). About 20 percent wanted to move to a federal agency, and 11 percent wanted to work in the White House.

TABLE 5.12. Congressional staff aspirations for future
occupations, within government

Ideal government job	%
Congress, different office	33
Congress, same office	31
Federal agency	20
State government	3
White House	11
Other / Don't know	4

Note: Calculated by authors. Percentages rounded.

TABLE 5.13. Partisan differences in aspirations for future occupations, outside of government

		By party (%)		
Ideal private-sector job	All (%)	Democratic	Republican	Difference
Lobbying firm	22	13	28	15
Trade/business association	22	16	27	11
Graduate school	15	21	9	−12
Research	11	15	7	−8
Issue advocacy organization	8	15	3	−12
Start business	6	6	5	−1
Law firm	6	4	7	3
Financial sector	4	2	4	2
Don't know / other	4	2	4	2
Political party	2	2	3	1
Election campaign	1	0	1	1
Labor union	1	3	0	−3
Independent political organization	1	2	0	−2
Campaign consulting	1	0	1	1

Note: Calculated by authors. Percentages rounded. Positive differences are ideal jobs favored by Republican staffers; negative differences are those favored by Democratic staffers.

Very few staffers (less than 3 percent) wanted to move to state government. In general, we found that self-identified Republican staffers were more enthusiastic about moving to the White House or federal agencies than were Democrats.

Table 5.13 describes the ideal jobs for respondents who indicated that they would like to move into the private sector. Here we see both broad tendencies overall for all staffers, as well as some significant partisan differences. By far, the most common private-sector destinations for staffers were lobbying firms and trade associations, at around 22 percent of respondents each. The least-desired positions included campaign consulting and working for independent political organizations, labor unions, or election campaigns (roughly

1 percent each). As table 5.13 indicates, however, self-identified Republicans were substantially more likely than Democrats to report wanting to move into lobbying firms and trade associations. In contrast, Democratic staffers were much more likely than Republicans to anticipate a future career working for an issue advocacy organization. Democrats were also more likely to say that they would like to pursue graduate education or a research-oriented career.

In general, these differences are consistent with a Republican Party that is closely aligned with the business community, and a Democratic Party coalition of issue advocacy groups representing diverse identity groups and policy objectives. Still, it is notable that Democratic staffers were about equally likely to say that they would work for a trade association as for a single-issue advocacy group or research outfit—and across both parties, a large proportion of senior staffers (43 percent) said that they would like to work for a trade association. The bottom line is that jobs lobbying on behalf of businesses, especially in trade associations, are appealing to congressional staff, and especially experienced staffers.

What If Congress Had More Money? Priorities for the Institution

What do staffers think should be done to improve Congress?[15] If office budgets could be magically doubled, staffers overwhelmingly thought the top priority should be pay increases. Sixty percent of staffers named this their top priority, and 89 percent put it in their top three priorities, as shown in table 5.14. The second most common top priority was hiring more legislative/policy staff—roughly one in five (21 percent) put it as their top priority, while 77 percent included it among their top three. Figure 5.4 shows the percentages of staffers listing each of these potential uses of additional money as the number one, two, and three top priority of any additional funds.

TABLE 5.14. Hypothetical preferences for spending additional legislative branch appropriations (percent)

Preferred expenditure	In top three	Top priority
Increasing pay for existing staff	89	60
Hiring more legislative/policy staff	77	21
Hiring more oversight staff	29	7
Hiring more staff to handle constituent demands	38	5
Getting additional office space	18	4
Hiring more communications staff	26	2
Increasing fringe benefits	24	1

Note: Calculated by authors. Percentages rounded.

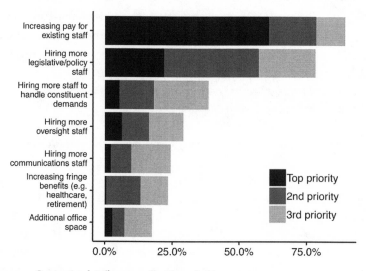

FIGURE 5.4. Congressional staff resource allocation priorities

Note: N = 419. Staffers were asked, "What would you do with double your current office budget?"

TABLE 5.15. Partisan differences for spending additional legislative branch appropriations (percent)

Preferred expenditure	Democratic (top 3)	Republican (top 3)	Difference
Hiring more oversight staff	25	33	8
Increasing fringe benefits	22	25	4
Hiring more staff to handle constituent demands	36	39	3
Hiring more communications staff	24	28	3
Getting additional office space	20	16	−4
Hiring more legislative/policy staff	80	74	−6
Increasing pay for existing staff	94	86	−8

Note: Calculated by authors. Percentages rounded. Positive differences are ideal jobs favored by Republican staffers; negative differences are those favored by Democratic staffers.

How uniform are these assessments? Republicans and Democrats have similar priorities, as shown in table 5.15. The most notable difference is that Democrats are a little more likely to want to increase pay for staff (8 ppd) and hire more staff (6 ppd). Republicans are slightly more likely to want to hire more oversight staff (8 ppd).

As shown in table 5.16, priorities showed some variance by seniority level. Senior staff are almost twice as likely to want to hire more communications staff (39 percent of senior staff put hiring more communications staff in their top three priorities, as compared with just 22 percent of midlevel staff), whereas midlevel staff are 10 percentage points more likely to want to hire more oversight (35 percent put it in their top three, compared with senior staff's 25 percent). Midlevel staff are also more likely to want to increase fringe benefits, though that's not commonly a top priority.

Patterns are mostly similar across chambers. But House staff are twice as likely to prioritize hiring more communications staffers (32 percent vs. 16 percent) in their top three preferences, whereas Senate staffers are notably more likely to want to do more oversight (37 percent vs. 24 percent), as shown in table 5.17. This finding may reflect some differences in the chambers. In the House, more offices have little opportunity to do oversight because they are not on the relevant committees, and hiring communications staff may seem to be more of a boost to their bosses' profile. They are also up for reelection every two years rather than every six as for their Senate counterparts.

The most significant prioritization differences are between members' personal and committee offices, as shown in table 5.18. Again, more pay and more

TABLE 5.16. Seniority differences for spending additional legislative branch appropriations (percent)

Preferred expenditure	Senior staff (in top 3)	Midlevel staff (in top 3)	Difference
Hiring more communications staff	39	22	17
Hiring more staff to handle constituent demands	40	33	7
Increasing pay for existing staff	94	90	4
Getting additional office space	16	19	−3
Hiring more legislative/policy staff	73	77	−4
Hiring more oversight staff	25	35	−10
Increasing fringe benefits	13	24	−11

Note: Calculated by authors. Percentages rounded. Positive differences are ideal jobs favored by senior staffers; negative differences are those favored by midlevel staffers.

TABLE 5.17. Chamber differences for spending additional legislative branch appropriations (percent)

Preferred expenditure	Senate (in top 3)	House (in top 3)	Difference
Hiring more communications staff	16	32	−17
Getting additional office space	16	19	−3
Increasing fringe benefits	23	24	−1
Increasing pay for existing staff	89	90	0
Hiring more staff to handle constituent demands	38	37	1
Hiring more legislative/policy staff	81	74	7
Hiring more oversight staff	37	24	13

Note: Calculated by authors. Percentages rounded. Positive differences are ideal jobs favored by Senate staffers; negative differences are those favored by House staffers.

TABLE 5.18. Office type differences for spending additional legislative branch appropriations (percent)

Preferred expenditure	Personal (in top 3)	Committee (in top 3)	Difference
Hiring more oversight staff	17	48	−31
Increasing pay for existing staff	79	94	−16
Hiring more legislative/policy staff	75	79	−5
Increasing fringe benefits	25	27	−2
Getting additional office space	27	20	7
Hiring more staff to handle constituent demands	25	14	11
Hiring more communications staff	53	18	35

Note: Calculated by authors. Percentages rounded. Positive differences are ideal jobs favored by members' personal office staffers; negative differences are those favored by committee staffers.

staff top the list of priorities, but committee staffers see considerably more need for oversight staff, and the least need for communications staff and constituent service—perhaps not surprisingly, since personal offices do most of that work.

Regardless of party, seniority, chamber, or office type, it is clear the vast majority of staff would prioritize paying existing staff more and hiring more legislative and policy staff if they had the money. This finding should give us confidence that if Congress were to allocate more for Members' Representational Allowances, most offices would wind up with better-paid staff and more policy staff. This survey also gives us some sense of how money would be allocated depending on whether it goes to members or committees. Notably, committees would spend more on additional oversight while, not surprisingly, personal offices would spend more on constituent service.

Conclusion

The Congressional Capacity Survey supplies empirical support for the observation that has frequently aired in media: life on Capitol Hill is not easy for staff, who come and go. The hours are very long, and staffers usually must serve as jacks-of-all-trades, mostly expecting to put out the next political fire that comes their boss's way. Many of them wish Congress would hire more staff. There simply are not enough of them to cover every subject their member of Congress must address.

Most congressional staff feel underpaid, and not many of them imagine themselves spending their whole careers on the Hill. Many arrive as interns, often unpaid, which means time spent in the legislature amounts to a short-term opportunity cost. Staffers stick around and tolerate the wages and other unpleasant aspects until they have banked several years, which they can parlay into jobs in the private sector (which pay more) or the executive branch (where the civil service pay scale, stable hours, and job security await). And if office budgets increased, staffers would prioritize spending it on increasing staff salaries and hiring more staff.

Staff play an essential role in the functioning of a healthy Congress. They should, when staff are too few and so many consider their time on the Hill merely, as one former intern put it, a "pit stop" en route to somewhere else (Bhattacharya 2017). This is genuine cause for concern.

What Do Congressional Staff Actually Know?

KRISTINA C. MILER

Conversations about congressional capacity generally focus on the many demands on legislators' time, including fund-raising, campaigning, and constituency service, with the concern being that these demands negatively affect legislators' capacity to do legislative work. One common response is that members of Congress have staff to help them. The logic is that while any one member of Congress cannot do everything, together with a team of professional staff, a member can successfully accomplish these many legislative and nonlegislative tasks. But are staff really up to the task? This chapter examines whether the staff who are necessarily entrusted with much of the legislative work in the US Congress have the knowledge of policy and procedure that is widely assumed. Staff knowledge is critical to congressional capacity, and a better understanding of what staff do—and do not—know should inform any efforts at congressional reform.

Although congressional staff members are rarely the focus of discussions about Congress, scholars have noted the critically important role they play in making public policy and navigating the legislative process. The predominant view of staff is rooted in Salisbury and Shepsle's (1981b) classic argument that members of Congress should be seen as heads of enterprises, which reconciles the centrality of legislators with the reality that much of the work in Congress is done by staff. Indeed, a variety of studies affirm the importance of staff. Scholars have found that differences in staff contribute to variation in legislators' behavior (e.g., DeGregorio 1995; R. Hall 1993; Montgomery and Nyhan 2017; Whiteman 1995). A few studies even raise concerns that staff members are too important in the legislative process (e.g., DeGregorio 1988; H. Fox and Hammond 1977; R. Hall 1996; Kingdon 1989; Malbin 1980; Price 1971; Salisbury and Shepsle 1981a). Others highlight the risk of staff members using Congress as a stepping-stone to other jobs, particularly given the diminished institutional support for congressional staff reflected in budget cuts and reorganizations (e.g., LaPira and Thomas 2017; Mann and Ornstein 1992; Salisbury and Shepsle 1981a).

Among congressional scholars, then, there is recognition that staff contribute to the legislative process, but one topic that we know relatively little about is what staff members know and how that knowledge varies. We have some expectations based on how Congress works or observations of staff members' behavior, but due to the time and labor-intensive nature of gathering data about staff members, there is little systematic evidence about staff. Previously, scholars interested in staff have conducted interviews with as many as several dozen staff, but the field has not had a large-scale survey of congressional staff to facilitate broader inquiries. Therefore, the Congressional Capacity Survey (Drutman et al. 2017b) provides a unique opportunity to examine congressional staff in a way not possible previously.

This chapter examines what staffers know about both substantive policies and congressional procedure in order to better understand Congress's current policymaking capacity. The data reveal new insights about staff knowledge, including the considerable variation in procedural and substantive policy knowledge among staff members. Six common preconceptions about Congress are identified and assessed: the deliberative Senate, committee expertise, party polarization, the "brain drain," the importance of experience, and the gender gap. Notably, there is strong evidence that staff members with more experience, regardless of whether it comes from specialization or longer careers on Capitol Hill, are more knowledgeable about both procedure and policy. Partisanship also affects staff members' knowledge of congressional rules and procedure with stronger partisans demonstrating more familiarity with how Congress works. An important implication, then, is that if we want to increase congressional capacity, reforms should incorporate staff specialization and staff retention, as well as broad efforts to increase and equalize staff knowledge of policy and procedure.

What Do Staff Members Know?

Uncovering what staff members know about congressional procedure and policy is valuable to the study of Congress because staff members play a key role in the day-to-day work of legislating. Staff members are responsible for developing the substance of legislation (e.g., Baumgartner and Jones 2015; DeGregorio 1996; Kingdon 1989; Malbin 1980) as well as for helping to move legislation through the complex process (e.g., Romzek and Utter 1997; Whiteman 1995).

Furthermore, staff are an important conduit of information to members as well as between congressional offices (e.g., Montgomery and Nyhan 2017; Romzek and Utter 1997; Sabatier and Whiteman 1985; Whiteman 1995). If Congress is to increase its capacity to define the policy agenda, develop proposals, make public policy, and oversee implementation, staff must be informed.

Indeed, poorly informed staff members can diminish the effectiveness of Congress in two critical ways. First, poorly informed staff are more likely to rely on shortcuts, or heuristics, when making decisions about sponsoring legislation, taking a position on existing proposals, and countless other decisions during the policymaking process. For example, staff may make decisions by taking cues from party leaders, lobbyists, or the executive branch rather than relying on their own assessment of the situation (e.g., B. Jones 1994, 2001; Kingdon 1989; Matthews and Stimson 1975). Although heuristics can be quite helpful in reducing the informational workload, reliance on heuristics is problematic because it can introduce bias and distortions (e.g., Kanwisher 1989; Kuklinski and Hurley 1994; Miler 2007, 2010; Tversky and Kahneman 1974). Put simply, decisions based on cues do not always approximate the decision one would have made if fully informed (e.g., Kuklinski and Quirk 2000; Lau and Redlawsk 2001; Miler 2009; Tetlock 2005). Therefore, to the extent that less-informed staff members are overly reliant on heuristics, they may be promoting incomplete or biased information within their network of staff and members of Congress. Such information may present just one perspective, or may omit the views of constituents, or may be misleading—all of which can produce suboptimal policy outcomes.

Second, low information levels among staff are problematic for Congress because they contribute to an information asymmetry that advantages the executive branch and interest groups over Congress. If staff are unable to verify or counter information from other political actors, and may even rely on information from these sources, this gives the executive branch (or lobbyists) greater influence in shaping policy outcomes. This is of particular concern in the political climate of the late 2010s, as several chapters in this volume address the risks of declining congressional capacity and rising executive branch power (see chapters 3 and 4) and interest group influence (see LaPira and Thomas 2017).

Thus, I examine staff members' knowledge of both policy and procedural information. The data come from the Congressional Capacity Survey (Drutman et al. 2017b), which is a unique survey of more than four hundred staff members across personal, committee, and party offices in both the US House of Representatives and the US Senate. Chapter 5 in this volume provides more details about the Congressional Capacity Survey, but it is worth highlighting here the key measures of staff knowledge. The procedural knowledge questions included in the survey asked about specific, yet accessible, information about the rules of the chamber in which the respondent works. House staffers were asked about rules pertaining to the Committee of the Whole, discharge petitions, appropriations process, and the process of filing and debating a bill. Senate staff members were asked about bypassing committee, amendments between the chambers, and cloture rules and strategy. The percentage of staff members answering these questions correctly ranged from 34 percent to 83 percent, depending on the question. Perhaps indicative of the current climate, the fewest Senate staff could identify the advantages of using amendments between the chambers to resolve differences, and most staff knew that Senate Rule XIV allows bills to bypass committee consideration.

To evaluate how much staff members know about substantive issues, respondents were asked a series of questions about one of three issue areas: budgeting and appropriations, health care, or national security. Staff members' responses to these questions again reveal a range of knowledge. In each policy area, there was at least one question that was answered correctly by the vast majority of respondents (i.e., 70 percent or more of staff members), as well as one question that stumped many staff members (i.e., 45 percent or less of staff members answered it correctly).

These sets of procedural questions and policy questions are then aggregated to create two knowledge "scores" that correspond to the percent of procedural (or policy) questions answered correctly.[1] Knowledge scores, therefore, provide summary measures of staff knowledge and facilitate comparisons among congressional staff. As a whole, staff knowledge of Congress is perhaps best characterized as middling. Although staff members answered more questions correctly than incorrectly, the average procedural knowledge score is 64 percent, and the average policy knowledge score is only 55 percent.

Figure 6.1 illustrates the distribution of procedural knowledge scores and reveals that most staff members answered three of four questions about the rules and procedures of their chamber correctly. Similarly, figure 6.2 shows the distribution of staff members' policy knowledge scores as a whole and when broken out by policy area. The pattern of policy knowledge is similar across the three policy areas, although the average level of knowledge of budget and appropriations policy (63 percent) exceeds that of health care (54 percent) or national security (58 percent). Considering the context in which the survey was administered and the frequency of budget crises, it is not hard to see why staff might be especially well versed in this policy area.

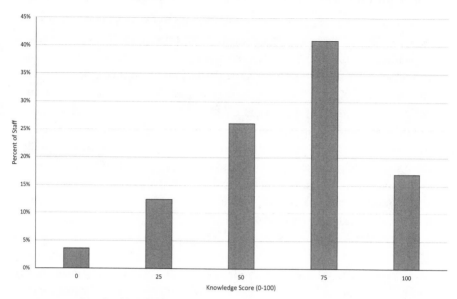

FIGURE 6.1. Procedural knowledge
Source: Data from Drutman et al. 2017b.

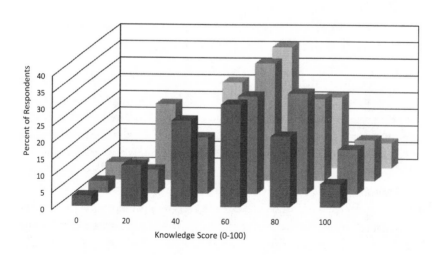

■ All policy   ■ Budget policy   ■ Health policy   ■ National security policy

FIGURE 6.2. Policy knowledge
Source: Data from Drutman et al. 2017b.

One can interpret these aggregate knowledge scores in a more—or less—favorable light. On the one hand, many congressional staffers scored high, indicating that staff are well positioned to increase congressional capacity for policymaking. In fact, 83 staff members scored a perfect 100 percent on either the policy or procedural knowledge scores.[2] An additional 217 staff members missed only one question when asked about substantive policy (82) or chamber rules and procedure (135). On the other hand, 15 percent of staff members did not answer more than one question correctly, and this was true for both the policy and procedural questions. The data also reveal that staff are more knowledgeable about congressional rules than they are about specific public policy areas, a finding which likely reflects the challenges of being (and staying) informed on complex and changing issues.

Regardless of how one interprets these aggregate scores, it is clear that there is considerable variation in staff members' knowledge of both policy and procedure. In the remaining sections of this chapter, then, I explore further variation among staff members by focusing on six expectations about how Congress works that have not previously been examined in the context of staff knowledge because we have not had the data to do so. Understanding how staff members' knowledge varies is critical to identifying the best way to increase staff expertise and thus improve the policymaking capacity of Congress.

Is the Senate the "Upper Chamber" When It Comes to Staff Knowledge?

The terms "upper chamber" and "lower chamber" are rarely used in public discussions of the Senate and House, but on Capitol Hill this distinction and the ranking it implies often rankle House members. The Senate is traditionally thought of as the more senior, deliberative, and policy-focused institution (e.g., Kramnick 1987; Matthews 1960; Sinclair 1989). The six-year election cycle is widely understood to allow senators more time to develop policy expertise and master the intricacies of Senate rules. The question, then, is whether this characterization holds true when focusing on staff members. Do Senate staff members know more about policies and chamber rules and procedures?

Comparisons of staff knowledge in the two chambers do not reveal a significant knowledge advantage (see figure 6.3). When asked about their chamber's rules and procedures, there is no discernible difference in the average scores of Senate and House staffers (62 percent vs. 65 percent, respectively). When asked about substantive issues, Senate staffers score only marginally higher than their House counterparts, with an average score of 56 percent as

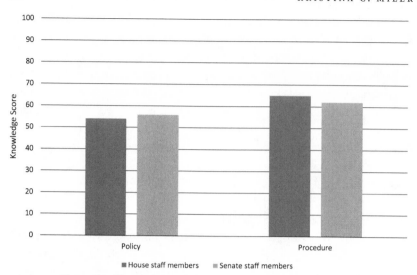

FIGURE 6.3. Bicameral staff knowledge comparisons
Source: Data from Drutman et al. 2017b.

compared with 54 percent, and the slight difference is not statistically mean-ingful. If each policy area is examined separately, only on national security issues is there any indication at all that Senate staff are more knowledgeable, which comports with the Senate's larger role on foreign policy.[3]

The overall finding that staff knowledge levels are similar across the House and the Senate adds a new dimension to the competitive bicameral dynamics evident in the legislative process. It also suggests that any efforts to improve staff knowledge (and thus increase congressional capacity) should be pursued in both chambers.

Are Committee Staff Members Actually More Knowledgeable?

Another preconception about Congress is that staff members for congres-sional committees are experts on policy. Committee staff are believed to be insulated from the day-to-day politics and electoral demands to which staff in personal offices must attend, which allows them to focus on substantive issue areas (e.g., Fenno 1973; R. Hall 1996; Krehbiel 1991; Smith and Deering 1984).[4] It would be logical, then, to expect committee staff members to have higher levels of policy-specific knowledge than their personal staff counterparts.

To examine this conventional wisdom, I compare the average policy scores for staff members in personal offices, committee offices, and party offices (see the left side of figure 6.4). Contrary to expectations, personal staff score

higher when asked about policy-specific information (57 percent) than committee staff (51 percent) or party staff (56 percent). This unexpected finding, however, could be because committee staff includes staffers from all
committees, regardless of their relevance to the policies being asked about.
When examining the knowledge scores of staff members only on committees relevant to the issue at hand (i.e., budget and appropriations, health care,
or national security), it is no longer the case that committee staff fall behind
personal staff. Rather, the data reveal that there is no statistically meaningful difference between the policy knowledge scores of relevant committee
staff and personal staff who work on the issue (61 percent and 63 percent,
respectively).[5]

The data, therefore, suggest that the source of informational advantage for
staff is likely in specialization—something that can occur through the committee system or within a personal office—rather than committees' separation
from politics. As expected, committee staff are somewhat better informed
on issues relevant to their committee and are poised to help move legislative
proposals through the committee process (see chapter 7 in this volume). However, personal office staff members are similarly knowledgeable about issues
in their portfolio. The key variation in policy knowledge seems to be rooted
in specialization rather than institutional position.

In the case of knowledge of congressional rules and procedures, the striking difference is that staff who work in party offices score significantly higher

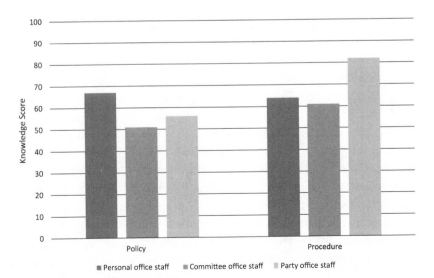

FIGURE 6.4. Staff knowledge by office type
Source: Data from Drutman et al. 2017b.

than their counterparts in personal or committee offices (see the right side of figure 6.4). Although the number of party office staff is small (fewer than twenty people), they score an average of 82 percent when asked about chamber rules and procedure, as compared with 64 percent for personal staff and 61 percent for committee staff. That staff in party offices are particularly well versed in the rules of the congressional game is consistent with research that highlights the use of rules and procedure to advance party preferences (e.g., Cox and McCubbins 1993, 2005; Lee 2009; Sinclair 1989). Thus, it is likely that staff in party offices have incentives to be well versed in the chamber's rules in order to advance their party's goals.

Is Everything on the Hill Polarized?

In today's highly polarized Congress, it seems as though partisanship affects every aspect of the legislative process. Staff members themselves carry party loyalties (e.g., Jensen 2011), and Democratic and Republican staff members are equally represented in the Congressional Capacity Survey (see chapter 5). Although knowledge levels do not vary by party per se,[6] is it the case that staff knowledge is affected by the intensity of staff members' party identification?

There is good reason to think that staff members' knowledge of the institution may vary according to the strength of their party affiliation. As noted, scholars have shown that parties and their leaders in Congress strategically use chamber rules and procedures to advance their preferred policies and partisan goals (e.g., Cox and McCubbins 1993, 2005; Evans and Oleszek 2001; Lee 2009, 2016; Theriault 2013). As a result, staffers who identify as strong partisans (from either party) should be more likely to be well versed in congressional procedure.[7]

When staff are grouped according to how strongly they identify with their party, a clear positive relationship emerges between strength of partisanship and knowledge of chamber rules (see figure 6.5). Staff members who only weakly identify as partisans have an average procedural knowledge score of 49 percent, but those who identify as partisans score 11 points higher with an average score of 59 percent.[8] Furthermore, staff members who identify as strong partisans demonstrate even greater familiarity with congressional rules and procedure, and correctly answer 68 percent of questions, on average.

The evidence that more-partisan staff members are more familiar with the rules of the House and Senate, combined with the earlier finding that staff members in party offices have greater knowledge of congressional procedures, offers new insight into the connection between party and procedure in today's Congress. Potential efforts to reduce partisanship in Congress and

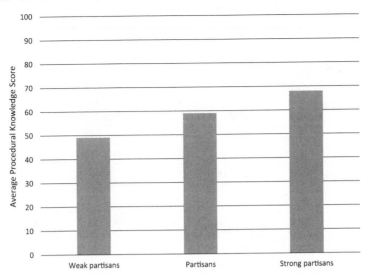

FIGURE 6.5. Partisanship and procedural knowledge
Source: Data from Drutman et al. 2017b.

decentralize the legislative process should consider the partisan-based variations in staff knowledge that underscore the extent to which party leaders use rules to advance partisan goals. In addition, since weak partisans have the lowest levels of procedural knowledge, reform advocates should seek out venues that appeal to less-partisan staff rather than rely on party-based channels for educating staff on congressional procedure.

Is There a "Brain Drain" of Congressional Staff?

A source of concern for advocates of a strong Congress is the possibility that the best and brightest are being courted away from the Hill, particularly into more lucrative private-sector jobs. Indeed, there is evidence of a well-worn path between Capitol Hill and K Street, one that both members of Congress and their staff tread (e.g., Cain and Drutman 2014; LaPira and Herschel 2014, 2017; Lazarus and McKay 2012; Lazarus, McKay, and Herbel 2016; Mann and Ornstein 1992). In fact, scholars have shown that lobbyists who previously worked in Congress are paid better than their colleagues, which reflects the value of their unique knowledge of Congress (e.g., LaPira and Herschel 2017). However, we know less about whether staff members who intend to leave Congress are distinct from staff who plan to continue working in Congress. One might expect that the most knowledgeable staff members also will be the ones to leave Congress for the private sector. Evidence of such a pattern

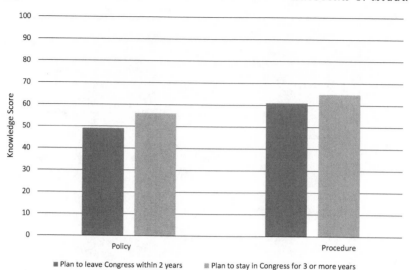

FIGURE 6.6. Staff knowledge by expected departure from Congress
Source: Data from Drutman et al. 2017b.

would be troubling because it would leave Congress weaker relative to lobbyists, the executive branch, and other political actors.

In short, the data do not support fears that the most knowledgeable staff
are the ones leaving. When staff members were asked how long they envision working in Congress, approximately 35 percent replied that they intend
to leave Congress within two years, while 65 percent intend to stay on the
Hill for longer. When these two groups are compared, there is no evidence
that those more likely to leave Congress in the near future are more knowledgeable (see figure 6.6). In fact, the data show that staff who plan to stay in
Congress for three or more years score significantly higher on policy questions than do staff who plan to leave the Hill soon (57 percent vs. 52 percent).[9]
When it comes to procedural knowledge, staff members who plan to leave
in the next two years have an average score of 61 percent as compared with
65 percent for staff who plan to stay in Congress longer, although this difference is not statistically significant at conventional levels.

When staff members are compared based on their long-term career goals,
there still is no evidence of a brain drain. Staff members who hope to leave
Capitol Hill do not demonstrate greater procedural or policy knowledge than
their colleagues who want to stay in Congress. Figure 6.7 presents the average knowledge scores for staff members who report their ideal next step to
be staying in Congress, working in other parts of government, or working in
the politically relevant private sector (i.e., lobbying firms, advocacy, political

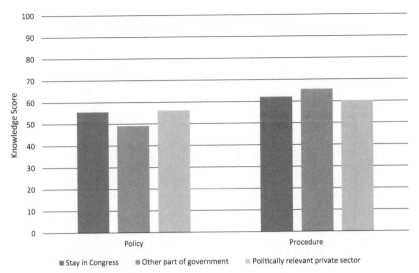

FIGURE 6.7. Staff knowledge by future career path
Source: Data from Drutman et al. 2017b.

consulting, campaign finance, and parties), and there is remarkably little difference.[10]

Altogether, the data are not consistent with the idea of a staff brain drain away from Capitol Hill. While there exists a revolving door between Congress, K Street, and the executive branch, these unique survey data reveal that the staff who leave are not necessarily the most knowledgeable. This is an encouraging finding for those who would like to see Congress retain a strong role in the policymaking process because it means that at least some highly knowledgeable staff members are choosing to stay in Congress.

Is Experience the Best Teacher?

Congressional scholars regularly associate a legislator's tenure in Congress with increased expertise, and there is evidence that those who have been in the institution longer are more knowledgeable and effective (e.g., Kingdon 1989; McCrain 2018; Volden and Wiseman 2014). It is easy to imagine the same to be true for legislative staffers who learn from recurring policy debates and the repetition of the legislative process. Indeed, chapter 13 in this volume focuses specifically on the impact of experienced staffers on legislative effectiveness. Here, then, I examine whether staff with more experience working on the Hill are more informed about congressional rules as well as substantive policy areas.

I first examine whether longer-serving staff members know more about Congress than their colleagues do. Both policy and procedural knowledge are positively correlated with the number of years a staff member is employed on the Hill, although the relationship is weaker for policy information.[11] This finding likely reflects the fact that procedural knowledge varies less over time whereas policy details often change over time. Additionally, staff members' policy portfolios may shift over their career, which reduces the advantages of a longer career on the Hill.

The Congressional Capacity Survey also affords a second measure of experience: the frequency with which staff members work on a given policy. If experience is the root of staff members' knowledge, then there should be a positive relationship between how much time staff spend working on an issue and how much they know about it. As figure 6.8 shows, staffers who work on an issue daily correctly answer an average of 62 percent of relevant policy questions, while those who work on the issue only occasionally correctly answer 51 percent, and staff members who never work on the issue correctly answer just 44 percent of questions. Furthermore, this relationship holds true when looking at each of the three issues separately.[12]

Taken together, there is strong evidence that experience goes hand in hand with greater knowledge of policy and procedure. This relationship has important implications for improving staff knowledge and the capacity of

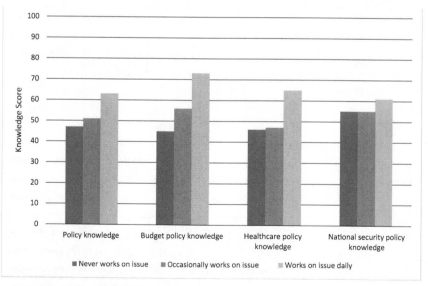

FIGURE 6.8. Staff knowledge by time spent working on issue
Source: Data from Drutman et al. 2017b.

Congress. First, it suggests that efforts to retain staff will have the benefit of increasing aggregate knowledge in Congress, especially procedural knowledge, since information levels increase with longer tenure on the Hill. Second, the evidence that staff members who work on an issue daily are more knowledgeable indicates that specialization is an important element of congressional capacity. Moreover, this reinforces the earlier finding that the informational advantages enjoyed by committee staff are rooted in the specialization that is the hallmark of the committee system. Therefore, if the goal is to have better-informed staff to increase congressional capacity, the data suggest that staff specialization and staff retention are essential.

Is There a Congressional Staff Gender Gap?

As the topic of gender equity in the workplace has risen in salience, so has interest in the gender dynamics of Capitol Hill. Women make up nearly half of all congressional staff, but they are underrepresented in the top positions on the Hill (Burgat 2017; Gangitano 2016).[13] Moreover, even among Hill staff in similar positions, there are striking differences in the policy portfolios of men and women (Burgat 2017). One possible explanation for this gender disparity is that it has little to do with gender itself, but instead reflects differences in policy knowledge that happen to correlate with gender.

The data on staff knowledge, however, provide no evidence of gender disparity in staff members' knowledge of policy issues, regardless of whether the focus is budget and appropriations, health care, or national security. The scores of male and female staffers simply cannot be distinguished from one another. The absence of a gender-based difference in knowledge of policy areas undercuts the argument that disparities in staff members' portfolios are reflections of knowledge of the substantive policy area. For instance, only 29 percent of congressional staff working on homeland security and defense are women (Burgat 2017), yet women score 60 percent on the national security questions compared with 57 percent for men.[14]

However, the data also indicate that women score lower than their male colleagues when asked about the rules and procedures of Congress. Across both chambers, female staffers answer 59 percent of procedural questions correctly while men provide the correct answer 66 percent of the time.[15] To the extent that knowledge of congressional procedure gives one an advantage in the legislative process—a point famously made by the late Representative John Dingell (D-MI)—the gender gap in procedural knowledge may be cause for concern. In addition to possible implications for staff members' career trajectories, a gender gap in procedural knowledge has the potential to hinder the progress of issues that female staff members work on if they are less able to use the rules of the institution to advance those policies.

Bringing It All Together

The insights presented in this chapter are drawn when considering each factor in isolation. What happens, then, if these factors are examined together? Are they still important determinants of staff knowledge when other considerations are taken into account? To examine staff knowledge in a more complex and realistic setting, I estimate two separate models—one for policy knowledge and one for procedural knowledge—using ordered logistic regression with robust standard errors. The two models are identical, with two exceptions. First, the frequency with which staff work on a given policy issue is only included in the model of policy knowledge. Second, the model of policy knowledge includes indicator variables for the various policy areas (minus one) to account for any unique features of the issues.

As shown in table 6.1, the results largely confirm the bivariate relationships, albeit with greater confidence, now that we've accounted for a host of other explanations. The first column of table 6.1 estimates staff members' scores on procedural knowledge and shows the importance of partisanship. Both the strength of staffers' partisan orientation and whether they work in a party office are key predictors of how much staff members know about congressional rules and procedure. The reported results also show that experience in Congress continues to be an important determinant of staff members' procedural knowledge: staff who have worked on the Hill for longer are more knowledgeable about the institution. Lastly, there continues to be evidence that female staff members score lower than their male colleagues do when asked about congressional rules and procedure, all else equal.

The second column of table 6.1 presents the estimates of staff members' knowledge of policy information. Most obvious is that staff members who have more experience in an issue area—whether over a longer career or through daily activity—are significantly more likely to have accurate knowledge of that policy area, even when accounting for other factors. The relationship between experience and substantive knowledge is positive and statistically significant for each of the policy areas when evaluated separately as well (see appendix 6.1 online). The data also reveal that Senate staff members demonstrate greater knowledge about policy issues than do their House colleagues when controlling for other factors. This effect is driven primarily by Senate staff members' informational edge when looking at national security policy, which is consistent with the Senate's traditionally larger role in matters

TABLE 6.1. Models of staff knowledge

	Procedural knowledge score	Policy knowledge score
Democrat	0.017	−0.225
	(0.230)	(0.229)
Strength of partisanship	0.559**	0.215
	(0.150)	(0.154)
Senate office	−0.051	0.740**
	(0.221)	(0.244)
Committee office	−0.207	−0.730**
	(0.253)	(0.247)
Party office	1.14†	0.348
	(0.620)	(0.428)
Years working in Congress	0.081**	0.049*
	(0.022)	(0.020)
Female	−0.471†	0.214
	(0.256)	(0.241)
Time spent on issue	—	0.693**
		(0.147)
Next step: Stay in Congress	0.172	0.306
	(0.268)	(0.276)
Next step: Relevant private sector	−0.377	0.164
	(0.300)	(0.278)
Number of observations	296	296
Wald χ^2	41.91	85.81

Note: Column 2 includes a dummy variable for two of three policy blocks not reported in the table. All coefficients were estimated using ordered logistic regression with robust standard errors. Cut points (4) for procedural knowledge: −1.97, −0.12, 1.38, 3.54. Cut points (5) for policy knowledge: −1.94, 0.01, 1.72, 3.45, 5.34.
$†p < 0.10; *p < 0.05; **p < 0.01.$

of foreign policy.[16] It is also worth noting that the negative relationship between committee staff and levels of policy information persists, but a closer look at each issue (see appendix 6.1) reveals that this relationship largely reflects the dynamics of national security.

Looking Forward

This chapter reveals that congressional staff members' procedural and substantive knowledge varies considerably and that they know less on average than might have been expected given their front-row seat to the legislative process. Efforts to improve congressional capacity, such as the House Select Committee on the Modernization of Congress, therefore should include efforts to increase and equalize information levels among staff. The findings presented here also have several implications for what those efforts might look like. Most notably, the analyses of substantive knowledge among staff members show that specialization matters. Whether in a committee or personal office, staff members who devote more time to an issue area are better informed. We cannot expect a multitasking staff member who handles four issues to have the same deep, policy-specific knowledge as a lobbyist or agency staff member who is dedicated to a single issue area. If Congress is to assert its prerogative and capacity in policymaking, then allowing staff to be specialists is an important—and relatively easy—step in that direction. One way to achieve greater specialization may be to hire more staff, but specialization also may be achieved through reorganizing existing staff and resources. Greater substantive knowledge also may generate new ideas and different legislative proposals as staff are better able to evaluate existing claims and perhaps think more creatively about policy solutions. Indeed, increased capacity for information-driven policymaking within Congress should help achieve a broader, more diverse range of policy alternatives to address the complex problems facing the country (see chapter 11 in this volume, as well as Baumgartner and Jones 2015).

Staff retention is another important goal for Congress, since longer-serving staff are systematically better informed about the rules of the institution as well as the details of policy areas. Staff with greater seniority are better able to provide members of Congress with the objective information necessary to make good public policy and to use the rules and procedures to advance their goals. Although some amount of staff turnover is unavoidable, the key is that there is no evidence that better-informed staff members are more likely to leave Congress. Thus efforts to retain staff will both increase aggregate knowledge in Congress and improve the balance of information relative to the executive branch and interest groups who seek to promote their own interests in the legislative process.

The data also reveal that information levels among congressional staff are not immune from the dynamics of heightened partisanship and the incentives it creates. The parties' use of institutional rules to advance partisan goals makes procedural information more valued among strong partisans and staff members who work in party offices. This knowledge may help advance more-partisan legislation at the expense of more-moderate legislative proposals. Thus, efforts should be made to increase procedural knowledge among less-partisan staff members, which could have the benefits of increasing staff knowledge, advancing less-partisan legislation, and countering partisans' use of procedure to advance party preferences. Additionally, more-informed staff are less likely to rely on partisan cues when making decisions or advising members of Congress, which could help lessen polarization in policymaking.

In sum, staff are central to the information environment, the development of public policy, and consequently the balance of power between Congress, the executive branch, and interest groups. To increase capacity, Congress could hire more staff to attend to the ever-increasing demands on members' offices, but the data presented here suggest that more staff is not necessarily the answer. If Congress wants to better represent the wide-ranging interests of the American people, develop policy to address complex problems, and oversee existing programs, its staff must have a command of procedural and substantive information. Such knowledge will allow staff members to engage relevant actors outside of Congress from a position of strength, rather than deference. Reforms that emphasize staff specialization and retention will help Congress achieve that position. More broadly, the country will benefit from multiple, independent sources of information to help identify problems that need to be addressed and to develop innovative policy solutions. Increasing staff knowledge, then, is an important component of increasing congressional capacity to legislate, as well as to govern and to represent the people.

How Committee Staffers Clear the Runway for Legislative Action in Congress

CASEY BURGAT AND CHARLES HUNT

So my chief counsel . . . he's a lawyer, and he'd been doing it for a long while, so he was an expert on that whole process. How do you choose the issues in your committee that you want to investigate? How do you bring witnesses in and how do you interrogate, so to speak, before they testify? What documents do you gather, and all that sort of stuff. And he's the guy who would be sitting next to me through all those hearings whispering in my ear, passing me notes. He knew the political process. He knew the legislative process. He spent a ton of time developing expertise and knowledge on each one of these issues. And, we usually had several investigations going at once, so we have—I don't remember how many staff we had, probably five or six, maybe seven—staff that were just helping me with an investigation.

FORMER MEMBER OF CONGRESS

Much of the recent scholarship on policymaking and legislative productivity in the United States Congress has focused primarily on partisanship (i.e., Lee 2009, 2016), the centralization of policy crafting in congressional leaders (Curry 2015), and their multifaceted effects on who dictates the policymaking process and legislative outcomes. While not misplaced, this focus can short-change some of the many important ways in which Congress can improve the quality and quantity of its legislative output, particularly within the committee process by which Congress is supposed to develop policy and push it through the two chambers.

Congressional committees and the legislative outcomes they produce remain relevant in several key ways. From a policymaking perspective, committees are where issue expertise resides and where most deliberation on policy alternatives occurs. Issue area expertise possessed by the committee members is most often researched from the perspective of lawmakers and the expertise, experience, and policy interests they possess. Membership on committees is often purposeful, where members are assigned based on educational, occupational, or geographic interest in a particular policy area, partly because this matching is likely to lead to legislative productivity (Francis and Bramlett 2017). Committees delineate these jurisdictions to provide increased attention to specific issue areas. In doing so, the chambers achieve an efficient division of labor that facilitates lawmaker specialization across the vast number of government issues and produces more reasoned, thoughtful policy.

We argue that the benefits committees provide by cultivating issue specialization and efficiency are every bit as relevant in the composition of committee staff. We show not only that committees produce more meaningful legislation when staffed at higher capacity but also, perhaps more important, that committees are demonstrably more productive when equipped with staff whose job descriptions and expertise match the nature of the legislative function being performed. Even when controlling for specific committee, committee chair attributes, majority status in both chambers, and other political and committee-level variables, we find that committee legislative productivity is best facilitated by a robust staff presence—in particular, staff whose experience is best suited to each of three distinct types of legislative output we measure in this work.

This research closes a critical gap in our understanding of how committees operate. It extends to congressional staff the nuances of policy specialization we apply to lawmakers, and it shows that committees not only take these staffer-level characteristics into account, but that they are wise to do so due to the resulting boost in certain types of legislative productivity. Our results should induce congressional scholars to rethink how staffers can be used to reinvigorate the committee process, and how their expertise and experience might be more effectively applied to specific types of legislative outputs to increase productivity, efficiency, and quality.

The Legislative Impact of Committee Staff

Though they often remain nameless to the general public, and even to other legislative offices, much of the day-to-day work done on specific issue areas and policy proposals is executed by committee staffers (Aberbach 1987; Brady 1981; Deering and Smith 1997; DeGregorio 1988; Malbin 1980; Price 1972; Salisbury and Shepsle 1981b). Thus, it is not surprising that congressional studies and lawmakers themselves regularly contend that staffers increase the capacity of lawmakers and the institution (Malbin 1980). Despite their importance, staffers' influence on legislative capacity is often overlooked in the very places most scholars assume staffer expertise to be at their highest and their impact on legislative activity to be greatest: congressional committees (Polsby 1969). In contrast to personal office staffers who are often the focus of scholarly attention, committee aides are devoted full-time to their committee's specific issue jurisdictions "to provide committees with substantive expertise relevant to the subject matter of each committee" (Deering and Smith 1997, 163). A primary contention of this project is that staff impacts on legislative productivity are just as substantial at the committee level.

Unsurprisingly, scholars have found that members rely on committee aides for policymaking due to staffers' greater experience levels and longer congressional tenures (Aberbach 1987; Brady 1981; Deering and Smith 1997; DeGregorio 1988; Malbin 1980; Price 1972; Salisbury and Shepsle 1981a). However, as with differences in expertise and influence within personal offices, not all committee staffers automatically enjoy influential status. David E. Price (1971, 1972), for example, makes the distinction between "policy entrepreneurs" and "policy professionals"—the former are in constant search of opportunities to implement policy solutions, whereas the latter are willing to let committee members dictate where their policy attention should be spent. In either case, lawmakers view committee staffers as repositories of long-serving institutional memory and issue area expertise who enable lawmakers to "increase the efficiency of their explicit analytical activities and enhanc[e] their own knowledge and power" (Polsby 1969, 70–71).

As ample evidence within this volume has shown, members rely on their personal staffers for more efficient and productive operation of their office-enterprise. Dependence of committee members on committee staffers is likely even more pronounced for two reasons. First, and most important, committee activities are but one subset of a member's responsibilities and attention. Put directly, lawmakers spend only a portion of their time and attention on matters within their assigned committees; for committee aides, on the other hand, committee matters make up their entire job description.

Committee staffers largely serve at the discretion of the chair or ranking member, depending on which party employs them, and are expected to execute on the priorities of their respective party's leaders and committee members even when members are not actively engaged in committee activities. These member priorities manifest in a variety of committee outputs that are largely developed, researched, and advanced by full-time committee aides. In other words, common committee outputs—policy creation, oversight activities, and hearings—all occur and require significant and regular staffer attention relatively independent of committee members. Once the direction and focus of the committee is set by its leaders and members, much of the work toward specific outputs is executed by its aides. It is important to point out that members often act on the work of committee aides only at the culmination of staff work, such as voting to report a bill out of committee that was largely researched, negotiated, and written by committee aides.

The second reason member reliance is more pronounced at the committee level relates to the aforementioned issue expertise and institutional memory on committee policy jurisdictions that staffers provide. There are several reasons committee aides are so highly valued. First, they typically maintain longer congressional tenures than staffers employed in personal offices (Petersen, Eckman, and Chausow 2016). This longer tenure allows staffers to become well versed in the ways of the Hill, develop relationships across offices and parties, and become fluent in the intricacies of legislative research, policy crafting, and political motivations that often propel or stifle legislative action.

Second, committee staffers enjoy a more limited issue portfolio than personal aides do. Whereas committee staffers are expected to become experts on the issues relevant to their committee's jurisdiction, personal office staffers are more policy generalists whose portfolios are so broad that issue area expertise is much harder to develop. Narrower policy focus enables committee aides to be better versed in the minutiae of policy details, likely obstacles, and legislative histories that are vital to successful policy creation.[1] Moreover, longer-serving aides with concentrated portfolios develop and maintain relationships with policy stakeholders and pivotal players within and outside the institution, identify policy windows for legislative entrepreneurship, and anticipate likely consequences and costs associated with their legislative proposals.

Third, because committee staffers are employed by the entire committee rather than a member facing reelection every two years, committee work devotes less attention to "reelection" issues such as constituent service or direct district communication. Committees instead offer staffers an opportunity to execute on issues in greater depth and with less regard to the day-to-day political happenings of any individual member-boss or Congress as an institution. For staffers who have committed to a career in Congress, committees provide them a more concentrated issue portfolio and a more stable source of employment when compared with personal offices, where turnover among staffers is higher and tenures are generally shorter.

It is already apparent that staff support is helpful and necessary for legislative productivity for individual members of Congress and for the institution as a whole. But we argue that committee staff are just as, and likely even more, essential to the operations of committees and serving the needs of their elected members than the literature regularly finds with personal staffers. Even while concerns about congressional gridlock and productivity are paramount, increased staffer resources should increase committees' ability to execute on its specific priorities. Therefore:

Hypothesis 1: The higher the count of congressional committee staff, the greater the legislative output will be in committees.

The "Right Staff" at the Right Time

Though empirically untested, the impact of committee staff is not novel. As put by Deering and Smith (1997), "Committee staff influence the agenda-setting decisions of chairs, advocate or even champion legislative proposals, conduct investigations, negotiate on behalf of committees and their chairs, and work to build coalitions in committee, on the floor, and in conference. The assistance of quality staff can give a committee . . . a substantial advantage over competitors in legislative politics" (162).

But, to date, congressional observers have largely overlooked *which* committee staffers influence various committee outputs, instead most often referring to committee aides as a singular resource with few distinctions between their duties and respective influence on outcomes. Previous research overlooks the very different strengths, talents, and expertise required for different itemized tasks demanded of committee staffers. For example, conducting a fruitful committee oversight investigation requires a vastly different set of skills than authoring legislative proposals, and negotiating the scope of a committee hearing utilizes different talents than building a coalition for floor passage.

Though often grouped together, committee aides vary considerably in their job titles and responsibilities. Some are tasked with policy duties, such as researching and authoring legislative proposals for committee consideration; others are responsible for carrying out a communications strategy for the committee to present its work to interested parties; still others serve as leaders overseeing the staff and production, responsible for facilitating progress on committee priorities with outside actors. These staffers are also diverse in their personal and occupational experience as well as their levels of legislative and procedural expertise. Some are oversight experts with long tenures at federal agencies; others serve with significant congressional experience and a mastery in parliamentary procedure. Staffers are valuable in their respective roles, but they are valuable for different tasks and at different times.

Therefore, a second primary contention of this chapter is that congressional committee outputs are affected by the particular type of staffers executing its work. We argue that the particular types of staffers are better suited to influence production of varying types of committee outputs, and at varying stages of the legislative process. These stages of the process—our three dependent variables for this study—require certain levels of policy and political expertise which specific staffer types are in positions to provide, thus having positive effects on that particular output. First, we use the number of substantively important bills that are reported out of committee; second, the number of hearings conducted by that committee; and third, the amount of committee-reported legislation that eventually passes the House chamber.

We focus on the two contingents of committee aides most likely to influence the legislative productivity of their respective committees: *policy staffers* and *senior staffers*. Policy aides are those most responsible for researching and improving various potential policy proposals and authoring legislation that satisfies the members of the committee. Often policy aides have established expertise on these matters thanks to extensive vocational experience with the relevant issues. They are the most likely to be familiar with the intricate details and legislative histories of issues and have developed relationships with internal and external policy stakeholders.

This expertise is particularly valuable to committees in the early stages of policymaking as staffers work to craft members' policy goals into viable legislative proposals to be reported out for consideration. A great deal of substantively important legislation is considered within a congressional committee, but such legislation is of varying quality. The likelihood of any one piece of legislation being reported out of committee depends in part on how well crafted the legislation is and how it reflects the policy demands of at least a majority of committee members. Thus, the amount of policy expertise applied to that legislation is of great consequence. We argue that *policy staffers* are most likely to have influence at initial stages *within the committee* as policy proposals are being crafted and improved on, as opposed to in later stages of the process in which political and agenda-setting considerations become paramount (Kingdon 1984). Therefore:

> Hypothesis 2: The greater the number of policy-oriented House committee staff, the greater the number of important bills reported out of House committees.

However, this initial stage of the legislative process depends on more than just the quality of the policy. The postcommittee political viability of committee proposals also plays a significant role. Support within the committee is itself subject to a perception of how likely that legislation is to pass the chamber or become law. We argue that *senior staffers*—the vast majority of whom hold the titles of staff director or deputy staff director—are equipped to anticipate these political questions during the committee phase such that only the most politically viable legislation is reported out and is ultimately approved by the full House.

Senior staffers must also navigate the political and communications dynamics of legislative activity beyond the committee stage. Whereas policy staffers' main priority is to craft legislation that satisfies the policy demands of committee members, senior staffers are responsible for guiding this legislation out of the committee, onto the floor, and into law. To do so, senior staffers maintain strong networks with committee leaders, members, and personal staff, and as a result can align committee activities with broader party and institutional agendas. This increased cooperation between committee staff, outside stakeholders, and committee and chamber leaders makes senior staffers crucial to the ultimate success of committee legislation. We therefore predict:

> Hypothesis 3: The greater the number of House committee senior staff, the greater the number of important bills reported out of House committees and passed by the chamber.

Data and Methods

To test these expectations, we combine several preexisting data sets on committee activity with an original and comprehensive data set on committee staffing capacity. These data span from 2001 to 2017, thus capturing the effects of staffing as it varies within committee over time.[2] It also provides a particularly tough but important test for the power of congressional capacity in an age where much of congressional activity is thought to be governed by partisanship (Lee 2009) and/or party leaders (Curry 2015). If staff capacity can continue to have an effect in even the most party-dominated environments for policymaking, it is a signal that staffers are not merely helpful but truly essential in executing on committee priorities, including passing important legislation through regular procedures in Congress.

Notably, we study the impact of staffing on committee outputs only within the House of Representatives. We do so for several reasons. First, because there are far fewer members of the Senate, individual committees are composed of a greater proportion of the chamber across the board, significantly diluting the leverage gained by serving on such a committee relative to other senators who do not. Relatedly, the average senator serves on more than double the number of congressional committees than the average House member and nearly triple the number of subcommittees (Ornstein et al. 2013). As a result, senators are in a far better position to execute on policy concerns no matter whether it is one of their top priorities. Third, Senate rules and procedure grant more opportunities for individual members to affect policy changes independent of the committee process. Fourth, senators enjoy more personal office staff who are better able to execute on policymaking, constituent service, and communications efforts aimed at increasing the senator's visibility and prestige. For these reasons, in addition to senators' bigger and more diverse constituencies, our analysis is limited to committees within the House, where there are more significant distinctions in how members view committee assignments and responsibilities (Deering and Smith 1997).

To assess the impact of congressional committee staffing counts on committee activity, we employ three measures of legislative outputs: substantively "important" bills voted out of committee, important bills passed by the chamber that were under the jurisdiction of that committee during its life cycle, and total number of hearings held by each committee.[3] Vitally, these data categorize bills as "important" bills of substance as opposed to ceremonial bills of little importance.[4] These bills are a better measure of the impact of committee staffers on productivity, as more-substantive legislation demands increased committee aide experience, attention, and expertise relative to ceremonial measures. We use by-year counts of these "important" bills that have been reported out of the committee in which they were referred, as well as counts of bills which, after having been referred to this committee, passed the chamber in which they originated.[5] Both measures are indicators of substantive legislative committee output, and they also measure the committee's influence in the chamber. Our third measure of output is an original data set of aggregated counts of hearings held in all House committees.

Committee staffing data used in this project are drawn from LegiStorm's personnel compensation database, which dates back to 2001. LegiStorm cleans and digitizes official staffer compensation information submitted by all congressional offices, personal and committee, to the clerk of the House. These records itemize payments to each individual staffer, the staffer's title, and the staffer's office. The House reports these payments through a statement of disbursements every three months.

Our data break down the number of staffers assigned to a committee in a given year, as well as the types of positions they hold. These counts include any staffer paid by a committee within a given year, including paid interns, fellows, and part-time, shared, and temporary employees. While LegiStorm's data are rich in detail and comprehensive in their reach, its precleaning categorization of staffer position types was insufficient to address the relative impact of each type on committee productivity. The "Preclean" bars in figure 7.1 show that of the more than 62,000 staffer-years in our data set, nearly 60 percent were either uncoded (categorized in our data as "Other" staff members) or categorized as Professional Staff Members (PSMs), who are staffers with functions that vary widely between committees and therefore cannot be easily classified based on title.

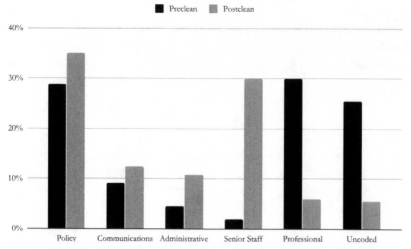

FIGURE 7.1. Committee staff types as percentage of total, 2001–2017
Source: Data from US House of Representatives 2018.

Using regular expressions on job titles listed within the official compensation records, we were able to bring the total percentage of uncoded staffers
(including PSMs)[6] down from 56 percent to just over 11 percent of all committee staffers over the eighteen-year period of our study. Figure 7.1 visualizes
the results of this coding and data-cleaning process, and a more complete
description of the operationalization of these regular expression groupings by
title can be found in tables 7A.1 and 7A.2 in the online appendix.

After this classification process, we aggregated counts of staffers into four
distinct position categories for each committee-year, labeled in figure 7.1 as
Policy, Communications, Administrative, and Senior Staff.[7] In total, this differentiation of staffers by job titles is a primary way in which our data is well
suited to addressing the question of whether staffers of a certain type and expertise are able to influence the legislative work undertaken by committees.

We incorporate six controls that also affect committee legislative outputs.
First, we obtained counts of number of members per committee-year to control
for the possibility that committees with more members would produce greater
legislative output. Second, we use the Policy Agenda Project's topic codes based
on *CQ Almanac* publications and aggregated by committee-year to determine
the number of major policy topics each committee addresses. This variable indicates which committees have wider policy jurisdictions and thus are in a better
position to produce more of our outputs under consideration. Third, we include
a dummy variable for instances in which the chair of the committee vacated the
post within the year as well as the tenure length of the committee chair. Fourth,

we include binary variables indicating whether there was a unified Congress (both chambers of the same party) in that year, and whether it was an election year, to account for House members being preoccupied with electoral politics rather than committee production. Fifth, we include a binary variable indicating whether a committee-specific authorization bill reemerged that year, as these bills can consume much, if not all, of the committee's attention and resources to secure its passage. Finally, we created a variable indicating exogenous policy shocks, which increase demand for legislative and hearing outputs.[8]

To hold as much committee-specific variation constant as possible, we employ conditional fixed-effects negative binomial regression to predict per-year counts of important bills reported out of committee, important committee-reported bills that passed the chamber, and committee hearings held. The effects measured by these models will therefore capture variation only within each committee itself to ensure that member- or committee-specific variables do not cloud the results. Full descriptive statistics of key variables can be found in table 7.1

TABLE 7.1. Descriptive statistics for key committee variables

Variable	Mean	SD	Min.	Max.
Important Bills Reported from Committee	16	22.4	0	143
Important Committee Bills Passed Chamber	11	15.1	0	91
Number of Hearings Held	50	30.1	0	164
Total Staff	67	33.1	25	160
Policy Staff	24	16.4	3	84
Communications Staff	5	2.6	0	18
Administrative Staff	14	8.4	1	52
Senior Staff	10	5.7	1	25
Unified Congress	0.7	0.5	0	1
Election Year	0.5	0.5	0	1
Committee Chair Turnover	0.0	0.2	0	2
Committee Chair Tenure Length	1.7	1.5	0	7
Committee Size (Members)	47	14.5	9	82
Exogenous Policy Shock	0.08	0.3	0	1
Committee Authorization Year	0.03	0.2	0	1
Committee Jurisdiction Count	7	3.5	2	14

Note: SD = standard deviation.

here, and a detailed explanation of each variable and its source data can be found in table 7A.3 in the online appendix.

Results

We ran a number of models to capture the differences expected by our hypotheses. First, we ran fixed-effects negative binomial regressions on each of our measures of legislative output in all House committees to assess hypothesis 1, which predicted that increases in total staff would lead to increases in legislative output. Table 7.2 shows the raw regression results of these models for each of our three measures of output.

These results are a clear confirmation of hypothesis 1. All three measures are positively affected by total staff support, with "important legislation reported" and "important legislation passed chamber" reaching statistical significance at the 0.05 level. The coefficients also tell us about substantive significance. For example, a 50 percent increase[9] in a committee's total staff support results in a 43 percent increase in the amount of legislation reported out of that committee

TABLE 7.2. Effects of staff support on committee outputs, 2001–2016

Dependent variable	Important Legislation Reported	Important Legislation Passed Chamber	Number of Hearings Held
Total Staff Support	0.86**	0.69*	0.14
	(0.26)	(0.29)	(0.19)
Unified Congress	0.06	0.16	−0.07
	(0.08)	(0.09)	(0.06)
Election Year	−0.84**	−0.83**	−0.15*
	(0.08)	(0.09)	(0.06)
Committee Chair Turnover	−0.57*	−0.43	−0.27
	(0.30)	(0.31)	(0.18)
Committee Chair Tenure Length	0.03	−0.01	−0.05*
	(0.03)	(0.03)	(0.02)
Committee Size (Members)	0.003	0.01	0.01
	(0.007)	(0.01)	(0.005)
Exogenous Policy Shock	−0.36*	−0.44*	0.01
	(0.16)	(0.18)	(0.10)
Committee Authorization Year	−0.16	−0.28	−0.33
	(0.25)	(0.28)	(0.18)
Committee Jurisdiction Count	−0.003	0.008	0.03
	(0.04)	(0.05)	(0.04)
Constant	−1.91*	−1.78	0.83
	(0.99)	(1.11)	(0.85)
N	254	254	254

Note: Results found using conditional fixed-effects negative binomial regression.
$*p < 0.05; **p < 0.01.$

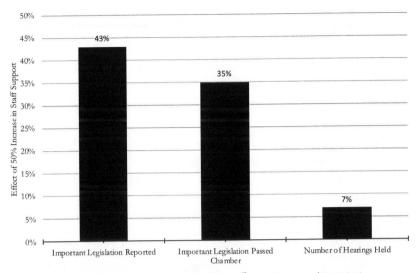

FIGURE 7.2. Effects of 50 percent increase in committee staff support on committee outputs
Source: Data from US House of Representatives 2018.

and a 35 percent increase in committee legislation that passed the chamber as a whole. It also results in a 7 percent increase in the number of hearings held in that calendar year. Clearly, having more staff support matters across the board in terms of producing legislative output from committees and successfully passing it. Figure 7.2 plots the predicted increases in committee outputs resulting from a 50 percent increase in committee staff support.

We propose that committees' ability to take up and accomplish legislative goals depends on whether they have the necessary staff resources to accomplish them. A possible alternative explanation for the importance of staff reverses this causal effect. That is, committees decide to pursue certain types of legislative activity and then staff their committees based on these specific goals. We believe this proposition is faulty on a theoretical level since appropriations for committees, and therefore funds available for staffing decisions, are set by Congress in advance of each year, pursuant to House rules.[10] Thus, within-year or within-Congress staffing adjustments would require supplemental appropriations. Though such instances have occurred, they are extremely rare.[11]

Hypothesis 1, however, reflects a weakness in previous work on both congressional committees and congressional staff: that all staff are created equal in terms of their expertise. Our findings that accompany hypotheses 2 and 3 aim to rectify this mistake by breaking down our primary independent variables by staff type. For these tests, in place of the total staff support variable, we substituted counts of the four substantively important groups of staffers by committee (policy, communications, administrative, and senior staff) to demonstrate the differential effects. Table 7.3 shows the raw regression results of these models for each of our three measures of output.

In these results, we first find confirmation of hypothesis 2: that higher numbers of *policy staffers* are particularly conducive to early-stage legislative output—in this case, the amount of legislation reported out of committee. The results indicate that a 50 percent increase in policy staff predicts a 17 percent increase in legislative output from a committee. Policy staff influence is also positive for the amount of committee legislation that passes the chamber, but the result is not statistically significant. These results confirm that staffing expertise in the policy/legislative realm is most valuable at initial stages of the legislative process, in crafting high-quality enough legislation to reach the next stage.

The results in figure 7.3 also confirm hypothesis 3: that the experience and multifaceted expertise provided by *senior staffers* lead to higher policy output at all points in the legislative process. In this case, a 50 percent increase in the number of senior staff leads to about a 15 percent increase in each of the three committee outputs and reaches statistical significance for two of them. These results indicate that senior staffers have consistent impacts on productivity driven by multifaceted expertise and leadership in both policy and political spheres on the Hill; extended social and political networks that enable them to organize support for legislative priorities; and prior experience shepherding through legislation, giving them a better intuition for its political viability at all stages of the process.

Interestingly, table 7.3 and figure 7.3 also show that senior staffers greatly influence the number of hearings held by committees. While not explicitly hypothesized, this finding aligns with our theoretical expectations. The public event of the committee hearing is the final presentation of the work conducted by staffers weeks and months prior. As previously theorized, senior staffers, by virtue of their extended networks, tenures, and expertise, are in the best position to recognize the policy and political implications that hearings offer, and they are responsible for aligning the work of the committee's policy and communications staff to carry out necessary research and preparation. Specifically, senior staff lead negotiations between the committee chair and ranking member as to the hearing's scope, potential witnesses, and lines of questioning. Just as senior staff manage committee efforts for the reporting and passing of important legislation, these senior aides also influence the production of committee hearings—another important, and public, committee output.

TABLE 7.3. Effects of specific types of staff support on committee outputs, 2001–2016

Dependent variable	Important Legislation Reported	Important Legislation Passed Chamber	Number of Hearings Held
Policy Staff Support	0.33*	0.14	0.01
	(0.13)	(0.15)	(0.11)
Communications Staff Support	0.29*	0.35*	−0.06
	(0.13)	(0.15)	(0.10)
Administrative Staff Support	−0.03	0.03	−0.07
	(0.12)	(0.13)	(0.09)
Senior Staff Support	0.32*	0.29	0.30**
	(0.13)	(0.15)	(0.10)
Unified Congress	0.09	0.19*	−0.04
	(0.08)	(0.09)	(0.06)
Election Year	−0.86**	−0.85**	−0.14*
	(0.08)	(0.09)	(0.06)
Committee Chair Turnover	−0.61**	−0.49	−0.30
	(0.30)	(0.31)	(0.18)
Committee Chair Tenure Length	0.02	−0.01	−0.05*
	(0.03)	(0.03)	(0.02)
Committee Size (Members)	0.008	0.02*	0.01*
	(0.007)	(0.01)	(0.01)
Exogenous Policy Shock	−0.35*	−0.47**	0.03
	(0.15)	(0.17)	(0.10)
Committee Authorization Year	−0.20	−0.31	−0.31
	(0.23)	(0.27)	(0.17)
Committee Jurisdiction Count	0.01	0.03	0.07
	(0.05)	(0.05)	(0.04)
Constant	−0.69	−0.99	0.67
	(0.64)	(0.72)	(0.60)
N	254	254	254

Note: Results found using conditional fixed-effects negative binomial regression.

$^*p < 0.05$; $^{**}p < 0.01$.

Finally, the results in table 7.3 show that *communications* staffers also produce substantive and statistically significant increases in legislation reported and legislation passed the chamber. These findings suggest that communications aides generate and capitalize on public narratives or policy windows in which a committee's legislative proposals can be characterized as viable solutions (Kingdon 1984) or as winning messaging for the majority party (Lee 2016). Their skills and media contacts help communications staffers induce positive media coverage of member and party-desired committee actions—such as framing a controversial policy proposal as a justified course of action—thereby increasing public demand and acceptance for the action. More fundamentally, the effects of communications staffers on a committee's legislative

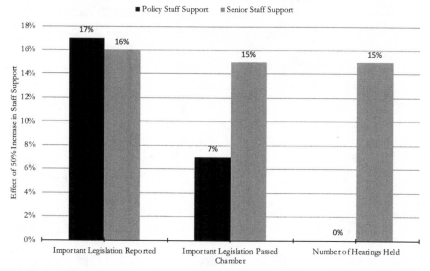

FIGURE 7.3. Effects of 50 percent increase in staff support by position groupings on committee outputs
Source: Data from US House of Representatives 2018.

productivity suggest that a strong committee media presence helps facilitate their passage out of committee and even by the chamber.

The results shown in tables 7.2 and 7.3 confirm our theoretical expectations discussed earlier: not only that staffers generally increase legislative productivity but also that this productivity depends on the type of staffer deployed at certain points in the legislative process.

Discussion

Results presented in this chapter should encourage congressional scholars and reformers to consider not just how staff can improve legislative productivity but also which types of staff are most effective at it. Our results indicate that committee staffers have positive effects on legislative output in the chamber in a general sense and that meeting particular staffing needs at particular points in the legislative process exponentiates these effects. At the same time, the trends suggested by our data and figure 7.2 suggest that if granted the increased committee staffing resources for which many reformers are advocating, committees are likely to put them toward communications rather than policy positions.

These findings comport with theories from earlier chapters in this volume that point out not a simple need for greater capacity to accomplish legislative goals in Congress (as we find in our first hypothesis), but also for more diverse applications of this capacity in order to maximize legislative productivity and quality.[12] Since the 1980s, the responsibilities of the federal government, and of Congress in particular, have grown in both size and complexity (Sinclair 1989, 2016), while congressional action has simultaneously been crippled by partisan gridlock (Layman and Carsey 2002; Theriault 2008) and increased competition between the two parties for majority control (Lee 2016). Our findings demonstrate that diverse types of staffers with distinct expertise are necessary to navigate the new political and legislative complexities that Congress now faces.

These parallel responsibilities are often in conflict with each other: ideal policy goals are political untenable to enough lawmakers to gain passage, and partisan political goals are thwarted by the reality of a diverse, complex nation with both old and emerging policy problems. Elected representatives are the embodiment of this conflict, often pulled in different directions by policy and political priorities alike. But at the committee level, legislative success can happen only when these differing goals converge not just in the individual, but between lawmakers.

We have demonstrated that staff members at the committee level are well suited to facilitate this convergence. Staffers can use their individual types of experience and expertise to pass more-substantive legislation that serves the policy and political needs of both members and constituents. Policy staffers can use their issue expertise to create better-quality legislation within the committee; and senior staffers can work alongside them to anticipate political complexities to make the legislation successful at both the committee and chamber levels. As for the committee structure at large, this division of responsibility clearly assists in passing substantive legislation, and particularized staffing resources help solve the broader problem of congressional inaction in an age of intense partisan conflict.

Legislative Branch Support Agencies: What They Are, What They Do, and Their Uneasy Position in Our System of Government

KEVIN R. KOSAR

Legislative branch support agencies have existed for more than a century, yet they remain remarkably little known to the public and are only occasionally studied by scholars.[1] For the purposes of this chapter, the term *legislative branch support agencies* includes the Congressional Budget Office (CBO), Congressional Research Service (CRS), the Government Accountability Office (GAO), and the defunct Office of Technology Assessment (OTA).[2]

That these organizations are so little known is due mostly to their position in the US system of governance. Generally, their job is to assist legislators in the execution of their legislative duties. Unlike the officials they serve, legislative branch support agency employees are civil servants—unelected persons—and it is not their duty to engage in politics or make policies.[3] They take an oath of office to uphold the US Constitution and tend to have long tenures in government service.[4] Their budgets are appropriated by the US Congress annually.

Thus, legislative branch support agencies personnel mostly tend to stay out of the public eye and well behind the politicians they assist. Their relative anonymity, however, should not obscure the important roles they play in the legislative process. These agencies' manifold activities are both formal (e.g., scoring the approximate cost of legislation) and informal (e.g., responding to requests for research assistance from legislators and their staff). Congress established legislative branch support agencies precisely because it needed assistance in various aspects of its workflow (e.g., comprehending whether an executive branch expenditure of funds on a particular good or service was legal).

Legislative branch support agencies, therefore, have a key role in augmenting congressional capacity. They lend much-needed expertise to a legislative body comprising mostly individuals with little experience developing federal policy or overseeing its execution, and they reduce legislators' dependency on lobbyists (LaPira and Thomas 2017). The civil servants who support Congress serve as attention expanders—extra sets of eyes, ears, and minds—who can identify matters as "problems" worthy of legislative focus and action (Baumgartner and Jones 2015). When they produce reports identifying agencies misusing public funds, many legislators, media, and interest groups often notice—and act.

Their effects also are felt within the chambers. The agencies, by virtue of their nonpartisan employees and nature, are a shared resource that individual legislators and committees may utilize to augment their own limited knowledge and staff capacity. The legislative branch support agencies augmented the power of the committees during the days of the "textbook Congress" of the 1940s–1960s (Shepsle 1989, 339–51) and the subsequent "pluralist adhocracy" of the 1970s (described in chapter 2 in this volume). Today, the agencies still augment the policymaking and oversight powers of committees, but they also empower individual legislators, whose access to information is consciously limited by power centers within the legislature during a time of what we described in chapter 2 as "adversarial clientelism" (see also Curry 2015, 78–119).

With policy outputs being the product of a struggle between competing branches sharing powers, these agencies help redress some of the intrabranch informational asymmetries that bedevil Congress (Kosar 2018a). And the asymmetries are significant, what with the executive branch being a roughly $4 trillion, global enterprise with 170 or so agencies operating under 180,000 pages of regulation that affect virtually every aspect of American life (see chapter 4 in this volume; Kosar 2015a).

These agencies, then, affect the balance of policy power in the two chambers and between the branches of government. As a result, they are significant institutions. The diminution of legislative branch support agencies therefore produces a diminution in congressional capacity and Congress's governance capacity.

This chapter provides an overview of what the legislative branch support agencies are, why they were established, and what they do. Legislative branch support agencies are essential to the operation of a modern legislature, yet as this chapter details, they occupy uneasy positions in the American system of government. Their institutional position and influence mire them in intense political controversies, which can provoke congressional retribution. Understanding the evolving institutional context they work within will be essential to future efforts to consider how legislative branch support agencies can support Congress in the twenty-first century.

Legislative Branch Support Agencies:
Why They Were Created and What They Do

The genesis of Congress's legislative branch support agencies has roots within a brute fact expressed by Thomas Jefferson in 1814: "There is, in fact, no subject to which a member of Congress may not have occasion to refer" (quoted in Stathis 2014, 9). The need for information prompted Congress to establish the Library of Congress in 1800 and fund its acquisition of books.[5] The first five clerks of the House of Representatives managed the library's collections, which were kept in the US Capitol (Library of Congress, n.d.).

The Library of Congress served as the sole legislative branch support agency for a century. Thereafter, Congress augmented its informational and analytical capacity by establishing the Congressional Research Service (1914), Government Accountability Office (1921), Office of Technology Assessment (1972), and the Congressional Budget Office (1974). As noted in the sections that follow, each had a particular role to play in support of the legislative process; however, collectively these agencies were intended to professionalize the legislature, and to strengthen Congress's position relative to the executive branch, which was better staffed with expertise.[6]

CONGRESSIONAL RESEARCH SERVICE

CRS began as the Legislative Reference Service (LRS), and was inspired by state legislative support agencies.[7] During its first few decades, the agency's duties largely consisted of providing reference services and preparing digests useful to legislators making laws, such as "Proposed amendments to the Constitution of the United States introduced in Congress from December 4, 1889, to July 2, 1926." On occasion, LRS published lengthy studies, and its attorneys assisted committees with bill drafting. Congress's demand for help grew quickly. LRS fielded an average of 1,260 requests per year by 1920 (Stathis 2014, 13).

The 1946 Legislative Reorganization Act expanded LRS's role in the legislative process and its staff. The statute directed it to "advise and assist any committee of either House or any joint committee in the analysis, appraisal, and evaluation of legislative proposals pending before it, or of recommendations submitted to Congress by the President or any executive agency, and otherwise to assist in furnishing a basis for the proper determination of measures before the committee."[8]

The law also authorized the hiring of experts in the areas thought most critical to the legislature and the nation: agriculture, industrial organization, international trade, banking, veterans' affairs, and more.[9] Expanding the role of LRS was part of the statute's larger objectives: strengthening Congress to better function and to better manage the executive branch, which had grown in immensity and complexity during World War I and the Great Depression.

Having more LRS experts enabled congressional committees to call on the agency more often—which it did. In the 1950s and 1960s, LRS experts aided committees assessing current policy and considering improvements on a broad range of topics, including national defense, international relations, government organization, and social policy (education and youth employment programs).[10]

Congress again expanded the Legislative Reference Service and rechristened it the Congressional Research Service in 1970.[11] The replacement of the word *reference* with *research* underscored the agency's heightened analytical duties. CRS was to support congressional oversight of the executive branch and identify policy issues worth the legislature's attention.[12] Congress expanded CRS's staff, and the agency went from around 360 employees in 1971 to just under 900 workers by 1985 (CRS 1976, 48; Library of Congress 1986, A23). CRS's staff count has decreased to around 650 today; however, the agency now assists Congress in every aspect of the policymaking process, from problem identification through policy formulation and oversight of executive branch implementation (Library of Congress 2016, 140). CRS staff train congressional staff and legislators in legislative procedure, issue legal opinions, draft the bill digests that appear on the Congress.gov website, write policy memoranda and reports,[13] help committees prepare for hearings, and assist staff in responding to constituents.[14] The agency's budget was $107 million in FY2016 (CRS 2017, 36).

GOVERNMENT ACCOUNTABILITY OFFICE

The Government Accountability Office began as the General Accounting Office in 1921. It was established by the Budget and Accounting Act, which aimed to establish a modern, professionalized system for budgeting for the federal government.[15] The statute created the Bureau of the Budget, which later became the Office of Management and Budget, and directed the president to annually submit a government-wide budget.

GAO's role was carved out of the US Treasury. It would be "independent of the executive departments" and would audit their outlays and prescribe the forms and system of accounting for expenditures of funds appropriated by Congress. The new agency was obliged to report to the president and Congress its recommendations for any legislation needed to improve government accountancy; to

report to Congress on any illicit executive branch contract outlays; and to respond to congressional committee requests for information and data on spending. Whereas the Treasury's comptrollers and auditors were accountable to the
president alone, GAO's comptroller general was given a fifteen-year term and
made removable only by a joint resolution of Congress or impeachment.[16]

Congress provided sufficient funds to staff GAO with 1,700 employees immediately. That cohort peaked at more than 14,000 during World War II to
contend with the tens of millions of executive branch payments. The agency's
work focused heavily on accountancy. A GAO history relates:

> Until the end of World War II, GAO primarily checked the legality and ad-
> equacy of government expenditures. The agency issued decisions on payment
> questions and helped process financial claims for and against the government.
> GAO's employees reviewed individual financial transactions by checking ex-
> penditure vouchers. They also audited and reconciled disbursing officers' ac-
> counts. The work was done centrally, which meant that government agencies
> had to send their fiscal records to GAO. Legions of audit clerks worked in the
> great hall of the Pension Building—GAO's home from 1926 to 1951—reviewing
> stacks of paperwork documenting government expenditures. (GAO, n.d.-c)

Congress subsequently expanded and deepened GAO's duties through
various statutes.[17] The agency was obliged to detail staff to congressional committees, to provide legal opinions to Congress on various matters, and to help
Congress review major regulations, to name just three additional responsibilities (F. Kaiser 2008; GAO, n.d.-a).

GAO is perhaps the most well-known legislative branch support agency.
Media often refer to it as Congress's "watchdog" because it publicly issues many
reports critiquing executive agencies' program management and use of funds.
GAO staff frequently testify before Congress and also do sit for interviews with
media. Its staff count has declined since the mid-1990s, yet it remains the largest of the four congressional support agencies. Its fiscal year 2016 budget was
$555 million, and it employed about 3,000 staff (GAO, n.d.-b).

OFFICE OF TECHNOLOGY ASSESSMENT

Congress established OTA in 1972. Congress's threefold justifications for creating a new agency were written into the statute.

[1] "As technology continues to change and expand rapidly, its applications
are—(1) large and growing in scale; and (2) increasingly extensive, pervasive, and critical in their impact, beneficial and adverse, on the natural and
social environment. (b) Therefore, it is essential that, to the fullest extent

possible, the consequences of technological applications be anticipated, understood, and considered in determination of public policy on existing and emerging national problems";

[2] "the Federal agencies presently responsible directly to the Congress are not designed to provide the legislative branch with adequate and timely information, independently developed, relating to the potential impact of technological applications"; and

[3] "the present mechanisms of the Congress do not and are not designed to provide the legislative branch with such information."[18]

Hitherto, the legislature had relied on the executive branch to brief it on technological issues. However, Congress had grown suspicious of what executive agencies had been telling them, as Keiper points out: "More than ever before, contentious questions related to science and technology were coming before Congress—including antiballistic missile funding, the supersonic transport project, the future of the Apollo space program, and numerous controversies related to energy and the environment. President Nixon's relationship with his science advisers was fraying. And members of Congress increasingly concluded that they needed their own advice, both to fare better in those particular legislative battles and to give their branch more power against the executive" (Keiper 2004–5, 27).

OTA had a narrowly focused mandate: study emergent technologies and advise Congress about their potential impact. OTA did not tell Congress what to do; rather, it offered its take on an emergent technology. It did so through its lengthy assessment reports, which reviewed the existing research and data on a technology (e.g., *Costs and Effectiveness of Cholesterol Screening in the Elderly*) and explained what the evidence demonstrated—or did not; the reports also included shorter-form executive summaries.[19] Unlike the other legislative branch support agencies, OTA had a research production model that networked diverse expertise. Its staff relied heavily on experts both inside and outside government to aggregate research and data, discuss it, and then help generate its reports; that is to say, peer review by academics was part of the process (Graves and Kosar 2018).

OTA was not free to research any topic it pleased. Congress maintained close supervision of its activities. The agency could initiate studies only at the request of a committee (either its chair, ranking minority member, or a simple majority), the OTA's board, or its director.[20] OTA's director was appointed by the agency's twelve-person board, whose members were six senators (three Democrats and three Republicans) and six representatives (also equally divided by party).[21] OTA's completed studies were reviewed by its board, which had to approve their release to the requesting committees.

At its peak, OTA employed around 140 civil servants, and its budget was $37 million in 2019 dollars.[22] Between 1972 and 1995, OTA produced nearly 750 assessments, background papers, and other research products (Office of Technology Assessment 1996). Congress defunded the agency in 1995, for reasons described in the following section. To ensure that OTA's work would not be lost, however, the Federation of American Scientists maintains an archive of OTA's research (see Federation of American Scientists, n.d.).

CONGRESSIONAL BUDGET OFFICE

CBO was the last legislative branch support agency established. Congress created it as part of a broader effort to strengthen Congress vis-à-vis the executive in the early 1970s (Wolfensberger 2013). The Congressional Budget and Impoundment Control Act of 1974 established new impoundment and budgetary procedures and empowered Congress to develop a budget independent of the president.[23]

CBO began work in February 1975 with 193 employees—many if not most of whom were trained in economics (Reynolds 2017a, 1–33). Its primary duty is to assist the House and Senate Budget Committees (created by the 1974 law), which produce the budget resolution determining the aggregate government spending and revenue levels.[24] CBO's analyses, estimates, and forecasts serve as the starting point for the budget committees' work. The agency also checks the veracity of presidents' budgets by using CBO's own methodologies (CBO 2016).

The agency serves other committees of Congress, most notably by producing cost estimates of legislation for bills reported by committees. These "scores" estimate the effects on federal spending over the five and ten years subsequent to enactment.

Among legislative branch support agencies, CBO's scope of work is the most narrowly focused. It reports—which do not advocate any particular policies—inevitably address federal spending and revenues, the funding of particular federal programs and agencies, and various large issues that have ramification for the federal budget and the economy (e.g., the role of immigrants in the US labor market).

CBO, in short, was designed to provide intellectually defensible, nonpartisan data that would be used by congressional committees and individual legislators to discuss, debate, and decide federal budgeting. As table 8.1 shows, CBO's budget for fiscal year 2016 was $46.5 million, and it employed 235 staff. The table presents budgets and staff counts for CRS, GAO, and OTA as well, along with descriptions of the services provided to Congress.

TABLE 8.1. Legislative branch support agencies: FY2016 budgets, staff counts, and services for Congress

Agency	Budget	Staff count	Services for Congress
CBO	$46.5 million	235	Assists budget committees; publishes analyses of president' budgets, cost estimates of bills, baseline budget and economic projections, and reports on expired authorizations, federal mandates, and other budgetary matters.
CRS	$107 million	650	Trains congressional staff and legislators; publishes digests of bills, legal opinions, reports on government operations and policies, and the *Constitution Annotated*; and provides reference services, in-person consultations, congressional testimony, oversight support, and occasional staff details.
GAO	$555 million	3,000	Publishes audits of agency handling of funds, reports on agency and program management and effectiveness, legal opinions on agency expenditures and certain actions; provides some consultations, congressional testimony, oversight support, and occasional staff details.
OTA (defunct)	$0	0	Published assessments of new technologies; offered some consultations with legislators and staff.

Sources: K. Hall 2016; Brudnick 2016b; Library of Congress 2016; GAO n.d.

Note: CBO: Congressional Budget Office; CRS: Congressional Research Service; GAO: Government Accountability Office; OTA: Office of Technology Assessment.

Legislative Branch Support Agencies: Outputs and Congressional Staff Perspectives

Legislative branch support agencies produce significant quantities of informational and analytical work for Congress. Some of this work is actively demanded by Congress (e.g., requests for GAO to testify before committees), while other work is done in anticipation of legislative demand (e.g., CRS reports) or pursuant to statutory mandate (e.g., CBO's budget reports to the budget committees). Table 8.2 displays data on the quantity of some these products and services.[25] The data depicting requests for testimony, briefings, requests for assistance, and CRS.gov pageviews are clear indicators of the significant congressional demand for help.

These data align with the findings of the Congressional Capacity Survey. Response data indicate Hill staff (including both committee and personal staff) use legislative support agencies often. Their frequency of use is listed in tables 8.3 and 8.4 for the issues of budget and health care, respectively. The finding that staff turn to the agencies so often might be considered a measure

TABLE 8.2. FY2016 output of legislative branch support agencies

Agency	Products and services output
CBO	600+ formal cost estimates and "thousands" of preliminary, informal cost estimates
	100 scorekeeping tabulations, including budget account-level detail for individual appropriation acts at all stages of the legislative process
	3 sets of detailed 10-year baseline budget projections and 2 sets of 10-year economic projections, as well as long-term budget projections
	90+ analytical reports and other publications
CRS	16 testimonies before Congress
	4,397 in-person briefings
	1,197 reports
	3,126 confidential memoranda
	52,000+ email and phone responses
	6,312 bill summaries
	1.7 million views of pages on CRS.gov (accessible only to Congress)
GAO	119 testimonies before 69 distinct committees/subcommittees
	Requests for work from 95 percent of the standing committees and 48 percent of their subcommittees
	800 reports (annual average)
	400 legal opinions
OTA (defunct)	No new output since defunded in 1995

Sources: K. Hall 2016; CRS 2017; GAO 2016.

Note: CBO: Congressional Budget Office; CRS: Congressional Research Service; GAO: Government Accountability Office; OTA: Office of Technology Assessment.

of their trust in them. To test this hypothesis further, staff were surveyed about the information sources they used when studying budget or health care issues. Tables 8.3 and 8.4 shows that for these issues, staffers trust information from the nonpartisan legislative branch support agencies very highly and more than nearly every other source—especially the executive branch.[26]

LEGISLATIVE BRANCH SUPPORT AGENCIES:
BUFFETED BY CONGRESS

The data presented in tables 8.1–8.4 on legislative branch support agencies' outputs and staff perspectives thereof might be read to suggest that CBO, CRS, and GAO hold a secure position on Capitol Hill. Yet, the agencies have faced two pressures that are, in some instances, interrelated: downsizing and political retribution. In aggregate, the legislative branch support agencies have seen their staff counts decrease, as illustrated in figure 8.1.

This decline is driven partially by Congress's appropriated funding of the agencies at rates that have not kept up with inflation. In 1984, CBO, CRS,

GAO, and OTA together were funded at $339,964,000, or $785,310,000 in 2016 dollars. Actual appropriations in 2016 were $684,445,000, about 13 percent lower. Since the per capita employment costs of the agencies tend to go upward, this decrease in funding adds further downward pressure on staff head counts as agencies simply cannot afford more full-time employees.

The reduction in total staff count also is the product of major cuts to OTA and GAO, which were clearly political retribution abetted by a somewhat bipartisan sense that the legislative branch—and Congress included—was overstaffed.[27]

TABLE 8.3. Frequency of staffer use of legislative branch agencies and other government resources and their perceived trustworthiness: budget

Source	Frequency of use		Trustworthiness	
	Mean	SD	Mean	SD
Professional committee staff	1.62	0.62	2.14	0.64
Congressional Research Service	1.56	0.64	2.46	0.65
Congressional Budget Office	1.37	0.63	2.13	0.79
Bureaucratic agencies	1.34	0.63	1.49	0.63
Party leadership	1.28	0.67	1.53	0.65
Government Accountability Office	1.24	0.70	2.26	0.68
Members similar to your own boss	1.23	0.74	1.47	0.56
Caucuses	0.91	0.68	1.38	0.71
The administration	0.88	0.65	0.91	0.76
State delegation members	0.80	0.72	1.34	0.63

Note: SD = standard deviation.

TABLE 8.4. Frequency of staffer use of legislative branch agencies and other government resources and their perceived trustworthiness: health care

Source	Frequency of use		Trustworthiness	
	Mean	SD	Mean	SD
Congressional Research Service	1.45	0.71	2.49	0.68
Professional committee staff	1.44	0.74	1.97	0.70
Congressional Budget Office	1.25	0.71	1.99	0.84
Party leadership	1.12	0.74	1.51	0.70
Bureaucratic agencies	1.09	0.70	1.48	0.70
Members similar to your own boss	1.11	0.72	1.55	0.70
Government Accountability Office	1.06	0.78	2.25	0.77
Caucuses	0.84	0.69	1.36	0.69
State delegation members	0.83	0.71	1.42	0.67
The administration	0.69	0.64	0.78	0.75

Note: SD = standard deviation.

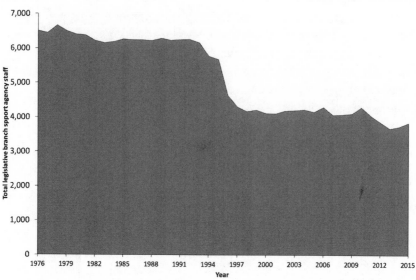

FIGURE 8.1. Legislative branch support agencies' staff head counts, 1976–2015
Note: Data compiled from CBO, CRS, GAO, and OTA appropriations requests and annual reports.

In 1995, Congress defunded OTA, and its 140 employees were separated from service. The agency had been criticized by some media and legislators for producing reports that were too long and difficult to read. Others made the inaccurate charge that the agency's work was redundant of work being done at other legislative branch or executive branch agencies (Lambro 1980, 248–51).[28] To a degree, the agency had never been able to shake off the stain of its operationally wobbly first years, which were tainted by legislative politics. Members of Congress dabbled in the agency's personnel practices, and conservatives cried foul that its first director was a former Democratic representative. The Right also complained that OTA's oversight board chair, Senator Ted Kennedy (D-MA), was heavy-handed and influenced agency's research (Bimber 1996). Additionally, in the mid-1980s, OTA also had raised questions about the feasibility of the Strategic Defense Initiative (SDI) missile defense system, which the Reagan administration and some members of Congress viewed as a critical bargaining chip with the Soviet leadership, if not a plausible defense technology, and which critics dubbed "Star Wars" in comparison to the popular fantasy–science fiction film franchise.

Similarly, cutting GAO's staff was both political punishment meted out by Republicans for the agency's purportedly too-friendly relationship with Democratic committee chairs over the late twentieth century into the twenty-first, and a way to make good on the "Contract with America" promise to prune government (Seelye 1994; Glastris and Edwards 2014).

Congress has not made similarly significant budget reductions to CBO and CRS; however, each agency has found itself buffeted by legislative pressures. CBO in 2017, for example, released a cost estimate for legislation to repeal the Affordable Care Act, which was viewed very unfavorably by congressional Republicans, who had dubbed the act "Obamacare" in reference to the Democratic president under whose administration the legislation was passed. Some members of the House prepared amendments to cut CBO's budget, remove its scoring authority, and outsource this work to private think tanks. The amendments failed (R Street Institute and Demand Progress 2017). CBO also faced criticism over how it calculates the baselines used for formulating the budget and its reestimations of the president's budget. To a degree, these criticisms are fomented by the high-stakes consequences of the agency's work. For example, per statute, CBO's cost estimates trigger legislative procedural consequences (points of order) that greatly affect the probability of enactment.

CRS, meanwhile, has been taken to task a number of times in the 2010s for producing reports or memoranda that offend political sensibilities (Kosar 2015c). About 2007, CRS quit providing counts of earmarks to Congress because the issue had become too controversial (Fund 2007). In 2012, in response to Republican criticism, the agency withdrew a report on tax policy it had issued (Weisman 2012).

There is evidence that fear of political retribution clearly has affected some of the agency's work and policies.[29] In 2018, CRS management rebuked a CRS legislative attorney for words deemed too strongly conclusive of a scientific consensus on the human contribution to climate change (Wyatt 2018, 6n9). To avoid needless controversies, agency management has diminished opportunities for CRS experts to participate in academic conferences, write for noncongressional audiences, and come to decisive conclusions in its written work.[30] Since 2004, the agency has been embroiled in an ongoing internal feud between its analysts and management over the conflation of "objectivity" and "neutrality" in research reports and memoranda, with analysts favoring the former and management the latter (Aftergood 2006; Kosar 2018a).

The internet has only exacerbated the situation. At the turn of the twenty-first century, hardly anyone except members of Congress and their staffs read CRS reports—the paper copies of which were kept in a room in the agency's building and were carried to Congress via interoffice mail couriers. Today thousands of PDF copies of CRS reports may be found on the internet and can be grist for media and bloggers, which legislators may see (Kosar 2015b). Rather than informing the debate, CRS—and the other legislative branch support agencies to a degree—can find themselves inadvertently instigating it or swept into it.

Conclusion: Legislative Branch Support Agencies' Uneasy Position

Legislative branch support agencies are well embedded in the congressional policymaking and oversight process. Various statutes requires them to carry out diverse tasks (e.g., conducting audits). In its day-to-day work Congress relies on assistance from the agencies (e.g., downloads of reports from their websites). The data presented in this chapter indicate that staff value the agencies' assistance. More fundamentally, Congress's need for expert assistance is sewn into the nature of self-governance in a mass democratic republic. Legislative branch support agencies bridge the gap between complex government and the elected officials who are expected to direct it. So, CBO, CRS, and GAO would appear unlikely to disappear.

Yet, as the evidence presented in this chapter indicates, these agencies have found themselves crosswise to Congress in the twenty-first century.[31] One of the four agencies was abolished, and another saw its staff cut. Congress has chosen to reduce the funding relative to inflation. Additionally, it is not hard to see the buffeting effects of polarization and the vacillating party control of Congress on the agencies. Both factors encourage legislators to view some forms of the agencies' research and assistance as helping or harming one side's struggle for agenda and narrative control. Both parties may call on civil servants for help, but inevitably calculations of trust and relative power make these collaborations more difficult and appear more perilous.[32]

But it also may well be the case that legislative branch support agencies' uneasy position is the product of a shift in the broader institutional context that fostered their growth. Between 1946 and the early 1990s, GAO and CRS occupied a secure and insulated position in the legislative branch. They worked closely with committees, whose staff were selected with the assent of both the committee chairs and the ranking members.[33] Thus, nonpartisan agencies did much of their work in concert with somewhat nonpartisan Hill staff and with the blessing of committee leadership. This professionalized arrangement was reinforced by idiosyncratic aspects of the political environment of the era: long-standing Democratic majorities in both chambers, strong committees, and a far less competitive and freewheeling media environment than exists today. (Media reports citing GAO or CRS/LRS reports prior to 1970 were rare.)

After 1970, these institutional pieces began to fall away. The 1970 Legislative Reorganization Act abolished the bipartisan hiring process. Chairs and ranking members separately chose their staffs, and chairs got far more employees. Unsurprisingly, slowly but surely, committee staff evolved into the disputatious camps of majority versus minority staffers that seem to be the norm today. Committees and their leadership also saw their power flow down to individual legislators and upward to chamber leadership. In November 1994, the Democrats' previously imagined permanent control of the chambers had clearly ended. The next year, the Drudge Report—a gossipy email newsletter on politics—was launched by the manager of a gift shop at CBS with no journalism experience.

All of which may mean that the legislative branch support agencies will continue to find themselves needed by, but often fearful of retribution by, the very elected officials they serve.

PART 3

The Politics of Capacity in the Legislative Process

Still Muddling Along? Assessing the Hybrid Congressional Appropriations Process

PETER HANSON

> We're flying blind.
>
> FORMER HOUSE APPROPRIATIONS CLERK

Discussions of the federal budget have taken on the desperation of NASA mission control in the movie *Apollo 13*. In the film, a NASA spacecraft is on its way to the moon with a crew of astronauts when it suffers an explosion. Amid alarms signaling cascading failures of key systems, flight director Gene Kranz gives up trying to keep track of all the things going wrong on the ship. Instead, he asks mission control a different question: "What have we got on the spacecraft that's good?" Observing a congressional budget process characterized by temporary shutdowns, long-term continuing resolutions, a breakdown in "regular order," and massive omnibus bills, many analysts wonder if anything about it is still functioning. Many conclude the answer is no.

I argue that sweeping generalizations about the budget process offer little insight into the actual capacity of the United States Congress to adopt a budget. So much has changed, so quickly, that analysts have difficulty separating features of the budget process that are genuinely dysfunctional from those that are just different from the recent past. In this chapter, I make two contributions to discussions about the capacity of Congress to adopt a budget. First, I offer a framework to describe the transformation of the budget process since the 1980s. Second, I assess the capacity of Congress to adopt a budget along two core dimensions: the capacity of Congress to draft appropriations bills and the capacity of Congress to adopt appropriations bills. Previous research and the evidence presented in this chapter suggest two broad conclusions.

First, the budget process since the 1980s has been a procedural hybrid that combines elements of both "regular order" and "unorthodox lawmaking" (Hanson 2014b; Sinclair 2007). Members of Congress have faced substantial difficulty in passing a budget since the mid-1970s for reasons that are well understood, including rising partisan polarization, close electoral competition, and

sharp differences in spending priorities. They have partially adapted their procedures in response to these pressures. Members have continued to follow a
model for the writing of the annual appropriations bills that has not changed
since the mid-twentieth-century "textbook Congress." Bills are drafted by
subcommittees of the House and Senate Appropriations Committees and reported to the floor after hearings and markups that provide an opportunity
for information gathering, deliberation, and public review. Members have
shifted their manner of passing appropriations bills. Prior the 1980s, members routinely adopted each bill on an individual basis. Since the 1980s, they
have been likely to follow patterns of "unorthodox" lawmaking in which they
bundle some or all spending bills together into a single package, known as
an *omnibus appropriations bill*, for consideration. The use of omnibus appropriations bills has been heavily criticized, but this criticism often misses
a central fact: it is an effective way to pass the budget. The hybrid budget
process has helped members muddle through near-constant budgetary crises
and fund the government for about forty years—a respectable record given
the contentious nature of the legislative environment.

Second, this hybrid process is not in equilibrium. The evidence presented
in this chapter shows that the apparently stable process of writing appropriations bills is undergoing a slow but profound change and becoming increasingly unorthodox. Members are moving deliberative processes behind closed
doors and adopting a more informal approach to drafting legislation. Observable measures of committee activity such as holding hearings and calling
witnesses are in steep decline. The once routine process of the committee
reporting legislation also has started to fray. This change has been accompanied by a reported decline in the capacity of the Appropriations Committee
to gather information and write legislation effectively. Policymakers say in
recent interviews that the difficulty reaching agreement on each year's appropriations bills means that the development of the following year's bills is
invariably rushed. Staff lack the time for oversight, to develop expertise, or to
maintain their standards of quality in the drafting of bills.

These findings suggest that the record since the 1980s may not predict
the capacity of Congress to adopt a budget in the years to come. The budget process has never been fully unorthodox, but it is becoming more so as
mechanisms for bill writing evolve. Additionally, reports from staff members
about their declining expertise and oversight may reflect a hollowing out of
the bill-writing capacity of the Appropriations Committee that could erode
its control over spending. In short, the full impact of the ongoing disruption of the appropriations process by the current polarized and competitive

political environment, and the impact of the adaptations Congress is making in response to that disruption, have not yet made themselves felt. Congress is not about to lose its core Article I power over spending, but its effectiveness wielding this authority may be affected by changes to the distribution of power over spending decisions and in the degree of expertise Congress can bring to those decisions.

Congressional Budget Capacity: What We Know

The congressional budget process has been characterized by two major elements since the passage of the Congressional Budget and Impoundment Control Act of 1974. The first is the writing of a budget resolution that sets overall spending levels for the year. It is important because it forces Congress to weigh competing priorities simultaneously and make broad decisions about how to distribute resources between major categories such as defense or social services. But, the budget resolution is only a blueprint and does not actually allocate funds. A failure to pass it will not shut down the government or have significant consequences for the American people. I do not focus on it here. The second component is the adoption of a dozen appropriations bills that allocate spending for federal programs. These bills are of immense importance because they provide the funding necessary for programs that touch the lives of all Americans. To a limited degree, they also set policy. If they are not passed (and no funding is provided in their absence), many programs will not be funded and the lives of the American people will be disrupted. They are the subject of this chapter.

I define *congressional budget capacity* as the capacity of Congress to write appropriations bills and to secure their adoption by the House and Senate. The capacity to *write* appropriations bills describes the ability of members to complete the technical and logistical work of gathering and interpreting information and then drafting legislation that is responsive to national conditions and the needs of various stakeholders. The capacity to *adopt* appropriations bills describes the ability of members to overcome the numerous veto points in the constitutional system to secure the enactment of spending bills. This is admittedly a narrow way of looking at the budget process, since it is agnostic toward the long-standing policy goals of budget reformers such as deficit reduction. It has the advantage of helping scholars to place the variety of problems that appear to be plaguing the annual passage of the budget into a framework and to sort out features that are problematic from those that are simply different from the past.

THE FIRST DIMENSION:
DRAFTING APPROPRIATIONS BILLS

The capacity to draft appropriations bills in Congress historically was the subject of intensive study by political scientists (Fenno 1966; Schick 2007; White 1989; Wildavsky 1979). The recent history of appropriations begins with the "textbook Congress" of the mid-twentieth century. Power in the House and Senate was decentralized during this era, and the responsibility for drafting legislation rested with committees. The task of writing the annual bills necessary to fund the government was delegated to the Appropriations Committee. It was powerful and independent. Each of its subcommittees was responsible for writing a bill funding a unique domain of federal activities, such as agriculture or defense. The core of this system remains intact today.

The heart of the committee's work drafting legislation consists of gathering information, assessing it, and making spending recommendations based on these evaluations and member priorities. Specifically, committee members evaluate the detailed budget requests made for every program in every federal agency by the executive branch and hold hearings with agency officials and interested stakeholders to assess the merit of spending requests (Wildavsky 1979). Past scholars regarded hearings as central to the committee's role writing legislation. Richard Fenno observed, "In its direct confrontation with agency officials, the Committee performs two of its House-prescribed tasks: law-making and oversight" (Fenno 1966, 324). Joseph White, author of the most recent large-scale study of the House Appropriations Committee, observes that in the 1980s hearings were the source of the committee's expertise and, by extension, its power and influence (White 1989). Hearings allowed members and staff to probe federal officials about programmatic needs, make independent and effective decisions when drafting bills, and defend their choices if questioned by other members. They were a robust and effective way of gathering information. White found that "on balance staff members feel they can get the information they need. There is ample reason to believe that they can keep the subcommittees as well-informed as they were in the 1950s" (1989, 296). In more recent years, scholars have questioned whether formal hearings still make a substantial difference in appropriations outcomes (see, e.g., Schick 2007).

The next step in the process is for each of the dozen subcommittees of the Appropriations Committee to draft an appropriations bill covering the federal agencies under its jurisdiction. The total amount of funds available to each subcommittee is determined by the full Appropriations Committee, but within that context, subcommittees have substantial autonomy to write their bills as they see fit (Schick 2007, 239). Historically, the chairs of the sub-committees were widely regarded as among the most important members of the chamber and called "cardinals" in recognition of their power. The chair of the subcommittee first releases the "chair's mark" of the bill. This draft of the bill is then refined and approved by subcommittee members in a markup. The full Appropriations Committee next reviews the bill, typically approving it without changes, and reports the bill to the floor with an accompanying report (Schick 2007, 240). At that point, the bill is formally introduced, available to the public, and ready for debate on the floor of the House or Senate.

Twenty-first-century studies have reported a general decline in the independence and power of committees as Congress has grown more polarized and power has become centralized in party leaders, but it is not clear to what extent these changes have influenced the drafting of appropriations bills. Scholars have described the politicization of the House Appropriations Committee in the wake of the 1995 "Republican Revolution" when Speaker Newt Gingrich attempted to force the Clinton administration to accept budget cuts or face a government shutdown (Aldrich and Rohde 2000b; Pearson 2015). Term limits for committee chairs made formerly independent chairs more dependent on leadership and reduced their collective expertise. Party leaders appear to be more involved in the drafting of appropriations bills than in the past. But no studies have systematically evaluated how deeply and routinely party leadership has become involved in spending decisions or how these changes have influenced the information-gathering and bill-writing capacities of the House and Senate Appropriations Committees, the relationship between subcommittee and the full committee, or the norm of the committee reporting legislation to the floors of the House and Senate for consideration. The committee's bill-writing practices in recent years are mostly a black box.

THE SECOND DIMENSION:

PASSING APPROPRIATIONS BILLS

The capacity of Congress to adopt the annual appropriations bills, the second dimension of capacity, has been well studied in the twenty-first century (Aldrich and Rohde 2000b; Drutman and Hanson 2019; Hanson 2014b, 2016; Sinclair 2012). Much of this work has focused on understanding the rise of unorthodox lawmaking in the appropriations process—specifically, the erosion of "regular order" and the corresponding rise in omnibus spending bills that bundle together two or more of the regular appropriations bills that are produced each year by the dozen subcommittees of the House and Senate Appropriations Committees. The findings are straightforward.

Congressional politics since the 1980s have been increasingly characterized by close margins of control, heightened electoral competition between
the Democratic and Republican Parties, and rising levels of partisan polarization (Lee 2015, 2016; McCarty, Poole, and Rosenthal 2006). These factors
have intensified conflict in the House and Senate and made it more difficult
for party leaders to navigate successfully the many veto points in the constitutional system and pass legislation. Threatened by gridlock, leaders have
turned to "unorthodox" methods of lawmaking to maintain their productivity (Curry and Lee 2019a; Sinclair 2012). For example, they have been more
willing to use ad hoc working groups rather than committees to write legislation or reduce opportunities for debate on the floors of the House and Senate
(Sinclair 2008; Smith 2014). In appropriations, unorthodox lawmaking has
manifested in the form of omnibus appropriations bills.

Members of Congress, acting through their leaders, utilize omnibus lawmaking for similar reasons in the House and Senate: it helps them maintain
their capacity to pass a budget. They create omnibus spending bills when they
face difficulty passing the dozen regular appropriations bills on an individual
basis in what members call "regular order" (Hanson 2014b). Within this context, there is important bicameral variation. The Senate has been more likely
than the House to stumble in passing the regular appropriations bills. The
Senate's individualistic rules expose spending bills to filibusters and politically charged amendments that often derail their passage. These problems are
less intense in the House due to its stronger tools of majority party control,
but House leaders have still faced high levels of amending activity that com-
plicates their task of passing spending bills (Drutman and Hanson 2019; Hanson 2016). Beyond those chamber specific problems, debate over the budget
has been characterized by sharp disagreements over top-line spending levels
driven by the presence of deficits and differences in party priorities. Leaders have found it helpful in this contentious environment to bundle bills together to broaden their coalition of support. Long-standing research shows
that bundling separate policy domains together in the same legislation (such
as defense and social spending) gives all members something to vote for and
can ease the passage of legislation (Black 1958; Krutz 2001; Riker 1982; Shepsle
and Bonchek 1997). Leaders also tend to bring up omnibus bills shortly before
government funding will expire, using the pressure of deadlines to reduce the
number of likely amendments and ease opposition (Hanson 2014b).

The transition to omnibus legislating has been met with criticism on the
grounds that members have experienced reduced opportunities for participation and deliberation. Rank-and-file members say they dislike omnibus bills
because they reduce opportunities for legislating relative to "regular order,"

including opportunities for credit claiming and position taking (Hanson 2014b). Scholars have suggested that "regular order" is more likely to create the conditions necessary for effective deliberation on legislation, including scrutiny that is likely to catch errors or opportunities to offer perfecting amendments on the floor (Green and Burns 2010; Mann and Ornstein 2006). However, research has not systematically identified clear, negative consequences arising from omnibus legislating. Nolan McCarty (2016) finds no major economic consequences associated with the decline of "regular order" in appropriations. Lee Drutman and Peter Hanson (2019) find that floor debate under "regular order" on appropriations bills has mixed deliberative value. Overall, more work needs to be done to understand the consequences of omnibus legislating.

Assessing the Appropriations Committee

Eric Schickler (2001) observes that congressional norms, rules, and practices are not a product of neat design. Rather, new practices are layered on top of the old in an untidy combination. Such is the case with appropriations. The appropriations process in practice is a hybrid in which an unorthodox method of passing bills has been layered onto a traditional method of writing them. Scholars and practitioners have not grappled with how this hybrid process functions as a system, and no assessment of budget capacity can be complete without evaluating how its components work together. The empirical section of this chapter begins the work of assessing the hybrid appropriations process by filling in the gaps on what is known about the internal workings of the Appropriations Committee and its effectiveness in writing appropriations bills since the mid-1970s. I draw on interview data to provide insight into internal committee processes, descriptive data tracking Appropriations Committee hearings, and patterns in reporting and passing bills. I conclude that committee members are slowly abandoning the formal procedures they have used in the past to write appropriations bills in favor of informal, closed-door practices. In short, bill writing is becoming more unorthodox. Additionally, staff report that their overall capacity to deliberate effectively on appropriations bills is declining.

APPROPRIATIONS COMMITTEE HEARINGS

Hearings have historically been central to the lawmaking and oversight capacity of the Appropriations Committee. They provide committee members with the opportunity to challenge agency officials, learn from stakeholders, and make decisions about appropriate spending levels for federal programs. The House Appropriations Committee reports on its oversight activities each Congress in its *Report of Committee Activities*. These reports outline the legislative history of all appropriations legislation and report the number of hearings held, witnesses called, and pages of documentation produced by the committee. They also report, with varying degrees of precision, the number of investigatory reports requested or produced by the committee's special investigations staff or of the Government Accountability Office. I collected all reports written by the committee from the 94th Congress (1975–76) to the 114th Congress (2015–16), a period of forty years. The aggregated results show a sharp decline in formal oversight activity by the committee.

Table 9.1 reports the number of hearings, witnesses called, pages of documentation produced, and special reports initiated or completed. Figure 9.1 reports the same findings as a proportion based on the maximum for each category to more clearly show trends over time. The number of hearings has declined steadily overall, from a high of 900 in the 94th Congress to 191 in the 114th Congress—a 79 percent decrease. The number of witnesses called to testify before the committee has fallen from a high of 10,781 in the 102nd Congress to just 664 in the 114th—a decline of 94 percent. The number of pages of documentation produced by the committee has held steadier. It peaked at 202,767 pages in the 96th Congress and has declined by 38 percent to 126,309 in each of the 113th and 114th Congresses.[1] The relatively mild decline in the number of pages of documentation produced is likely because the committee continues to request budget justifications and written testimony from witnesses without calling them in person. Interestingly, the number of special reports requested, which peaked at 140 in the 96th Congress and remained above 100 through the 100th Congress, dropped off sharply after then but rose significantly after the 112th Congress—to near historic levels in the 113th. These reports tend to be narrowly focused on particular programs and aimed at rooting out instances of waste. The rise in their number may signify an effort by members to signal that they are interested in reducing waste, but these reports likely have little overall impact on the ability of the committee to conduct its oversight work across all agencies.

Anecdotal evidence from policy advocates corroborates the obvious interpretation of the figures that the committee's use of hearings to oversee the federal budget has declined substantially. A lobbyist with a major interest group with more than ten years' experience advocating for federal funding reported observations about the Interior Appropriations Subcommittee in the 2010s.[2] In prior years, the subcommittee would hold a hearing devoted exclusively to the lobbyist's issue with four or five witnesses, including

TABLE 9.1. Key oversight indicators from report of committee activities

Congress	Hearings	Witnesses	Pages	Reports
94th	900	8,400	150,000	90
95th	700	10,700	158,000	95
96th	720	10,215	202,767	140
97th	700	11,772	200,000	124
98th	600	10,720	180,000	100
99th	510	9,363	193,809	130
100th	512	9,570	180,942	117
101st	569	10,187	174,687	53
102nd	525	10,781	196,352	66
103rd	547	10,036	187,282	87
104th	457	6,999	174,576	47
105th	315	5,928	184,608	72
106th	429	4,916	188,907	42
107th	365	4,014	174,748	39
108th	313	3,063	156,503	35
109th	304	2,463	155,056	26
110th	402	3,076	165,868	35
111th	332	2,481	139,278	28
112th	256	720	—	78
113th	212	1,898	126,309	123
114th	191	664	126,309	83

Sources: Data compiled from *Report of Committee Activities*, 94th–114th Congresses. Page totals for the 112th Congress were not included in the report from that congress.

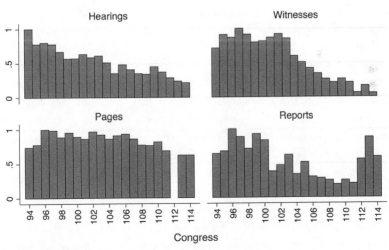

FIGURE 9.1. Key indicators of Appropriations Committee oversight
Sources: Data compiled from *Report of Committee Activities*, 94th–114th Congresses. Page totals for the 112th Congress were not included in the report from that Congress.

businesspeople, policy advocates, and military personnel. "It was a great . . . hour, hour and a half thing," the lobbyist said. By the time of the interview, that practice had ended: "We now have been reduced to a cattle call where the House Interior [Appropriations] Committee invites us to be one of literally scores of witnesses. We have two minutes, and you're just, one after another, getting up and talking about very, very high level things. . . . You know, let's talk about why you should fund the [policy area]. And that, obviously, is not a good way to make policy."

THE APPROPRIATIONS COMMITTEE'S RECORD REPORTING BILLS

The second major step in the bill-drafting process is for each Appropriations subcommittee to mark up its bill, adopt it, and send it to the full Appropriations Committee to be adopted. When that process is completed, the bill is formally introduced, along with an accompanying report explaining its details. Next, I examine whether the Appropriations Committee reliably reports its bills to the floor, drawing on the legislative history of appropriations bills from Congress.gov and the Report on Committee Activities. The data show that the once standard process of reporting bills is eroding.

The Appropriations Committee of each chamber was tasked with producing a total of thirteen bills each year from 1993 to 2004. In 2005 and 2006, the Appropriations Committees of the House and Senate reorganized their subcommittee structure. The House established ten subcommittees and the Senate twelve. The Appropriations Committees reorganized again in 2007 and established a parallel system of twelve subcommittees. Table 9.2 shows that it is rare for the full committee to fail to report appropriations bills drafted by its subcommittees. Only 9 percent of House bills and 5 percent of Senate bills were not reported from each chamber's Appropriations Committee, respectively, from 1993 to 2016. But, there is variation over time. Data for both chambers show that it became more common to fail to report a bill in later years than it had been in earlier years: all failures to report a bill in the House occurred after 2001. In two years, the House Appropriations Committee failed to report a majority of its bills: seven of the twelve in 2008 and ten of the twelve in 2010. Failures to report a bill appear across the time frame in the Senate data but are concentrated in its later half.

In some cases, the original data sources show that the subcommittee marked up legislation but the full committee did not act on the bill. For example, the *Report of Committee Activities* in the 111th Congress indicates that all bills in 2010 were marked up in subcommittee even though ten were not

TABLE 9.2. Bills not reported by House and Senate Appropriations Committees

Year	Number		Percentage	
	House	Senate	House	Senate
1993	0	0	0.00	0.00
1994	0	0	0.00	0.00
1995	0	2	0.00	0.15
1996	0	2	0.00	0.15
1997	0	0	0.00	0.00
1998	0	0	0.00	0.00
1999	0	0	0.00	0.00
2000	0	0	0.00	0.00
2001	0	0	0.00	0.00
2002	2	0	0.15	0.00
2003	0	0	0.00	0.00
2004	0	1	0.00	0.08
2005	0	0	0.00	0.00
2006	0	0	0.00	0.00
2007	0	0	0.00	0.00
2008	7	3	0.58	0.25
2009	0	0	0.00	0.00
2010	10	1	0.83	0.08
2011	3	1	0.25	0.08
2012	1	1	0.08	0.08
2013	2	1	0.17	0.08
2014	1	4	0.08	0.33
2015	0	0	0.00	0.00
2016	0	0	0.00	0.00
Total	26	16	0.09	0.05

Sources: Data compiled from *Report of Committee Activities*, 103rd–114th Congresses; CRS n.d.

reported from the full committee.[3] In others, original sources show that neither the subcommittee nor the full committee acted on the bill. For example, the *Report of Committee Activities* for the 112th Congress shows no subcommittee markup for the Labor–Health and Human Services bill.[4] Original sources do not report subcommittee activity for most years.

Consequences for Deliberation

The evidence presented in this chapter illustrates the slow erosion over time of the Appropriations Committee's formal process for bill development and raises a larger question: Is the committee still deliberating on bills effectively? There are three issues to consider. First, who is deliberating? Second, what constitutes effective deliberation? Third, how is deliberation taking place? I address these issue questions in turn in an effort to answer the larger question.

Who is deliberating on appropriations? Interviews indicate that the Appropriations Committee still retains primary authority over the drafting of appropriations bills despite the important role of party leaders in the finalizing spending agreements. This is true regardless of whether bills are produced through the textbook process or behind closed doors. In waves of interviews conducted in 2005, 2012, and 2019, staff members described the committee as playing a dominant role in drafting appropriations legislation.[5] A Senate leadership staff member observed, "When the subcommittee reports to full committee, you can say that they're 90-plus percent settled, and then once it goes from the full committee . . . to leadership, they are 95 percent settled, and you have that final 5 percent that you're going into the leader's office at the eleventh hour with" (Hanson-Reynolds Interview A). Leaders finalize top-line spending levels, settle controversial matters, and wrangle votes, but the vast majority of spending decisions remain with the Appropriations Committee.

What constitutes effective deliberation? Simone Chambers (2003) defines *deliberation* as "debate and discussion aimed at producing reasonable, well-informed opinions in which participants are willing to revise preferences in light of discussion, new information, and claims made by fellow participants." Effective deliberation leads to an informed consensus of opinion, or it has the effect of clarifying and structuring conflict that must later be resolved (Warren and Mansbridge 2016). In the congressional context, deliberation would appear to require access to an array of accurate information, diverse policy perspectives, and good faith discussions by all participants aimed at reaching informed conclusions. A related but distinct concept is *deliberative negotiation*, "a practice in which individuals . . . make and respond to claims, arguments, and proposals with the aim of reaching mutually acceptable binding agreements" that includes "arguments on the merits made by advancing considerations that other parties can accept; searching for zones of agreement and disagreement; and arguing about the terms of fair processes as well as outcomes" (Warren and Mansbridge 2016, 192–93).

How is deliberation taking place? The lack of recent studies on the Appropriations Committee makes this question difficult to answer with specificity. Policymakers say the answer is that the committee carries out its work using a mix of informal, closed-door methods and formal processes. Interviews in 2019 with two recently retired senior Appropriations staff members indicate that key sources of information for writing bills include detailed budget justifications provided by agencies, meetings with agency officials and advocates, and hearings (Hanson-Reynolds Interviews B and F). In their account, hearings are a helpful but not exclusive way of gathering information. Hearings create a public record and give federal officials an incentive to be responsive to informal committee inquiries (Hanson-Reynolds Interview B). But committee staff also noted that hearings could be an inefficient use of time relative to closed-door meetings: "Give me twenty minutes with the secretary or the agency head in my office, or give us staff an hour with your CFO and your budget officer and your program people, and we'll learn more" (Hanson-Reynolds Interview F). Markups remain an important way for the Appropriations Committee to negotiate the details of legislation, but staff members say that similar negotiations occur privately when public markups do not occur.

The use of informal, private methods of deliberation in place of formal, public methods raises questions about whether the quality of the committee's work has been affected by this change. In theory, informal and private methods of deliberation and deliberative negotiation could be as effective as—or even more effective than—public, formal processes for achieving the same goals. Warren and Mansbridge (2016) summarize research showing that deliberative negotiation may thrive in private settings in which members can candidly discuss and resolve their differences. Curry and Lee (2016) similarly find that unorthodox lawmaking has helped Congress maintain its productivity because deliberation and negotiation occur behind closed doors, allowing Democrats and Republicans to reach agreement outside the glare of attention from the media and interest groups.

Assessing the quality of deliberation is difficult due to the challenge of observing legislating that takes place behind closed doors, but interviews offer useful insight. The two recently retired Appropriations staff members interviewed by Hanson and Reynolds said they were generally satisfied that the committee had the information it needed to do its work, one of them asserting that "on the fundamental work of the committee, the making decisions about dollar amounts, the committee still does a damn good job" (Hanson-Reynolds Interview B). The other staff member also observed that the failure to mark up legislation may contribute to member cynicism about the appropriations process but probably did not dramatically change the content of bills: "The result's not going to look exactly the same as it might have had it gone through committee and particularly the floor. But again, that base product is still going to in many respects accommodate as much as could be reasonably accommodated, because why wouldn't we? We're trying to grow the vote. We're trying to fundamentally reflect the priorities of the membership writ large" (Hanson-Reynolds Interview F). By these accounts, the quality of the committee's work does not hinge on whether it uses formal or informal methods of deliberation.

Interviews with congressional staff conducted by Tim LaPira for the Congressional Staff Capacity Survey were less encouraging.[6] They describe a hollowing out of the Appropriations Committee's bill-writing capacity arising from the continual disruption of its work. The intense difficulty of lawmaking has simultaneously undermined the committee's formal *and* informal means of gathering information, building expertise, and overseeing programs. One former staff director for an Appropriations subcommittee explained:

> When I first went to the Hill we would take our time and read the budget. We would start with the secretary. We had a very thoughtful hearing. We would do all those things. That timeline changed. With the fact that Congress isn't enacting things on time, which forces the administration to submit the budget late, oftentimes we were writing our bill before we got the budget. In fact, our chairman at one point even said, "Ah, we don't even need the budget. Just write your bill." To a large degree he's right, because it's just a proposal. My comeback to him was, "Mr. Chairman, it will be a decidedly better bill if we had the administration's proposal so that we can counter some of their arguments or incorporate some of their needs that we don't know about. We're flying blind. I'm telling you what [I think]. It's a much better product if I get what OMB thinks, if I get what DHS thinks." He knew that, but he's like, "Okay, that's great. Go back. Write your bill." (Drutman et al. 2017a, Interview 25)

A second staff member with experience on a different Appropriations subcommittee offered a similar assessment: "You want to talk about insanity? The budget's going to drop, they just finished the [omnibus]. . . . How do you analyze a $600 billion budget in less than a month? You don't. It's impossible. It's absolutely impossible" (Drutman et al. 2017a, Interview 19). Staff time for meetings with agency staff, travel, or briefings off the Hill is compressed or nonexistent (Drutman et al. 2017a, Interviews 19 and 25). Turnover has increased as staff members suffer from burnout. "I can't tell you how many calls I'm getting where people are like, 'Man, I just can't do this' " (Drutman et al. 2017a, Interview 25). The staff member explained:

> The biggest thing for burnout though was inability to meet deadlines and so forth. At the end of the day the process, you've got to keep to keep them on process. What really is frustrating is that process then shifts constantly. How do you keep people motivated? Go back to my friend's comment: "I've been conferencing for seven months." You're the majority clerk of that subcommittee. You've been marching your team to a deadline, to a process. Then you get there, then it moves again. Then it moves again. Then it moves again. It keeps slipping. You're like, "Okay, it's very hard to keep people motivated in

that environment." That was part of the reason why I was like, "All right. I've got to step away because I don't know how to keep doing this and keep people focused." Sure enough, the answer is they lost focus. People start taking longer lunches. They start . . . "What are we doing?" That's tough because you're supposed to be doing oversight, but it's hard to do oversight when you haven't finished your bill and you haven't turned in your new bill. You're in this netherworld. (Drutman et al. 2017a, Interview 25)

Burnout also posed a risk to the quality of bill writing, the staff member explained. The drafting of appropriations bills is detail-oriented work in which staff members tediously proof bills by hand to ensure that they are correct. Burned-out staff are more likely to make errors. In the staff member's view, the key to improving the Appropriations Committee's capacity to write legislation would be to improve Congress's capacity to pass appropriations bills so that the committee could have time to devote to its work once again.

In short, interviews indicate that changes in process may not be as significant as the ongoing disruption of legislating by the challenging legislative environment. This evidence raises the concern that the pressures of partisanship and electoral competition may have led to an overall erosion of the ability of members to deliberate, conduct deliberative negotiations, and, by extension, carry out their lawmaking responsibilities as effectively as they may have done in the past.

Conclusion

Discussions of congressional budget capacity frequently focus on the perception that budgeting is "broken" or a "train wreck." But the budget is a reflection of the nation's priorities. Americans have diverse conceptions of the public good, and each year, their representatives must sort out how to pursue these multiple conceptions in the form of spending federal dollars. Budgeting should be contentious. Public clashes sorting out differing priorities are not a measure of Congress's budget capacity. Nor should changes to the norms of passing appropriations bills automatically set off alarms. Members acting through the hybrid system that has evolved since the 1980s have done a reasonably good job writing and passing appropriations bills. Indeed, the unorthodox methods they have adopted have likely allowed them to preserve their budget capacity even as the challenges of lawmaking have grown.

If that's the case, does the long-term decline in traditional bill-writing activities such as hearings, markups and reporting legislation matter? It is tempting to answer this question by assessing whether, in principle, informal methods of gathering information, conducting oversight, and drafting legislation can replace traditional methods. However, an abstract analysis of this sort may be beside the point. The evolution of the budget process since the 1980s can be summarized as a story of disruption and adaptation. Partisanship, rising polarization, and electoral competition have interfered with routine legislating, forcing members of Congress to adapt with new strategies to write and pass the budget. They have done so with some success, but the disruptive pressures they face are ongoing. Appropriations staff report encountering serious obstacles that limit their ability to gather information and conduct oversight, suggesting that Congress has not yet settled into a new equilibrium to do its work. The long-term result may be erosion in the expertise of staff and, by extension, the members they serve.

The consequences of such an erosion would be potentially serious. Congress is a resilient institution, but its capacities can be degraded over time. One important source of evidence about the effects of reducing expertise comes from studies of state legislatures that have implemented term limits. Although the comparison is not perfect, term limits reduced legislative expertise by forcing the replacement of veteran legislators with comparative rookies. Studies of the effect of this change show a decline in "innovative" legislation and a rise in the relative power of alternative sources of expertise such as the executive branch and interest groups (Kousser 2005). Term-limited legislators are less likely to have the capacity to make independent judgments and more likely to rely on the assessments of experts outside the legislature. Studies of the US Congress show that informational asymmetries among members are a source of power and influence (Curry 2015; Krehbiel 1991). An erosion in the expertise of the Appropriations Committee is likely to diminish the influence of Congress relative to the president and interest groups in Washington, DC, and alter the distribution of power within Congress in ways that are difficult to predict but likely to reduce the committee's control over the production of legislation.

Can the capacity of Congress to write and adopt appropriations bills be strengthened? "Reform" is always a tempting call in troubled times—but there is no easy reform that can help members of Congress to improve their budget capacity. For example, expanding the number of staff members available to the Appropriations Committee will probably not improve its ability to produce legislation. Appropriations staff are already some of the most well-qualified and highly respected staff members in Congress. The issue here is not staff number or quality—it is a legislative environment that makes it hard for them to do their job effectively.

The experience of the Joint Select Committee on Budget and Appropriations Process Reform also should serve as an important cautionary tale for reformers. This committee was established by the Bipartisan Budget Act of 2018 for the purpose of recommending improvements to the budget process. Its members were divided evenly between Democrats and Republicans from the House and Senate to maximize the likelihood that its recommendations would win widespread support. After months of hearing testimony, committee members tried to move forward a small package of process-oriented reforms including biennial budgeting, but their efforts collapsed amid disagreement on how the proposals would be considered by the full membership of Congress (Werner 2018). The committee's recommendations went nowhere.

There are two lessons to draw from the failure to adopt this modest package of reforms. The first is to recognize the tendency of reformers to recommend minor changes to process that are designed to be easily palatable and win bipartisan support. As this chapter suggests, the underlying causes of instability in budgeting include high levels of partisanship, polarization, and electoral competition that have disrupted routine legislating. Tinkering with the nuts and bolts of the budget process by shifting deadlines or making other incremental changes is unlikely to contain those forces and make a meaningful difference in the ability of members to complete their work. The second lesson is that any process reforms that are significant enough to make budgeting more stable and efficient in this challenging environment, such prohibiting senators from filibustering appropriations bills (Hanson 2017), are likely to generate significant opposition because they would substantially redistribute power. The implication is that the budget process is unlikely to stabilize until the political environment stabilizes on its own, or until members decide—as they did when exercising the "nuclear option" to eliminate filibusters for judicial nominees—to risk bold changes in procedure to further adapt to the perils of the current environment.

There is good news and bad news in assessing the capacity of Congress to write and pass a budget. The good news is that Congress is a resilient institution that is able to carry out its duty to pass a budget under adverse conditions. The bad news is that its respectable record to date in passing the budget may obscure a larger deterioration in its ability to perform its core work of gathering information, evaluating federal programs, and making effective funding decisions. There is no easy solution to these challenges, and time will tell whether members of Congress and their staffs are able to regain their footing and do their work—or whether we will observe a long-term erosion in Congress's budgeting capacity.

Congress and the Capacity to Act: Overcoming Gridlock in the Senate's Amendment Process

JAMES WALLNER

Congress is broken. According to the conventional wisdom, the reason why is because its members are unable to reach agreement on important legislation given the polarized political environment in which they deliberate.[1] The legislative process has all but stalled in the United States House of Representatives and Senate. And it has been years since members in either chamber engaged regularly in meaningful deliberation. The result is gridlock.

Most observers blame the Senate for this dysfunction. Unlike in the House, the minority there can influence policy outcomes in several ways. Chief among them is the fact that the Senate's rules permit a minority of its members to filibuster (i.e., block) legislation they oppose. The filibuster effectively forces the majority to negotiate with the minority to pass controversial bills, meaning that at least some of the latter's ideas are typically incorporated into legislation before it clears the Senate.

In theory, polarization makes it harder for senators to compromise by increasing the distance between the two parties. As that gap widens, senators agree on less and less and, as a consequence, the majority goes to greater lengths to avoid negotiating with the minority. "Polarization-induced gridlock" results when the gap becomes unbridgeable (Barber and McCarty 2016, 77).

Although they are compelling, such explanations do not account for what happens in the Senate on a regular basis. This is because polarization is not the proximate cause of gridlock in the institution. Rather, it is the unwillingness of its members to act that is responsible for the Senate's present dysfunction. Put simply, Democrats and Republicans alike appear uninterested in expending the effort required to legislate successfully in a contentious environment.

When controversial bills do pass, it is almost always without the involvement of rank-and-file members in either party. Party leaders instead routinely craft must-pass legislation behind closed doors with little or no input from senators. Once an agreement has been reached, leaders wait until the last minute to unveil it in order to confront members with a fait accompli and thus increase the likelihood of the legislation's passage.

Despite their clear frustration with making decisions in this way, senators do not use the resources currently at their disposal to participate in the legislative process. Instead, those who end up supporting legislation crafted via such a process often declare their opposition to it in principle before announcing their begrudging support and blaming the necessity of the particular situation for why they have no choice but to vote for it. The only role senators play in the process is to vote yes or no at its end.

While senators feel like they have no choice but to go along with this state of affairs, routinely making controversial decisions this way has important consequences for Congress's ability to perform its responsibilities in the political system more broadly. Relying on leaders to craft proposals in lieu of its committees and using self-imposed deadlines to force action on the floor limits the number of controversial proposals Congress can consider in any given year. This decline has been accompanied by a subtle, yet consequential, shift in how members of Congress understand the role they play in American politics. Specifically, developments in the 2010s suggest that members no longer see Congress as the preeminent venue where they engage in politics on behalf of the people they represent to resolve their differences and compromise. In lieu of the conflict that such a process would inevitably generate between members with different policy views, there appears to be a bipartisan consensus that administrative agencies and courts in the federal judiciary are more appropriate venues for making controversial decisions. Such sentiment shifts the locus of the government's decision-making process from the legislative to the executive and judicial branches.

This shift has serious implications for the health of the American republic. Far from being the preeminent branch of government originally envisioned by the framers of the Constitution, Congress, at present, is a phantom whose presence is felt only by its absence.[2] Albeit in different ways, both administrative agencies and the courts make decisions by substituting reason and technocratic expertise for the messy realities of republican politics. When that happens, the American people lose their ability to inform the decisions their government makes because they can't hold officials in the executive and judicial branches accountable as easily as their elected representatives in the legislative branch. Conversely, officials in the executive and judicial branches are unable to legitimize the decisions they make in the eyes of the American people. To do that, they need the active involvement of legislators in the lawmaking process.

Growing awareness of congressional dysfunction has sparked renewed interest in congressional reform among those concerned about the health of the political system. For example, a consensus is emerging among academics that the dysfunction is the consequence of Congress's inability to act. Put another way, scholars see the problem as one of members being unable to participate effectively and intelligently in the legislative process. The implication of such a view is that fixing Congress requires improving the capacity of its members to act.

To that end, scholars have proposed reforms aimed at increasing congressional compensation for members and staff, ending term limits for committee chairs and ranking members, streamlining the budget process, bringing back earmarks, eliminating the Senate filibuster, and strengthening legislative support agencies such as the Congressional Research Service and the Government Accountability Office. The cumulative aim of such reforms is to combat the centrifugal forces inherent in Congress's current environment by giving its members, especially in the Senate, the resources and expertise needed to fulfill their lawmaking responsibilities.

Yet notwithstanding the merits of such proposals, they are unlikely to fix Congress on their own or taken as a whole because Congress's dysfunction at present does not stem from an inability of its members to act. Rather, the problem is their unwillingness to act. This is evident in that members do not use the resources currently at their disposal to participate in the legislative process but instead acquiesce voluntarily to their own disenfranchisement. Improving Congress's capacity for action is thus insufficient for curing its dysfunction as long as this underlying dynamic persists.

To understand how empowering the rank and file combats congressional dysfunction requires first recognizing the dynamic and evolving relationship between Congress's internal and external environments. It requires acknowledging that the way in which the House and Senate order their internal proceedings changes over time in response to new challenges in their environments. In other words, there is no "correct" form of congressional organization that will produce efficient outcomes in perpetuity.[3] Thus, reformers should be careful to do more than merely apply solutions from Congress's past to solve its problems today: an institutional reform that worked in the past will not automatically work again in the future if the environment in which Congress operates has changed. Only when reformers acknowledge this premise is it possible to thoroughly evaluate the likely effectiveness of specific reforms to fix the problems that arise out of Congress's current environment.

Granting the contingency of congressional organization underscores the extent that Congress is structured poorly to foster deliberation and lawmaking given the challenges in its environment. Casting the problem underlying Congress's dysfunction in these terms illuminates the obstacles to enacting the reforms needed to overcome gridlock, especially in the Senate. Specifically, those who will lose power if the rank and file are persuaded to use the resources already at their disposal to play an active role in the lawmaking process can be expected to oppose doing so in the first place. And since party leaders are the most powerful actors in the Senate today, efforts to decentralize the chamber cannot succeed without accounting for their opposition.

To that end, I examine in this chapter the Senate's amendment process to demonstrate that members have the ability to act but choose not to. Specifically, I detail some of the ways in which senators can leverage their procedural rights to play an active role in the legislative process over the objections of the majority leader. My analysis of the ways in which leaders combat such efforts underscores one reason why members are unwilling to flex their institutional muscles in spite of their growing frustration with the leadership-driven status quo.

I chose the Senate as the unit of analysis because it is easier to observe in the institution the inherent contradiction that members are unhappy with the status quo but are nevertheless unwilling to change it despite having the capability to do so. Unlike in the House, senators have a number of well-known procedural tools that they can use to force their way into the lawmaking process. Chief among these are the right to debate and offer amendments on the Senate floor. Therefore, claims that senators lack the capacity to act cannot explain why they currently refrain from doing so, especially with regard to the amendment process. Highlighting just one example of the procedures that senators regularly forgo (so-called third-degree amendments) suggests that improving congressional capacity in itself is not likely to result in a more inclusive and deliberative decision-making process absent other more fundamental changes in how the rank-and-file members understand their role in the Senate. Examining the Senate's amendment process also highlights some of the subtle ways leaders persuade, or pressure, rank-and-file members to acquiesce in a decision-making process that renders them irrelevant.

I conclude by considering the implications of this perspective for the reform effort more broadly, and I offer a two-phase approach to the task of fixing Congress.

Conflict and Congressional Organization

Keith Krehbiel (1991, 2) provides a definition of congressional organization that captures both its structural and procedural characteristics: "legislative organization refers to the allocation of resources and assignment of parliamentary rights to individual legislators or groups of legislators." "Resources" and "parliamentary rights" are distributed more broadly in the Senate than in the House, and the constraints imposed on individual members by the Senate's internal organization are typically informal. As a result, the Senate is an ideal place to observe otherwise capable members who are simply unwilling to act.

Failure to understand the implications of particular forms of congressional organization for efforts to order the legislative process inhibits a broader understanding of today's congressional dysfunction. According to Krehbiel (1991, 14), "to understand legislative organization is to understand *legislative institutions*, that is, rules and precedents that act as binding constraints on legislators' behavior."

The literature on Congress includes a theoretically diverse collection of approaches to understanding the legislative process. The most prominent approaches focus on member behavior and the strategic calculations they make to achieve their goals in Congress. According to these behavioral and rational choice approaches, member action shapes Congress as an institution and determines the legislative process within it (Riker 1962; Fenno 1966; Mayhew 1974; Polsby 1975; Riker 1980; Calvert 1995; Crawford and Ostrom 1995; Eguia and Shepsle 2015). More recently, a historical-institutional approach has proliferated in the literature that focuses on how Congress itself shapes the goal-driven behavior of its members, as well as the legislative process (Evans and Oleszek 1999; Mayhew 2000; Binder 2003; Wawro and Schickler 2006; Lee 2009, 2016; Evans 2018).

Regardless of the approach employed, the literature shares a common interest in the nature of conflict within Congress and the manner in which it is limited. Indeed, the question of conflict limitation is central to any study of Congress because its ability to resolve conflict is directly related to its ability to pass legislation. According to Barbara Sinclair (1990, 97), "there is broad general agreement that the chief congressional function is lawmaking." Nelson Polsby (1968) argues that the viability of Congress depends on its ability to successfully limit conflict and pass legislation. Put simply, Congress "works" when it can successfully limit excessive political conflict within and between the House and Senate.

Limiting conflict is, above all, a question of order. Specifically: What kind of institutional organization serves to order the internal deliberations of Congress through which compromise is reached? The internal organization of the House and Senate regulates member participation in the legislative process, and its particular structure at any given moment is best understood as a response to a particular form of conflict originating in the broader political environment.

The importance of congressional organization in structuring the legislative process has also been acknowledged in the literature. For example, Polsby (1968, 165) argues, "the House's institutional structure does matter greatly in the production of political outcomes." Examining the Senate, Randall Ripley (1969) observes that the institution has periodically changed its internal structure and manner of making decisions in response to new forms of conflict in order to maintain its legislative productivity. Sinclair (1990, 99) maintains that "how well Congress performs its legislative function depends, in part, upon how it is organized."

Congressional organization will inevitably change if its particular "structure of decision-making" fails to "promote reasonably responsive, reasonably coherent, and reasonably expert lawmaking" (Sinclair 1990, 99). According to Sinclair (2007, 108), "modification and innovations can be seen as responses to problems and opportunities that members—as individuals or collectively—confronted, problems and opportunities that arose from changes in institutional structure or challenges in the political environment." Moreover, this institutional change occurs in the Senate despite the partisan control of the chamber. According to Ripley (1969, 49), "two factors pushed senators of both parties to organize themselves so as to have a consistent and important impact on legislative matters. First, by the mid-1870's the Democrats became strong enough to pose a constant threat to Republican control of the Senate. Second, the lack of party control led to chaotic conditions in the late 1860's, 1870's, and early 1880's. This frustrated the senators in their attempts to be legislatively effective."

Elaine Swift (2002) adopts a similar approach to explain the development of the Senate's system of standing committees. She argues that standing committees emerged with bipartisan support because of the increased demands placed on the Senate by a growing electorate and an expanding national agenda. Notably, both of these developments limited the Senate's ability to consider and pass legislation in an efficient manner. The Senate instituted a new system of standing committees in response to these external developments in an effort to maintain its legislative productivity. Viewed from this perspective, the internal organization of the Senate and its particular way of making decisions in any given period can be interpreted as resulting from efforts to maintain the institution's legislative productivity.[4]

The way in which Congress orders its internal proceedings today is perfectly logical. First, all legislatures, including the House and Senate, are characterized by two fundamental features (Loewenberg 1971). They are collective

institutions comprising members who represent separate and distinct constituencies. They are also egalitarian institutions in that their members are
inherently equal and possess the same authority over their vote. Put simply,
no member's vote counts more than another's.[5] Yet notwithstanding these
fundamental features, legislatures in general and Congress in particular are
governed by a mixture of formal rules and informal norms and precedents.
These rules necessarily restrict the authority of individual members to participate in the legislative process.

Second, members cede power to enforce these rules to others to ensure
that Congress performs its primary function of lawmaking (Mayhew 1974;
Rohde 1991; Cox and McCubbins 1993, 2005; Sinclair 1995). Doing so permits
members to maintain Congress's legislative productivity. This is important
because an unproductive Congress makes it more difficult, if not outright
impossible, for members to achieve their goals in the institution.

Third, party leaders limit conflict in Congress by enforcing the institution's rules and norms. They do this by exercising power to influence their
colleagues (Smith 2007), thereby affecting legislative outcomes. Members
cede power to their leaders to maintain order because they believe that the
leaders are the institutional actors best situated to ensure that Congress is
productive.

Fourth, members of the majority party work collectively to pass their
agenda. Such collective action is made possible by broad agreement on a
party program, which itself depends on the ideological cohesiveness of the
two political parties. The development of centralized control of Congress under the auspices of the party leaders was made possible by significant shifts
in the electorate during the second half of the twentieth century that led
the Democratic Party to become more liberal and the Republican Party to
become more conservative (see, e.g., Rohde 1991). Similarly, Cox and Mc-
Cubbins (1993, 2005) present a theory of "legislative cartels" to account for
the behavior of majority parties in Congress. According to their approach,
majority parties seek to structure the decision-making process in a way that
advantages policy outcomes favored by their members.

But this form of congressional organization breaks down in the presence
of significant intraparty divisions. The growing heterogeneity of Democrats
and Republicans today makes it difficult for a Congress organized along these
lines to operate. Such divisions prompt leaders to avoid taking up bills addressing controversial issues and to structure the legislative process to discourage other members of Congress from doing so over their objections.
Leader control of the House and Senate is thus crucial to perpetuating the
mirage of partisan unity in the Democratic and Republican caucuses. That

is why leaders work hard to keep divisive issues off the agenda for as long as possible. When that is no longer an option, leaders resort to crafting must-pass legislation behind closed doors with little or no input from the rank and file. Leaders then wait until the last minute to unveil the legislation to confront members with a fait accompli and thus increase the chances of the bill passing while minimizing the public exposure of partisan divisions.

The Senate's Amendment Process: A Case Study in Dysfunction

Notwithstanding the growing intraparty divisions among Democrats and Republicans, their heterogeneity has not resulted in disgruntled members challenging the way in which Congress orders its proceedings on a sustained basis. This lack of challenge is reflected in the complete collapse of the Senate's amendment process, about which almost all members complain but few act to prevent. Senate majority leaders today have utilized a complex assortment of rules and practices to exert greater control over the institution's decision-making process than at any point in its history. The principal means by which they establish such control is their ability to block amendments on the Senate floor. Recent work captures this dynamic (Beth et al. 2009; Den Hartog and Monroe 2011; Koger 2010; Sinclair 2007; Smith 2014). This work identifies the ability of the majority leader to use his or her priority of recognition to fill the amendment tree. When coupled with cloture and employed early in the process, filling the tree may be successful in passing the majority's preferred bill through the Senate unchanged. At a minimum, the tactic protects members of the majority from having to cast tough votes that could be used against them in their effort to secure reelection.

While Senate majorities have increasingly exercised negative agenda control over the Senate in the twenty-first century, it would be inaccurate to view Senate minorities as powerless. Individual senators, and the minority party collectively, can employ the Senate's rules and practices to circumvent the majority leader's efforts to control the agenda by blocking votes on amendments. Specifically, a senator may circumvent the majority leader's ability to prevent amendments by offering an amendment despite a filled tree and then appealing the subsequent ruling of the chair that the amendment is not in order. Doing so forces a recorded vote directly related to the amendment in question or the majority to filibuster the appeal, or both.

The process of filling the amendment tree follows precedent to block members from offering their own amendments. However, any senator may attempt to offer an amendment even though the amendment tree has been filled. In this situation, the chair would rule that the amendment is not in order pursuant to the Senate's precedents. At that point, the member could appeal the ruling of the chair and request a recorded vote. If a simple majority of the Senate votes for the appeal, the underlying amendment is pending. No further action is required.[6]

The tactic of offering a third-degree amendment has a number of advantages for individual senators, as well as Senate minorities more generally. First, it is permitted under the Senate's current rules (not precedents, although it is consistent with the principles on which they are based and were designed to facilitate for much of the Senate's history). For example, Rule XX stipulates, "A question of order may be raised at any stage of the proceedings . . . and, unless submitted to the Senate, shall be decided by the Presiding Officer [*Chair*] without debate, subject to an appeal to the Senate" (US Senate 2007, 15). Second, it reinforces the minority's narrative that the majority is unwilling to vote on their amendments and therefore blocks them. Third, offering amendments despite the filled tree and appealing the ruling of the chair that they are not in order forces the majority to cast tough votes on procedural questions directly related to the amendment being offered. Procedural votes have been viewed as substantive votes when the question is directly related to the underlying policy and the tactic is employed on a regular basis. For example, cloture's meaning over the years has changed from being widely perceived as a procedural vote to now being understood by nearly everyone as a substantive vote (Sinclair 2006, 150, 164). It is likely that third-degree amendment votes would eventually be understood in the same way.

Recent developments in the Senate support this claim. For example, Senator Pat Toomey (R-PA) offered a third-degree amendment to legislation extending emergency unemployment benefits (S. 1845) on January 15, 2014. The tree had been filled and, as a result, members were not allowed to offer amendments on the Senate floor. Kelly Ayotte (R-NH) had previously moved to table the blocker amendment in the amendment tree so that senators could then offer their own proposals to the legislation. However, the Democrats easily defeated Ayotte's effort on a 54–42 vote. Toomey then subsequently ignored the blocker amendment and offered an amendment directly to the legislation instead of moving to table the tree. His amendment would have prohibited people with annual incomes greater than $1 million from receiving unemployment benefits. In contrast to how it handled the Ayotte motion to table, the majority pulled the legislation from the Senate floor before adjudicating the Toomey appeal of the chair's ruling that his amendment was not in order under the Senate's precedents. Despite their previous unwillingness to allow a vote on the amendment, the majority ultimately included the text of the Toomey amendment in the Emergency Unemployment Compensation Act of 2014 (H.R. 3979), which eventually passed the Senate in April 2014.

Similarly, Senator David Vitter (R-LA) offered an amendment during later consideration of H.R. 3979 even though the majority leader had filled the tree in an effort to again block amendments. While Vitter's appeal of the chair's ruling that the amendment was not in order was tabled, 67–29, the vote illustrated the tactic's utility in imposing costs on rank-and-file senators when used in conjunction with efforts by outside advocacy groups to publicize it. That these procedural votes may be characterized as substantive votes if used on a regular basis was demonstrated after the vote when several conservative advocacy groups sent Vitter a letter thanking him for employing the tactic. In the letter, these groups asserted that offering third-degree amendments "put senators on record for their willingness to allow legislative deliberation in the Senate." Significantly, the letter stated that of the organization signatories, those with scorecards "intend to treat these procedural votes as policy votes" moving forward.[7]

Threatening to ignore a filled tree by simply offering an amendment and appealing the ruling of the chair that it is not in order may encourage the majority leader to return to an open process by giving senators leverage with which to negotiate for amendment opportunities on legislation in the future because the threat to offer a third-degree amendment imposes significant costs on the majority leader directly. If used on a routine basis, the tactic effectively ends the majority's ability to exercise negative agenda control and substantially alters the balance of power between the majority and minority parties in the institution, as well as between individual senators and the party leadership. Instituting a new norm that a filled amendment tree need not be followed in this manner would undermine the ability of the majority leader to block amendments to begin with. In short, filling the amendment would no longer be effective in deterring members from offering amendments on the Senate floor. In practice, the only time the amendment tree is followed literally in the contemporary Senate is when the majority leader would like to block other senators from offering amendments. Without this ability, it would be very difficult for the majority leader to block senators from offering amendments on the Senate floor.

Because of the threat represented by third-degree amendments to their ability to control the agenda, Senate leaders have resisted efforts by rank-and-file members to employ the tactic. They do so principally by distorting the costs associated with limiting their ability to fill the tree in the first place. For example, Lamar Alexander (R-TN) took to the Senate floor during a rare

Sunday session in late July 2015 to speak against the effort of one of his Republican colleagues to force a vote in relation to an amendment. Senator Ted Cruz (R-TX) had tried unsuccessfully two days before to offer an amendment to the Hire More Heroes Act (H.R. 22). He was unable to do so because the majority leader, Mitch McConnell (R-KY), had previously filled the amendment tree on H.R. 22 by offering several measures to the bill that would reauthorize the highway bill, revive the Export-Import Bank (Ex-Im), and repeal the Affordable Care Act. McConnell then filed cloture on the underlying bill and each of the blocker amendments.

Despite the fact that the majority leader's actions technically prevented Cruz from offering his amendment, he chose to call it up anyway and asked for its immediate consideration. Predictably, the chair ruled that the Cruz amendment was out of order, stating, "The amendment is not in order to be offered, as it is inconsistent with the Senate's precedents with respect to the offering of amendments, their number, degree and kind."[8] Cruz subsequently appealed the ruling of the chair. The Senate's adjudication of the appeal was scheduled to take place the following Sunday, immediately after cloture was invoked on the first pending amendment.

That Sunday, Alexander, a three-term senator, close McConnell ally, and widely recognized expert on the Senate's rules, warned his colleagues of the dire consequences that would result if they joined Cruz in voting to overturn the decision of the chair later that morning. Specifically, he made two claims regarding the effort. First, Alexander equated Cruz's appeal with the "nuclear option" employed by Senate Democrats in November 2013. He suggested, "If . . . a majority of Senators agree with the Senator from Texas, the Senate will be saying that a majority can routinely change Senate rules and procedures anytime it wants on any subject it wants in order to get the result it wants." Alexander's goal was to link Cruz's appeal with the effort of Senate Democrats to circumvent the filibuster for judicial and executive nominations on a simple-majority vote in the previous Congress—a move that had been widely criticized by Senate Republicans at the time. Alexander believed that by framing Cruz's appeal in such terms, he would make it less likely that Republican senators would vote to overturn the chair, regardless of how they felt about the substance of the underlying amendments. He intimated this point in his closing remarks, observing that "a Senate in which a majority routinely changes the rules by overruling the Chair is a Senate without any rules."[9]

Second, Alexander asserted that Cruz's appeal would, if successful, "destroy a crucial part of what we call the rule of regular order in the U.S. Senate." The consequence would be the creation of "a precedent that destroys the orderly consideration of amendments." As a result, he confidently predicted,

"There will be unlimited amendments. There will be chaos."[10] This assertion would be particularly concerning to members accustomed to being in Washington Tuesday through Thursday when the Senate was in session.

The majority whip, John Cornyn (R-TX), echoed Alexander's description of the consequences that would befall the Senate if Cruz were successful in his effort: "If the rule the junior Senator from Texas is arguing for is embraced, we will lose all control of the Senate schedule; there will be chaos; and, indeed, we won't be able to meet simple deadlines." He concluded by asserting, "To overrule the Chair on something this important to the orderly consideration of the Senate's business would be a terrible mistake."[11]

Cruz responded by pointing out where he believed these statements to be inaccurate and inconsistent. For example, Cruz argued in reply to Alexander that his effort was very different from the nuclear option even though both used the same mechanism to accomplish their goals (i.e., an appeal of the chair's ruling): "The senior Senator from Tennessee gave a learned speech on changing the rules of this body through appealing the ruling of the Chair, and I very much agree. When the former majority leader used the nuclear option, it was wrong to violate the rules. But the amendment tree does not come from the rules, the amendment tree comes from the precedents, and precedents are set precisely through appealing the rulings of the Chair by a majority vote."[12] He also pointed out that many of his colleagues, including Alexander, McConnell, and Cornyn, had voted on several occasions in the past to overturn rulings of the chair.[13]

Cruz then asserted that the practice of filling the amendment tree was inconsistent with the Senate's institutional character and urged his colleagues to vote to overturn the ruling of the chair to allow his amendment to be made pending to the bill: "A great many Members of this body have given long, eloquent speeches on how this body operates when each Member has a right to offer amendments—and even difficult amendments. We debate and resolve them. That is the heart of this vote, and I would encourage each Member here to vote his conscience or her conscience on both substance and the ability of the Senate to remain the world's greatest deliberative body."[14]

The implication was that the centralization of power in the office of the majority leader, represented here by the filling of the amendment tree, was inherently destructive of the Senate's deliberative nature.

By exaggerating the effect of Cruz's actions, Senate leaders intended to discourage his colleagues from similarly asserting their capacity to play an active role in the legislative process. They feared, correctly, that they would not be able to maintain control over the amendment process if members used the resources at their disposal to offer amendments over their objections.

Conclusion

An analysis of the Senate's amendment process suggests two reasons why most members refrain from acting on the Senate floor. First, it takes a lot of work. While rank-and-file senators in both parties can offer third-degree amendments to legislation even though the majority leader has filled the tree, doing so creates the expectation that they would do it again in similar situations in the future. Such hardball tactics thus deprive members of a convenient excuse for inaction when their rhetoric and policy positions are not aligned.

Second, the unpredictable nature of the lawmaking process in the Senate compounds the work required to act. Outcomes cannot be known in advance because members are able to propose amendments on the Senate floor that may change significantly the content of the underlying legislation. The associated effort and uncertainty makes acting less appealing than not acting in the eyes of Democrats and Republicans. The Senate's declining legislative record over the 2010s suggests that its members increasingly prefer convenience and certainty over inconvenience and hard work.

This analysis also provides support for my claim that the root problem underlying Congress's present dysfunction is the unwillingness of its members to act. That is, an analysis of the Senate's amendment process illustrates one of the ways in which most members of Congress refrain from using the resources currently at their disposal to participate in the legislative process and instead acquiesce voluntarily to their own disenfranchisement. Although capacity is important and rank-and-file members could certainly use more of it, improving Congress's capacity for action is thus insufficient for curing its dysfunction as long as this underlying dynamic persists.

Given the results of my analysis, I suggest that reformers should approach the task of fixing Congress in two phases. First, they should identify reforms that will encourage individual members to play a more active role in the legislative process using the resources already at their disposal. Only after getting rank-and-file members to reassert themselves will efforts to improve Congress's capacity for action help members perform their lawmaking duties in a more effective and intelligent way. Second, reformers should change how the House and Senate make decisions to create more opportunities for those reassertive members to influence policy outcomes.

This prescription may seem counterproductive given the present nature of American politics. After all, increasing the influence of all members to participate in the lawmaking process not only generates more conflict, and thus more gridlock, but increasing Congress's lawmaking capacity in the current environment also counterintuitively requires more conflict, not less. That is, the gridlock we observe today results from the absence of conflict inside Congress.

To the extent that fixing Congress requires empowering its rank-and-file members to participate in the legislative process on their own terms, it also means more political conflict and divisive debates in the near term. Some observers will likely see this as problematic to the extent that they understand congressional dysfunction as the consequence of excessive political conflict. In contrast to the approach recommended here, many reformers typically advocate walling off the legislative process from political conflict in order to fix Congress.

Yet political conflict is inherent in Congress's identity as a representative assembly, and reforms that seek to insulate its deliberations from its external environment can only offer temporary solutions and thus are not likely to succeed. To wall off congressional deliberations from conflict may make negotiating deals easier, thereby increasing Congress's legislative productivity in the short term, but doing so may also undermine its overall lawmaking capacity over time. Routinely making important decisions in this way exacerbates the very conflict that the reforms are designed to mitigate.

Viewing conflict as incompatible with lawmaking reinforces congressional dysfunction and thus blinds members to the possibilities inherent in deliberation. Indeed, the collective tendency today is to immediately look for ways to insulate decision making from conflict as soon as we are presented with a controversial question of public policy. With such a mind-set, it is unlikely that we will ever acknowledge fully that conflict can be harnessed and used as a productive force in making compromise possible.

Yet according to the political theorist Hannah Arendt (1958, 190), political action, and thus the conflict it produces, "always establishes relationships and therefore has an inherent tendency to force open all limitations and cut across all boundaries." For that reason, political action makes new beginnings, and compromises, possible. Similarly, Bertram Gross (1953, 1) observed that compromise agreements arise out of the "development of the group struggle itself, for the vicissitudes of this struggle create the conditions that promote cooperation and make it possible." Put another way, Congress is designed to produce the *right* compromise through conflict.

Rather than to seek ways to protect members of Congress from conflict, reformers should consider instead how to structure the legislative process so that members can successfully negotiate bipartisan agreements in spite of it. At a minimum, this requires increasing their ability to participate in the process. Yet it is difficult to do so unless that process is structured so that members are afforded the opportunity to participate.

Congress, not the presidency or the federal judiciary, is the place where politics appropriately occurs under the US Constitution. As long as Americans are unable to acknowledge this as a society, the nation's members of Congress will continue to be unwilling to act.

11

The Issue Dynamics of Congressional Capacity

JONATHAN LEWALLEN, SEAN M. THERIAULT, AND BRYAN D. JONES

One of the key questions posed in this volume is, "Congressional capacity for what?" What should we expect out of the institution and its members? In our view, Congress has two major responsibilities in the US political system. The first is making public policy, either through legislation or in conjunction with the executive branch. The second is the collective representation of the diverse array of interests in American society: paying attentions to issues the public thinks are important. When we consider the question of "congressional capacity for what," then, we need a way to evaluate congressional capacity that incorporates the many separate activities that fall under Congress's twin responsibilities that sometimes conflict with one another.

Congress is certainly experiencing difficulties living up to its policymaking and representational responsibilities. The government shutdown that spanned the 115th and 116th Congresses is perhaps the most vivid example of fiascos that have damaged Congress's reputation. In the end, Republican President Donald Trump capitulated to Democratic demands and at the same time issued his emergency declaration to facilitate funding for a wall at the US-Mexico border, which led Congress to spend time reconsidering the powers it has delegated to the president and leave a host of other policy problems unaddressed.

Many observers view this example and others like it—multiple government shutdowns in the 2010s; gridlock over an international nuclear research agreement with Iran, federal assistance for the water crisis in Flint, Michigan, and disaster relief in Puerto Rico; failure to reauthorize numerous government programs in time—as symptoms of a partisan divide; we view them as information-processing capacity problems rooted in the committee system. Information processing involves translating inputs to outputs, and those outputs can range from simple issue attention to major policy changes. Thinking about Congress in terms of information processing thus incorporates both of the institution's responsibilities: policy and representation. The opposing sides in the shutdown debate may have been representing their constituents' views in their Twitter debates, but it was only when members consulted policy experts about the appropriate protections at the US-Mexico border that a solution began to take form.

We evaluate changes to information processing through committee hearings, which serve several functions. The public nature of hearings corresponds to the dissemination and transmission of information throughout the institution, and hearings themselves also serve as an output for issue attention, which contributes to both the policy process and collective representation (Lewallen 2018). In this chapter we explore whether changes to committee information processing have occurred across a wide range of issues or been concentrated among a few policy topics, particularly those issues related to the scope of government activity and its role in the national economy that tend to divide the two parties.

Our chapter first discusses our explanation for a dysfunctional Congress rooted in changes to how the committees process information through their public hearings and describes the coding we derive to measure these changes. We next present data on close to 22,000 committee hearings from 1971 to 2010. We find that the changes to committee information processing do not affect all issues equally; rather, some issue areas have experienced rapid declines in obtaining "good" information while other issue areas are much less affected. The final section concludes with some ideas for future investigation into the issue dynamics of Congress's information-processing capacity.

The Information Dimension of Congressional Capacity

In 1950, the American Political Science Association (APSA) issued a report titled "Toward a More Responsible Two-Party System." The report responded to the loose linkages between state and national party organizations that made it difficult for whichever party gained control of the federal government to establish and implement a coherent agenda. The report made several recommendations based on its diagnosis, including "a party system with sufficient party loyalty" and "tightening up the congressional party organization" (APSA 1950, 2–8).

In many ways we have the party-centered Congress today that APSA wanted (Sinclair 2003); members of the two parties in Congress are voting in patterns that are internally cohesive and distinct from each other. Furthermore, they are doing so at higher rates than at any other time in the institution's history (Rohde and Aldrich 2010). Party leaders have more tools at their disposal to enforce discipline and structure the institution's agenda (Curry 2015; Theriault and Lewallen 2012). Such patterns were, for many decades, an ideal to which most political scientists believed Congress should aspire. Yet citizens, journalists, current and former members of Congress, and political scientists alike now lament the increase in party polarization along with the decline of comity and bipartisanship within the legislative branch and the decline in trust in government among voters (Bipartisan Policy Center 2014; Galston 2010; Mann and Ornstein 2012; Mansbridge and Martin 2013). We do not doubt that polarization and partisan warfare within Congress have contributed to increased gridlock and breakdowns in the legislative process, but we also believe that the solution to these problems is rooted in a broader concern: the committee system's capacity to process information about policy problems and solutions.

The term *information processing* refers to how organizations acquire, synthesize, distribute, and use information; how they translate inputs into outputs (Cyert and March 1963; G. Huber 1991; Simon and Newell 1964). Information and analysis are critical to governance; Congress in particular is responsible for gathering information and defining problems as a means of meeting the American public's policy needs (C. Jones 1975). As James Madison wrote in the *Federalist* in 1788 in arguing against annual elections, "No man can be a competent legislator who does not add to an upright intention and a sound judgment a certain degree of knowledge of the subject on which he is to legislate" (quoted in Kramnick 1987, 328). While Republicans and Democrats in Congress may not always agree on matters of governance, more consensus should exist on the importance of obtaining good information. Without it, the parties offer the voters a distinct choice between policy positions, but the policies themselves may suffer and, in the end, frustrate the parties' efforts.

The 2017 tax revision law is a prime example of the consequences of bad information processing on public policy. For all of the tax code's complexity, Republican majorities in the House and Senate moved a bill through the institution in five weeks. Although the Senate Finance Committee had held several hearings on the idea of revising the tax code in preceding years, the specific bill that was enacted into law never received a hearing and infamously included handwritten revisions in the margins made on the Senate floor to facilitate agreement among Republicans (R. Rubin 2017). The result was a law both vague and self-contradictory: "Republicans' tax-rewrite plans are riddled with bugs, loopholes and other potential problems that could plague lawmakers long after their legislation is signed into law. . . . 'It's crazy,' says one Republican lobbyist. 'I don't think anyone could explain it, let alone comply with it'" (Faler 2017).

With good information, the parties can still present voters distinct agendas of ideologically opposed ideas, but they can do so with solutions—either from the Left or the Right—that might actually solve the problems they have identified and in turn lead to more favorable evaluation from their constituents.

The committee system is where Congress primarily processes the myriad information it receives. Committee hearings allow members to acquire information and simultaneously signal that information to the rest of the institution and to other institutions (Diermeier and Feddersen 2000; Katzmann 1989). By connecting outside expertise to the members of Congress who actually make the decisions, committees are critical stages in the flow of information within the institution (Krehbiel 1991; Porter 1974; Sabatier and Whiteman 1985). The testimony and witness responses gathered in hearings become part of the public record and foster participation in the legislative process.

Partisan warfare in policymaking and in committee information processing are undoubtedly related; committees often respond to the partisan environment in which they operate (Fenno 1966). We further believe that breakdowns in the committee process feed back into the partisan war. If and when committees restrict their attention or receive slanted testimony, then the information available to members of Congress becomes limited, which reinforces partisan cue taking and hinders effective problem solving.

Consider a human trafficking bill taken up in the Senate in March 2015. Just as the bill was scheduled for debate, Senate Democrats noticed a provision that limited spending on abortion services in other countries; the provision had been in the bill since its introduction two months prior, but Democrats had not asked whether the bill addressed abortion funding and Republicans did not volunteer that information. The antitrafficking bill finally passed the Senate by a 99–0 vote, but not before senators engaged in heated rhetoric and a largely partisan series of procedural votes. The debate and gridlock over this bill even spilled over into other institutional responsibilities, as it delayed a vote on Loretta Lynch's nomination to be attorney general.

We can trace this breakdown in congressional problem solving back to the Senate Judiciary Committee. While we should not necessarily expect a committee to search high and low for pro–human trafficking advocates, the committee's hearing featured four senators, including Democrats Barbara Mikulski and Kirsten Gillibrand, and four antitrafficking advocates, all of whom expressed their support for the bill but none of whom addressed the legislation in much detail. Had the abortion restriction provision been identified earlier in the process and Democrats' objections been raised during the committee's hearing, a floor fight—and a lot of embarrassment—could have been avoided. Inadequate information processing in this case fed back into the partisan war and limited the institution's capacity to manage its agenda and make policy.

To understand the breakdown in information processing at a more systematic level, we have coded committee hearings based on hearing and testimony summaries of the Congressional Information Service (CIS) as well as the Policy Agendas Project's Congressional Hearings data set. In addition to the issues they address and the types of witnesses testifying, we code information gathering in committee hearings along two dimensions—what we call *purpose* and *stance*.

The first dimension we use to describe committee information processing is a hearing's *purpose*: whether it addresses a problem, policy implementation, or a proposed solution. The problems and solutions discussed in these committee hearings may not be new; what is "new" in this context is the relative attention they receive. *Problem-focused* hearings are those asking if a particular issue needs to be addressed and how. They tend to address recent studies, policy trends (such as an increase in childhood obesity), natural disasters, and national or international events. *Implementation-focused* hearings ask whether the government's current approach to addressing a particular problem is working or even appropriate. The important distinction for implementation hearings is whether the bureaucratic solution already has been adopted. If so, the hearing tends to assess how an agency is carrying out that solution, and so the "implementation" code is most appropriate. If the agency has not yet acted on a proposal, then the hearing focuses on the "solution" aspect and whether the proposal is appropriate. *Solution-focused* hearings address the benefits or costs of a particular proposal; the problem is taken as given.

The second dimension we code is a hearing's *stance*. We find that a hearing can take one of two stances: positional or exploratory. *Positional* hearings ascertain information from only one side of the debate. All of the witnesses may praise (or, alternately, criticize) a program or idea, or the hearing itself may focus only on the positive (or negative) aspects. *Exploratory* hearings, by contrast, gain testimony from more than one side of a particular debate or impart information and analysis without a witness's personal opinion.

Positional language in the CIS summary includes "objections to," "need for," "importance of," "preference for," "negative impact of," "charged inadequacy of," and "disagreement with." Language that would indicate an

exploratory hearing or individual's testimony includes "discusses," "explanation of," "analysis of," "views on," "briefing on," "status of," and "differing (or
conflicting) views on." According to our coding rules, only one witness needs
to have provided a view that differs from other witnesses in order for a hearing stance to qualify as exploratory.

Anecdotal evidence suggests that congressional information-processing
capacity has not suffered equally across all issues. Congress has struggled to
reauthorize transportation agencies and programs such as the Federal Aviation Authority and the Highway Trust Fund, yet the two parties have come
together during such "polarized" times to enact laws on drug enforcement
issues such as combating prescription drug abuse and reducing the disparity in criminal penalties for possession of powder and crack cocaine. If we
ultimately wish to see congressional capacity improve, we first need to understand where it needs such improvement. The next section presents our data
on committee hearings to assess how changes to committee information-
processing capacity vary across issues.

Data on Congressional Hearings

We first obtained our sample of hearings from the Policy Agendas Project's
Congressional Hearings data set, which uses a topic coding scheme to trace
issue attention in Congress across time. Our own data collection efforts began in the first Congress after the passage of the Legislative Reorganization
Act of 1970, the 92nd Congress (1971–72) and concluded with the hearings
that took place in the 111th Congress (2009–10), the most recent Congress for
which the Policy Agendas Project had data when we began our coding efforts. We gathered data by committee, initially following Deering and Smith's
(1997) findings on perceptions of conflict in different committees' environments. While we did not subsequently build on their analysis, collecting data
this way leaves us with a broad representation of issues (see table 11.1). Our
data set includes 21,830 hearings, which represents more than one-third of the
total number of hearings held by all congressional committees during this period. We have also collected data on the number of witnesses who appeared at
each hearing to assess the volume of information gathered in these fora. Our
data set excludes Senate hearings on nominations.

Our analysis here focuses on three measures: the average number of witnesses
per hearing in a Congress, the percentage of hearings that attend to proposed
solutions, and the percentage of exploratory hearings. We highlight solution-
focused hearings rather than either problem-focused or implementation-focused
hearings, though patterns on the three hearing purposes are connected; higher

TABLE 11.1. Hearings coded by issue

Issue	No. of hearings
Defense	2,873
Government Operations	2,248
Banking and Commerce	1,872
Public Lands and Water	1,562
Agriculture	1,509
Health	1,476
Environment	1,364
Education	1,354
Labor and Employment	1,300
Macroeconomics	1,266
Energy	940
Law, Crime, and Family	847
Social Welfare	596
International Affairs	584
Civil Rights and Liberties	537
Transportation	406
Housing	361
Trade	343
Science and Technology	309
Immigration	83
Total hearings	21,830

Source: Policy Agendas Project Congressional Hearings
data set for 92nd through 111th Congresses.

levels of solution-focused hearings mean fewer problem- and implementation-focused hearings, and vice versa. Effective problem solving (however defined) requires good information about the solution under consideration to address that problem. A decrease in attention to proposed solutions would suggest that committees no longer are "lay[ing] an intellectual and political foundation" for good problem solving (R. Kaiser 2013, 27).

Committee hearings during this period averaged eleven witnesses, while 44 percent of hearings addressed a proposed policy solution and 69 percent of hearings were exploratory (see table 11.2). We find large cross-sectional differences in committee information processing by issue. Many more witnesses have testified on hearings related to agriculture and the environment—seventeen and fifteen on average, respectively. Hearings on these two policy areas also tend to be more exploratory (78 and 75 percent, respectively) and more focused on proposed solutions (46 and 51 percent, respectively). Relatively more defense hearings have been exploratory, 81 percent, than any other policy area, while 61 percent of hearings on public lands and water issues have been devoted to proposed solutions.

TABLE 11.2. Committee information processing by issue, 1971–2010

Issue	Avg. no. of witnesses	Solution (%)	Exploratory (%)
Average across issues	11	44	69
Macroeconomics	*9*	45	**72**
Civil Rights and Liberties	10	43	68
Health	10	*30*	65
Agriculture	**17**	**46**	**78**
Labor and Employment	12	**52**	*67*
Education	12	**51**	*55*
Environment	**15**	**51**	75
Energy	12	43	75
Immigration	*8*	*28*	*64*
Transportation	11	*41*	*67*
Law, Crime, and Family	*9*	*30*	**71**
Social Welfare	**15**	**55**	*61*
Housing	11	*32*	*63*
Banking and Commerce	*9*	*30*	*55*
Defense	*9*	**47**	**81**
Science and Technology	*8*	*31*	**71**
Trade	*8*	*34*	*59*
International Affairs	*6*	*21*	**73**
Government Operations	*8*	**46**	65
Public Lands and Water	11	**61**	70

Note: Cell entries in bold represent above-average values; cell entries in italics represent below-average values.

Hearings in other areas have focused much more on policy problems and implementation and been more positional over the forty-year span of our study. Just 21 percent of hearings on international affairs have focused on proposed solutions; instead, 45 percent of them have been devoted to new and emerging problems. Hearings on this topic also involve almost half as many witnesses (six) as the overall average. Commerce and education issues are 14 percentage points below the overall exploratory average at 55 percent each.

We now turn to longitudinal trends in committee information processing by issue with slope coefficients from regressing a given issue's witness, solution, and exploratory measures on a time trend. A positive coefficient indicates that the relevant indicator increased over time for a particular issue, while a negative coefficient indicates that an indicator decreased over time. Comparing the slope coefficients across issues reveals the relative magnitude of those changes.[1]

The average number of witnesses at a given hearing has decreased for sixteen out of the nineteen issues we analyze; only science and technology, international affairs, and environment issues have seen no statistically significant

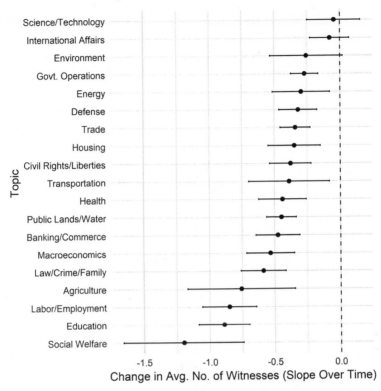

FIGURE 11.1. Changes in average number of hearing witnesses, 1971–2010

Note: The data represent the slope coefficient estimates with standard errors for a series of OLS regression equations $Y_i = \beta_0 + \beta_1 X + \varepsilon$, where Y represents the average number of witnesses called to hearings on a given issue i in Congress t and X represents a time trend counter. Immigration hearings have been excluded from this analysis due to a small number of hearings.

change in the number of witnesses called per hearing between 1971 and 2010 (see figure 11.1). The largest decreases in witnesses have been in hearings devoted to social welfare, with a little more than one fewer witness per hearing with each successive Congress. Education, labor, and agriculture issues exhibit the next-largest decreases.

Nearly two-thirds of the issues we analyze saw significant decreases in their attention to proposed solutions (see figure 11.2). Put another way, twelve out of nineteen topics have seen significant shifts away from hearings that help members learn about proposed government action, either bills or regulations. Science and technology hearings exhibit the largest shift by far—a 4 percentage point decrease in solution-focused hearings with each successive Congress—followed by defense, education, agriculture, and government operations (which includes multiagency appropriations measures along with

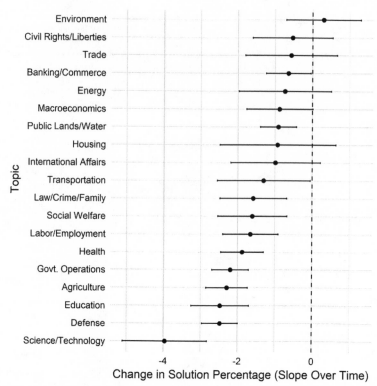

FIGURE 11.2. Changes in percentage of hearings devoted to policy solutions, 1971–2010
Note: The data represent the slope coefficient estimates with standard errors for a series of OLS regression equations $Y_i = \beta_0 + \beta_1 X + \varepsilon$, where Y represents the average number of witnesses called to hearings on a given issue i in Congress t and X represents a time trend counter. Immigration hearings have been excluded from this analysis due to a small number of hearings.

matters related to government employees, tax administration and enforcement, and electoral campaign regulation).

Finally, hearings on five of the nineteen issues we analyze have become more one-sided over time. Once again social welfare shows the biggest increase in positional hearings, followed by trade, housing, public lands and water, and health (see figure 11.3). The percentage of exploratory hearings has increased over time for science and technology and defense, and in the former case the change appears to be quite large, an increase of about 2 percentage points with each successive Congress. The time trend has positive slope coefficient estimates for four additional issues—transportation, international affairs, macroeconomics, and government operations—although they are not statistically significant.

To summarize our findings, three issues have seen significant decreases in all three of our capacity indicators: health, social welfare, and public lands and water (see table 11.3). During the forty-year period between 1971 and 2010, these issues all have seen fewer witnesses called to testify (and thus fewer sources of information), fewer hearings devoted to learning about proposed solutions, and fewer exploratory, analytical hearings. Social welfare issues saw the largest decrease of any issue in two of our three measures. Health hearings were consistently below average in their attention to proposed solutions throughout this period but dropped even lower in the 1990s and the first decade of the twenty-first century and fell to just 12 percent solution-focused in 2009–10. Health hearings were consistently average or above average in our exploratory measure throughout the 1980s but similarly became more

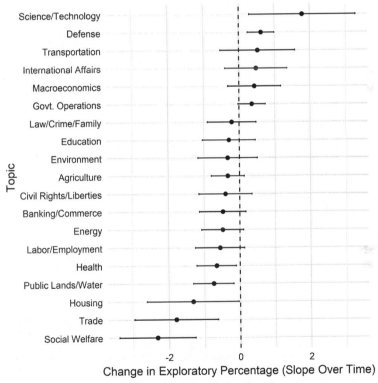

FIGURE 11.3. Changes in percentage of exploratory hearings, 1971–2010

Note: The data represent the slope coefficient estimates with standard errors for a series of OLS regression equations $Y_i = \beta_0 + \beta_1 X + \varepsilon$, where Y represents the average number of witnesses called to hearings on a given issue i in Congress t and X represents a time trend counter. Immigration hearings have been excluded from this analysis due to a small number of hearings.

TABLE 11.3. Summary of changes to committee information processing by issue

	Witnesses	Solution percentage	Exploratory percentage
Increase	None	None	Defense
			Science and Technology
No change	Environment	Macroeconomics	Microeconomics
	Science and Technology	Civil Rights and Liberties	Civil Rights and Liberties
	International Affairs	Environment	Agriculture
		Energy	Labor and Employment
		Housing	Education
		Trade	Environment
		International Affairs	Energy
			Transportation
			Law, Crime, and Family
			Banking and Commerce
			International Affairs
			Govt. Operations
Decrease	Macroeconomics	Health	Health
	Civil Rights and Liberties	Agriculture	Social Welfare
	Health	Labor and Employment	Housing
	Agriculture	Education	Trade
	Labor and Employment	Transportation	Public Lands and Water
	Education	Law, Crime, and Family	
	Energy	Social Welfare	
	Transportation	Banking and Commerce	
	Law, Crime, and Family	Defense	
	Social Welfare	Science and Technology	
	Housing	Govt. Operations	
	Banking and Commerce	Public Lands and Water	
	Defense		
	Trade		
	Govt. Operations		
	Public Lands and Water		

Note: Policy areas in each cell are listed in the order of their Policy Agendas Project major topic code.

positional in the late 1990s and the early part of the first decade of the twenty-first century.

Two additional issues consistently have exhibited no significant change in committee information-processing capacity: international affairs and the environment. Recall from table 11.2 that international affairs exhibited the lowest witness average and the lowest percentage of solution-oriented hearings of all twenty issues. While these patterns have stayed relatively consistent over time, data from the most recent congresses in our data set suggest they are declining even further, with just three witnesses called on average and only 8 percent of those hearings being devoted to proposed solutions in 2009–10.

An Issue-Focused Approach to Congressional Capacity

Many proposed solutions for increasing congressional capacity are universal, aimed at the institution as a whole. We first need to understand the problem better, which our systematic study of committee information processing sets out to do. Our findings suggest that more targeted remedies that speak to differences in how the institution addresses different issues may be more appropriate.

We are cognizant that change does not always imply worsening conditions; the decline in solution-focused hearings is not in itself negative as it may simply reflect a change in Congress's view of what information it needs to fulfill its responsibilities, which include monitoring emerging policy problems and exercising oversight of the executive branch. But the combination of changes we find gives us reason to believe that Congress's capacity to make policy and represent the views of diverse groups in society has declined. Fewer committee hearings and fewer witnesses at those hearings may not directly produce worse policy. But they undoubtedly reduce the scope and volume of information available to members of Congress as they make their decisions and the scope and volume of viewpoints and societal groups that participate in the legislative process, which contributes to a decline in Congress's capacity for pluralist representation.

As the 2017 tax bill example shows, such a decline can have negative consequences for Congress's ability to do what it wants to do well, even if the majority party wants to find something on which it can claim credit or highlight differences with the minority party. As committees spend less time learning about proposed bills and regulations, members of Congress increasingly turn to party leaders about the effect of those proposed solutions, which reinforces partisan warfare and creates downstream problems for policy implementation and judicial interpretation. Spending so much Senate floor time debating one provision of a human trafficking bill held up consideration of other measures and reduced Congress's agenda capacity.

Jochim and Jones (2013) previously examined the extent to which voting on various issues has become structured to polarize the two parties. They find that six issues became significantly more amenable to party polarization over time: education, science and technology, public lands and water, transportation, health, and domestic commerce. All six of those issues also saw decreases in the percentage of solution-focused hearings in our data, which suggests a connection between committee information processing and how party leaders structure members' voting choices; how Congress attempts to solve public problems.

Congress cannot simply rely on its previous record of information processing to guide it. The nature of policy problems changes over time, requiring
political institutions to update their understanding and develop new combinations of solutions. Turnover within Congress, among both elected membership and staff, depletes institutional memory and brings new participants into
different issue environments with which they may not have experience. At the
same time, the trends we uncover in issues such as science and technology
and the environment may hold answers for increasing Congress's problem-
solving capacity in the policy areas that have seen the biggest declines, such
as health, social welfare, and public lands and water.

In closing, we stress that good information processing and solution search
can be carried out in a partisan environment. But in such an era, a robust
committee process becomes even more vital for exploring effective policy solutions. High-quality information through and from the committee system
should render more effective Congress's ability to solve problems regardless
of the solution, partisan or otherwise, which would render American representative government more effective as well.

12

Congressional Capacity and Reauthorizations

E. SCOTT ADLER, STEFANI R. LANGEHENNIG, AND RYAN W. BELL

The conventional view of the contemporary United States Congress is that of an ineffective lawmaking body plagued by partisan conflict and gridlock. For years close observers have told us that Congress is "broken" (Mann and Ornstein 2006; Shapiro 2018), that "it's worse than it looks" (Mann and Ornstein 2012), and that it is "in crisis" (Davis, Frost, and Cohen 2014). Commentators on the cable news shows endlessly recount lawmakers incapable of governing.

With this being the narrative surrounding Congress, scholars have sought to describe that dysfunction with various estimates of the body's performance. Measures have ranged from straightforward accounting of days of work in Washington, DC, law output, or the frequency of its inability to perform basic budgetary functions, to more-complex accounting of historic statutes over time, and even included explorations of Congress's success in meeting the demands placed on it by the public.

These innovative metrics of lawmaking activity provide meaning for our discussion of whether Congress has the *capacity* to adequately govern. As we see in this volume, there are many ways to think about this—from explorations of budget making and floor procedures to examinations of congressional staff and support agencies. In this chapter, we study the question of congressional performance from an often overlooked but central duty Congress has set for itself: revising and updating the hundreds of existing federal programs and agencies that come up for renewal on an ongoing basis. Next to the appropriations process, short-term authorizations have for decades been the key mechanism of control and routine oversight of policies and agencies touching almost every realm of federal policy.

Assessment of its ability to keep authorizations of legislation current is a gauge of both Congress's oversight of the executive branch and its functioning as a policymaking body. As well, it permits a more nuanced examination of governing within individual policy areas than we have seen previously. If we want to understand the process of legislative deliberation and negotiation, statutes that require reauthorization are where we are very likely to see the dynamics of governance play out. Specifically, we devise a method that allows us to track and assess the expiration and renewal of programs and agencies by Congress down to the level of legislative provisions (or statutory sections) rather than entire laws.

This chapter begins with a brief overview of the various ways in which congressional accomplishment is measured. Next, we discuss expiring legislation as a gauge of congressional capacity. We provide an overview of the *United States Code*, the primary data source that we use to provide insight into the renewal rate of expirations in laws spanning the period from 1994 to 2016. We also explore the impact of political factors—such as unified versus divided government, the divisiveness of issues, the public's demand for particular issues, and the size of Congress's agenda—on legislative accomplishment vis-à-vis reauthorizations. We find that Congress is having increasing difficulty keeping pace with the array of expiring programs and agencies that require renewal and that the contentiousness of policy areas is a large contributing factor in its lack of meaningful governance.

Assessing Congressional Accomplishment

With growing concern that polarization and rancorous political discourse in Washington is leading to intransigence and gridlock with regard to governance, it is natural that observers of politics would seek to gauge the degree of that dysfunction. In fact, a cottage industry has grown up around assessing Congress's achievements over time. This accounting often starts with basic indicators of procedure (e.g., days in session, hearings held), audits of obstruction (such as cloture votes), or operational openness (e.g., majority versus minority amendments adopted). Observers even tally outputs such as laws produced, sometimes distinguishing in very basic ways between laws of lesser or greater consequence.[1]

While certainly informative of lawmaker effort, measuring congressional achievement by a sheer count of public laws or days in session is not a complete picture. Therefore, congressional scholars have devised new, more-complex measures to capture the body's activity and performance levels. At the forefront of this effort is David Mayhew's (1991) catalog of historic statutes. His accounting of the pace of "landmark" or major legislation concluded that production of historic legislation did not vary much from era to era and that key conditions such as unified versus divided government did not make much of a difference. Following in Mayhew's footsteps, others attempted improvements on the enumeration of landmark laws, such as a more refined categorization of laws (e.g., Kelly 1993; Howell et al. 2000).

An important innovation in the assessment of congressional accomplishment was the introduction of a *denominator*—a baseline metric of Congress's obligations. In large respect this has been seen as "what constituents are demanding." George Edwards, Andrew Barrett, and Jeffrey Peake (1997) used *CQ Almanac's* inventory of major bills considered each term to see what policy proposals made it off of the agenda and into law. Sarah Binder (2003) studies the flip side of productivity—gridlock—and defines the agenda of issues through an appraisal of the unsigned editorials of the *New York Times*, contrasted against Mayhew's landmark legislation as the index of legislative supply. Alternatively, examining the variety of "required" activities of governance, one could assess on-time budget resolutions (Heniff 2015) or the failure to produce annual appropriations (Woon and Anderson 2012; Anderson and Woon 2014; Hanson 2014a, 2014b; McCarty 2016).

An equally important duty that makes up an enormous amount of substantive lawmaking on Capitol Hill involves revisiting laws that govern federal agencies and programs. Regular governance and oversight by Congress in a wide array of policy areas is often accomplished through statutes authorizing the existence and defining the duties of departments and programs. Keeping these laws fully updated and active is a duty Congress has set for itself. It compels this ongoing vigilance through the use of short-term or temporary authorizations; authorizations that need periodic updating. Exploring how well it performs this function allows us to go beyond the macrolevel of congressional lawmaking—we can learn much about the body's capacity to govern by examining issue areas individually. Separating authorizing obligations into their respective issue areas allows us to examine congressional accomplishment with an eye toward characteristics of policy subsystems and other dynamics within issue domains.

Congressional Capacity and Expiring Legislation: The Importance of Reauthorizing Legislation

The ongoing existence and funding of nearly all federal programs and agencies depend on two forms of legislation: authorizing and appropriations. Alone these two types of laws make up the bulk of substantive legislating each congressional term (Schick 2007; Tollestrup and Yeh 2014). *Authorizing legislation* provides the specific statutory framework for federal programs and agencies and their respective responsibilities. It gives instructions to agency officials about their priorities and their required plan of action. *Appropriations legislation*, on the other hand, provides for the funding out of the federal treasury of programs and agencies previously authorized, but is not permitted to include authorizing language.[2]

Recent interviews with a wide variety of congressional staff highlight the importance of the authorization process to both the functioning of government and Congress's place in a system of shared federal powers (Drutman et al. 2017a). As one staffer put it, "Reauthorization is an essential part of oversight, oversight is an essential part of reauthorization" (Drutman et al. 2017a). Similarly, officials in federal agencies also see the directives provided through authorizing legislation as critical. "Those authorization levels are really important to us," said Amanda Greenwell, head of the office of legislative and public affairs at the National Science Foundation, whose authorization ran out in 2013. She added, "A lot of times the committee will not put any authorizations in at all, and that really worries us because then you're putting in all these new requirements [and] there's nothing in there to say this is what the [funding] level should be for this agency" (Vinik 2016).

Congressional staffers often highlight the widespread use of expiring provisions, emphasizing some of the biggest and most frequently noted reauthorizations handled by Congress, such as the annual Defense authorization, the Farm Bill, the Higher Education Act, and the Children's Health Insurance Program (Drutman et al. 2017a). At the same time, these insiders note the increasing difficulty of reauthorizing programs on time. A wide array of critical federal departments and programs have gone years without a full reassessment and reauthorization. The Federal Bureau of Investigation, the Drug Enforcement Agency, and the Bureau of Alcohol, Tobacco, Firearms and Explosives have not been reauthorized since 2009, and the Department of Homeland Security has not been reauthorized since it was created in 2003 (Vinik 2016). One involved staffer noted that the State Department went seventeen years (2002–16) without a reauthorization (Drutman et al. 2017a). Sometimes referred to as "zombie" programs, one expert noted, "government is mindlessly expanding programs that should be reviewed to see whether or not they are truly effective" (Tapper 2016). Failing to renew and update agencies and laws results in Congress having a much more difficult time holding administrators accountable for their actions or in correcting policy deviations, and it ultimately means surrendering much of their authority over agencies to the executive branch (Strand and Lang 2017).

There are a variety of political and practical reasons Congress cannot or will not reauthorize some existing agencies and laws. For supporters of existing government agencies, there is a real fear that coveted programs will not make it through the partisan gauntlet and thus disappear. As well, a loss of policy knowledge and historical memory through lawmaker and staff turnover can result in little know-how and political skill in accomplishing the complicated task of reauthorizations. But ultimately the process of reauthorization is an imperative for proper governance and a congressional responsibility. The notion that different lawmaking entities should be responsible for policy directives and spending decisions is a principle that dates back to the First Congress and was ensconced in congressional rules in the early nineteenth century (Schick 2007, 191). The House and Senate mandate that programs be currently authorized in law before lawmakers can appropriate funds for their operations.[3] Since the 1960s, Congress has frequently limited the period between reconsideration and updating of federal programs to between three and six years, though with some wider variations as well. Such laws are often the primary or even sole task of Congress's various authorizing committees.[4]

The gears of government can grind to a halt when a short-term authorization expires. For example, in the summer of 2011, Congress was unable to pass the reauthorization of the Federal Aviation Administration, thus rendering government incapable of collecting the tax on airline tickets and forcing the shutdown of hundreds of airport improvement projects and the unpaid furlough of about four thousand federal employees for several weeks. Such a shutdown is, however, more the exception than the rule. Frequently programs and laws that Congress cannot reauthorize will continue to exist through their appropriations, along with a waiver adopted on any point of order in the chamber rules prohibiting unauthorized appropriations. The result of such action is that lawmakers have not reevaluated and updated critical existing programs.

Given the centrality of authorizations to Congress's duties, it seems natural that we would look to its record of reauthorization as a way to gauge performance. Indeed, this has been a focus of a limited number of assessments in the twenty-first century (for academic studies, see T. Hall 2004; Adler and Wilkerson 2012). Commonly the source of information demonstrating the failure of lawmakers to reauthorize programs is data collected by the Congressional Budget Office (CBO) indicating "appropriations that go unauthorized." In an annual report, CBO staff have been mandated since the mid-1980s to identify all appropriations that are funded but lack a proper authorization (CBO 2015). Therefore, we often see references to CBO data from this report. Observers point to an ever-increasing appropriations amount or proportion of the federal discretionary spending that is unauthorized (Tapper 2016;

Vinik 2016). Advocacy groups and lawmakers (see McMorris Rodgers, n.d.) who have waded into the debate over reauthorizations usually rely on these same data (Reich 2016; Strand and Lang 2017).

While examining the amount of appropriations that go unauthorized offers a useful representation of congressional inactivity, it does not paint a complete picture. Not all programs and agencies that expire necessarily exist only by appropriated funds. Moreover, the only thing that can be accounted for here are specific dollar amounts of the obligation, not what is referred to by the CBO as "indefinite" authorizations (these are authorizations that frequently distinguished with an obligation of "such sums as may be consumed"). Moreover, while the CBO's objective is to provide a general report to Congress on programs and activities whose authorization has expired or will expire, questions remain about whether this inventory is a comprehensive and quantifiable accounting of either laws or provisions expiring in any given year or congressional term (Adler and Wilkerson 2012).

Temporary Legislation as a Measure of Accomplishment

As the foregoing discussion demonstrates, laws of limited duration create a political and policymaking imperative for legislators to revisit policies as they come up for renewal. Renewal and updating of these temporary authorizations of appropriations effectively represent the agenda that Congress sets for itself in advance and constitute an enormous portion of substantive lawmaking activity during a congressional term. We are able to gauge Congress's ability to fulfill its governance responsibilities and oversight of executive branch agencies by assessing its success in revising and improving the hundreds of existing programs and laws that expire each term. Examining the fate of such legislation offers a metric by which to measure congressional accomplishment along with an important baseline of expected performance.

USING THE *UNITED STATES CODE*

To study Congress's ability to fulfill the duties of renewing and updating existing laws and programs, we examine the framework it uses to keep track of changes in policy over time: the *United States Code*. The *Code* is a systematically organized and comprehensive collection of the substantive provisions containing the general and permanent laws of the United States federal government. To make sense of how a new statute affects existing federal policy, Congress compiles each statute's various provisions into a document that is a single corpus of federal law. In effect, the *Code* is a thorough catalog of most federal policy annually updated, effectively recording the year-by-year policy accomplishments of Congress.

The *Code* is a relatively underutilized source for detailed accounting of changes to federal policy by subject matter. It has not heretofore been compiled in a form that could be aggregated and assessed in a linear fashion. There have been a few instances where it has been employed to measure policy change. For example, in the work of Valerie Heitshusen and Garry Young (2006), they employ the *United States Code* and find that divided government does not appear to influence legislative productivity as measured by the changes in positive law titles. However, legislative activity is depressed when parties become more cohesive and following "critical elections." Similarly, the work of Michelle Whyman (2017) uses the *United States Code* to examine the durability of laws over time.

Briefly, the *United States Code* is compiled by the Office of Law Revision Counsel (OLRC) of the House of Representatives through yearly updates that include all newly enacted and repealed statutory language. It divides each law into provisions in accordance with how the legislation is organized within the *United States Statutes at Large* (Tress 2009). The *Code* is broadly organized by subject matter into fifty-four titles. With increasing specificity, the contents of a public law are categorized into a hierarchy. Below a title (the highest level), are subtitles, parts, subparts, divisions, subdivisions, chapters, and subchapters (not all subunits exist under every title). Sections, at the most granular level, are "as nearly as may be, a single proposition of enactment" and serve as the building blocks of the *Code*.[5] Sections are often identical in content to what would be a provision in a statute, and the *Code* is made up of more than fifty thousand sections. Twenty-seven of the titles and their corresponding sections have been enacted into *positive* law, meaning that the full title itself was codified into law, while the remaining titles are *nonpositive*, meaning that the title has been editorially compiled by the OLRC from different laws.

The *Code* provides an opportunity to track the evolution of policy change at the provision level.[6] Given the sorting of laws into subject matter and their division by section, newly created and amended provisions can be tracked over time in a way not previously possible.[7]

Although the modern version of the *United States Code* dates back to 1947, the 1994 edition is the first one to have been made available electronically, as are all subsequent editions (which appear every six years) and their annually updated supplements. Each section contains the name, section number, location, text, enacting and amending legislation, amendment notes, and the year in which the provision was enacted, as well as additional information. After compiling the complete text of every section for every year, corresponding sections were matched from one year to the next, creating a data set of information on all sections within the *Code* for the twenty-two-year period beginning with 1994 and ending with 2016 (the second session of the 103rd Congress through the 114th Congress).

Though made up of fifty thousand sections, coding each for its subject matter (using *Comparative Agendas Project* codes) was a relatively straightforward task using the existing aggregations of sections into chapters. While the substantive titles are somewhat informative for the many hundreds of chapters and thousands of sections located within each, they are also wildly inconsistent and, in some cases, misleading. For example, Title 42—"The Public Health and Welfare"—contains a wide range of policy areas, such as "Leprosy" (ch. 3), "Disaster Relief" (ch. 15), the Civil Rights Commission (ch. 20A), the United States Synthetic Fuels Corporation (ch. 95), and "Aeronautics and Space Activity" (ch. 155).

By tracking changes in these expiring sections over time—paying particular attention to amendments that updated (or, occasionally, eliminated) expiration dates—we are able to observe the creation, expiration, and reauthorization of expiring provisions in law at the most precise level possible. With sections coded by subject matter and committee of jurisdiction (through their enacting or amending public law number), we can analyze the effects of policy area conditions and institutional circumstances on congressional performance regarding its authorizing responsibilities.

IDENTIFYING EXPIRATIONS

The individual title-year files publicly available from the OLRC were used to create the section-level data identifying expirations for our analyses. The OLRC provides a classification table with information on new, repealed, omitted, or renumbered sections for each year. In most cases, a section's heading and section number were used to locate its succeeding section the following year. However, due to occasional section renumbering or changes in legislation, other information was required to match sections over time, such as text of the section or the full *Code* citation and enacting legislation.

After the sections were parsed and matched across time, information on authorizations and their respective expirations was extracted from the sections' text using a variety of word combinations. The vast majority of temporary authorizations that are intended to be reviewed and updated are commonly referred to as *simple authorizations*, or authorizations of appropriations. The initial terminology used to identify these authorizations was based on the Office of the Legislative Counsel's drafting manual, specifically the section "Appropriations Authorization."[8] Additional terminology was developed by locating within the *Code* provisions from the CBO's data on unauthorized appropriations and identifying the authorizing language. These expiring authorizations usually included some combination of a specific dollar or percentage amount or the phrase "such sums" and a defined time period such as "for fiscal years." After these criteria were established, random sections of the *Code* were examined to locate additional authorizations, remove nonauthorization language, and then update the criteria again. This process was repeated numerous times until there were no further updates made to the criteria.

Finally, since our focus is on those programs, agencies, and laws that are set for reconsideration and formal renewal, we eliminated from our count a variety of statutory provisions that have expirations or are renewed but are not formally reauthorized by Congress on a periodic basis. First, because a large number of mandatory government programs renew automatically through their appropriations, we identified these through a variety of sources and disregarded the relevant *Code* sections.[9] As best we could, we also eliminated from the data set sections of the *Code* that have expirations but were never intended to be renewed—commonly referred to as "sunset" provisions.[10] Finally, we removed sections that contain the expiration of reports, boards and commissions, demonstration, and pilot programs.

Renewals across Issue Areas

Our first look at reauthorizations compares the degree to which particular issue areas are governed by legislative expirations (table 12.1). To study this, we examined expiring provisions or sections of the *United States Code* aggregated to the issue area level. Like the concept of policy subsystems (Baumgartner and Jones 1993; Jenkins-Smith, St. Clair, and Woods 1991), we presume that the key factors influencing whether an expiring provision is renewed typically occur at a higher level, such as the statute, the committee, or the policy arena.

Using all years of the *United States Code* available to us (1994–2016), with sections coded into *Comparative Agendas Project* (Comparative Agendas Project, n.d.) major topic area as shown in the first column of table 12.1, we examine the breadth of expirations across issue areas. The second column presents the average number of sections for any given year per issue area in the *Code*.[11] These numbers include all sections that are amended, new, omitted, repealed, and transferred, as well as those that exist without any action taken over the period examined. Issue areas vary quite a

TABLE 12.1. Sections governed by expirations

Policy topic	Total number of sections	Number expiring	Percentage of sections with expirations	Percentage of active sections with expirations
Energy	1,860	161	8.66	5.89
Education	2,296	142	6.18	5.55
Environment	1,672	116	6.94	4.33
Social Welfare	1,173	58	4.94	3.99
Law, Crime, and Family	2,483	107	4.31	3.91
Community Development and Housing	1,123	52	4.63	3.40
Immigration	271	14	5.17	3.40
Agriculture	2,680	95	3.54	3.17
Science, Space, Tech, and Communications	916	37	4.04	2.84
International Affairs	2,511	131	5.22	2.69
Transportation	2,782	91	3.27	2.57
Civil Rights	515	11	2.14	1.66
Public Lands and Water	8,134	155	1.91	1.39
Foreign Trade	1,127	18	1.60	1.21
Labor and Employment	891	14	1.57	1.07
Health	1,884	28	1.49	0.95
Banking and Finance	2,794	50	1.79	0.94
Defense	5,248	40	0.76	0.67
Government Operations	4,025	31	0.77	0.54
Macroeconomics	1,744	4	0.23	0.16

Source: Data compiled from *United States Code*, 1994–2016.

bit in their scope of federal policy, with the largest number of sections falling into the area of public lands and water, followed by defense. Immigration policy constitutes the fewest number of sections in the *Code*. The third column represents the average number of sections that were identified as having an expiration date. Energy issues top the list, with an average of 161 expiring sections, while macroeconomic issues have the fewest average number of expiring sections (4).

We narrow our examination of expirations to those "active" sections of the *Code*—sections that were amended or created at any point during the twenty-one-year series.[12] Out of these sections, the fifth column shows the percentage that have an expiration. Energy provisions top the list, with about 6 percent of active sections being governed by expirations. Not surprisingly, this includes provisions from such pivotal legislation as the Federal Energy Administration Act and Rural Electrification Act. Expiring statutory provisions dealing with education are a close second on this list, containing portions of landmark laws, such as the Higher Education Act. Environment and social welfare legislation round out the top four issue areas governed by expiration. Each of these two contains familiar pieces of legislation with expiring sections, such as the Endangered Species Act and the National School Lunch Act. Macroeconomics placed last on this list.

Renewal Rates over Time

Our first assessment of reauthorization patterns examines the overall renewal rate by topic area, rather than the individual renewals of each expiring section. Figure 12.1 shows the distributions of the expiring sections and their accompanying renewal rate by congressional term for four representative issue areas: (a) agriculture, (b) education, (c) transportation, and (d) health. We separate our examination of expiring *Code* sections into two groups—(1) the total agenda of currently or previously expired provisions, and (2) what items Congress actually addressed on the agenda by reauthorizing or repealing expiring or expired provisions. The total agenda (the left bar for each congressional term) is split into two types of expiring sections. The bottom part of the left bar (very light gray) represents the *Code* sections that expire during that given congressional term (*current agenda*). The top part of the left bar (dark gray) represents those *Code* sections that expired prior to that term but had not been renewed up to that point (*previous agenda*). Similarly, what Congress addressed through reauthorizations (the right bar for each congressional term) is composed of two parts. The bottom part of the right bar (medium gray) represents those *Code* sections that expired that term and were reauthorized (*renewed (current)*). The top part of the right bar (black) represents those *Code* sections that had previously expired but were finally reauthorized that term (*renewed (previous)*).[13]

As the four-part figure 12.1 illustrates, there is variation in both the total agenda and what actually gets renewed for any given issue area across congressional terms. A good example of the pattern in expirations and reauthorization is figure 12.1A, tracking expiring sections in agriculture policy. Three very evident spikes occur in renewals during the 107th, 110th, and 113th

Congresses. The first two account for the expiration and reauthorization of the huge farm bill in the same term that the prior authorization expired. In the last instance, the farm bill expired in 2012 (the 112th Congress) but was not renewed until 2014 (the 113th Congress). Similarly, in figure 12.1C, spikes occur in reauthorization of expiring transportation sections, in the 105th, 108th, 112th, and 114th Congress, all representing the renewal of the important Highway Bill. In many instances the expiring programs were reauthorized a congressional term after the prior legislative provisions expired. The pattern in expiration and renewal of education-related sections shown in figure 12.1B is wrapped up primarily in the troubled history of two major laws: the Elementary and Secondary Education Act and the Higher Education Act. Both have

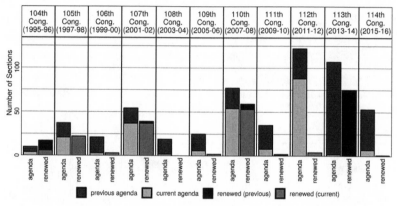

FIGURE 12.1A. Distribution of renewal rate: agriculture policy

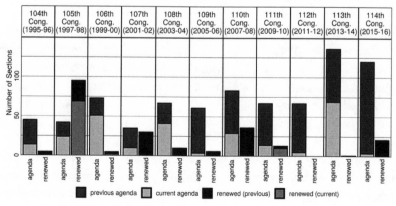

FIGURE 12.1B. Distribution of renewal rate: education policy

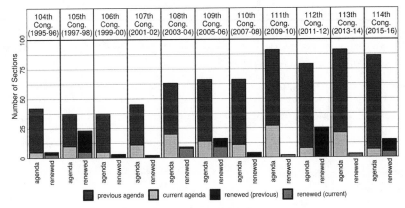

FIGURE 12.1C. Distribution of renewal rate: transportation policy

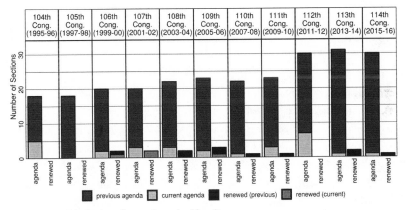

FIGURE 12.1D. Distribution of renewal rate: health policy

had major legislative provisions sit for years at a time un-reauthorized. Alternatively, the failure of lawmakers to pass much legislation can reveal itself in these figures, such as immigration policy. Lawmakers have been unable to keep pace with the growing number of expiring and expired provisions in immigration law over time.

Determinants of Reauthorization Rate

Finally, to explore further the patterns of reauthorization rates by issue area and over time, we test statistical models where the rate of renewal is the predicted outcome.

The dependent variable is the count of renewed sections in a given Congress (C) and topic area (P).[14] It is defined as

(1) Total Renewals$_{C,P}$ = | renewed$_{C,P}$ |.

Likewise, the amount of previously and currently expired provisions is

(2) Total Expirations$_{C,P}$ = | expired$_{C,P}$ |.

Finally, Congress C's renewal rate for topic area P, defined as the percentage of work completed out of all work to be done, is identified as

$$(3)\ \text{Renewal Rate}_{C,P} = \frac{\text{Total Renewals}_{C,P}}{\text{Total Expirations}_{C,P} + \text{Total Renewals}_{C,P}}$$

We test a number of factors that are commonly believed to have an impact on congressional lawmaking output and overall legislative performance. The first is that lawmakers, as representatives, respond to the policy priorities of constituents. We examine this responsiveness in two ways: the priority issue areas of the general public (*Public Salience*), and those policy areas that political elites are highlighting (*Elite Salience*). We employ a relatively common gauge of public salience of particular issue areas—Gallup's Most Important Problem (MIP) questions coded by *Comparative Agendas* major topic areas. Since the data are annual, we averaged the two years of each congressional term together and created a measure that reflects the percentage of people by issue area who perceived issues in each topic area to be the most important problem facing the country. To measure *Elite Salience*, we use Sarah Binder's *New York Times* newspaper editorials coded by PAP major topic area (Binder 2003, 2014).[15] Unsigned editorials from the *New York Times* serve as a proxy for the changing levels of attention being paid to salient issues by political elites (Binder 2003). The measure aggregates the count of mentions for any particular issue found in the editorials across major topic area (within each congressional term).

Additionally, we explore representation further in a different specification, by accounting for the overall disposition or "mood" of the public toward lawmaking activism within each realm of policy (*Public Mood*). Public mood within specific policy areas utilizes the Stimson (2015) mood measure and adapts the global public mood measure to specific CAP major topic areas. Each topic mood measure has various questions that cover the subtopics nested within the major topic areas. Again, we average together the issue area mood score for each of the two years in a congressional term. Higher values of policy mood indicate that the public prefers a more activist government in certain issue areas.

We also test two specific conditions in Congress: First, we examine the degree to which an issue area itself is a divisive one on Capitol Hill, particularly between the two parties (*Issue Divisiveness*). To measure *Issue Divisiveness*, we aggregate party unity roll call votes by *Comparative Agendas* major topic area. Previous literature uses party unity scores as a proxy for issue divisiveness, demonstrating that some issues produce more conflict than other issues do (Rohde 1991; Crespin, Rohde, and Vander Wielen 2013; Gelman, Wilkenfeld, and Adler 2015). We operationalize this measure as the percentage of votes in each major topic area (by congressional term) that consist of a majority of Democrats opposed to a majority of Republicans. Second, we test the degree to which the partisan configuration of the various chambers and the presidency—specifically unified versus divided government—facilitates or inhibits reauthorizations (*Unified Government*). The variable for *Unified Government* is a dichotomous variable that takes a value of one when the president's political party is the same as both the House and the Senate and zero otherwise.

Finally, we inquire whether the size of the workload within an issue area affects renewals of expiring statutory provisions (*Agenda*). To take account of the immediate agenda before Congress within each issue area, we measure the number of sections from the *United States Code* that expire in the issue area during that current congressional term. This measure captures the fluctuating size of Congress's workload that needs to be addressed imminently.

Analysis

The data structure is time series cross-sectional, with congressional terms as the time component and *Comparative Agendas* major topic areas as the panel component. We include a lagged dependent variable to model the temporal effects, as well as fixed effects and robust clustered standard errors to account for panel heteroskedasticity and autocorrelation. After the inclusion of the independent variables, the number of observations for the analysis is 180, with twenty distinct panels (or major topic areas). The analysis spans the 104th through 114th Congresses (1994–2016).

RESULTS

In this section we present the results from the analysis. The coefficients shown in table 12.2 illustrate the renewal rate of expiring legislation on average by issue area across congressional terms. A positive coefficient indicates an increase in the renewal rate of expirations in sections. Alternatively, a negatively signed coefficient indicates a decrease in the renewal rate of expirations in sections.

The results provide evidence that external factors are not particularly important in reauthorization rates. Public or elite salience regarding an issue is not meaningful in effecting the renewal rate of expiring provisions. The same is true of public mood—it is not important in altering reauthorization activity.

We see much clearer evidence of Congress's dysfunction when examining indicators of its internal dynamics. First, Congress does not seem to be able to react to the agenda it sets for itself. As the size of its issue area agenda grows, its reauthorizing capacity seems to decrease. The more expiring provisions there are on Congress's to-do list, the lower the renewal rate of reauthorizations within that issue area. This finding demonstrates that Congress simply cannot react in time to surges in expirations, even though it knows in advance that they are coming. Moreover, we also see, unsurprisingly, that more-divisive

TABLE 12.2. Predictors of renewal rate

Independent variable	Dependent variable: Renewal rate
Public Salience	0.315***
	(0.099)
Elite Salience	−0.000
	(0.000)
Public Mood	0.0001**
	(0.000)
Divisiveness	−0.116*
	(0.065)
Unified Government	−0.016
	(0.021)
Agenda	−0.002**
	(0.000)
Constant	0.327***
	(0.056)
Observations	180
Groups	20
R^2	within = 0.1957, between = 0.0225
F statistic	2.87** (df = 7; 19)

Note: OLS with fixed effects; robust standard errors in parentheses.
$*p < 0.1; **p < 0.05; ***p < 0.01.$

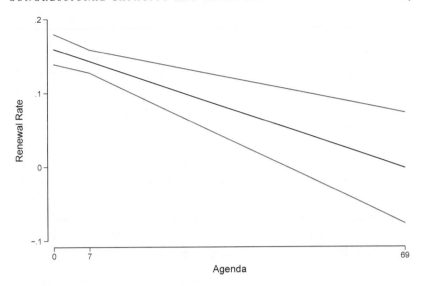

FIGURE 12.2A. Substantive results: agenda

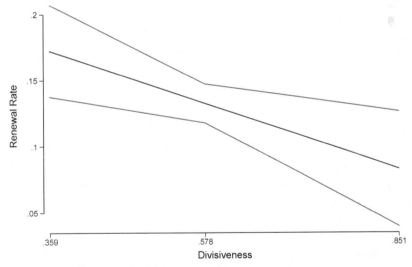

FIGURE 12.2B. Substantive results: divisiveness

issues have a significantly lower renewal rate for expiring legislation. This finding strongly comports with received wisdom that Congress often struggles to
reauthorize programs and agencies in controversial or divisive policy arenas.

Figure 12.2 examines the substantive relationships between the size of the
congressional agenda or the divisiveness of issues and its impact on the renewal

rate of expiring legislation. For figure 12.2A, there is a substantial decrease in the renewal rate for legislation as the congressional agenda grows. As the agenda moves from its smallest size (left) to its largest (right), there is an approximately 16 percent drop in the renewal rate of expiring legislation. We see in figure 12.2B that moving from the least divisive (left) to the most divisive (right) issues results in an 8 percent decrease in renewals of expiring legislation.

Discussion

In this chapter, we have proposed and tested a method of understanding Congress's capacity to govern by examining the rate at which lawmakers update expiring provisions enacted into law. Revisiting and renewing expiring laws is an enormous part of what Congress must do from year to year. As a result, studying this phenomenon serves as a fertile proving ground for our many notions of congressional performance. The *United States Code* provides an ideal opportunity to track the creation, updating, and elimination of these limited-term statutory authorizations. Here, we have presented one account of authorizations and their renewal—tracking them by their policy arena and gauging their rate of reauthorization, whether on time or expired. In doing so, we tested a few of the more prominent notions of what affects congressional accomplishment— unified versus divided government, issue divisiveness, elite and voter salience, public mood, and the size of the congressional agenda within the policy area.

The findings suggest that examining expiring provisions in legislation is an important and often understudied way of thinking about Congress's capacity and ability to govern. By examining the trends in the renewal rate of expiring legislation by policy area over time, we find that when the issues on the legislative agenda become more divisive, members of Congress are less willing to renew expired provisions. Preliminary evidence also suggests that an increase in the size of the legislative agenda decreases Congress's willingness to renew expiring provisions of law. Finally, other factors, such as elite or voter salience, and unified versus divided government, show little evidence of impacting the renewal rate of expiring legislation.

These results confirm that Congress is increasingly having a difficult time completing items on its legislative agenda. More important, by looking at the renewal rate of reauthorizations, we have moved closer to answering a key question raised by this research: Is Congress engaging in ways to do its most basic constitutional job—creating legislation for the well-being of the public—despite conditions and pressures that may make this hard to do? Using reauthorizations as a measure of congressional performance indicates that Congress is frequently not living up to its basic governing obligations.

How Experienced Legislative Staff Contribute to Effective Lawmaking

JESSE M. CROSSON, GEOFFREY M. LORENZ, CRAIG VOLDEN, AND ALAN E. WISEMAN

Legislative staff are integral to the functioning of the United States Congress. In each legislator's district, congressional staff fulfill important representational roles for their member of Congress, as they answer service requests from constituents, alert the legislator to key local events and needs, and maintain contact with influential local interests.[1] In Washington, DC, congressional staffers serve as a legislator's engines of policy production, as they draft bills, seek out cosponsors, meet with lobbyists, and network with other key staffers on the legislator's behalf. Indeed, for those who have worked in or around the US Congress, the importance of staffers to the functioning of the institution is nearly universally appreciated, with some staffers even earning titles such as a member's "secret weapon" (BeShears 2015). Consequently, allocation of scarce resources to various types of staff represents a vital strategic decision that each member of Congress must face. Moreover, whenever Congress as an institution considers fortifying its own position relative to the executive branch and modernizing its activities, the issue of the support and retention of staff rightly receives considerable attention.

While scholars have focused on the relationship between legislative staff and the incumbency advantage (e.g., Johannes and McAdams 1981; Cain, Ferejohn, and Fiorina 1987) or the value of experience to staff's future compensation as lobbyists (e.g., LaPira and Thomas 2017), less research has explored how legislators' cultivation of their policy staff affects their ability to produce and advance legislation. One recent notable contribution, however, is that of Jacob Montgomery and Brendan Nyhan (2017), who find that members of the US House of Representatives who exchange legislative staff across Congresses display similarities in their patterns of legislative effectiveness, which the authors attribute to their common staff members. Additionally, Joshua McCrain

(2018) finds a positive correlation between the aggregate staff experience in a congressional office and a representative's legislative effectiveness.

In this chapter, we build on these early findings to explore the extent to which staff contribute to a representative's ability to effectively legislate. In drawing on congressional data about representatives' staff allocations in the 103rd through the 113th Congresses (1993–2014), consistent with McCrain (2018), we find a positive relationship between staffers' total legislative experience and a representative's ability to advance legislation. However, unlike McCrain, we find this benefit to be highly conditional on a representative's circumstances. Specifically, committee chairs in the House receive a substantial legislative boost when working with experienced staff, whereas nonchairs typically do not obtain similar benefits. Second, new representatives benefit significantly from hiring experienced legislative staff when they first arrive. Finally, we show that a greater length of prior service by a representative's most experienced legislative staffer increases the effectiveness of chairs and nonchairs alike.

These results suggest that specific, targeted attempts to enhance congressional lawmaking capacity are likely to be more fruitful than broad-brush reforms. We find no evidence, for example, of greater lawmaking effectiveness overall among representatives with large staffs or with greater spending on legislative staff. Rather, providing experienced staff to new lawmakers who are just learning the ropes and to committee chairs, who have substantial capacity for lawmaking, seems to yield the greatest return on investment. Additionally, targeted efforts to retain the most experienced staffer in each office seem likely to be more beneficial than trying to cultivate experience across the board in this high-turnover environment.

Measuring Lawmaking Effectiveness and Staff Experience

To explore the relationship between experienced legislative staff and lawmaker effectiveness, we employ the Legislative Effectiveness Score (LES). As developed and defined by Craig Volden and Alan Wiseman, the LES measures the "proven ability to advance a member's agenda items through the legislative process and into law" (Volden and Wiseman 2014, 18). Legislative Effectiveness Scores combine fifteen bill-level indicators for every member of the US House of Representatives, based on the bills they sponsor, how far those bills move through the lawmaking process, and how important their proposals are (ranging from commemorative to substantive and significant). Scores are constructed in each Congress and normalized to take an average value of one within each two-year Congress, which facilitates easy comparison across legislators.[2]

From a normative perspective, it is not crucial for all members of Congress to excel at the lawmaking part of their jobs. That said, an ability to formulate proposals that are perceived to be sufficiently beneficial so as to overcome the significant lawmaking hurdles built into the American constitutional system is an important skill that serves as a prerequisite to Congress addressing the country's most pressing public policy challenges.

Experienced legislative staff promise to help with such efforts, as well as to support lawmakers' many other goals, activities, legislative styles, and reelection strategies (e.g., Fenno 1973, 1978; Grimmer 2013; Bernhard and Sulkin 2018). Given our focus on effective lawmaking, we are interested in measuring the experience cultivated among each member's personal legislative staff.[3] To do so, we rely upon a comprehensive new data set (Crosson, Furnas, and LaPira 2018) of all personal staff who served in the US House of Representatives from 1994 to 2013. Using publicly available *Statements of Disbursement for the U.S. House of Representatives*, quarterly publications of Leadership Directories' *Congressional Yellow Books* (Leadership Directories 1994–2008), and staffer data provided by the company LegiStorm, the data set provides a wealth of information regarding who has served as a staffer in Congress, when he or she served, and how he or she was compensated. Perhaps most important, the data set classifies each staffer into one of five staffer "types," based on his or her responsibilities within the congressional office. More specifically, staffers are classified as legislative staff, political staff, communications staff, office management staff, or constituency service staff.[4]

We trace the employment history of the group of "legislative staffers" to determine their earliest appearances in the data set, generating a count of years served in Congress. We then add these counts together within each representative's office for each Congress to generate our *Total Legislative Staff Experience* variable.[5] The variable therefore represents the total number of years served in Congress among all legislative staffers in a representative's office. This measure is similar to the work experience variable that is employed by McCrain (2018), but our metric captures the experience of legislative staff specifically, and not all work experience among a staff, some of which is potentially irrelevant.[6]

In addition to examining overall legislative staff work experience, we also generate a *Most Experienced Legislative Staffer* variable. Specifically, we measure how long each representative's most experienced legislative staffer has served in Congress, either in the current representative's office or with others in the institution. Because values of this variable are particularly susceptible to measurement error due to left-censoring (i.e., we cannot measure how long staffers served on Capitol Hill before they entered our data set in 1994), we confine our analyses of this variable to the period after the 106th Congress (i.e., post-2000), at which point the mean and variance of our *Most Experienced Legislative Staffer* variable become fairly stable.

In the analysis that follows, we explore the relationships between the cultivation and retention of experienced legislative staff and a representative's legislative effectiveness, as measured by a representative's LES. We also explore how staff investments interact with a representative's institutional positions and personal experience (or lack thereof) to influence legislative effectiveness.

Do Experienced Legislative Staff Promote Effective Lawmaking?

It is commonly believed that skilled staff are crucial for a lawmaker's success. By engaging with stakeholders, negotiating legislative details, and navigating the practices and procedures of the House more effectively, experienced staff may provide their bosses with a crucial edge in their lawmaking efforts. If so, we might expect that as the total number of years of work experience of a representative's legislative staff increases, so too does the representative's legislative effectiveness.

To examine this relationship, we estimate a series of linear regression models in which a representative's LES in each Congress is the dependent variable, and the independent variable of interest is the total years of experience possessed by that representative's legislative staff. Our models also include a wide range of conventional control variables (consistent with Volden and Wiseman 2014, 2018), and we employ legislator fixed effects to account for idiosyncratic factors that are associated with individual legislators, which might influence their effectiveness. For example, some legislators might be more interested in lawmaking and hence cultivate and retain more-experienced legislative staff than do those who focus on other activities. Given these fixed effects, the source of variance informing our results presented in this chapter comes from the frequent hiring, retention, lateral movement, and turnover of staff that are so common in Congress today. Table 13.1 presents summary statistics for data that we use in our analysis to engage with these questions.

Based on our analysis of all House members from the 105th through 113th Congresses (1997–2013), we find that, on average, House members with more-experienced legislative staff appear to be somewhat more effective lawmakers, although not at conventional levels of statistical significance ($p = .11$), as shown in table 13.2.[7] The small size (coefficient of 0.00539) and lack of significance suggests that the average member is unlikely to notice any benefit from cultivating and retaining an experienced legislative staff.

TABLE 13.1. Summary statistics for legislative effectiveness scores and staff experience in US House of Representatives

Variable name	Description	Mean	SD
LES[a]	Member's Legislative Effectiveness Score	1.003	1.532
Total Legislative Staff Experience[b]	Total years of congressional service by member's legislative staff	12.180	8.111
Most Experienced Legislative Staffer[b]	Total years of congressional service by member's most experienced legislative staffer	4.775	2.910
Total Legislative Staff Spending[b]	Average annual spending on legislative staffers employed by member ($100,000 increments)	2.899	1.835
Total Legislative Staff Size[b]	Average number of legislative staffers employed by member	5.675	1.856
Majority Party[a]	Equals 1 if member is in majority party	0.542	0.498
Seniority[a]	Number of terms served by member in Congress	5.367	4.202
Majority Leader[a]	Equals 1 if member is in majority-party leadership	0.023	0.149
Minority Leader[a]	Equals 1 if member is in minority-party leadership	0.023	0.150
Committee Chair[a]	Equals 1 if member is a committee chair	0.048	0.214
Subcommittee Chair[a]	Equals 1 if member is a subcommittee chair	0.211	0.408
Power Committee[a]	Equals 1 if member serves on Rules, Appropriations, or Ways and Means	0.258	0.438
Distance from Median[a]	| Member i's DW-NOMINATE score – Median member's DW-NOMINATE score |	0.444	0.275
Size of Congressional Delegation[a]	Number of districts in state's congressional delegation	19.01	15.10
Vote Share[a]	Percentage of vote received in previous election	66.69	12.97

Note: SD = standard deviation

[a]Data from Volden and Wiseman 2014 and the Center for Effective Lawmaking (www.thelawmakers.org).

[b]Data from Crosson, Furnas, and LaPira 2018.

Of course, representatives vary widely in their experiences and institutional positions. Some House members, for example, hold committee chairs, which allow them to wield a disproportionate level of influence over the lawmaking process. Indeed, our analysis in table 13.2 shows that members attaining committee chairs approximately quadruple their lawmaking effectiveness, all else equal. Do experienced staff complement such members' institutional advantages? On the other hand, new members of the House often find that they must learn deeply about a set of issues, personalities, folkways, and procedures, such that they may lag behind their longer-tenured peers in terms of legislative effectiveness. Do experienced legislative staff supplement the efforts of these novice legislators? And for the many members of the House who are neither new nor institutionally empowered, is there any benefit from cultivating experienced legislative staff?

TABLE 13.2. Experienced legislative staff do not improve average lawmaking effectiveness

	Model 2.1
Sample:	Full
Dependent variable:	LES
Total Legislative Staff Experience	0.00539
	(0.00335)
Majority Party	0.424**
	(0.144)
Seniority	0.0109
	(0.0124)
Majority Leader	0.479**
	(0.170)
Minority Leader	−0.0446
	(0.164)
Committee Chair	3.292***
	(0.120)
Subcommittee Chair	0.452***
	(0.0716)
Power Committee	−0.262**
	(0.0953)
Distance from Median	−0.215
	(0.273)
Size of Congressional Delegation	−0.0363
	(0.0261)
Vote Share	0.0390*
	(0.0184)
Vote Share Squared	−0.000251*
	(0.000120)
Constant	−0.193
	(0.863)
Legislator fixed effects?	Y
R^2	0.367
AIC	8,681.5
BIC	8,761.2
F	118.6
N	3,391

Note: Standard errors in parentheses. Model 2.1 shows that the total years of legislative staff experience have a statistically insignificant effect on the average House member's Legislative Effectiveness Score when controlling for other factors.

$^*p < 0.05$, $^{**}p < 0.01$, $^{***}p < 0.001$.

Legislative Staff Experience and Committee Chairs

Committee leaders exert substantial control over the legislative agenda. With the ability to grant preliminary consideration to legislation (or not), chairs sit at the first and most dramatic winnowing point in the legislative process (Krutz 2005; Adler and Wilkerson 2012). Chairs also advance their own legislation much more consistently than do rank-and-file members of similar seniority (Volden and Wiseman 2014; Berry and Fowler 2018). And chairs can also draw on a specialized committee staff whose hiring and duties are largely at their discretion (Deering and Smith 1997). Thus, chairs have substantial advantages in advancing their proposals through the lawmaking process. Experienced staff may serve as a force multiplier given these advantages. Their knowledge of policy details and their connections with interest groups and with other lawmakers may allow chairs to take fuller advantage of their powerful positions, in ways that are more limited from rank-and-file members.

Indeed, we find that committee chairs benefit from experienced legislative staff much more than do other legislators (see table 13.3).[8] Among committee chairs, a one-standard-deviation increase in personal legislative staff experience is associated with a full one-point rise in LES.[9] Put another way, gaining about seven years of total legislative staff experience is equivalent to doing the work of an entire additional lawmaker or to shepherding another "substantive and significant" bill into law. In contrast, legislators who are not committee chairs do *not* appear to enjoy increased legislative effectiveness from retaining experienced legislative staff. Indeed, when committee chairs are excluded from the full sample that is analyzed, the meager and suggestive effect of legislative staff experience on a representative's LES collapses further toward zero. On average, lawmakers who do not hold institutionally privileged positions do not benefit from having experienced legislative staff.

Can Legislative Staff Experience Overcome Lawmaker Inexperience?

As the newest members of the House, freshman representatives face some of the toughest obstacles to effective lawmaking. Lacking the legislative expertise, political networks, and knowledge of congressional folkways possessed by their longer-tenured peers, freshmen may choose to supplement their inexperience by hiring more-experienced legislative staff. However, relatively few choose (or are able) to do so. In fact, the average level of aggregate legislative staff experience for freshmen (6.4 years) is less than half that of non-freshmen (13.3 years). Do freshmen who invest in experienced legislative staff benefit from doing so?

TABLE 13.3. Benefits of experienced staff accrue to committee chairs

	Model 3.1	Model 3.2
Sample:	Full	Nonchairs only
Dependent variable:	LES	LES
Total Legislative Staff Experience	−0.000597	0.00257
	(0.00335)	(0.00248)
Committee Chair	1.155***	
	(0.250)	
Total Legislative Staff Experience × Committee Chair	0.134***	
	(0.0138)	
Other controls?	Y	Y
Legislator fixed effects?	Y	Y
R^2	0.391	0.225
AIC	8,555.7	6,087.6
BIC	8,641.5	6,160.6
F	120.9	60.66
N	3,391	3,230

Note: Standard errors in parentheses. Model 3.1 shows that legislative staff experience has a positive and statistically significant effect on the Legislative Effectiveness Score (LES) of committee chairs, based on the interaction term. The main effects in models 3.1 and 3.2 show no significant impact of legislative staff experience on the LES of nonchairs.

$*p < 0.05$, $**p < 0.01$, $***p < 0.001$.

    To engage this question, we replicate our analyses on subsamples of legislators at varying levels of seniority, and we find (in results reported in tables 13.4 and 13.5) a strong positive association between legislative staff experience and legislative effectiveness for freshman and sophomore representatives.[10] However, that association becomes much weaker for representatives beyond their first two terms in Congress. For a freshman, a five-year increase in total legislative staff experience is associated with a 10.7 percent increase in that representative's LES.[11] This trend is illustrated in the leftmost panel of figure 13.1, with a large positive slope in the association between legislative staff experience and a representative's predicted LES. That score increases by more than 50 percent for new lawmakers who hire staff with twenty years of legislative staff experience, compared with those representatives who instead hire their campaign workers to serve as their legislative staff. Moving left to right across figure 13.1, this slope remains sharply positive in the second term before flattening out in the third and fourth terms. This result indicates no additional lawmaking benefits from experienced staff once the representative

TABLE 13.4. Inexperienced House members benefit from experienced staff

	Model 4.1	Model 4.2	Model 4.3	Model 4.4
Sample:	1st term	2nd term	3rd term	4th term
Dependent variable:	LES	LES	LES	LES
Total Legislative Staff Experience	0.0131* (0.00656)	0.0160* (0.00664)	0.00700 (0.00547)	−0.00532 (0.00587)
Other controls?	Y	Y	Y	Y
R^2	0.166	0.191	0.275	0.237
AIC	1,027.6	987.6	871.4	788.6
BIC	1,066.0	1,024.6	907.5	823.4
F	12.97	13.02	18.87	13.32
N	529	449	407	352

Note: Standard errors in parentheses. Models 4.1 and 4.2 show a positive and statistically significant effect of experienced legislative staff on subsets of House members in their freshman and sophomore terms, as reflected in their Legislative Effectiveness Score (LES). Models 4.3 and 4.4 show that this effect diminishes and becomes statistically insignificant beyond their second term in office.

$*p < 0.05, **p < 0.01, ***p < 0.001.$

TABLE 13.5. Benefit of legislative staff experience declines beyond freshman term

	Model 5.1
Sample:	Nonchairs, first four terms
Dependent variable:	LES
Total Legislative Staff Experience	0.0255*** (0.00763)
Seniority	0.102** (0.0329)
Total Legislative Staff Experience × Seniority	−0.00704** (0.00255)
Other controls?	Y
R^2	0.212
AIC	3,660.6
BIC	3,731.5
F	23.27
N	1,737

Note: Standard errors, clustered by legislator, in parentheses. Model 5.1 shows a positive and statistically significant effect of legislative staff experience on new House members' Legislative Effectiveness Score (LES) that declines as their seniority increases.

$*p < 0.05, **p < 0.01, ***p < 0.001.$

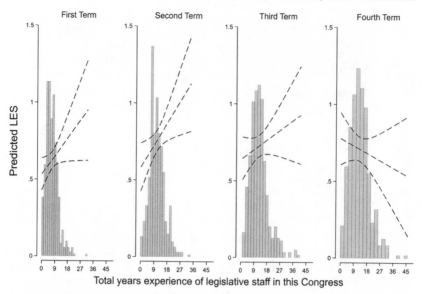

FIGURE 13.1. Congressional staff experience and legislative effectiveness, by term in office
Note: The positive and statistically significant slopes in the first two panels of the figure show the extent
to which increased staff experience boosts the predicted Legislative Effectiveness Score (LES) of freshman
and sophomore representatives. As legislator experience increases further, the effect of staff experience
becomes insignificant. All results shown here are based on models in table 13.4. Graphs include 95 percent
confidence intervals and show the distributions of staff experience across lawmakers' first terms in office.

has accrued a moderate level of experience, apart from the findings for committee chairs noted in earlier discussion.[12]

These results suggest that legislative staff experience can supplement legislator inexperience. However, as representatives gain more experience, which
likely corresponds with their developing more expansive political networks,
they gain less of a benefit from their legislative staff's experience. This finding
may reflect the existence of a kind of ceiling on the degree to which experienced staff can make up for legislator inexperience.

The Benefits of Retaining the Most Experienced Legislative Staffers

Perhaps the largest human resources challenge facing Congress is the retention of high-quality staff. Even a handful of years on the Hill affords a staffer
enough experience and personal connections to render him or her a potentially valuable asset to lobbying firms and interest groups. Moreover, current
staffers often cite poor working conditions and lower salaries as the main

reasons that many of their colleagues have departed the Hill to work as lobbyists (Drutman et al. 2017a).

In the previous section, we demonstrated that, apart from committee chairs and new members, lawmakers do not benefit on the whole from a more experienced staff. However, there may be a significant qualitative difference between the large numbers of young staffers with just a few months or years of experience and the small number of very experienced legislative hands who are immensely valuable in the lawmaking process. Do these most long-serving legislative staffers contribute to their bosses' lawmaking success in a meaningful way? To answer this question, we replicate our staff experience analysis, but we replace the *Total Legislative Staff Experience* variable with a new variable, measuring the tenure of each representative's *Most Experienced Legislative Staffer*.

Whereas total legislative staff experience is associated with only a weak increase in overall legislative effectiveness, those representatives whose most senior legislative staffer is among the most experienced in the House appear to benefit greatly from having that person on their payroll (see table 13.6). Specifically, an increase in five years of experience in a representative's most experienced legislative staffer is associated with a 17 percent increase in that representative's LES.[13] Similar to our earlier findings on the relationship between aggregate staff experience and legislative effectiveness, we see that committee chairs benefit more than nonchairs do from retaining a highly experienced legislative staffer. For committee chairs, a three-year increase in the experience of their most experienced legislative staffer is associated with a full-point increase in their LES, which roughly corresponds with their advancing and having passed into law one more "substantive and significant" bill.

While chairs benefit tremendously from retaining these highly experienced legislative staffers, substantial benefits also accrue to rank-and-file members for retention of high-end staff, as shown in model 6.3 of table 13.6. For a nonchair, a five-year increase in the experience of the representative's most experienced legislative staffer is associated with nearly a 14 percent increase in that legislator's LES.[14] Hence, even those representatives who do not hold committee chairs can benefit (in their legislative effectiveness) by having a highly experienced staffer in their offices.

This targeted investment in highly talented and highly experienced legislative staff differs dramatically from more blunt instruments, such as attempts to increase the overall experience levels of the thousands of congressional staff members, to expand those ranks substantially, or to pay them all significantly more. Earlier, we showed that an overall increase in staff experience

TABLE 13.6. Influence of most experienced staffer, staff spending, and staff size

	Model 6.1	Model 6.2	Model 6.3	Model 6.4	Model 6.5
Sample:	Full	Full	Nonchairs	Full	Full
Dependent variable:	LES	LES	LES	LES	LES
Most Experienced Legislative Staffer	0.0336**	0.0159	0.0223*		
	(0.0124)	(0.0124)	(0.00887)		
Committee Chair	3.696***	1.370***		3.270***	3.285***
	(0.142)	(0.322)		(0.104)	(0.104)
Most Experienced Legislative Staffer × Committee Chair		0.324***			
		(0.0405)			
Legislative Staff Spending				0.0108	
				(0.0104)	
Legislative Staff Size					−0.00168
					(0.0117)
Other controls?	Y	Y	Y	Y	Y
Legislator fixed effects?	Y	Y	Y	Y	Y
R^2	0.422	0.443	0.264	0.397	0.399
AIC	6,472.0	6,379.9	4,322.9	11,158.1	11,183.5
BIC	6,548.0	6,461.7	4,392.5	11,240.7	11,266.1
F	103.9	104.4	51.98	172.1	173.6
N	2,549	2,549	2,426	4,233	4,240

Note: Standard errors in parentheses. Models 6.1 to 6.3 show that a longer-serving most experienced staff member contributes significantly to the lawmaking effectiveness of committee chairs and non–committee chairs alike, as reflected in their Legislator Effectiveness Score (LES). Models 6.4 and 6.5 show no effect from greater spending or larger legislative staffs on lawmaking effectiveness for the average representative, respectively.

*$p < 0.05$, **$p < 0.01$, ***$p < 0.001$.

has little impact on lawmaking effectiveness for the average representative, with benefits accruing only to new representatives and to committee chairs. In models 6.4 and 6.5 of table 13.6, we show that such null results extend also to staff spending levels and staff size. Specifically, we replicate our analysis on a representative's LES from the full sample, but we replace *Total Legislative Staff Experience* with *Total Legislative Staff Spending* (which measures each representative's total annual expenditures on that representative's legislative staff) and *Total Legislative Staff Size* (which measures each representative's average legislative staff size in each Congress). Neither of these variables is associated with higher levels of LES. Hence, those representatives who are unable to hire or retain highly experienced staffers cannot compensate for this shortcoming by simply spending more money or hiring more (relatively inexperienced) legislative staffers.

Congressional Capacity and Legislative Effectiveness:
Implications and Conclusions

Congressional staff contribute in many ways to the job performance of House members, from aiding constituents, to communications, to lawmaking. We focus on the extent to which representatives' personal legislative staff, in particular, help enhance their effectiveness at moving their proposals through the legislative process and into law. We find that the experience of legislative staff does seem to improve legislative effectiveness, particularly when an experienced staff includes especially long-serving individual staffers. However, such experience does not benefit all members of Congress equally.

Figure 13.2 concisely summarizes our results with respect to how legislative staff experience influences representatives' Legislative Effectiveness Scores—a comprehensive measure of their abilities and activities in advancing new policies. The figure illustrates the percentage increase in lawmaking effectiveness upon attaining five more years of experience among a legislator's staff.[15] The first result displayed shows the lack of any statistically significant effect of more staff experience on all lawmakers in the House grouped together. This finding, combined with the evidence reported in this chapter of no systematic lawmaking benefit from greater staff spending overall or from larger staffs, argues against a wholesale investment in congressional lawmaking capacity via legislative staffs.

However, the overall effect illustrated at the top of figure 13.2 masks the specific conditions under which staff experience is particularly beneficial. The next finding in the figure shows that staff experience is especially helpful for committee chairs, with five more years of staff expertise associated with about a 14 percent increase in the LES for chairs. The size of this effect is remarkable if we consider the baseline effectiveness of chairs. On average, the committee chairs in our data set receive an LES of 4.66, accomplishing five times as much in the lawmaking space as the average score across all lawmakers. The 14 percent increase in effectiveness for these lawmakers, then, is approximately another 0.7 LES points. Volden and Wiseman (2014, 27) point out that one point is equivalent to introducing and shepherding into law one additional major (what they call "substantive and significant") piece of legislation. This is, indeed, quite a large return on the expertise of legislative staff. Committee chairs also have access to committee staff, whose expertise undoubtedly enhances the lawmaking activities of all committee members, but especially the chair.

Excluding chairs, these aggregate results show few additional benefits from legislative experience. One clear exception to this pattern, however, is for

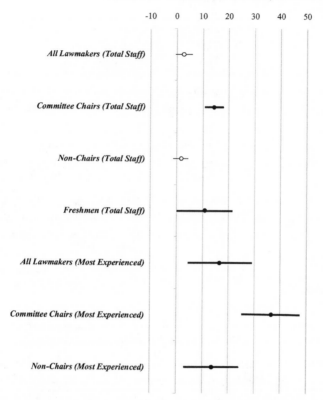

FIGURE 13.2. Percentage increase in legislative effectiveness with five years more staff experience
Note: Illustration of enhanced Legislative Effectiveness Score (LES) for various groups of lawmakers upon receiving five more years of legislative staff experience. Calculations are percentage increase in LES relative to the average LES for the group, based on models shown in tables 13.2–13.6. Point estimates and 95 percent confidence intervals shown, with bold indicating statistically significant differences from zero. Results labeled "(Total Staff)" are based on the *Total Legislative Staff Experience* variable from models 2.1, 3.1, 3.2, and 4.1, respectively. Results labeled "(Most Experienced)" are based on the *Most Experienced Legislative Staffer* variable from models 6.1, 6.2, and 6.3, respectively.

freshman and sophomore lawmakers. New members of the House of Representatives face a steep learning curve in putting their first bill in the hopper and steering it through committee, to passage in the House, and into law. Having an experienced hand among their legislative staff is invaluable to these novice lawmakers. Quantifying such experience, we find an approximately 11 percent increase in legislative effectiveness among first-term lawmakers who have staff with five more years of experience than among those assisting an average freshman.

The bottom three results in the figure show perhaps an even more attractive way to boost lawmaking effectiveness through a reliance on legislative staff. These results focus on the most experienced legislative staffer in each representative's office. In the most recent Congress in our data set (2013–14), the longest-serving legislative staff member in an average office had seven years of prior experience. A little under a quarter of representatives employed a staff member with at least a decade of legislative experience. Those who did tended to enjoy a significant boost in their lawmaking effectiveness.

As shown in figure 13.2, among all lawmakers, an increase of five years in the experience of a representative's most senior legislative staffer is associated with a 17 percent rise in that representative's LES. That boost is about 14 percent for nonchairs (i.e., rank-and-file lawmakers, whether in the majority or minority party), and a whopping 36 percent for committee chairs. Indeed, even a three-year increase in a chair's most senior legislative staffer's experience is equivalent to the capacity increase of guiding one additional substantive and significant piece of legislation through the policymaking process and into law.

One may respond to this finding (and the rest of those throughout this chapter) by arguing that members of Congress who have an interest in lawmaking will hire more legislative staff and be sure to retain them for a longer period of time, relative to members without such policymaking interests. However, the fixed-effects analysis used throughout this chapter fully counters that argument: all of the findings presented here for the House of Representatives are on the basis of variance within each representative's staff over time, rather than across representatives. Moreover, the analyses control for the representative's own seniority, which has an independent and positive influence on effective lawmaking. Controlling for all these considerations, legislative staff experience is strongly linked to effective lawmaking, especially for new legislators and for committee chairs.

In sum, these findings offer four main takeaways for the cultivation of expert legislative staff in Congress. First, experienced legislative staff are among the important factors that help explain which lawmakers succeed in advancing their legislative agendas and which fail.

Second, the largest bang for the buck comes from experienced staff aiding committee chairs. Due to their powerful institutional positions, chairs sponsor much more legislation that moves through the legislative process and into law than do others. Whether those bills are being put forth on behalf of the chair, the committee, or the majority party, having expert staff to aid in the lawmaking process yields significant returns. Experienced personal legislative staff seem to add to the beneficial design of staff tasked to specific committees.

Third, at the other end of the spectrum, early-career lawmakers benefit substantially from hiring experienced legislative staff, as opposed to hanging on to campaign staff who lack experience within Congress.

Fourth and finally, relevant to ongoing reform efforts, such as the ongoing work of the Select Committee on the Modernization of Congress as this book goes to print, proposals to increase congressional capacity for lawmaking need not be massive overhauls. Our analysis shows that a targeted effort to retain the most long-serving legislative staff would likely be much more effective than would broad (and highly costly) attempts to increase staff size or staff compensation across the board.

Along these lines, targeted subsidies or bonuses available on a competitive basis for long-serving staff, additional clear career progression opportunities for staff within Congress itself, and support aimed at cultivating policy expertise among staff are all proposals worthy of serious consideration.

Capacity in a Centralized Congress

JAMES M. CURRY AND FRANCES E. LEE

The erosion of decentralized and committee-led legislative processes is often blamed for declines in the lawmaking capacity of the United States Congress. Under this diagnosis, many scholars and observers argue that Congress should restore "regular order" processes. We argue that while decentralized approaches to lawmaking worked in earlier, less partisan eras to resolve legislative conflict, those approaches are not well suited to contemporary conditions. Drawing on data on congressional lawmaking and interviews with longtime members of Congress and congressional staff, we argue that Congress often employs centralized processes in an effort to *maintain lawmaking capacity* in a contentious political environment prone to gridlock. To make this case, we show that laws passed using centralized procedures are not more partisan than those enacted via "regular order." Rather than tools to jam through partisan laws, centralized processes are often employed because they confer advantages—including efficiency, secrecy, and flexibility—that enable congressional negotiators to pass legislation under challenging circumstances.

Congress's capacity as a legislative institution provokes anxiety on the part of many scholars and congressional observers (see chapters 1 and 2 in this volume). Concerns include declining staff expertise (chapters 3 and 6 in this volume; Clarke 2017; Drutman and Teles 2015b; Goldschmidt 2017; LaPira and Thomas 2017), an erosion of "deliberative" "regular order" processes (Bendix 2016), decreased committee activity (chapters 9 and 11 in this volume; Lewallen, Theriault, and Jones 2016), and the empowerment of partisan leaders (Drutman 2017). These changes—coupled with rising party conflict (Barber and McCarty 2016; Lee 2016), evidence of mounting congressional gridlock (Binder 2014), and concerns over "dysfunction" (Mann and Ornstein 2006, 2012)—have spurred calls for reform.

Reform proposals largely aim to restore a previous state of affairs on Capitol Hill, including (1) expanding staff resources on committees and at service agencies (i.e., the Congressional Research Service), and (2) reestablishing "regular order" lawmaking processes by decentralizing policymaking power back to committees, downgrading the role of party leaders, and reducing the frequency of backroom dealmaking. While we do not dispute that Congress could do well with more staff and that Congress worked well in the past using a committee-based division of labor, we are doubtful of the feasibility of returning to earlier ways of doing business. What facilitated congressional capacity in an earlier era may not work well under contemporary conditions.

We argue that the centralization of power and process in party leaders has occurred as an adaptation to an exceptionally challenging political environment and that centralization has for the most part helped Congress maintain lawmaking capacity in the face of today's challenges. Today's political environment—characterized by pervasive partisan conflict inside and outside of Washington, narrow congressional majorities, frequent divided government, and tight budgets—differs markedly from that of the mid-twentieth century, when party conflict was muted, congressional majorities were large and long-lasting, and federal dollars were easier to come by. A changing environment necessitated changes in how Congress does business. That members of Congress will purposively reform congressional processes is well established among political scientists (chapter 16 in this volume; Binder 1996; Schickler 2001), including in response to environmental pressures (Cooper and Brady 1981; Polsby 1968; Smith 1989).

Drawing on analyses of congressional processes and partisanship, as well as interviews with longtime congressional lawmakers and Hill staff, we argue that centralization is better understood as an adaptation to today's difficult environment than as a driver of it. First, we show there is no evidence that centralized processes are used disproportionately to jam through partisan enactments. Laws developed via centralized processes are frequently no more partisan than those crafted via "regular order." Second, centralization affords several key advantages that maintain Congress's capacity to make laws under challenging circumstances.

The Case for Decentralization

A strong and effective Congress is thought to feature decentralized power, including an internal division of labor organized around committees, and an automatic and universalistic "regular order" decision-making process.[1]

Among scholars, the works of Nelson Polsby (1968, 1975) and Richard Fenno (1962, 1966) underlie this perspective. Polsby (1975) defined *transformative legislatures*—those with significant lawmaking capacity—as well institutionalized (Polsby 1968), with a complex division of labor among their members and committees. Formalized deliberative processes—what we might think of today as "regular order"—help Congress shape legislative proposals and mute external influences, including from parties. Fenno (1962, 310; see also 1966) argues that committee processes facilitate what he termed "integration"— minimizing "conflict among [the institution's] roles and its subgroups" and building institutional consensus for action.

Other scholars since have likewise emphasized the deliberative value of decentralized, committee-led processes for congressional policymaking capacity. Committee-led policy development helps Congress uncover knowledge and consider policy alternatives (Adler and Wilkerson 2012; Bendix 2016; Bessette 1994; T. Hall 2004; Maass 1983; Quirk 2005). A division of labor spurs committee members to specialize their legislative portfolios, develop expertise, and produce well-crafted legislation that can win broad support (Gilligan and Krehbiel 1990; Krehbiel 1991). "Traditional" processes promote legislative entrepreneurship by "provid[ing] incentives for members to undertake legislative activity" (Wawro 2000, 158), thereby making Congress more "dynamic" (Baumgartner and Jones 2015; Drutman 2016). Decentralized processes are even expected to make Congress more "capable of attracting and retaining talented and ambitious politicians" (Shepsle 1988, 463).

Since the 1970s, Congress has increasingly abandoned formal, decentralized, committee-led policymaking processes in favor of centralized, leadership-led, and informal approaches (Sinclair 2016; Tiefer 2016). Today, legislation frequently bypasses committee stages of the legislative process (Bendix 2016), and fewer bills are subject to committee hearings and testimony (Lewallen, Theriault, and Jones 2016). More bills are considered under restrictive procedures limiting debate and amendment on the floor of each chamber (Bach and Smith 1988; Finocchiaro and Rohde 2008; Reynolds 2017b; Wallner 2013). Congressional resources and procedural powers have been centralized in party leaders (Aldrich and Rohde 2000b; Curry 2015; Rohde 1991), who have assumed more responsibility for legislative dealmaking (Hanson 2014b; Sinclair 2016) and moved legislative processes behind the scenes (Curry 2015).

These changes have raised concerns about "a virtual collapse of genuine deliberations" (Mann and Ornstein 2006, 106), ceding of power to the executive branch (chapter 4 in this volume; Crespin and Madonna 2016), and an erosion of bipartisan lawmaking (Aldrich and Rohde 2000a). There appears little doubt among scholars and observers that these changes have harmed Congress's capacity to build bipartisan coalitions in order to make law and have been drivers of partisan conflict.

Are Centralized Processes Tools for Partisan Lawmaking?

If changes to congressional organization and procedure are important drivers of partisan conflict, and if centralized processes harm bipartisan coalition building in Congress, one would, at minimum, expect to find a correlation between the use of centralized procedures and the levels of partisanship on lawmaking efforts. After all, Congress does not uniformly turn to centralized, leadership-driven processes for bill development and consideration. The legislative process is variable, with centralized processes employed on some bills and committee-led, "regular order" processes employed on others.

Procedural variation from law to law can give us some leverage on the question of how centralization relates to institutional capacity. It should be noted at the outset, however, that analyzing the relationship between process and partisanship is fraught with thorny problems of causal inference. Even if unorthodox legislative processes correlate with partisan lawmaking, correlation alone would not establish causation. Indeed, leaders might just turn to centralized processes when faced with partisan conflict, but these processes themselves might not have any independent effect. If centralized processes *do* correlate with more-partisan outcomes, scholars need to delve more deeply to gauge whether partisanship drives process, process drives partisanship, or the two mutually interact. However, at this juncture, the literature has not even established that there is a correlation between unorthodox processes and partisan lawmaking.

We analyzed the legislative histories of 621 important laws enacted by Congress from 1987 through 2016 and constructed two process indexes for each law. First, an *unorthodox development index* assesses the degree to which traditional committee processes (holding committee hearings and issuing committee reports) were employed in the House of Representatives and the Senate during the development of each law. The index ranges from zero (hearings held and a committee report filed in both chambers—a fully "decentralized" and committee-led approach) to one (all committee steps skipped—a fully "centralized" approach). Second, an *unorthodox management index* assesses the processes used to consider those laws on the floors of the House and Senate. This index ranges from 0 percent unorthodox (open floor proceedings allowed—a fully "decentralized" approach) to 100 percent unorthodox (proceedings are tightly restricted and managed by party leaders—a

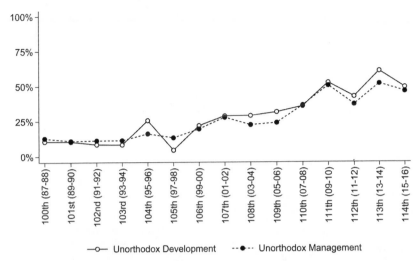

FIGURE 14.1. Bill development and bill management indexes, 1987–2016

fully "centralized" approach). Further details on these data and measures are found in the online appendix.[2]

Figure 14.1 presents the average of our indexes over time, from 1987 through 2016 (100th–114th Congresses). As shown, Congress has increasingly used unorthodox and centralized tactics to develop and manage legislation. However, much legislation is still considered using traditional, decentralized approaches. Were every law considered using a fully centralized process during a Congress, the index values would be equal to one. However, even in the 114th Congress, the development and management indexes equaled 49 and 46 percent, respectively.

The two-part figure 14.2 shows the predicted statistical relationship between these indexes and levels of partisanship on the final passage lawmaking votes in the House (figure 14.2A) and the Senate (figure 14.2B).[3] Strikingly, there is no meaningful relationship between *unorthodox development* and partisanship. At least since 1987, the use of the traditional committee processes versus centralized processes to develop laws has had no relationship to the levels of partisanship found on those lawmaking efforts. Laws developed via "regular order" and in committee are simply not more likely to be bipartisan than laws negotiated in leadership offices.

In contrast, there is something of a relationship between *unorthodox management* and partisanship. Laws managed on the floors of the House and Senate using more centralized processes are, on average, slightly more partisan. Even so, many laws considered under such processes were bipartisan as well. For instance, as illustrated by the graph on the left side of figure 14.2A, while

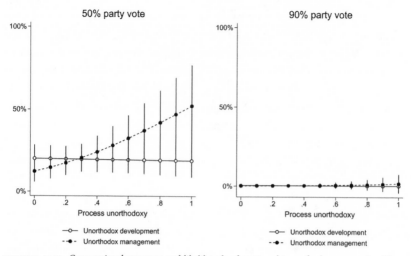

FIGURE 14.2A. Congressional processes and likelihoods of partisanship on final passage votes: House of Representatives.

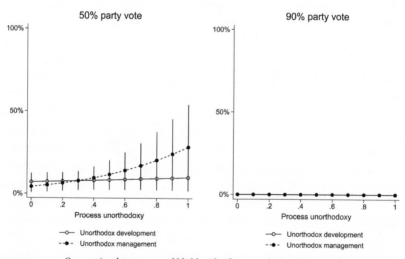

FIGURE 14.2B. Congressional processes and likelihoods of partisanship on final passage votes: Senate

the likelihood of a 50 percent party vote (at least 50 percent of one party voting opposed to at least 50 percent of the other) on a House final passage vote increases to 52 percent as the *management* index increases from 0 percent to 100 percent unorthodox, this also means almost half of laws managed under fully centralized processes still garnered broad bipartisan support.

Moreover, the likelihood of a 90 percent party vote (at least 90 percent of each party opposed to the other) on final passage in the House, depicted by the graph on the right side of figure 14.2A, is unlikely under any form of processes. In the Senate, even more bipartisanship exists among laws managed using centralized processes. Just 28 percent of laws passed under the most unorthodox management processes are expected to be 50 percent party votes, as illustrated by the graph on the left side of figure 14.2B, and none are expected to pass on a 90 percent party vote, as shown by the straight line at the 0 percent level in the graph on the right side of figure 14.2B.

These analyses suggest that the relationship between centralized legislative processes and partisanship in Congress is simply not as clear as some expect. At the most observable level—partisan conflict on lawmaking votes— the laws developed via party leadership-led and centralized legislative processes look quite similar to those developed via decentralized approaches. Congress builds broad, bipartisan coalitions to pass laws whether or not committees take the lead in developing legislation, and it frequently does so even when party leaders tightly manage the consideration of bills. In fact, party leaders often take the lead to negotiate bipartisan agreements.

Centralization as Adaptation

The contemporary Congress struggles with gridlock, stalemate, and partisan conflict, but the centralization of power and processes is not necessarily to blame for these problems. In fact, centralization may be a feature of the contemporary Congress that guards it from greater impotency as a lawmaking institution. Paraphrasing Barney Frank (D-MA), who served in the House from 1981 to 2013, things might have "sucked worse" without centralization.[4]

For insight into the reasons legislators turn to centralized legislative processes, we draw on twenty-four interviews we conducted with longtime Hill staffers and members of Congress,[5] as well as the forty-seven senior staff interviews conducted for the broader Congressional Capacity Survey (CCS) project (see chapter 5 in this volume).[6] Generally speaking, interview subjects describe centralized processes as adaptive, meaning that they help Congress find policymaking success in a challenging political environment. According to these interviews, centralized, leadership-led processes *work* to achieve a legislative outcome and sometimes are the only processes that will work. Interviewees consistently point to three reasons: (1) centralized processes are more efficient, and they provide (2) greater secrecy and (3) greater flexibility as compared with "regular order" processes.

EFFICIENCY

Interview subjects frequently describe "regular order" processes as inefficient and prone to deadlock under current conditions. Open, decentralized legislative processes often fall victim to partisan politics. Committee markups and open floor proceedings create numerous opportunities for obstructionists to throw a wrench in the proceedings, resulting in unnecessary headaches and delays. According to one staffer, if "you try to work through an open markup or something, the bill gets weighed down in partisan attacks and nothing happens. There's no product."[7] Another senior staff member explained the problem with open processes: "Everybody then decides to use that opportunity to fight every culture war. . . . The entire appropriations process was shut down two years ago, because of a Confederate flag amendment. . . . Last year, they almost shut down the entire appropriation process on the energy department over LGBT hiring practices of federal contractors. . . . Leadership, I think prudently, tries its best to shield those bills from coming to the floor."[8]

Rather than facilitating deliberation over the pending legislation, open markups and amending processes often just get exploited for partisan and ideological position taking. Members use amending opportunities to raise hot-button issues that can, in turn, endanger legislative efforts and bring "down the whole bill over a little political amendment."[9] Faced with these prospects, leaders instead often opt for tightly managed floor processes. As one staffer remarked, "When the other side isn't really trying to legislate through the process but is just putting up these partisan 'gotcha' amendments, you have to move on. You have to close it down."[10]

Interview subjects describe a party leadership that usually prefers a more decentralized process, provided it can succeed in obtaining a legislative result. Generally speaking, party leaders like to see committee chairs take the lead developing legislation. Said one staffer, "[Speaker Ryan] wants the committees to be doing the work and he wants to have chairmen take ownership and responsibility for things. He wants freshman members to be involved. I think that in some cases leadership's hand gets forced" because the process deadlocks.[11] In fact, the difficulties of moving legislation in the party-polarized Congress are so severe that committee chairs often look to party leaders for help. "As far as giving power back to the committees, I think that's a work in progress because there's often times where the committee chairmen don't want to take the responsibility," another staffer commented.[12] When problematic issues arise, chairs often look to House leaders for a resolution rather than try to work problems out on their own, even when leaders are telling them, "Hold on, this is your world."[13] In other cases, as one of our interviewees observed, committee leaders themselves often "punt to the leadership to make key decisions."[14] As one committee staffer put it, "When we just couldn't resolve things with the Democrats we'd have to kick it to the leadership to work it out."[15]

Crises almost always require leadership to take charge. Centralization can happen in a number of ways and for various reasons, but one staffer claimed that "the number one reason it happens is timing."[16] When facing a deadline, the leadership is expected to step up, as two of our interviews revealed:

> It's a crisis model. Leadership steps in when backs are against the wall and something has to be done.[17]

> There is legislation done at the end when crisis looms. The House has passed something extreme. The Senate is logjammed or passed something really different. In these processes, the leadership takes the lead.[18]

Centralized processes are not anyone's ideal. Our interviewees lamented, "It's a shame you can't do things differently. . . . The time cycles we are working in speeds things up so you can't."[19]

Even absent a deadline or crisis, there are some legislative issues that at the outset do not seem amenable to "regular order" processes. In such cases, the leadership may preempt the committees.[20] As one staffer described it, leadership will sometimes work around a committee, putting "together groups of senators to work on a bill. They essentially create ad hoc committees because they don't believe the regular committees can do it anymore. And they're right. They can't."[21]

Whether the leadership takes the initiative to centralize or intervenes at the behest of a committee, concerns about the capacity of decentralized processes to achieve a legislative result are often a critical consideration in centralized lawmaking. Our interviews did not turn up examples of members or staffers who saw leadership as usurping power that appropriately resided elsewhere. Instead, centralization is portrayed as a second-best alternative that is more adaptive to contemporary challenges. The implication is that decentralized processes may have worked well in the past but are poorly suited for the intensely partisan atmosphere of today.

SECRECY

Another advantage of centralized processes is that they are less transparent and more secretive. Not only can open and traditional processes—such as freewheeling committee meetings and open floor debate and amendment—make it easier for opponents to obstruct and try to kill legislation, they can make it harder for a bill's proponents to engage in meaningful deliberations.

As one staffer put it, "Transparency is a good thing in principle but it makes Congress more dysfunctional."[22]

Centralized processes allow lawmakers to move sensitive negotiations out of the view of lobbyists. Traditional processes allow well-financed interest groups to monitor the proceedings and use their clout to influence reelection-minded legislators. As the politics and public affairs scholar R. Douglas Arnold (1990, 275) put it, "Open meetings filled with lobbyists, and recorded votes, on scores of particularistic amendments, serve to increase the powers of special interests, not to diminish them." According to one of our interviewees, such efforts can bog down a legislative effort: "I know transparency is good, but it's very difficult with an issue like health care. There are so many interested parties on the outside. There is so much money involved; 15,000 lobbyists who want to be involved."[23] Another reflected, "Once K Street knows you have a train leaving the station, they have umpteen things they want to get on it."[24] To cut a deal and get it through Congress, one staffer asserted, "you need the backroom discussions outside the view of the lobbyists, even if that's sacrilege to the open-government people."[25]

Centralized processes enable Congress to mute pressures emerging from both parties' activist bases. A zealous party base can color the reactions of rank-and-file lawmakers to specific proposals, even those that compose a small part of a larger deal, as there are "hyperpartisans on both sides that will turn everything into a wedge," one staffer said.[26] While at one time "regular order" processes allowed Congress to resolve conflicts, today, an interviewee noted, "regular order is too messy and it's covered instantly in the media and it can create problems."[27]

If information gets out about negotiations, one committee staffer said, "you run the risk of some members getting all riled up and the snowball starting rolling down the mountain and picking up steam. You just have to do it in a kind of secretive way."[28] Today, another staffer added, "the politics of each party's base has made [regular order] impossible."[29] Negotiating in the open in this environment makes reaching any deal difficult. Lawmakers cannot make offers that sound like capitulation—or even just engage in a give-and-take. If congressional leaders often appear overly secretive in their approach, it's because they feel they have to be, one of our interviewees explained: "There's so much divisiveness inside in the parties' caucuses that you render yourself pretty vulnerable if you're putting out your gives that publicly. I'll admit there is an increasing trend toward opaqueness and nondisclosure to the broader group, but part of it is this sense that the broader group will not handle the information responsibly."[30]

Secrecy and behind-the-scenes processes allow negotiators to explore opportunities and manage sensitive issues: "Secrecy was critical. . . . We needed to have the trust on both sides to be able to float things and have a real discussion."[31] Negotiators need to be sure anyone they speak with will promise secrecy: "When we talked to outside experts, we pledged them to secrecy."[32] Another put it, "Everyone we talked with we pledged them not to tell anyone."[33] Sometimes the mere fact that negotiations were ongoing had to be kept secret to keep a deal alive. As one staffer confided, "On occasions when [Speaker John] Boehner and [House Minority Leader Nancy] Pelosi would need to meet during the negotiation, we made up reasons to cover for them" because otherwise, "my side would be so mad if they knew the two leaders were working together!"[34]

Keeping things quiet is essential, another staffer pointed out, as "a leak can short-circuit the negotiations."[35] However, when negotiators all emerge unified around a single legislative package, it becomes hard to oppose, other staffers observed. Instead, "everyone could say, 'Well, this or that part of it stinks, but at least it solves the overall problem.'"[36] Simply, in today's Congress, "it's in the backroom where the deal is made."[37]

FLEXIBILITY

Finally, the flexibility of centralized processes is another advantage, one that enables leaders to negotiate broader legislative packages that might not otherwise be possible. Several of our interviewees noted that some deals, and some decisions, are just too big for committees to take the lead. As one senior staffer explained, "I think there are some issues that, yeah, are leadership driven, but it's because maybe they're the only ones that can bring all of the parties together and have a sit down and be like 'Okay what's the common ground that we can move forward on.'"[38] A committee chair or individual member can't "bring the Freedom Caucus, the RSC [Republican Study Committee, the party's conservative caucus], and the Blue Dog Democrats in here and come to some agreement," the senior staffer added.[39]

Committees are hemmed in by their jurisdictional boundaries. When looking for trades or logrolling across issues to build legislative support, committees can only work within the policies and programs under their jurisdictions. "The committee process chops issues up, making larger negotiations impossible," one staffer explained.[40] Another noted that "committee chairs are always a bit too in the weeds to some extent."[41] Discussing a health care effort, one staffer reflected that committee members and staff "were so focused on the little pieces. They had something like seventeen meetings on just the nursing home provisions. They'd debate two lines, a comma, etc. It's just too much detail!"[42] In contrast, party leaders are often better suited to strike "grand bargains" because they can explore policy solutions across policies, programs, and jurisdictions, and put together legislative packages that can draw broad support for passage. As one staffer explained, "Leadership can open up the universe of policy to find the solution, taking into account the whole picture—the politics, the budget. These decisions get chased up to the leaders. . . . There's no other decision maker who can get a deal to do things like keep the government open."[43] As another staffer said simply, in the contemporary Congress, "all the big deals tend to be leadership driven."[44]

This flexibility is particularly valuable in helping figure out how to pay for legislation in an era of tight budgets and large deficits. "Deficits and debt . . . [that's what] animates most of the battles up here," remarked one senior staffer.[45] Identifying the necessary offsets requires creativity and the ability to look across jurisdictional boundaries, another staffer noted: "For anything you do, you have to find the money. Handling things at the leadership level allows you to go outside the relevant committee to find the money. Whatever problem you're trying to resolve—FAA [Federal Aviation Administration], highway trust fund, whatever. The committee may not have jurisdiction over the policies that would allow you to get the pay-fors. So, the leadership needs to step in. The leadership is the place you go when you need to find [budgetary] offsets."[46] Simply, one staffer said, "leadership has more flexibility to find the pay-fors" because it can work "outside the jurisdiction of any particular committee."[47] Finding offsets to pay for legislation entails political pain—cuts will have to be imposed or revenues raised: "When pain is involved, the leadership has to handle it."[48]

Even when "pay-fors" are not the issue, leadership can be more adept at cutting deals across jurisdictional boundaries created by the committee system. As one staffer put it, "If you've got two bills in two different committees, it's up to you in the leadership to figure out what you're going to do. That's the leadership's job."[49] A senior committee staffer noted that only "the leadership could clear the path for our committee. Leadership can work with the other committees and get them to back down, figure out what deals can be made. They can break—or maybe interpret—the rules in a certain way to help out."[50]

Centralized legislative processes are hardly ideal from the perspective of legislative deliberation, but participants describe them as enabling Congress to negotiate agreements, manage difficult trade-offs, and pass legislation. In other words, centralization helps Congress preserve lawmaking capacity in a political environment hostile to legislative action.

Conclusions

In recent years, alarms have been raised regarding Congress's capacity to play its role in the American political system. Once revered as the archetypical "transformative legislature" (Polsby 1975), Congress today finds far less esteem. That Congress is frequently unable to break through gridlock is undeniably troubling. However, we find no evidence in our data or interviews that the centralization of power and process in the House and Senate is an important *cause* of Congress's struggles to legislate. In fact, as we detail here, centralization is often a *solution* that helps break legislative impasses, build bipartisan coalitions, and pass laws. Centralization may be helping Congress maintain some of its lawmaking capacity, rather than weaken it further.

Comparing bills developed and considered by the House and Senate under different processes offers no evidence that centralization of power systematically undermines bipartisanship in lawmaking. Congress frequently passes laws on a bipartisan basis whether it employs centralized or decentralized legislative processes. Our interviews underscore that when processes are centralized, moved behind the scenes, or taken over by party leaders, it is only occasionally done with the motivation of ramming through a partisan law. Rather, it is usually done because centralized processes are seen as the most feasible path to a successful legislative outcome. On some occasions leadership may well block viable bipartisan compromise from coming to the floor, but interview subjects simply did not point to this as a primary consideration driving the centralization of power in party leadership. Instead, they consistently portrayed centralized processes as a means of achieving legislative results that would otherwise founder in deadlock.

Those advocating for reforms to the internal processes of Congress should consider these findings. Calling for a return to "regular order" may sound right and just, and it may remind us of days past when less partisan acrimony filled the halls of Congress and the institution successfully managed a larger legislative workload (Binder 2014). No doubt, there are trade-offs in choosing between centralized and decentralized approaches to congressional organization and process (see chapter 2 in this volume). One obvious downside of a legislative process centered in party leadership is that it cannot take full advantage of the committee system's division of labor. Committee-led processes allow Congress to move forward on multiple issues simultaneously. Leadership, by comparison, has much more limited policy bandwidth than a functioning committee system. "We joke around here where it's really hard for leadership to do more than one big thing at a time," said one senior staffer.[51] But that does not mean that a return to decentralized processes would allow

Congress to be more productive *under current conditions*. It might instead result in even more legislative futility.

Long before the parties in Congress polarized, Fenno (1962, 317) observed that committee-led processes would not work well under highly partisan conditions: "nothing would be more disruptive to the Committee's work than bitter and extended partisan controversy." "Regular order" legislative processes prevailed in a completely different congressional environment characterized by much lower levels of two-party conflict (Barber and McCarty 2016), dormant party caucuses (Forgette 2004), a large, seemingly permanent Democratic majority party (Lee 2016, 74–81), and a more favorable budgetary situation. Indeed, "regular order" processes with autonomous committees may well have emerged precisely because the majority party was so internally divided over issues of race and region that it was incapable of asserting centralized authority (Bensel 2011).

Indeed, the broader political environment is likely more to blame for the contentious state of affairs on Capitol Hill than any congressional organization or process. Our interviewees repeatedly referred to the parties' zealous activist bases as the underlying drivers of leaders' decisions to move processes behind the scenes and depart from "regular order." Those who wish to see Congress return to a previous way of doing business might focus their reform efforts on forces outside the institution. Our research suggests that actors inside the institution are typically adapting to those outside forces as best they can.

We would be wise to remember that Congress has been an institution in near-constant evolution throughout its history and that no process regime has been permanent in either chamber (see chapters 2 and 16 in this volume). Processes that prevailed under markedly different conditions may not be well adapted to contemporary challenges. Attempts to return to "regular order" could even yield additional dysfunction. If centralized processes often help contemporary congressional leaders break legislative impasses, reviving "regular order" may undermine congressional capacity rather than bolster it. Congress has time and again altered its institutional rules and processes to meet its collective and individual needs (Schickler 2001). The changes of the current era should be considered in a similar light.

Congressional Capacity and Bipartisanship in Congress

LAUREL HARBRIDGE-YONG

Policy gridlock and an inability to negotiate successful agreements in the United States Congress stand at the forefront of concerns by scholars (Mansbridge and Martin 2016) and the American public.[1] In fact, in June 2016, just 13 percent of Americans rated the job Congress was doing as excellent or good, and almost half of those who said it was doing a poor job cited congressional inaction as the top reason for their view (Newport and Saad 2016). One of the chief explanations for gridlock is the rise of polarization and the resulting lack of bipartisanship (Binder 2014). Though gridlock may be a common complaint in recent years, it may be just one component of broader concerns about *congressional capacity*—the resources that Congress collectively has available to perform its role in resolving public problems through its primary tools of legislating, budgeting, holding hearings, and conducting oversight.

This chapter explores the interplay between bipartisanship and congressional capacity though a focus on two questions. First, why is bipartisanship important for Congress to solve problems and govern? I provide a range of empirical evidence from my own research and from others suggesting that bipartisanship among members contributes to legislative productivity as well as to members' legislative and electoral success. Second, how are the institutional structures underlying congressional capacity—the distribution of staff across personal, committee, and leadership offices, and whether staffers are focused on policy or public relations—tied to bipartisanship? The results from a collaborative survey of congressional staff (Drutman et al. 2017b) show that these types of institutional arrangements shape the likelihood of bipartisanship among staff. Across both questions, I supplement the empirical evidence with interviews of congressional staffers conducted in 2017 by the Congressional Capacity Working Group (Drutman et al. 2017a). Combined, the results highlight the importance of institutional structures and investment in resources for legislative interactions, bipartisanship, and productivity.

Why Care about Bipartisanship?

Before we can even ask questions about whether Congress enacts laws that are responsive to public preferences or that reflect careful deliberation among competing views, Congress has to act in the first place, moving bills through the legislative process and into law. Throughout much of the literature on gridlock, problem solving, and legislative effectiveness, bipartisanship is seen as an important feature of successful policymaking—in part because the legislative process often requires cross-party coalitions. Unless institutional conditions are favorable for a single party to advance its agenda alone, bipartisanship is an important component of achieving a record of success.

Empirical evidence from the US House of Representatives shows that bipartisanship is strongly related to legislative success. Given the majority party's agenda-setting power, most bills that the majority party brings to a vote on the House floor pass the chamber. However, a much smaller fraction of these bills go on to become public law, and the success rate varies across Congresses. Figure 15.1 shows how often bills that passed the House go on to become public law. The left panel shows the overall percentage of House bills that passed in the chamber that went on to become public law from the 94th (1975–76) to 112th (2011–12) Congresses. Over this same period, polarization has risen dramatically. The statistical correlation between the percentage of House-passed bills becoming public law and polarization (that is, the difference in party means on DW-NOMINATE) is a significant −0.64 (p = .003). This suggests that as polarization in Congress has risen, the majority party in the House has become less successful at moving bills into law.

However, bipartisan bills fare much differently than their partisan counterparts. The right panel of figure 15.1 illustrates how the content of the legislative agenda is related to legislative success. Both lines show the percentage of House-passed bills that became public law, but, following my earlier work (Harbridge 2015), uses the cosponsorship coalition of the bills to split them between those with bipartisan coalitions (20 percent or more of the cosponsors from the party opposite the party of the bill's sponsor) and those with partisan coalitions (less than 20 percent of the cosponsors from the party opposite the party of the sponsor). The solid line shows that the bipartisan cosponsored bills that the House majority pursued on the floor became public law at surprisingly similar rates across the period. The correlation between the percentage of House-passed *bipartisan* bills becoming public law and

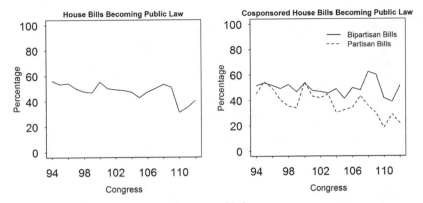

FIGURE 15.1. Bills that passed the House becoming public law
Note: Y-axis is the percentage of H.R. bills that passed the US House of Representatives that were enacted into public law. The left panel includes all House-passed bills. The right panel includes cosponsored House-passed bills and breaks bills into bipartisan and partisan coalitions.

polarization is an insignificant −0.12 ($p = .62$). In contrast, *partisan* cosponsored bills fare increasingly poorly as polarization increases ($r = -0.77$, $p < .001$). The lack of productivity in the last several Congresses (seen in the left panel) is driven by the lack of legislative success on partisan agenda items (seen in the right panel).

The connection between productivity and pursuing bipartisan legislation is reiterated by the negative relationship between House leaders' pursuit of partisan bills on the roll call agenda (that is, partisan agenda setting) and the percentage of House-passed bills that were enacted into law (that is, legislative success).[2] Between the 94th and 112th Congresses, the correlation between partisan agenda setting and legislative success was −0.56 ($p = .01$). These patterns indicate that when House leaders pursue partisan legislation on the agenda, fewer of their bills become law. Put simply, the institutional design of the US federal government, with multiple veto players and need to build broad coalitions, often requires support from legislators of both parties to enact legislation (Krehbiel 1998; Brady and Volden 2006).

While there is an empirical relationship between bipartisanship and legislative success and polls find that the public is frustrated by inaction, it is important to consider why electorally motivated members and their leadership should value legislative success in the first place. One reason is that legislative accomplishments may contribute to the valance component of the party brand (Stokes 1963; Butler and Powell 2014). In some instances, inaction and the resulting policy drift achieve conservative policy aims (Hacker 2005), but in many cases both Republican and Democratic majorities need legislative action

242   LAUREL HARBRIDGE-YONG

to achieve campaign promises, confront problems, and fulfill basic governing requirements. Another reason is the connection between institutional and individual approval; a growing body of work suggests that legislative productivity affects party and institutional approval (Arnold 1990; Adler and Wilkerson 2012) and that institutional approval affects legislators electorally (D. Jones 2010). These findings suggest that members of Congress, and the majority party in particular, should be wary of legislative inaction.[3] Legislators' own statements align with the presumption that productivity is important and seen as a core job of Congress. For instance, legislators are quick to blame other actors for legislative inaction, with members complaining about gridlock in communication with constituents and even using the Twitter hashtag #StuckInTheSenate (Blackburn 2014; House Republicans 2014).

Bipartisanship is important not just for legislative success on the floor agenda but at earlier stages of the legislative process as well. Committees, in particular, are often known for fostering bipartisanship, and both the leadership and staff play important roles building cross-party collaboration. For instance, in the case of energy reform in 2016, the ability of the Senate to maintain bipartisan support was attributed to Senate Energy Committee Chair Lisa Murkowski (R-AK) and ranking member Maria Cantwell (D-WA) working closely together and discarding potential deal-killer proposals (Agri-Pulse 2016). In speaking about the Senate Agriculture Committee, Ross Baker (2015, 29–30) highlights the role of staff. He quotes one Democratic staff member as saying, "I'm really good friends with my Republican counterpart. I go out and have drinks with him. I love that dude. He and I could cut a deal tomorrow that would be a good deal and get a farm bill." Although these examples point to the risks of partisanship that may come with using leadership teams rather than committees to draft major legislative initiatives (see Curry 2015), James Curry and Frances Lee in chapter 14 in this volume point out that even with centralized processes, it is possible to build bipartisan coalitions.

Bipartisanship is not only valuable for Congress as a collective entity or as committees, it is also important for individual members. Bipartisanship can help members be more effective lawmakers (Volden and Wiseman 2016) and more successful electorally, particularly when they represent districts that are not well aligned with their party (Harbridge 2015). Legislative effectiveness connects directly with congressional capacity, while electoral success may help indirectly (especially if it keeps members in office who have built up relationships with members across the aisle).

Finally, bipartisanship also has the potential to bring broader benefits, which are related to legislative success and to whether legislative initiatives garner support by the public. Bringing in viewpoints from both parties early in the legislative process has the potential to expand the number of stake-holders in the policy (Huntsman and Manchin 2014) and can improve the quality of the legislation by bringing in a more diverse set of viewpoints and avoiding groupthink (Sunstein 2006). Moreover, bipartisan support can affect how the public views legislators (Paris 2017) and the perceived legitimacy of laws (Wolak 2017). These findings suggest that bipartisanship can be tied to perceptions of representation and responsiveness.

CHALLENGES TO BIPARTISANSHIP

Yet bipartisanship is not without its opponents, suggesting that even if members can work across the aisle, they may not want to in today's political climate. Bipartisanship may be seen as capitulation or selling out, and some legislators perceive that their primary electorate will punish them for compromising (Anderson, Butler, and Harbridge-Yong 2020). More broadly, efforts to compromise or find common ground may conflict with a party's efforts to emphasize the two parties' differences (Harbridge 2015; Lee 2016). Partisan legislation provides a means of signaling to voters (including primary constituents), interest groups, donors, and others who may want to know how the two parties differ and to see the parties promote core principles. Thus, when party leaders have a choice over which bills to pursue on the floor agenda, bills that achieve partisan priorities and point out the differences between the two parties may be appealing.

A focus on partisan legislation, including highly partisan "messaging" bills, may hamper legislative success (Lee 2009, 2016; Koger and Lebo 2017). One staffer commented that the Veterans Affairs Committee is "a pretty bipartisan committee" but that the Republican leadership forced the chair to push through the most conservative version of a bill on VA accountability (that would strip collective bargaining rights from federal employees) even though they knew the bill would likely die in the Senate (Drutman et al. 2017a, p. 4.10). Not surprisingly, when leaders push extremely partisan legislation, it often ends in legislative inaction. This evidence suggests that sometimes party leaders ignore bipartisan initiatives; yet to the extent legislative success is valued, bipartisanship on some pieces of legislation may still be necessary. And legislative staff may play a key role in developing bipartisan buy-in for legislative initiatives.

Bipartisanship among Congressional Staff

Bipartisanship among congressional staff may be linked to congressional capacity for several reasons. First, bipartisanship among staff may be tied to legislative productivity. Cross-party interactions among staff have the potential to help Congress identify those legislative priorities where bipartisanship may be possible, helping grease the wheels of the legislative process and bringing forward legislation that has the support of wide-ranging constituencies. Since staff are engaged from the early stages of developing bills, efforts to cross the aisle may be consequential for policy content and coalitions of support. Second, bipartisanship among staff may be tied to many of the dimensions that Lee Drutman and Timothy LaPira in chapter 2 in this volume consider for evaluating congressional capacity—representativeness, responsiveness, deliberativeness, and oversight. For instance, given the distribution of public preferences (Fiorina, Abrams, and Pope 2005), collective representation of the public may be higher when Congress develops bipartisan solutions. Moreover, building a bipartisan coalition from early in the legislative process—a step at which staff members are key—may lead Congress to seek out and incorporate a more diverse set of information, producing greater deliberativeness in the process. The incentive for staff to work across the aisle may be highest among committee staff—who are focused on building support for policies in their jurisdiction—and weaker among members' personal staff and leadership staff, however. Yet even staff who serve ideologically extreme members of Congress or the leadership may have incentives to reach across the aisle on some issue areas.

Examples from interviews with staff highlight the role that staffers can play in building coalitions around legislation and improving the chances of moving a bill into law. For instance, one Democratic House staffer told the story of how extended bipartisan conversations among staff helped pave the way for the Toxic Substances Control Act of 2016. The staff had started working on the bill six to seven years earlier when the Democrats were in the majority and then worked with the Republican majority in subsequent years. The staffer recalled, "We had hundreds of hours of meetings amongst staff to go over proposals. . . . We put out discussion drafts. When one side would do something the other wouldn't like we were careful not to blow the whole thing up because we always thought that there was a common ground there. I couldn't have helped [him or her] hammer out that final deal . . . unless we had that process for the five years that I was there" (Drutman et al. 2017a, p. 2.3).

The staffer's efforts at bipartisanship and finding an acceptable compromise extended not just to staff and members of Congress in the opposing party but to other stakeholders as well, such as the American Chemistry Council (Drutman et al. 2017a, p. 2.6). This sentiment was repeated across staffer interviews. For instance, another staffer connected his or her efforts to work with staff in other offices to their ability to draw in cosponsors on their boss's legislation. "I got to know a lot of members personally, and a lot of other chiefs of staff so that's been incredibly valuable to be able to call them and say hey, what do you think about this? Someone that you can get a beer with is somebody that'll say 'okay, if this does no harm my boss will cosponsor it'" (Drutman et al. 2017a, p. 7.6).

To better understand the extent to which staffers work across the aisle and seek input from those in the opposing party, and how this effort might be affected by the institutional organization of Congress and the patterns of staff within that organization, I examine the characteristics of staffers who are more or less likely to engage across the aisle, and to what end. How often do staffers reach out to staff from the other party, and how does this outreach vary across types of offices and roles? How does their engagement with staff from the opposing party differ from their interactions with staff in their own party? The answers to these questions speak to several of the underlying concerns about changes in congressional capacity and the role that structures of staffing have played in reducing capacity as well as bipartisanship.

There are a number of factors that may shape the extent to which staffers work across the aisle. Some of these factors may be rooted in individual differences and demographics. Others may be rooted in the institutional organization of Congress and how the institution allocates its human resources (Galvin 2012). To the extent that a staffer's focus on policy increases the need to work across the aisle while a focus on party competition decreases incentives to work across the aisle, we may expect differences in cross-party interactions by staff in different types of institutional roles. For instance, bipartisan interactions among staff may be higher among committee staff than among leadership or personal staff. Committee staff are often policy focused and may seek to incorporate multiple viewpoints as they build coalitions around legislation. Even within a given type of office, however, there may be variation in cross-party interactions depending on the type of position. To the extent that policy-focused staff are more likely to think about legislating (rather than messaging), cross-party interactions may be more common (and more important for the policy outputs). Public relations (PR)-focused staff, by contrast, may be less likely to work across the aisle. Other features of staffers and their institutional environment may matter as well, including their tenure on Capitol Hill and whether they want to stay as a career staffer or see this role as a short-term stepping-stone to a role outside of Congress. If more-experienced staff are more likely to work across the aisle and cross-party collaboration is valuable for advancing legislation, this may explain part of why legislators with more-experienced staff are more effective at advancing bills through the legislative process (see chapter 13 in this volume).

As part of the Congressional Capacity Staff Survey (Drutman et al. 2017b), we asked several questions related to staffers' interactions with staffers from their own and the other party, including the frequency of those interactions and the goal or focus of those meetings.[4] The results presented in this section are weighted using poststratification survey weights based on chamber, party, and gender.

To examine how often members communicate with staffers from each party, we asked a series of two questions: (1) "When working to advance legislation, how often do you communicate with staffers from your own party?" and (2) "When working to advance legislation, how often do you communicate with staffers from the opposing party?" The response options to both questions corresponded to a five-point scale, ranging from "Never" to "Always." In the analyses that follow, these variables are treated as continuous variables ranging from 0 to 4. Most staffers communicate "often" or "always" with staff in their own party (mean = 3.5), while communication with staff in the opposing party is significantly lower (mean = 2.6, $p < .001$).

The patterns of how staff demographics and institutional characteristics affect communication with staffers in the opposing party are presented in table 15.1. The models are linear regressions estimated via maximum likelihood, though the results are similar if ordered logit models are used. For models 1–3, the dependent variable is how often the staffer communicates with staff in the opposing party; higher values indicate greater frequency of communication. For model 4, the dependent variable is the difference between how often the staffer communicates with staff in his or her own party versus the other party. In this case, higher values indicate that staffers communicate with staff in their own party more frequently than with staff in the opposing party.

I focus on several characteristics of staffers, including their office, role, and demographics, to predict these behaviors. Model 1 includes indicators for whether the staffer is in a party or administrative office or in a personal office (the excluded category is a committee office), whether the staffer's job is public relations focused,[5] the total number of calendar years the staffer was employed in any congressional office as well as tenure squared (which allows the effect of this variable to change over time), whether the party of the employing office is a Republican, the gender of the staffer, whether the staffer serves in the Senate,[6] and the staffer's own ideological extremity.[7] Model 2 adds a control for how often the staffer communicates with staff in his or her own party. Model 3 further adds staffers' future time horizon as a predictor.[8]

The results indicate that bipartisanship differs substantially across types of staff. Relative to the excluded category of committee staff, cross-party communication is significantly less common among staffers in members' personal

TABLE 15.1. Staff communication with staffers in the other party

	Model 1 (Other)	Model 2 (Other)	Model 3 (Other)	Model 4 (Own–Other)
Constant	3.3***	1.0***	1.1**	0.53†
	(−0.25)	(−0.29)	(−0.34)	(−0.3)
Party/Administrative Office	−0.37	−0.14	−0.15	−0.037
	(−0.33)	(−0.28)	(−0.28)	(−0.32)
Personal Office	−0.5***	−0.34**	−0.33**	0.21†
	(−0.12)	(−0.11)	(−0.11)	(−0.11)
Public Relations Focused	−0.97***	−0.81***	−0.81***	0.68**
	(−0.15)	(−0.18)	(−0.17)	(−0.22)
Tenure	0.068†	0.071*	0.079*	−0.079*
	(−0.041)	(−0.035)	(−0.035)	(−0.038)
Tenure Squared	−0.0036	−0.0033†	−0.0036†	0.0033
	(−0.0023)	(−0.0019)	(−0.0019)	(−0.002)
Republican	−0.35**	−0.32**	−0.31**	0.28*
	(−0.13)	(−0.11)	(−0.11)	(−0.11)
Male	−0.27*	−0.21*	−0.18†	0.15
	(−0.1)	(−0.097)	(−0.095)	(−0.1)
Senate	0.24*	0.25*	0.27**	−0.29**
	(−0.12)	(−0.099)	(−0.098)	(−0.1)
Ideological Extremity	−0.62*	−0.57**	−0.55**	0.52*
	(−0.25)	(−0.21)	(−0.21)	(−0.21)
Frequency of Communication with Own Party Staff	—	0.58***	0.57***	—
		(−0.054)	(−0.052)	
Expected time in Congress 1–2 years	—	—	−0.17	0.28
			(−0.21)	(−0.22)
Expected time in Congress 3–5 years	—	—	−0.039	0.11
			(−0.21)	(−0.21)
Expected time in Congress 6–10 years	—	—	−0.013	0.15
			(−0.22)	(−0.22)
Expected time in Congress > 10 years	—	—	−0.51*	0.58*
			(−0.25)	(−0.26)
N	300	300	300	300
R^2	0.17	0.33	0.36	0.15
Adjusted R^2	0.15	0.31	0.33	0.12
Log likelihood	243	197	189	215

Note: Standard errors in parentheses. Linear regression using poststratification survey weights based on chamber, party, and gender. In models 1–3, the dependent variable is the extent of communication with staffers in the opposing party. In model 4, the dependent variable is the difference in communication between staff in their own party and the opposing party.

†$p < 0.1$, *$p < 0.05$, **$p < 0.01$, ***$p < 0.001$.

offices. There are no significant differences between staff in leadership offices versus committee, but the survey includes a relatively small number of leadership staff, which reduces the power to detect an effect. Other features of staffers' institutional environment also matter—staffers in PR-focused roles are significantly less likely to communicate with the other party, while staffers in the Senate are significantly more likely to communicate with staff in the other party. When interviewed, one Republican House staffer noted several differences between House and Senate staffers: "The other side of the capital, the staff say for a lot longer, their portfolios are much more narrow. And they salvage that expertise" (Drutman et al. 2017a, p. 1.16). The significance of these measures of staff organization suggest that the institutional organization of Congress, and not just member interests or ideology, matters and that changes in congressional staffing may be hurting the prospects for bipartisanship.

Individual characteristics of staffers are also important. Staffers with a longer tenure working in Congress are more likely to work across the aisle. This finding suggests that turnover of staff and short stints for staffers, both increasingly common in recent years, may hamper bipartisanship. Party matters as well; Republican staffers are less likely to communicate with staff in the other party. However with a sample from just one point in time, it is unclear whether Republicans are different from Democrats, majority party staffers are different from minority party staffers, or both. Given that the majority party controls access to the agenda, it is likely that minority staffers have greater incentives to reach out to staff in the majority party than vice versa. Male staffers are also less likely to communicate with those in the other party than female staffers are—a pattern that is consistent with scholarship suggesting that women in leadership roles are often more willing to compromise and find consensus (Eagly and Carli 2003; R. Fox and Oxley 2003). Perhaps if there were more women in Congress—as members and staff—there would be more bipartisanship (for the limitations of this argument, see Lawless, Theriault, and Guthrie 2018). Finally, staffers who hold more ideologically extreme views are less likely to communicate with staff in the opposing party, suggesting that the polarization that hurts bipartisanship among legislators (Harbridge 2015) affects staffer interactions as well.

As shown in column 2, staffers who are more likely to communicate with other staff in their *own* party are also more likely to communicate with staff in the opposing party, suggesting that some staffers are more inclined to communicate with other staff than others, regardless of party. However, even controlling for this characteristic, all of the variables that were significant in column 1 remain significant, suggesting that the offices and positions that staffers occupy affect how often they seek out the perspectives of those in the opposing party. In this specification, tenure squared is also marginally significant ($p < .10$) and negative, suggesting that the number of years a staffer has worked in Congress increases bipartisanship up until year 11, followed by a decrease in the effect of tenure on bipartisanship. Similar patterns hold when controlling for staffers' future time horizons as well (column 3). For the most part, time horizons have no impact on cross-party interactions, though planning to stay for more than ten years reduces bipartisanship relative to planning to stay for less than a year.

Column 4 shifts the dependent variable to the difference in communication between staffers in one's own party and the opposing party, where higher values indicate a larger differential in favor of one's *own* party. Relative to committee staffers, personal staff are more likely to spend time with staff from their own party. Similarly, PR-focused staff spend more time consulting staff from their own party, as do Republicans and more ideologically extreme staffers. Both tenure as a staffer in Congress and serving in the Senate, by contrast, are associated with a decreased skew toward working with one's own party—that is, toward greater cross-party interactions.

Regardless of whether staffers are communicating with staff in their own party or the other party, the dominant focus of interstaff communication is policy content. After the question about how often staffers communicate with other staff, we asked, "When working to advance legislation, which of the following do you focus on the most when communicating with [staffers from your own party/staffers from the opposing party]?" Response options were policy content, the likely voting coalition for the bill, and conveying policy positions to groups outside Congress. Patterns were similar for communication with staff in their own and the opposing party. When staffers communicated with staff in their own party, 67 percent focused on policy, 28 percent focused on the voting coalition, and 4.8 percent focused on conveying positions to outside groups. Similarly, when staffers communicated with staff in the opposing party, 64 percent focused on policy, 30 percent focused on the voting coalition, and 5.5 percent focused on conveying positions to outside groups.[9] This finding highlights the centrality of congressional staff in developing the policy content of legislation, and how their efforts to work across the aisle can shape the policies that move forward.

TRENDS IN CONGRESSIONAL STAFFING

While this survey shows a snapshot at one point in time, a brief review of some of the changes in congressional staffing patterns since the late 1970s, in conjunction with the findings presented in this chapter, suggests that Congress is shifting toward an organizational structure that is increasingly less likely to produce staffers who work across the aisle. Since the 1980s, the number of personal staff has remained fairly constant, the number of leadership staff has risen dramatically, and the number of committee staff has declined (Lee 2009, 16). Between 1977 and 2016, House committee staff were cut by 31.4 percent (Petersen, Reynolds, and Wilhelm 2016a). Compared with the 1979–80 congressional session, when there were 2,027 House committee staff in total, there were only 1,164 House committee staff in 2015 (Brookings Institution 2019). Since committee staffers are significantly more likely to work with staff from the opposing party, a decrease in staff among committees likely reduces the extent of cross-party collaborations and the policy-focused interactions that follow. Another parallel trend in staffing also works against bipartisanship. In both leadership and committee offices, the proportion of staff devoted to public relations has increased since the 1980s (Lee 2016, 117). In the analyses presented in this chapter, PR-focused staffers are significantly less likely to work across the aisle. Finally, the pay gap between what staffers make in Congress and what they could make in the private sector may encourage staff to seek better opportunities elsewhere (Schuman 2010). Since this pay gap may reduce staff tenure, and since tenure is related to how often staff consult with the opposing party, this shift is likely to reduce the likelihood of bipartisanship. Staffers recognize the importance of long tenures for many aspects of the policymaking process. As one staffer remarked, "If you've been here for 10 years, chances are you're not approaching a whole lot of new things when you're dealing with them. So there's a lot of experience, institutional experience that it comes with that. And that's where I would suggest where members are harmed the most by not [keeping] a routine staff" (Drutman et al. 2017a, p. 1.17).

In sum, the underlying institutional arrangements of Congress affect the likelihood that staffers reach across the aisle, which is central to sharing insights about policy and building coalitions around legislation. Yet changes in the organization of Congress over time suggest that the institution is shifting away from one that incentivizes bipartisanship among staff and efforts to understand where the other side stands on policy.

Conclusion

The motivation for this chapter was to better understand the connections between congressional capacity and bipartisanship, both in terms of why bipartisanship matters for legislative success and other aspects of capacity and in terms of how the organization of Congress shapes bipartisanship among staff. Bipartisanship can help Congress produce a record of success, can help build coalitions at the committee stage, and can help members of Congress both legislatively and electorally. Bipartisan legislation is more likely to be enacted into law than more heavily partisan bills are, and the extent to which the House majority pursues bipartisan versus partisan legislation on its agenda is significantly related to the success of its agenda, particularly in recent years. The centrality of bipartisan legislation to the output of Congress is also seen in the fairly consistent degree of minority party support for major public laws since the 1970s (Curry and Lee 2019b).

This chapter suggests that recent trends in congressional staffing patterns have hurt the prospects for bipartisanship. While party leaders have built up their own capacity by investing in leadership staff (Glassman 2012), this increase has come at the expense of investing in committee staff and building the human and informational assets that might foster greater bipartisanship. Combined with decreases in congressional support staff through the Congressional Research Service, the Government Accountability Office, and the Congressional Budget Office (Kramer 2017; see also chapter 8 in this volume for more details), decreases in committee staff and a shift from policy-focused to public-relations-focused staff leave Congress with relatively few internal resources for understanding policy, and few reasons to work with the opposing party. Legislators turn to lobbyists instead (LaPira and Thomas 2014), which may further drive wedges between the two parties. If the institutional structure of staffing and the strategy of leaders on the floor is focused on messaging via partisan bills rather than legislating, there is little reason to expect much bipartisanship. Yet, this structure and strategy likely come at the expense of legislative success.

Legislators and staff understand that making deals and finding bipartisan agreement constitute an important part of how Congress gets things done, addresses important issues, and produces high-quality legislation that responds to constituent concerns. Yet, they are increasingly facing challenges to this effort, both through decisions that handicap themselves—such as a ban on earmarks, structuring staffer positions to prioritize public relations, or reducing committee resources and staff—and through external electoral pressures. While there is no single easy fix to capacity or bipartisanship, this research suggests several routes that reformers might consider for increasing bipartisanship and improving capacity. First, strengthen committees and committee staff. Second, incentivize staff to stay in Congress for reasonably long tenures and to develop policy expertise. Third, foster opportunities for both staff and members of Congress to listen to the other side. For instance, one staffer commented on the success of efforts to build a bipartisan consensus on defense through meetings with members from both parties. Rather than focus on the things that divided the parties, including sequestration and spending, they had a breakfast and lunch series that brought together roughly fifty Democrats and Republicans. They discussed defense issues on Asia, Iran, surveillance, and other topics, bringing in experts and having a conversation. As the staffer noted, "It's actually pretty amazing, because it's Congress and you just never know. . . . Most of the time if you close your eyes, you wouldn't know who the Republican was or who the Democrat was on any of these issues" (Drutman et al. 2017a, p. 14.3). And the staffer thought members found it beneficial too "because they said outside the hearing room, which [is] mostly playing to the cameras anyway, there really is not [a] forum that brings together folks to have kind of a discussion of just the issues" (Drutman et al. 2017a, p. 14.14). Increasing the opportunities and incentives for both legislators and staff to listen to the other side and find common ground may be the first step toward increasing bipartisanship and ultimately toward working together to address major problems confronting the country.

PART 4

Capacity and the Politics of Reform

Lessons from the History of Reform

RUTH BLOCH RUBIN

As Woodrow Wilson observed more than a century ago, Congress is "subject to constant subtle modifications" (Wilson [1885] 1981, 19). These are developments that take place incrementally, inadvertently, and without concerted effort to amend chamber rules. Consider changes to the filibuster. Throughout the nineteenth century, filibusters rarely prevented majority-supported proposals from passing the Senate. Today, however, simply the threat of obstruction is sufficient to compel party leaders to pull bills lacking a supermajority. The rules of filibustering didn't change, but the Senate's ever-expanding legislative agenda meant that the costs to the majority of obstruction did. Unable or unwilling to wait filibusters out, Senate leaders now seek to avoid them at all costs. And, as a result, merely threating to filibuster has become a routine tool of partisan brinksmanship (Wawro and Schickler 2006).

While developments of this kind are commonplace, every so often lawmakers make an explicit break with the past and deliberately seek to conceive anew how Congress operates. It is these moments of *conscious reform* that animate this chapter. Indeed, since about the middle of the twentieth century, Congress has been reshaped by three major reform movements. We can derive four general lessons or logics from these episodes, which vary in scope and durability. After outlining these logics in the next section, this chapter revisits the three formative moments in twentieth-century congressional history—in the 1940s, 1970s, and 1990s—where lawmakers sought to revise, eliminate, or impose altogether new parliamentary procedures and structures.

Logics of Reform

Political historians often describe episodes of congressional reform as contingent on an idiosyncratic confluence of temporal and political circumstances. For political scientists, however, efforts to revise and reorganize congressional institutions are more alike than they are different. As I will argue, they are governed by a series of common constraints.

First, *reform is difficult.* As political scientists have long recognized, an institution's inherited rules and routines are sticky. Once in place, congressional practices and procedures are hard to modify or supplant because they help structure lawmakers' interests and incentives. Members who fear that reform may unfavorably disrupt the institutional environment to which they have successfully adapted—especially those who benefit most from existing arrangements, such as party leaders or committee chairs—may reflexively reject attempts to change the status quo (Davidson and Oleszek 1977).

Uncertainty over who will benefit from, or be hurt by, reform further increases its costs. With limited time and resources, members of Congress are unlikely to invest in procedural or organizational projects with uncertain payoffs when they could instead devote their attention to pursuits more likely to deliver electoral or policy benefits (Adler 2002). To be sure, it is sometimes quite clear who the winners and losers of a reform effort will be, but that in itself does not make change any easier. When the benefits of reform are diffuse but the costs are concentrated, those hurt by a proposed procedural or organizational change are more likely to mobilize in opposition than those members who stand to benefit. Consider efforts to streamline policymaking by reducing the number of standing committees and redrawing the remaining committees' jurisdictions. While the entire chamber may indirectly benefit from the resulting efficiency gains, the costs fall disproportionately on those members who lose their committee posts or see their jurisdictions limited. As we will see, efforts to reform the committee system have foundered on just this problem.

Even in cases where a proposed reform has many potential beneficiaries and creates few losers, it may *still* fail if members cannot overcome their collective action and coordination problems. Just because enough lawmakers can agree on the need for change does not mean they will be able to settle on a specific proposal. To return to our previous example: How many committees should be eliminated? How should committee jurisdictions be redrawn? How can stakeholders be compensated for their losses? Widely distributing the benefits of reform—often a means of creating a winning coalition—exacerbates these problems. The greater the number of legislators who stand to benefit from a proposed change, the more each lawmaker is encouraged to free ride on the efforts of reform-minded colleagues.

Second, *reform requires entrepreneurs.* Given Congress's strong status quo bias, lawmakers must find ways to mollify reform's certain losers, clarify the benefits of their desired procedural change, and lower the barriers to members' collective and coordinated action. "Procedural entrepreneurs"— legislators who "seek innovation out of political self-interest"—play an essential role in achieving these ends (Davidson 1990, 360). By strategically framing a procedural problem and crafting a reform package, entrepreneurs can buy off critical stakeholders with targeted concessions or assurances of support for members' pet projects, thus minimizing the size and intensity of opposition (Riker 1986). Alternatively, they can structure a reform proposal to serve as a "common carrier"—a single policy that different individuals or congressional constituencies support for different reasons, each believing it will promote their own interests (Schickler 2001, 13). To diminish members' uncertainty, procedural entrepreneurs can provide their colleagues with information about the proposed reform's intended operation, offering members a kind of "legislative subsidy" (R. Hall and Deardorff 2006). Perhaps most important, entrepreneurs can reduce the costs of their colleagues' free riding by assuming responsibility for a reform bill's drafting and passage. With a self-interested entrepreneur at the helm, legislators need not devote their own energies to devising and advocating for reform—they need only show up to vote.

Who are these procedural entrepreneurs? Often, they are the chamber's "have nots"—junior backbenchers and members of the minority party (Davidson 1990). But party leaders and loyalists, too, may embrace reform, pursuing "changes that help their party . . . gain additional power and perquisites" (Schickler 2001, 15, 252). Not surprisingly, the latter have a decided advantage. When congressional parties back reform, they offer entrepreneurs critical organizational and informational support. For example, party whips, acting with the blessing of their leadership, can help reformers navigate Congress's fragmented institutional terrain to build a winning coalition.

Third, *reforms are not equally durable and often have unintended consequences.* The stickiness of congressional institutions is both burden and boon. Although Congress's rules may be hard to change, once a reform is passed, it becomes difficult to dislodge, as legislators readjust to the new status quo. And yet, not all reforms are equally durable. What explains variation in the stickiness of institutional change? One answer: when a new reform is enacted without dismantling conflicting features of existing institutional arrangements, it may be vulnerable to attack from constituencies dedicated to preserving the old status quo, who still benefit from preexisting power structures. So, too, when a reform seems unbalanced in favor of one interest or party, the disadvantaged are especially likely to pursue counterreforms of their own. In short: "the 'losers' in one round of institutional reform do not go away; instead, they (or successors with similar interests) typically remain to fight another day" (Schickler 2001, 255). Thus, reforms are likely to be stickiest when they successfully supplant existing organizational or procedural structures, or when they satisfy multiple crosscutting interests, such that it is difficult for opponents to make common cause.

Congressional reforms often produce unintended consequences. "Layering" new reforms atop existing institutional arrangements makes it difficult for legislators to accurately predict how a proposed change will alter the political terrain. This is likely to produce "haphazard" results, rather than a rationalized "master plan" (Schickler 2001, 15). The potential for policies and procedures to "drift"—that is, remain constant in the face of major social and economic shifts—presents yet another opportunity for the unexpected (Hacker, Pierson, and Thelen 2015). While in the short and medium term, a reform may predictably reconfigure legislative practice, over time, the surrounding institutional environment may change and with it the reform's effect. Drift can be pernicious, but in creating an adverse status quo, it can give members new reason to pursue reform.

Finally, *formal rules changes are not the only avenue for reform*. It may certainly be true that formal changes to chamber rules are the most democratic and direct avenue to improving the function and capacity of congressional institutions. But there are alternative, if imperfect, pathways for aspiring reformers. Here, we might think about efforts by the liberal Democratic Study Group (DSG) to supplement members' staffing support when existing arrangements proved insufficient to meet the demands of governing in the mid-twentieth century. Lacking the parliamentary and policy expertise of their more senior conservative colleagues—but unable to persuade majority leaders to reallocate clerk-hires—DSG members agreed to pool their own resources to employ additional staff. With an independent, auxiliary staffing operation, liberal members were able to conduct their own policy research and in later years provide substantial fund-raising support (Polsby 2004; Bloch Rubin 2017). To be sure, the liberals' staffing arrangement was a second-best solution. But in an era of increasing polarization, procedural entrepreneurs would be well served to consider alternative paths of reform when changing chamber rules proves intractable.

Against this backdrop, we can now turn to a brief history of the three major congressional reform efforts that have occurred since the mid-twentieth century, describing the ways in which they have altered—or reinforced—congressional capacity and patterns of lawmaking.

Reform in the 1940s

In the aftermath of the Civil War and throughout the Industrial Revolution, Congress was central to national decision making. But the dramatic expansion of administrative authority in response to the Great Depression and World War II radically altered the balance of power between the legislative and executive branches. While the presidency benefited from the creation of a modern administrative state and the explosive growth of the armed forces, these developments ballooned the legislative agenda and strained members' oversight capacity. As Lawrence Dodd observes, "By the early 1940s many congressional committees were overwhelmed by the executive: their staff work was conducted by the staffs from the agencies; their legislation came from the president" (Dodd 2012, 59).

Imbued with progressive spirit, a bipartisan group of procedural entrepreneurs—led by Sen. Robert La Follette Jr. (Progressive-WI) and Rep. Mike Monroney (D-OK)—formed a Joint Committee on the Organization of Congress in 1945. Their task: to study and ultimately recommend reforms that would "strengthen . . . the Congress, simplifying its operations, improving its relationships with the other branches . . . and enabling it better to meet its responsibilities under the Constitution."[1] With the enthusiastic participation of northern progressives, including Sen. Francis Maloney (D-CT) and Rep. Emmanuel Celler (D-NY), and southern moderates like Sen. Claude Pepper (D-FL) and Rep. Estes Kefauver (D-TN), the committee authored a detailed proposal. It recommended changes to committee jurisdictions and oversight authority, members' staffing and salaries, and the legislative budget process—as well as the creation of a personnel director who would oversee the hiring and allocation of legislative staff.

Although a majority of lawmakers were committed to defending Congress's institutional prerogatives, several of the Joint Committee's provisions proved controversial. In the Senate, opponents objected primarily to consolidating standing committees on the ground that it would reduce the number of leadership posts for both the majority and the minority. Nevertheless, with the support of senior members of both parties, the bill passed by a 49–16 vote. The Joint Committee's report drew greater ire in the House. The Rules Committee rejected proposals to establish a personnel director, joint House–Senate hearings, a legislative–executive council, and party policy committees. With the sometimes grudging aid of Speaker Sam Rayburn (D-TX) and his deputy John McCormack (D-MA), a stripped-down bill passed the House, 229–61. Determined to pass a reform measure even if it was imperfect, La Follette and his Senate colleagues on the Joint Committee moved that the chamber accept the House amendments (Galloway 1953).

The Reorganization Act of 1946, though a more limited intervention than many on the Joint Committee had hoped, succeeded in streamlining the committee system and providing committee members with professional and clerical staff. The number of personnel at the Legislative Drafting Office and Legislative Reference Service increased as well. To improve lawmakers' capacity to oversee the executive branch and to counter the president's powerful Bureau of the Budget (now Office of Management and Budget), a joint budget committee was also established (Galloway 1951).

What made these reforms possible? First, although reform imposed clear costs on more senior members, majorities in both chambers agreed that Congress's reduced role in national policymaking was untenable. Second, procedural entrepreneurs were critical to the process, devising specific proposals—in the words of one reformer, the "ice cream"—to encourage support for more controversial "spinach" provisions (Schickler 2001, 144; Davidson 1990, 360–61). They included, for example, a pay raise and a pension system in the hopes that "members would be more willing to sacrifice some committee power bases if doing so would lead to a better salary" (Schickler 2001, 143). Third, reformers benefited substantially from the strong support of leaders in both parties. Together, Republican and Democratic leaders managed the passage of the reform bill and, in the Senate, succeeded in limiting hostile amendments. Taken together, these factors proved sufficient to overcome Congress's strong status quo bias.

At the same time, the Reorganization Act created several unintended consequences. While the reform substantially reduced the number of standing committees from thirty-three to fifteen in the Senate and from forty-eight to nineteen in the House, the act did not limit the growth of subcommittees, which soon proliferated (Haeberle 1978; Kravitz 1990). Likewise, allocating additional staff to committees did strengthen oversight as intended, but it also heightened the importance of seniority in elevating members to committee and subcommittee posts (Dodd 2012, 61). Furthermore, not all of the Reorganization Act's provisions were equally durable. Within three years, Congress abandoned the measure calling for an annual budget resolution with enforceable spending caps in the face of resistance from entrenched legislative appropriators.

Reform in the 1970s

Just as the rapid expansion of executive power and administrative capacity motivated lawmakers to embrace procedural change in the postwar period, similar fears galvanized them to pursue reform again as the nationwide debate over American involvement in Vietnam intensified. Amid charges that Congress was forfeiting its responsibility to police the presidency, particularly on matters of foreign policy, a coalition of senior liberal Democrats and junior members of both parties pushed to establish a new Joint Committee on the Organization of Congress to study deficits in legislative capacity and recommend appropriate reforms. Armed with his experience cochairing that same committee in 1945 with LaFollette, veteran reformer Monroney sponsored the resolution to create the new Joint Committee in 1965.

As before, this committee was staffed by veteran reformers from both parties, eager to "shore up our fences and increase the effectiveness of the Congress in dealing with the tremendously diversified and complex issues [with] which it is faced, and the growing power of the executive branch." Principally concerned that lawmakers lacked "sufficient information . . . to deal effectively with the myriad of legislative problems," the Joint Committee made recommendations that were relatively narrow in scope, calling for further increases in staff and new procedural mechanisms to make the committee process more transparent and inclusive (Schickler 2001, 214).

Balking at the committee's modest proposal, a cadre of junior reformers pressed for more aggressive changes. Liberal members of the DSG, in particular, were determined to discipline committee chairs who used their posts to bottle up progressive legislation (Zelizer 2004). But devolving the power of committee chairs would not be easy, as party leaders feared disrupting existing power structures for uncertain reward. Naturally, members with considerable seniority—the current beneficiaries of existing party rules—had little to gain and everything to lose from committee reform. But even members with more limited seniority were hesitant to back it. Some hoped to benefit in the future from existing practices; others admitted they lacked sufficient knowledge to evaluate competing proposals (Bloch Rubin 2017).

Chastened but undeterred, the liberals refrained from pursuing chamber-wide reform, where their strength "would have been diluted by Republican participation," and concentrated instead on the Democratic caucus (Rohde 1991, 18). By 1970, under increasing pressure from the DSG's growing membership, Democratic leaders agreed to institute confidential up-or-down votes for individual committee posts at the request of as few as ten caucus members. To further limit the power of committee chairs, the caucus also agreed to grant subcommittee chairs additional staff, an effort that mitigated the skewed distribution of staff resources within the committee hierarchy (Bloch Rubin 2017).

That same year, the House and Senate passed a modified version of the 1965 Joint Committee's reform measure. At the core of the Legislative Reorganization Act of 1970 was a so-called committee bill of rights, which required committees to adopt formal rules, set regular meeting days, decentralize agenda-setting powers, enhance minority party rights, and make public committee hearings, votes, and transcripts. Yet again, members of the DSG sought to strengthen the reform bill, pressing the House to mandate recorded teller votes on floor amendments (Kravitz 1990). Working together with "Young Turk" Republicans and the sometimes-maverick Rep. Tip O'Neill (D-MA)—who served as a broker between the DSG and Democratic leaders— the reformers negotiated a package of amendments that coupled the recorded teller vote provision with measures strengthening the role of the minority party (Schickler 2001). Although the bill easily passed both chambers—59–5 in the Senate and 325–19 in the House—many members privately worried that "its provisions went too far," while others "believed it did not go far enough" (Kravitz 1990).

As was true of the 1946 act, some of the reformers' most desired changes created significant, if unintended, problems. Consider the DSG's demand for recorded teller votes. Although liberal members had hoped the measure would compel conservative Democrats to toe the party line, the Republican minority's amending activity quickly outpaced that of Democrats. But Republican lawmakers were quick to recognize that recorded votes were good for more than just position taking. They could "draft . . . amendments that confronted Democrats with an unpalatable choice, pitting their policy preferences against their reelection needs" (Sinclair 1995, 77). With the party's ideological fissures publicly exposed, Democratic leaders struggled to control a floor majority capable of passing party initiatives (Smith 1989, 32–33).

Subsequent reform efforts were attempted in the mid-1970s to rectify some of the Reorganization Act's perceived deficits. In 1973, the House created a bipartisan Select Committee—headed by the brilliant but aloof liberal Rep. Richard Bolling (D-MO)—to study potential ways to reform committee jurisdictions. As chair, Bolling advocated bold changes to consolidate and eliminate overlapping jurisdictions, often over the objections of his fellow committee members who worried that such changes, even if desirable, were not politically feasible. Believing that Bolling's proposal represented a power grab for the Rules Committee (of which he was a member), both liberal and conservative chairs of standing committees opposed the Select

Committee's recommendations. Junior liberals, too, feared they were going to be "screwed" by the proposal, which targeted popular progressive subcommittees like Education and Labor. With few allies, the House rejected Bolling's plan and passed a far weaker measure pertaining to only a handful of minor committees (Zelizer 2004). Reformers met with greater success in the Senate. The recommendations of the Senate's own bipartisan Select Committee were adopted, 89–1, in 1977, abolishing several standing committees and four select and joint committees, restricting the number of committee seats each senator could be assigned, and providing the minority party with additional staff.

Although reformers devoted much of their energy to increasing congressional capacity, they also pursued changes limiting executive discretion and authority. Reflecting concern that presidents of both parties were stretching the authority delegated by the 1964 Gulf of Tonkin Resolution to commit more troops in Southeast Asia without legislative approval, Congress passed the 1973 War Powers Resolution, which limited the executive's power to unilaterally escalate military conflicts for more than sixty days and mandated reporting of troop deployments. But lawmakers did not fully appreciate at the time that the resolution in effect "gave congressional war-making powers to the president for sixty days *unless* Congress chose to enforce them" (Dodd 2012, 67–68).

A year later, in response to Richard Nixon's use of impoundments to limit federal spending authorized by Congress, lawmakers passed the Budget and Impoundment Control Act. This bipartisan bill created dedicated budget committees to propose spending and revenue totals, limited the president's power to impound funds, and established the Congressional Budget Office to provide members with independent expertise (Schickler 2001). Although liberal Democrats were strong supporters of committee-based reforms and the War Powers Resolution, they resisted the Budget Act, fearing it would lead to reduced domestic spending. Still others worried the bill would encroach on other committees' jurisdictions. To pass the act, reformers had to alleviate these concerns, but, in so doing, they created an "ambiguous and permissive process" with procedures intended to centralize the budget process layered atop a fragmented appropriations and authorizations framework (Schick 1980).

The core logics of reform outlined at this chapter's outset can help explain both the profusion of reform efforts in the 1970s and their mixed success. As we have seen, canny and dedicated entrepreneurs are necessary to overcome their colleagues' bias toward the status quo. Here, liberal reformers operating through the DSG proved critical. Meaningful reforms—including the Budget

and Impoundment Control Act and the 1970 Reorganization Act—passed
both chambers, but only when intransigent stakeholders were mollified or
otherwise neutralized and proposals succeeded in bridging divergent interests. On other occasions, institutional obstacles forced entrepreneurs to pursue alternative pathways for reform—as liberal members' efforts to revamp
their party's seniority rules evidence. Sometimes, however, reformers like
Bolling failed to build winning coalitions altogether, becoming so "carried
away with the logic of reform" that they ignored political realities (Zelizer
2004, 143). It is also clear that reformers have a poor track record when it
comes to accurately predicting how a measure will alter the political terrain.
At best, procedural and organizational changes create additional red tape;
at worst, as in the case of the recorded teller vote measure and War Powers
Resolution, they can substantially disadvantage a party or the chamber body
as a whole.

Reform in the 1990s

A decade after the passage of the Legislative Reorganization Act of 1970, much
about Congress had changed. Despite reformers' intention to empower rank-
and-file members, by the 1980s their efforts were responsible for revitalizing
majority party leadership in both chambers. By granting the Speaker greater
influence in committee assignments, as well as the power to refer bills to multiple committees, the Reorganization Act enabled the House's Democratic
majority to structure committee and floor debates to the party's advantage
(Schickler 2001). Senate leaders also expanded their influence, relying on reconciliation measures and unanimous consent agreements to limit minority
filibusters and postcloture debate (Zelizer 2004). The centralization of power
in the hands of majority party leaders brought much-needed coordination to
a system fragmented by reform. Nevertheless, the act's key provisions—including the committee bill of rights and sunshine laws—gave minority party
members many of the tools necessary to foment rebellion.

By the 1990s, minority party dissidents were not the only threat to the
status quo. A series of legislative scandals, partisan investigations, and forced
early retirements had eroded public approval of Congress as an institution.
Determined to improve their public reputation by "clean[ing] house," a bipartisan coalition agreed to form another Joint Committee to "address how
to make Congress more effective, accountable, and credible" (Adler 2002,
175).[2] In contrast to previous reform efforts, the new Joint Committee had limited support from the Democratic Speaker and Senate majority leader, who
feared that the committee's conclusions might undermine the party in the

1992 elections. These fears were not entirely unfounded, as House Republicans were in the midst of drafting a sweeping reform agenda that would ultimately form the backbone of their 1994 "Contract with America."

After agreeing to delay any activity until after the election, the Joint Committee's chairs, Sen. David Boren (D-OK) and Rep. Lee Hamilton (D-IN), convened a series of hearings in January 1993 that included presentations by the Speaker and the House and Senate majority and minority leadership.[3] To supplement that testimony, the committee also tasked the Congressional Research Service with organizing a survey of senators, representatives, and their staff. Despite members' testimony defending the status quo, the Joint Committee concluded that "the simplification and rationalization of committee jurisdictions" should be a key priority. The committee also hoped to address the budget process, which "ha[d] become so complex and unwieldy that it [was] difficult for the public and even Members to follow."[4] More-radical reorganization proposals were offered by junior Republicans and liberal members of the DSG, although both groups' "recommendations were ambiguous about the details regarding which committees needed restructuring" (Adler 2002, 176).

While procedural entrepreneurs in previous eras successfully secured cooperation from both chambers, the 1992 Joint Committee was not so fortunate. Rejecting House Democrats' demand that the upper chamber consider filibuster reform and measures to curb nongermane amendments, the Senate's Democratic majority insisted on a separate markup and report. The House committee also faced pressure from embattled Speaker Tom Foley (D-WA), who vocally opposed further efforts to reform the committee system and held up the proposal in the Rules Committee for several months. Threatened by a discharge petition, Foley relented, only to block further consideration of the proposal when Democrats on the Rules Committee began to entertain Republicans' proposed ban on proxy voting as well as a more aggressive committee restructuring plan (Evans and Oleszek 1997).

Many of the proposals considered by the Joint Committee resurfaced as part of House Republicans' Contract with America. In addition to a ban on proxy voting in committees and a vague promise to cut their number by a third, incoming Republican Speaker Newt Gingrich (R-GA)—a self-identified reformer—proposed opening all committee meetings to broadcast coverage, creating term limits for committee and subcommittee chairs and the speakership, and further expanding minority amending power on motions to recommit. Unlike previous reform efforts, "this was not an instance in which pressure from freshmen insurgents played a major role. . . . Well before the Republican Conference could meet . . . Gingrich and his allies asserted the[ir] power" (Aldrich and Rohde 1997–98). Deviating from the recommendations of all three

Joint Committees, the new Speaker also sought to reduce committee staff allocations. However, much as in previous eras, when it came time for Gingrich's forces to articulate a clear plan for reorganizing the committee system, the party's newly appointed chairs became "'jealous guardians' of their jurisdictions," permitting the elimination of only three committees (Adler 2002, 183).

What made procedural change and congressional reorganization at the end of the twentieth century so challenging? For one, reformers often lacked the backing of party leaders. Without the blessing of the majority leadership, procedural entrepreneurs struggled to navigate their respective chamber's gatekeeping mechanisms. For another, even when Republican leaders prioritized reform, the former revolutionaries found it difficult to balance their public commitments with political reality. An aggressive agenda risked enraging key stakeholders and fracturing the Republican conference. As a result, the reforms passed under Gingrich were more modest in scope than initially imagined and enacted without dismantling conflicting features of previous institutional arrangements. Other procedural changes—particularly Gingrich's move to eliminate funding for legislative service organizations like the DSG and its Republican counterpart, the Republican Study Committee—generated unintended consequences. Without congressional sources of funding, legislative service organizations developed independent donor networks separate from those of congressional party leaders. Consequently, organized intraparty blocs like the contemporary House Freedom Caucus have free rein to grind legislative action to a halt, in defiance of the preferences of party leaders and the chamber majority (Bloch Rubin 2017).

Prospects for Further Reform

For pessimists, there are many reasons to question whether a new wave of meaningful reform is possible. Indeed, throughout this chapter, we have seen that bipartisan investment is often necessary, if not sufficient, to enact procedural and organizational change. In our current era of partisan distrust and stiff party competition, one would be forgiven for doubting whether enough lawmakers of both parties would be willing to set aside their differences and look past the next election cycle to collectively pursue reform. Relatedly, party leaders in both chambers appear increasingly committed to observing the Hastert Rule, whereby only those bills that garner support from a majority of the majority party are brought to the floor. Given that reform proposals often expose, and sometimes create, intraparty divisions, procedural entrepreneurs will have their work cut out for them to craft common-carrier proposals that a majority of their party—let alone a floor majority—can back.

Yet the optimists among us should not lose hope. Many of the same pressures that led to successful past reform efforts are present today. Both lawmakers and the public express deep dissatisfaction with Congress as an institution, and a recent rash of early retirements (including in very safe districts) may be some evidence that the status quo is now intolerable. Indeed, pundits and political scientists alike have observed that the executive's informational advantage vis-à-vis the legislature has only grown since the 1990s—particularly in the aftermath of the 9/11 attacks. Some issues of congressional capacity still cross party lines; identifying and retaining expert staff and expanding research services may serve as common ground.

Moreover, while scholars have long argued that electoral concerns militate against reform, the fact that an increasing number of campaigns are run "against Congress" may create new opportunities for procedural entrepreneurs. For legislators elected on promises to bring common sense back to Washington, championing reform efforts may represent one way for ambitious members to put their money where their mouth is. The fact that a bipartisan coalition of House members successfully pressured incoming Speaker Nancy Pelosi (D-CA) to establish a new Select Committee on the Modernization of Congress as part of the Democrats' rules package offers reason to think we may be closer to achieving reform than the pessimists would have us believe. Charged with studying and offering recommendations for potential changes in congressional rules, procedures, and schedules, the new Select Committee has the opportunity to set the agenda for both present-day and future reformers.

Nevertheless, we cannot be blind to the reality that partisan divisions may yet undermine the Select Committee's efforts to achieve sweeping reform. As we have seen, bipartisan reform committees often struggle to translate their recommendations into durable legislative results—and here, the fact that, as of this writing, the Senate has yet to join the House in its modernization efforts may put a ceiling on what the committee can achieve.

Aspiring procedural entrepreneurs may therefore continue to find it profitable to seek out alternative pathways for change. One possibility is to learn from the DSG and focus their efforts on the party caucus. But, if party organizations prove similarly hostile to change, reformers have still another avenue to pursue. Rather than simply accept their existing institutional environment, they can build organizations of their own. Here, too, the DSG is instructive. Created by members for members, the liberal intraparty organization succeeded in devising reforms that improved the capacity of some, if not all, lawmakers. In short, the current conditions in Congress may require aspiring *procedural* entrepreneurs to be *institutional* entrepreneurs as well.

Dodging Dead Cats: What Would It Take to Get Congress to Expand Capacity?

ANTHONY MADONNA AND IAN OSTRANDER

The thing that is wrong with Congress is fear; not fear of lobbies, not fear of criticism, not fear of the dead cats that are thrown at us ever so often; it is a fear that I observed years ago of doing something for ourselves as an institution.

REP. EVERETT DIRKSEN (R-IL)[1]

Responding to claims made by executive branch officials that the United States was losing World War II, Rep. Everett Dirksen (R-IL) put the blame on members of Congress. The legislature had not equipped itself with enough staffing resources to investigate the military and was completely reliant on executive branch experts, he claimed (see Barkley 1942; Dickson 1942). According to Dirksen, the reason for this shortsightedness was fear. Members had been so accustomed to voters and the media criticizing them for "mythical" perks and benefits (or throwing "dead cats" at them, as he called it), they assumed that actual reforms would lead to electoral consequences. Four years after his speech, Congress overcame this fear and expanded staffing resources through the Legislative Reorganization Act of 1946.

More than seventy years later, Congress finds itself in a similar situation. Staffing resources have stagnated, and the branch has found itself overly dependent on expertise provided by special-interest lobbyists (Drutman 2015; Drutman and Teles 2015b; LaPira and Thomas 2017) or executive branch personnel (Mills and Selin 2017). In this chapter, we explore the circumstances in which Congress might again expand its staff resources, presented in two parts.

First, we briefly highlight the history of congressional debates over staff resources. As Dirksen argued, electoral concerns about expanding staffing resources are not new: "running against Congress" has been a frequently employed campaign tactic. However, historical debates suggest that reforms have been able to overcome electoral concerns by arguing that staff resources were needed to rein in the executive branch.

Second, we examine the viability of "running against Congress" by running against staff. We argue that despite its common usage, members of Congress should be skeptical of effectiveness for a number of reasons. Most prominently, the public lacks the ability to monitor changes in congressional staffing. Using new survey data, we find that public attitudes toward and knowledge of congressional staff are the same today as they were *prior* to the significant cuts ushered in during the mid-1990s (as described in chapter 16 in this volume). Even if voters were able to monitor staff changes, we argue it is unlikely they would prioritize that issue over their more substantive policy preferences.

We conclude the chapter with an examination of the practical politics of reform.

History and Congressional Debates

Professional congressional staff support emerged slowly over time in an accumulation of several small steps and a handful of large leaps. Assistance to members of Congress and congressional committees was virtually nonexistent prior to the 1840s. The first congressional staffers were clerks arranged and paid for by the members themselves. Individual senators and representatives did not gain congressionally funded personal staff until a series of reforms in the 1880s, for the Senate, and 1890s, for the House of Representatives (H. Fox and Hammond 1977).

Even though these early reforms provided for fairly limited staff resources, they were generally met with aggressive opposition. This opposition almost always highlighted the electoral consequences of staff increases. For example, in 1886 when an amendment to H.R. 9726 sought to provide an extra month's pay to House employees, the *Washington Post* dubbed the endeavor "The Latest Salary Grab" and suggested that supporters would "be compelled to give an account of themselves to their constituents" (*Washington Post* 1886). Later, in 1892, Rep. George Dionysius Tillman (D-SC) memorably assured House members that if they voted to give themselves staffers, "as sure as God is in heaven . . . [they] will not need them long."[2] These electoral arguments were persuasive, and early reforms tended to occur only after a number of failures in previous years (H. Fox and Hammond 1977).[3] Electoral opposition to staff increases would continue throughout the twentieth century.

Successful advocates of increasing congressional staff support often rested their case on increasing the capacity of Congress in order to meet the demands of representation in an era of expanded government services as well as to vie for power with an expanded executive branch (Galloway 1951). Members worried not just about the workload but also about who was doing the work. Before significant expansions of congressional staff, committee chairs would often rely on executive branch staffers or lobbyists for basic expertise

(Schickler 2001). In 1967, Senator Millard Tydings (D-MD) echoed many other members in claiming Congress "has lost pace with the executive branch in providing itself with the necessary manpower to analyze and criticize administration recommendations for legislation."[4] In addition to these arguments, successful expansions of staff support occasionally benefited from lame-duck sessions and unrecorded voting.[5]

In the early twentieth century, Congress continued to expand its capacity through small increases in the size and pay of staff as well as the creation of congressional support organizations such as the precursor to the Congressional Research Service, chamber parliamentarians, and the Office of Legislative Council. The two largest congressional staffing reforms were the 1946 and 1975 Legislative Reorganization Acts. These reforms are significant because they altered many aspects of congressional staffing at once. In each case, the reforms came about with bipartisan support during a period of congressional resurgence in which Congress was attempting to reclaim power from an expanded executive branch. Both reforms dramatically increased staffing resources available to individual members, committees, and congressional support agencies as well as including many other provisions changing how Congress operates such as altering committee jurisdictions. In addition to the proponents' aforementioned arguments and procedural advantages, these reforms were generally accompanied by support from political elites in the media (Schickler 2001).

During the 1980s and 1990s, the debates surrounding congressional staffs and benefits became more ideological and partisan. Democratic control of Congress for nearly forty years allowed minority Republicans to make any unpopular increase in benefits the fault of the majority party while still enjoying those benefits. When benefit issues would arise, Speaker Tom Foley (D-WA) claimed Republicans leaders frequently told members to "vote no and take the dough" (Biggs and Foley 1999, 140).

In the early 1990s, Republicans called for the dramatic reduction of the size of government, including congressional staff, making the issue a central plank in their Contract with America. Like the opponents of the early congressional reforms, Republicans believed the issue would resonate with voters concerned that government was out of touch and that the size of Congress was an example of congressional bloat (Mayer and Canon 1995). They believed their dramatic victories in the 1994 midterm election validated this view. On the first day of the 104th Congress (1995–96), the new Republican House and Senate majorities ushered in reforms that cut committee staff by one-third, eliminated the Office of Technology and Assessment, and eliminated legislative service organizations and their staff positions.[6] Minority party Democrats also believed in the electoral effectiveness of the Republicans arguments, as most voted in support of these proposals.[7] In the next section, we examine this idea of "running against Congress" and its staff, arguing that there are good reasons to be skeptical of its effectiveness.

Running against Congress

In 1882, Mark Twain famously remarked, "Suppose you were an idiot, and suppose you were a member of Congress; but I repeat myself" (Paine 1912, 724). The quip, while appreciated at the time, was not met with shock. Congress has always been an unpopular institution, and the modern-day Congress is no exception. Accordingly, the tactic of running for Congress by "running against Congress" has long been described by scholars of political science as a pervasive and effective strategy (see, e.g., Fenno 1978). While campaigning, candidates regularly attack each other for being "part of the Washington elite," for taking perks and benefits in the form of high salaries, lavish pensions, and paid vacations and for being too close with special interests.

As the 1994 election suggests, members view running against Congress as a viable strategy, and political scientists often assume it to be effective (Lipinski, Bianco, and Work 2003). However, scholarly support for the effectiveness of "running against Congress" is limited.[8] There is even less evidence to suggest that campaigning against staff resources is an effective strategy. The closest example of this is the polling data from Hibbing and Theiss-Morse (1995, 67) that demonstrate that the public view staff as a "special perk" of members. And while respondents expressed overwhelming support for cutting legislative staff, it is doubtful the public would be able to monitor such a policy—let along be likely to vote on the issue.

Despite a lack of empirical support connecting electoral success to reducing staff budgets, members behave as if the public would be responsive. In addition to the stagnant resources and cuts since the 1994 election, the five-year debate over the "Vitter Amendment" in the Senate underscores member attempts to run against Congress by running against congressional staff. In 2013, Senator David Vitter (R-LA) introduced an amendment that effectively barred the federal government from making contributions toward congressional staffers' health insurance premiums. Despite criticism from members of both parties, he unsuccessfully attempted to attach it to a number of bills from 2013 to 2015 (Hudak 2013). Vitter featured opposition to congressional staff exemptions prominently in his gubernatorial campaign in 2015.

However, despite his very public effort on this issue, he was defeated by John Bel Edwards (D-LA), who painted the senator as being "too Washington."

This example highlights reasons to be skeptical about the electoral benefits of running against Congress by running against congressional staff. The general public lacks basic information on matters internal to Congress. Scholars have demonstrated that not only do voters frequently fail to identify members of Congress's positions on issues, but they do worse when it comes to identifying factors specific to congressional rules (see, e.g., Smith and Park 2013). Hibbing and Theiss-Morse (1995) reported that roughly 75 percent of survey respondents supported cutting the size of congressional personal staff. However, respondents also thought members had approximately half the personal staff they actually possess. Given this lack of information, we should expect voters to find monitoring changes to matters internal to Congress costly and difficult.

Monitoring change is also challenging because campaigns frequently spin dueling "running against Congress" narratives in television attack ads. For example, in the 2012 Senate race in Montana, Rep. Denny Rehberg (R-MT) ran ads asserting that Senator John Tester (D-MT) voted to "raise his own pay." However, Tester ran a similar ad asserting that Rehberg voted to "raise his own pay five times" (Dennison 2012a, 2012b). The ads are common and generally based on either procedural votes taken out of context or votes on large appropriation bills that members oppose for other substantive reasons. Given the frequency of these attacks and their dubious substantive basis, we should be skeptical of any electoral benefit. At a minimum, we are doubtful voters will actually be able to identify and reward members of Congress for their positions on staff resources. The next section examines public perceptions.

Public (Mis)Perceptions about Staff

In addition to general opposition to staff increases, public perception of congressional staffing has one other important characteristic: ignorance of the role of professional staff. This point is not lost on members. Rep. Barney Frank (D-MA) has claimed "the American people [don't] understand what a bargain they get with the people who work on our staffs, who are so talented and hard-working and could make a great deal more money elsewhere but really put in very, very long hours under difficult circumstances" (R. Kaiser 2013, 255). Public opinion surveys support the assertion that the public is both largely ignorant about and in opposition to congressional staff. As previously noted, Hibbing and Theiss-Morse (1995) found that about 75 percent of survey respondents supported cutting congressional office staff, but nearly all respondents had *underestimated* the actual size of such staffs by about half.

Hibbing and Theiss-Morse's work was based on a national survey conducted in 1992. In 1995, Republicans took control of the House and, in keeping with their campaign promises, slashed congressional staff. Since then, staff levels in Congress have decreased even further in many other areas.[9] Given the high levels of popular support for staff cuts reported by Hibbing and Theiss-Morse (1995), we should expect public attitudes toward Congress to reflect these changes.[10] Specifically, if "running against Congress" by attacking staff is a successful electoral strategy, we should expect voters to both be aware of the changes made by the institution and demonstrate more support for it.

To examine this hypothesis, we draw on data from the 2014 Cooperative Congressional Election Study.[11] Using this survey, we asked respondents whether they agreed with the statement, "There are too many staffers or assistants in Congress." While many respondents answered "don't know," almost 92 percent of respondents who did provide an opinion agreed with the statement.[12] This was an *increase* from the 75 percent reported in the 1992 survey, after nearly twenty years of reductions in congressional staff. Data from the 2014 survey are presented in figure 17.1. Additionally, there is no strong correlation between respondent belief that there are too many staffers and overall congressional approval. While 82.98 percent of respondents who agreed that there were too many staffers also disapproved of the job Congress was doing, congressional disapproval was also nearly 70 percent among those who *disagreed* with the statement or selected "don't know."

These survey results suggest that voters lack any ability to monitor staff-related policy changes. When asked how the size of congressional staff has changed over the last twenty years, 24.70 percent selected "don't know." Of the remaining respondents, just 2.27 percent selected "decreased," 12.67 percent selected "stayed about the same," and 85.10 percent responded with "increased." Responses regarding staff budgets were comparable.[13] And consistent with the 1992 survey, respondents drastically underestimated the number of staffers members of Congress employ. When asked how many staffers are employed by members, the median answer was ten—nearly half the maximum number allowed to House members.[14]

So while the public is predisposed against congressional staff, the evidence suggests that this is a low-salience issue and remains unmonitored.[15] Voters are thus unlikely to electorally reward members who support staffing cuts. However, members still behave in a way that suggests they fear electoral

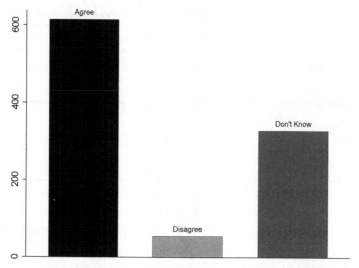

FIGURE 17.1. Answers to 2014 survey question "Do you agree or disagree with the following statement: There are too many staffers or assistants in Congress?"
Source: Madonna and Ostrander 2015.

consequences if they increase staff capacity. This misconception on the part of members suggests that substantial increases to congressional staff capacity in the near future are unlikely. However, the next section discusses potential reform strategies and some reasons for optimism.

Reform Potential and Process

Congress faces strong headwinds with respect to increasing its professional staff support. Our evidence suggests that the public is hostile to staff expansion, and members of both parties clearly fear electoral consequences of increasing staff benefits. This is nothing new. The historical record suggests that a fear of electoral consequences has frequently reined in attempts to increase congressional staff capacity. The question is, How far is Congress willing to cede power to outside interests and the executive branch before doing something to benefit the institution as a whole?

However, reformers have overcome similar difficulties in the past, suggesting that change is possible. Modern reformers lack the benefits provided by lengthy lame-duck Congresses, unrecorded voting, and one-party dominance. But several factors provide some reason for optimism. Would-be reformers should follow the lead of their historical predecessors by outlining the degree of influence the chamber has ceded to the executive and special interests. Cultivating support in the media would also likely be beneficial and mirror previous successful efforts.

There is some evidence that such an attempt at reform appears to be happening. There are bipartisan concerns over growing executive branch influence.[16] Additionally, members of both parties also appear to be concerned over the increased influence of leadership and the advantages provided to them by increased leadership staff. Finally, as with the reforms of the mid-twentieth century, media elites appear to be increasingly supportive of increasing congressional capacity (see, e.g., Glastris and Edwards 2014; Bernstein 2015; Bowman 2015; Klein 2015; Stein and Gurwitz 2015).

We have also demonstrated here that there are many reasons we might be skeptical that "running against staff" is a viable electoral strategy. The public appears unable to monitor policy changes in the area, the public is oversaturated by dubious campaign ad claims, and the topic lacks the salience of major substantive issues likely to impact votes. Reform efforts would be greatly assisted by a more detailed, systematic examination of the effectiveness of "running against Congress" and the salience of congressional staff.

Ultimately, the politics of reform will be dictated by the political contexts of the moment. Significant reform may require a larger push toward congressional resurgence. Congresses in which both parties are vying for majority status may have disincentives for bipartisan cooperation, often a necessity for congressional reform measures (Lee 2016). In the midst of a "do nothing" Congress, even minor reform measures with bipartisan backing may not get votes. Prior dramatic staff reforms often came on the heels of significant crises such as world wars, the resignation of a president, or upheavals within the parties. On a long enough timeline, such events are inevitable, but the exact timing of reform depends on there being a prochange environment in which to grow.

We must also note that other barriers to expanding congressional staff capacity exist. First, there is still no consensus on the types of staff reforms that should be enacted. The fact that members increasingly devote personal staff resources to media and district-specific positions suggests that not all reforms will increase policy capacity (Lee 2016). Second, as Ruth Bloch Rubin has argued in chapter 16 in this volume, any staffing reform will require procedural entrepreneurs who can devise proposals that will also provide enough benefits to other members to ensure their support.

Finally, more mundane concerns also exist. A significant staff increase would require space to operate, and existing office space on Capitol Hill is filled to capacity. Similarly, increasing staff pay and benefits, even substantially, may not be enough to counteract factors outside of congressional control, such as the high cost of living in Washington, DC, and long commutes to and from the capitol that may contribute to high turnover. As a result, reforming congressional staff remains a complex issue with almost as many barriers as avenues of approach.

Conclusion

Congress is faced with a dilemma when it comes to its staff resources. It struggles with dwindling capacity vis-à-vis outside interests and the executive branch, and yet the optics of expanding congressional staff while "running against Congress" may make reform votes too tough. Interestingly, this predicament has been present for more than one hundred years of congressional politics. Senator Dirksen once remarked that "through fear of public reproach we have in the years failed to staff and implement ourselves as a coordinate agency of government, and until we do we are not going to be able to do a real job."[17] Sadly, this sentiment remains as true today as it was back in 1942. Perhaps the main lesson from the past is that Congress often delays an increase in its own staffing resources until well after it begin to need it.

Previous debates on staff increases provide a good guide to the kinds of barriers Congress will face with future reform efforts. Reformers should frame the debate in terms of opposition to an expanded executive, centralized power among legislative leadership, or so as to avoid the influence of powerful lobbying interests. In this way, Congress may bypass prior ideological entrenchments and images of government bloat. History also suggests that a crisis—such as the growth of an "imperial" presidency, the administrative burden of a war, or a scandal—is fertile ground for increasing congressional staff resources.

There is a widespread public perception that adding extra staff is akin to a salary increase or a mere perk of the office. But as we have demonstrated here, this does not necessarily translate to electoral votes. While future work is needed, it seems likely that internal congressional issues such as staffing are of such low salience that they are unlikely to overtake substantive policy concerns during an election. Members will have "dead cats" thrown at them during elections, but they appear to do minimal damage.

Acknowledgments

An edited volume cannot help but be the product of many hands. This volume has three editors—Timothy LaPira, Lee Drutman, and Kevin Kosar—whose families and friends endured their endless musings about congressional capacity and the future of representative self-government. You know who you are, and we promise to stop. Eventually.

This volume purposely tries to bridge the gap between academe and the political reform advocacy community to address a problem long in need of a solution in Congress. Our intent was to bring the best possible evidence and arguments to bear on the critical question of congressional capacity. None of this could have been accomplished without the generous support and encouragement of the William and Flora Hewlett Foundation and the Democracy Fund. We thank Larry Kramer, Daniel Stid, Jean Bordewich, Lara Flint, Chris Nehls, Sean Raymond, and Nathaniel Turner for helping us turn our vision into reality.

This support permitted us to design and field what we believe is the largest and most comprehensive survey of congressional staff to date. Along with the editors, Zander Furnas and Alex Hertel-Fernandez made up the 2017 Congressional Capacity Survey team, which collected original qualitative and quantitative data from January through September 2017. All five members of the team contributed to the multimethod design, and helpful contributions were made by Casey Burgat, Heather Hurlburt, and Lorelei Kelly. LaPira spent three months traveling to Capitol Hill to conduct interviews and occasionally was joined by Furnas and Drutman. In June 2017, Furnas and LaPira spearheaded fielding the survey, which could not have been done without the timely email server expertise of Tim Ball. We could not have pulled off this feat without the hundreds of hardworking professionals who took time out of their schedules to sit for interviews or respond to a survey, though Institutional Review Board protocols dictate they must remain nameless here.

Many friends, colleagues, and former students played key roles in helping us boost the signal for the Congressional Capacity Survey, which undoubtedly improved response rates and quality. Shoshana Weissmann of the R Street Institute and Marian Currinder, editor of LegBranch.org, helped us encourage staffers to complete the survey, as did Michele Stockwell at Bipartisan Policy Center, Brad Fitch of the Congressional Management Foundation, Marci Dale at PopVox, and Rex Buffington of the Stennis Fellows Program. LaPira is particularly grateful to former students turned congressional staffers Hannah Aiken, Josh Althouse, Matt Silver, Heather Smith, and Kelly Waters, as well as James Madison University politicos Frank Cavaliere, Gina Foote, Jamie Jones Miller, and Carrie Meadows, for helping spread the word in their networks.

The Legislative Branch Capacity Working Group, a nonpartisan gathering of experts, congressional staff, and Congress watchers, also proved a fine place to venture hypotheses and get new ideas. The hundreds of attendees are too many to enumerate, but we do want to give special thanks to regulars Daniel Schuman, Max Spitzer, and Michael Stern.

We also benefited from feedback offered by attendees of the 2018 Congressional Capacity Conference at New America. We want especially to thank Charles Stewart III for "dropping bombs" in his summary reflection. On behalf of all the contributors, we appreciate feedback from discussants Jim Curry, Josh Huder, Zander Furnas, and Matt Glassman. Other attendees offered useful thoughts as well, including Ashley Antoskiewicz, Frank Baumgartner, Sarah Binder, Nick Carnes, Matt Green, Michele Nellenbach, Ellie Powell, and Michele Swers.

We also are in debt to Chayenne Polimedio and Elena Souris of New America, who assisted with survey administration, helped organize the Congressional Capacity Conference, and prepared the manuscript for submission to the press. We also thank Mark Schmitt at New America, who directs the political reform program and whose enthusiasm for this project was crucial in getting it going. Kudos also go to Lauren Rollins, editorial director of R Street Institute, who helped out.

None of this would have happened without Chuck Myers, who supported the project from the moment we pitched it, bent over backward to identify reviewers who weren't already in the table of contents, and then shepherded it through production with patience and insight.

Though it took a village to produce this volume, any shortcomings or errors in these pages are owned by the editors.

Notes

Chapter One

1. See online appendix materials for methodological details.

Chapter Three

Thanks are due to Curtlyn Kramer for research support and assistance with *Vital Statistics on Congress*; to Lee Drutman, Kevin Kosar, Tim LaPira, and the participants at New America's State of Congressional Capacity Conference for helpful comments; and to R. Eric Petersen of the Congressional Research Service for additional information about CRS staff data.

1. "Congressional Reorganization: Options for Change," Report of the Congressional Research Service, Library of Congress, to the Joint Committee on the Organization of Congress, S. Prt. 103-19, 103rd Cong., 1st Sess. 60 (1993).

2. A separate effort, known as the Hansen Committee, focused principally, though not exclusively, on reforms to the Democratic Caucus rules in the House between 1970 and 1974.

3. The two principal sources I will use here to discuss staff levels and distribution are *Vital Statistics on Congress* (see Brookings Institution 2019), and the Congressional Research Service (CRS). The former largely, but not exclusively, uses disbursement records from the House and Senate to estimate staff figures. The latter relies primarily on information from House and Senate telephone directories. In both cases, capturing an accurate picture of staff levels is difficult, and figures should be treated as estimates.

4. Data in this paragraph are from Brookings Institution 2019, Table 5-1; Chausow, Petersen, and Wilhelm 2016a.

5. See Brookings Institution 2019, Table 5-1; Chausow, Petersen, and Wilhelm 2016b. The two data sources disagree on the overall decline in committee staff size since the late 1970s; CRS puts it at approximately 8 percent, while *Vital Statistics* estimates it at roughly 32 percent.

6. For a thorough discussion of an earlier version of this data, see Glassman 2012. In the House, the most recent data for leadership staff include the following offices: Speaker, Majority Leader, Majority Whip, Chief Deputy Majority Whip, Minority Leader, Minority Whip, Assistant Minority Leader, Senior Chief Deputy Minority Whip, Democratic and Republican Cloakrooms, House Republican Conference, House Republican Policy Committee, House Republican Study Committee, House Democratic Caucus, and House Democratic Steering and Policy

Committee. In the Senate, the most recent data for leadership staff include the following offices: Assistant Democratic Leader, Assistant Majority Leader, Democratic Cloakroom, Democratic Floor Staff, Democratic Leader, Democratic Policy and Communications Center, Democratic Steering and Outreach, Majority Leader, Republican Cloakroom, Republican Conference, Republican Conference Vice Chairman, Republican Policy Committee, Secretary for the Majority, Secretary for the Minority, and Senate Democratic Media Center.

7. "Congressional Reorganization: Options for Change," Report of the Congressional Research Service, Library of Congress, to the Joint Committee on the Organization of Congress, S. Prt. 103-19, 103rd Cong., 1st Sess. 60 (1993). The CRS report attributes this idea originally to Maisel (1981).

8. All inflation adjustments are made using the CPI Research Series Using Current Methods (CPI-U-RS); see BLS 2019.

9. Data from 2001 to 2015 from Petersen and Chausow 2016a, 2016b. Data for 2016 for House and Senate, respectively, from Rates of Compensation Disbursed by Chief Administrative Officer of House, 2 U.S.C. § 4532; Senate Pay Adjustments, 2 U.S.C. § 4571.

10. Both chambers have made reports containing this information available digitally (since 2009 in the House, 2011 in the Senate), but that information is not machine readable.

11. Beginning for fiscal year 1996, the House made a major change in how it allocated committee funding, making it difficult to compare funds from pre- and post-1996 periods (Vincent 1997).

12. Data on requests to the Office of the Senate Legislative Counsel are from Endicott 2016. Data on staff levels are tabulated from Senate telephone directories. Notably, the number of bills actually introduced in the Senate did not see a similar growth over the same period.

13. *CBO's Appropriation Request for Fiscal Year 1998: Hearings Before the Committee on Appropriations, Subcommittee on the Legislative Branch*, 105th Cong. (1997) (statement of June E. O'Neill, director, Congressional Budget Office).

Chapter Four

1. Congress also often embeds substantive policy commitments in the structure of the agencies it creates quite apart from any desire to achieve the public good efficiently (Moe 1989).

2. A. L. A. Schechter Poultry Corp. v. United States, 295 U.S. 495 (1935); quotation at 553.

3. Included in the Legislative Reorganization Act of 1946 were the Federal Tort Claims Act and the General Bridge Act. The former created a procedure for suing the federal government for routine harms, which previously were addressed by Congress passing private bills to grant case-specific relief. The latter relieved Congress of the burden of having to approve every bridge being built over a navigable stream. Collectively, they did a great deal to free up legislators' time and attention for weightier issues.

4. An influential school of 1980s political scientists saw Congress as the dominant party in the relationship, bringing agencies into line whenever they departed from what the current legislative consensus could support and effectively monitoring executive branch activities through a system of reactive, interest-triggered "fire alarms" (McCubbins, Noll, and Weingast 1987; McCubbins and Schwartz 1984). Others have noted that as Congress built up the administrative state throughout the postwar era, it made systematic agency design choices that reflected the political environment of the time and especially divided government (Epstein and O'Halloran 1999; Huber and Shipan 2002; Lewis 2003).

5. The selected figures overstate the linearity of this progression.

Chapter Five

1. *Organization of the Congress: Final Report of the House Members of the Joint Committee on the Organization of Congress*, 103rd Cong., 1st Sess. (1993), http://archives-democrats-rules .house.gov/archives/jcoc2.htm.

2. We distributed a questionnaire to all individual staff who worked for a member, committee, or party leader in the US House or Senate in Washington, DC. We excluded interns, fellows, and congressional staff working in state and district offices. We began distributing the surveys in August 2017, and we closed the survey on November 4, 2017. We sent questionnaires to 8,485 individuals and received 441 responses. The margin of error at the 95 percent level of confidence is 4.5 percent.

3. These summary figures account for all 9,558 staffers in House offices and 6,801 Senate staffers, including staff in offices that were excluded from our sampling frame. LegiStorm updates these tallies "in real time" as it processes data.

4. Note: It is not uncommon for individual staffers to be employed by multiple offices.

5. The LegiStorm database is limited to congressional payroll disbursements back to 2000, making some respondents' actual tenure right-censored.

6. To maintain respondents' confidentiality, table 5.5 reports salary data in five bins of roughly $30,000. The median and mean estimates are from actual reported salary payments for each respondent, as reported by LegiStorm calculations of congressional payroll data.

7. Median salary data for the United States and the Washington–Arlington–Alexandria–District of Columbia metropolitan area are based on American Community Survey estimates (American Community Survey, n.d.). Estimates are from 2016, the most recent year available.

8. The median staffer reports working between fifty and fifty-nine hours per week.

9. For example, the median member's personal office in the House of Representatives has five staffers with policy responsibility (Crosson, Furnas, and LaPira 2018).

10. To get a sense of how staffers were spread across the issues, we asked how often they worked on particular issue areas: "Never," "Occasionally," or "Daily." We asked this question for each of the twenty-two Policy Agendas Project issue areas.

11. The survey asked a series of short knowledge batteries on three of the most commonly worked on issues: budget, health, and national security (defense and international affairs). We measure respondent issue knowledge with simple Guttman scales of the number of correct answers to these knowledge questions for each issue area.

12. Such staffers include those with some version of the title legislative director, legislative assistant, legislative correspondent, legislative counsel, policy advisor, or policy director.

13. We asked survey respondents the following question: "Thinking about your future career path, how long do you envision working in some position INSIDE Congress?"

14. There is also the potential for a prospective effect of these career aspirations on staffers' behaviors in Congress. To the extent that staffers know that they would like to move into the private sector—or at least would like to keep that option open for the future—they might change their behavior while working in Congress to build relationships and goodwill with potential future employers. In this way, the prospect of a lucrative private-sector career post-Congress might influence staffer behavior even independently of any interactions that corporate lobbyists might have with a staffer. In sum, there are good reasons for investigating what staffers say that they would like to do after leaving their jobs.

15. In our survey, we asked staffers a hypothetical question: "Imagine that your office budget were to double tomorrow. If it were up to you, how would you prioritize spending these new resources?"

Chapter Six

1. There are a total of four questions about House procedure, Senate procedure, and health policy, and a total of five questions about budget and appropriations policy and national security policy.

2. Stated another way, 17 percent of respondents correctly answered all procedural questions, and 7 percent of respondents received a perfect score on policy-specific questions.

3. Staff members who work in the Senate score 5 points higher on national security questions than their House counterparts on average (61 percent vs. 56 percent), and this difference approaches standard levels of statistical significance ($t = -1.56$, $p = .12$).

4. See also chapter 7 in this volume for a discussion of the role of staff on committees.

5. Since the data do not identify the committee on which a staff member works, I assume that committee staff who report working daily on a given issue work for a committee with jurisdiction for the issue. The comparison group of personal staff members is constructed similarly: personal office staff who report working on a given issue daily are assumed to be the policy specialist in their office.

6. The average Democratic staff and Republican staff scores are 60 percent and 56 percent, respectively, on policy questions ($t = -.217$, $p = .83$), and 65 percent and 63 percent, respectively, on procedural questions ($t = -.954$, $p = .34$). The multivariate analysis in appendix 6.1 online, however, reveals that Republican staffers did score higher on health policy questions, which likely reflects the Republican focus on attempting to repeal the Affordable Care Act in 2017 when the survey was conducted.

7. There is no clear expectation that strength of partisanship should affect staff members' policy knowledge, and this is borne out by the data. Substantive knowledge scores across weak partisans (50 percent), partisans (56 percent), and strong partisans (58 percent) are not statistically distinct as confidence levels do not surpass 75 percent.

8. Difference of means tests between weak partisans, partisans, and strong partisans establish that these differences are significant at conventional levels of statistical significance (e.g., 95 percent or higher).

9. The difference of means is statistically distinct at the 95 percent level ($t = -1.97$, $p = .05$).

10. Difference of means tests confirm that there is no significant difference in average knowledge scores (policy or procedural) between staff members whose ideal path is to stay in Congress, move to another branch of government, or move to a politically relevant private-sector job.

11. The correlation coefficients between staff tenure and policy and procedural knowledge are .15 and .26, respectively.

12. Difference of means tests for the issues pooled, budget policy alone, and health care policy alone confirm that the scores are distinct with greater than 99 percent confidence. For national security policy, the difference between staff who work on the issue daily and those who do not approaches conventional levels of statistical significance ($t = 1.44$, $p = .15$).

13. In addition, racial and ethnic minorities are significantly underrepresented on Capitol Hill according to studies by the Joint Center for Political and Economic Studies (2015) and Congressional Hispanic Staff Association (2010). Reflective of that reality, there are too few minority staff respondents in the data to analyze differences in staff knowledge by race or ethnicity.

14. Given 161 staff members who were asked about national security policy, 56 were women and 105 were men. The difference of means test fails to reject the hypothesis that there is no difference between their scores ($t = -0.89$, $p = .38$).

15. In total, 110 women and 220 men were asked about rules and procedures, and the difference of means for these two groups is statistically significant at the 99 percent confidence level $(t = 2.48, p = .01)$.

16. As shown in appendix 6.1, Senate staff score significantly higher on the knowledge test for national security $(p = .01)$, but chamber has only a marginal impact on knowledge of health policy $(p = .10)$ and is not a significant predictor of staff knowledge on budgeting $(p = .38)$.

Chapter Seven

1. In chapter 6 in this volume, Kristina Miler finds that staffers who engage in issues more regularly, such as committee aides who are responsible for consistent attention on issues within their committee's jurisdiction, maintain higher levels of policy knowledge when compared with aides who never or only occasionally work on an issue.

2. While it is a critical policymaking committee, we have removed the Appropriations Committee from our models for two reasons. First, due to the sheer scope of the appropriations process, each member of the committee is assigned a staffer who is responsible for tracking various legislative processes within the committee for the respective member. Such an arrangement is not true of any other House committees. Second, in part due to these supplemental staffer assignments, Appropriations is an outlier in the balance of staff types as well as the sheer size of total staff. The committee is three full standard deviations above the maximum in the sample of House committees that does not include them.

3. From the Congressional Bills Project (Adler and Wilkerson, n.d.-b).

4. Congressional Bills Project describes their process for coding "important" versus "not important" bills as "based on the presence of certain words in a title and can be used to exclude bills that are arguably of minor importance. For example, bills to name buildings are fairly common and a large proportion of the laws that are passed" (Adler and Wilkerson, n.d.-a). A full explanation of their coding methods is available via the "Codebooks" tab of their website (see Adler and Wilkerson, n.d.-a).

5. Congressional Bills Project captures all bills that passed or did not pass the chamber, whether they were in fact reported out of committee or not. Therefore, the "number of important bills passed" variable captures both reported bills and nonreported bills that went to the floor. We also are not concerned about overdispersion of individual bills: More than 80 percent of all bills were referred to only one committee in one chamber, and greater than 95 percent were referred to only two—and most of these were the two appropriate committees from each chamber.

6. As figure 7.1 indicates, the total Uncoded and Professional staffers amount to around 11 percent of all staffer-years postclean, and all committee-years used in our models fell within a range of 7 to 15 percent. Such low uncoded counts give us confidence that uncoded aides are not biasing our results for any one committee.

7. PSMs and Uncoded staffers were not included in the committee-level analysis.

8. For example, the House Homeland Security Committee, which is in charge of the budget for the Federal Emergency Management Agency (FEMA), was given a positive value for this variable in 2005 and 2006, when and shortly after Hurricane Katrina devastated the Gulf Coast; similarly, the House Financial Services Committee was given the same designation during and following the financial crisis of 2008–9.

9. Due to nonnormal distributions of our primary independent variables—committee staff counts—we have taken the natural logarithm of these variables to capture percent change rather

than per-staffer change for more accurate specification, even distribution, and generalizability of results. We also do this because one additional staffer is likely to have a different effect in a committee that already has seventy staffers, as opposed to one that only has ten. Similarly, we also use the original interpretation of the coefficients, which is to predict percentage change in the legislative outputs dependent variables. This allows us to standardize causes and effects across committees to a greater extent, which is particularly valuable in a fixed-effects model that captures within-committee variation.

10. House Rule X, clause 6.

11. A more explicit test of the alternative hypothesis just discussed is to lag staff variables in the opposite direction, effectively testing the causality of committees preemptively "staffing up." If we expected anticipated legislative action to drive staff hires in committees, we could confirm this by using a committee's legislative action in a given year to predict the following year's staffer counts as the dependent variable. However, models constructed to test this alternative hypothesis failed to converge, much less predict any kind of positive result. Each of these tests give us greater confidence in the causal direction of our argument.

12. See chapter 2 in this volume in particular.

Chapter Eight

1. Studies produced since 1990 are modest in number. They include Bimber 1996; Blair 2013; Joyce 2011; Relyea 2010, 2012a, 2012b; Trask 1991. A bibliography of early works on the GAO may be found in F. Kaiser 2008, 5n5.

2. This limited definition is not meant to slight the Library of Congress and its Law Library, which also assist legislators and their staff, nor the Government Publishing Office, whose employees produce key legislative documents (e.g., statutes and the *Congressional Record*). It also should be noted that the definition excludes important intrachamber organizations, such as the Office of the Clerk of the House of Representatives, the Parliamentarian of the US Senate, and the Joint Committee on Taxation, which provide day-to-day operational support.

3. Like other civil servants, workers in the legislative branch support agencies must abide by the Hatch Act and other legal proscriptions against partisan and campaign activities on the job. See Maskell 1998.

4. For example, the Government Accountability Office reports an annual retention rate of employees of 96 percent (not counting retirements) each year from 2012 through 2017 (GAO 2017, 23).

5. 2 Stat. 55. James Madison first proposed a congressional library in 1783. See Murray 2012, 155.

6. Here to "professionalize" refers to efforts to integrate civil servants and other staff into more aspects of the legislative process and to increase the legislature's information collection and utilization in decision making. Examples of this professionalization include hiring clerks to transcribe hearings and employing nonpartisan professional committee staff.

7. Sen. Robert LaFollette Sr. (R-WI) supported the establishment of LRS and as governor had signed into law similar state legislation creating a Wisconsin legislative research agency. See Stathis 2014, 10–14.

8. Legislative Reorganization Act of 1946, Pub L. No. 60-812, 60 Stat. 812 (1946), at § 203(a)(1).

9. Legislative Reorganization Act of 1946, Pub L. No. 60-812, 60 stat. 812 (1946), at § 203(b)(2).

10. LRS studies may be found by searching books and printed materials through the Library of Congress website, https://www.loc.gov/books/?q=%22legislative+reference+service%22&fa

=contributor%3Alibrary+of+congress.+legislative+reference+service&all=true&sp=8&sb=date
_desc.

11. Legislative Reorganization Act of 1970, Pub. L. No. 91-510, 84 Stat. 1140 (1970); Congressional Research Service, 2 U.S.C. § 166.

12. The statute reads: "[CRS shall provide] each committee of the Senate and House of Representatives and each joint committee of the two Houses, at the opening of a new Congress, a list of programs and activities being carried out under existing law scheduled to terminate during the current Congress, which are within the jurisdiction of the committee . . . [and] to make available to each committee of the Senate and House of Representatives and each joint committee of the two Houses, at the opening of a new Congress, a list of subjects and policy areas which the committee might profitably analyze in depth." Legislative Reorganization Act of 1970, Pub. L. No. 91-510, 84 Stat. 1140 (1970), at § 203(d)(2)-(3); Congressional Research Service, 2 U.S.C. § 166(d).

13. Unlike GAO, CRS does not possess investigative authority. Nor does it have field offices and employees. Hence, CRS reports do not include original data collection or reportage based on interviews. CRS analysts use open source materials and data. In the rare instances when CRS analysts are detailed to committees, they are endowed with congressional committee investigative authority and can demand information from agencies.

14. For a description of CRS's day-to-day work, see Kosar 2015c.

15. Budget and Accounting Act of 1921, Pub. L. No. 67-13, 42 Stat. 20 (1921).

16. Budget and Accounting Act of 1921, Pub. L. No. 67-13, 42 Stat 20 (1921), at §§ 301, 309, 312, and 303, respectively.

17. For the GAO's current duties and authorities, see Government Accountability Office, 31 U.S.C. § 701.

18. An Act to Establish an Office of Technology Assessment for the Congress, Pub. L. No. 92484, 86 Stat. 797 (1972), at § 2(a)–(c); Office of Technology Assessment, 2 U.S.C. § 471, at § (2)(a)–(c).

19. For the *Costs and Effectiveness of Cholesterol Screening in the Elderly* report, see Office of Technology Assessment 1989.

20. OTA's director was "authorized by the TAB to commit OTA resources on his or her own initiative for follow up studies based on earlier assessments, or in smaller scale research projects. But, for any major commitment of staff and resources generally in excess of one staff-year, the Director obtains approval from the TAB before committing OTA resources to the project." *Organization of the Congress: Final Report of the House Members of the Joint Committee on the Organization of Congress.* 103rd Cong., 1st Sess. (1993), http://archives-democrats-rules.house.gov/archives/jcoc2.htm.

21. Office of Technology Assessment, 2 U.S.C. § 472.

22. OTA's final budget was $23 million in 1995, which is equivalent to $37 million in 2019 dollars.

23. Congressional Budget and Impoundment Control Act of 1974, Pub. L. No. 93-344, 88 Stat. 297 (1974); Congressional Budget Office, 2 U.S.C. § 601 (1976); see also Schick 1975, 51–70.

24. The resolution also sets spending levels for each functional category of the budget and provides reconciliation instructions. Also, the duties of the budget committees also are set through chamber rules. See CRS 2009.

25. The outputs listed are not all inclusive. Data for some activities were not available (e.g., how many legislative branch agency staff served on committee details in Congress or how many podcasts and videos were produced by the agencies).

26. Our Congressional Capacity Survey data also indicate that staffers tend to use and trust information and data from the intragovernmental resources listed in tables 8.3 and 8.4 more than external sources (e.g., campaign donors, labor unions, political action committees, etc.).

27. "Congressional Staff and Management," in *Organization of the Congress*.

28. On the stark differences between the OTA's technology assessments and other legislative branch agency reports, see Rowberg 2016.

29. Certainly, there is nothing ipso facto inappropriate about legislators criticizing the analysis of a legislative support agency. But when criticism is delivered publicly and coupled with explicit or implicit threats of funding reductions, agencies will feel strong incentives to become more cautious.

30. For some recent CRS policies endeavoring to reduce the probability of political controversies, see Aftergood, n.d.

31. To be clear, the position of expertise in the United States never has been an easy one. Public suspicion of elites goes way back, and experts have been rightly blamed for many spectacular policy errors. See Hofstadter 1966; Nichols 2017.

32. The growth in the quantity of think tanks and research organizations since the 1970s also has enabled committee staff to shop for the perspectives they prefer and use the legislative branch support agencies more selectively.

33. The 1946 Legislative Reorganization Act "provided that each standing committee in the House and Senate be provided with a basic grant of 10 staffing positions, 6 professional and 4 clerical staff" (these basic positions have since come to be called "statutory" staff positions). The language of the act required that staff in such positions be hired upon a formal vote of each committee, without regard to the political affiliation of the staff member. To attract and retain highly skilled and experienced personnel, the maximum salary levels for committee professional positions were set at a level comparable to that paid an assistant secretary in a cabinet department. The 1946 act further stipulated that no work other than committee business could be assigned to these aides. See "Congressional Staff and Management."

Chapter Nine

1. Page totals for the 112th Congress were not included in the report from that Congress.

2. This interview was conducted in person by the author in February 2018 in Grinnell, Iowa, and is reported here for the first time. The identity of the subject is confidential.

3. Report of Committee Activities, H.R. Rep. No. 111-423 (2010).

4. Report of Committee Activities, H.R. Rep. No. 112-748 (2012).

5. The 2005 wave of interviews was conducted by the author, Ken Shepsle, and Robert Van Houweling (see Shepsle et al. 2009), and the 2012 wave was conducted by the author (see Hanson 2014b). The 2019 wave of interviews was conducted by the author and Molly Reynolds and is reported for the first time here, hereafter cited parenthetically as Hanson-Reynolds Interview, with letter labeling the interview subject, whose identity remains confidential.

6. These interviews, conducted in 2017, are found in Drutman et al. 2017a, cited in text with number labeling the interview subject, whose identity remains confidential.

Chapter Ten

1. For example, Thomas E. Mann and Norman J. Ornstein's book, The *Broken Branch: How Congress Is Failing America and How to Get It Back on Track*, gave rise to an entire academic

genre on Congress that has shaped how we think about congressional dysfunction today. See Mann and Ornstein 2006.

2. Contrast the Congress of 2019 with the institution described by James Madison in the *Federalist*. Madison writes, "The legislative department is every where extending the sphere of its activity, and drawing all power into its impetuous vortex" (Madison 1999, 281).

3. This is not to suggest that some forms of congressional organization are not better than others.

4. For an argument about the evolution of Senate rules in response to efforts to maintain the institution's productivity, see Wawro and Schickler 2006. For a contrary argument—that the Senate's procedures did not evolve in response to a growing workload, see Binder and Smith 1997.

5. This does not exclude chamber-imposed hierarchies.

6. According to the Senate's precedents, "Decisions of the Chair are subject to appeal and by a majority vote the Senate may reverse or overrule any decision by the Chair" (Riddick and Frumin 1992, 146).

7. Letter to Senator David Vitter, April 10, 2014, in the author's possession. The leaders of several advocacy groups signed the letter, including American Conservative Union, Americans for Prosperity, Concerned Women for America, Family Research Council, and Heritage Action for America.

8. 114 Cong. Rec. S5675 (July 24, 2015).

9. 114 Cong. Rec. S5706 (July 26, 2015) (statement of Sen. Alexander).

10. 114 Cong. Rec. S5706 (July 26, 2015) (statement of Sen. Alexander).

11. 114 Cong. Rec. S5708 (July 26, 2015) (statement of Sen. Cornyn).

12. 114 Cong. Rec. S5708 (July 26, 2015) (statement of Sen. Cruz).

13. It can be inferred from the past voting behavior of Republican senators then serving in the 114th Congress that appealing the ruling of the chair, in itself, is not perceived to be synonymous with the nuclear option as used by Senate Democrats in November 2013. For example, during the period between 1987 and 2014, forty-two Republicans serving in the 114th Congress voted to overturn the chair's ruling (or against a motion to table an appeal of the chair's ruling) at least two times. Of these, thirty-seven members voted to overturn the chair's ruling (or against a tabling motion) three or more times. Seven members voted against the chair nine or more times, four did so ten or more times, and two voted to overturn the chair (or against a motion to table an appeal) fourteen times. Alexander voted to overturn the ruling of the chair (or against a tabling motion) four times. Cornyn and McConnell did so five and fourteen times, respectively.

14. 114 Cong. Rec. S5708 (July 26, 2015) (statement of Sen. Cruz).

Chapter Eleven

1. We have excluded immigration hearings from this analysis due to the low number of hearings in our data set.

Chapter Twelve

1. For a sample of such congressional indicators, see the Bipartisan Policy Center's Healthy Congress Index (Bipartisan Policy Center, n.d.) or the Pew Research Center's occasional accounting of the public law productivity (Desilver 2017).

2. House Rule XXI, clause 2; House Rule XXII, clause 5; and Senate Rule XVI prohibit the inclusion of legislative provisions in appropriations measures (Saturno, Tollestrup, and Lynch 2016).

3. House Rule XXI, sec. 2(a)(1); Senate Rule XVI, sec. 1.

4. Technically, the requirement that authorization exist before Congress appropriates funds for a program or agencies is not a constitutional or statutory obligation. Accordingly, the Government Accountability Office has long recognized that if Congress enacts appropriations without an active authorization, such funds are legally binding and can be obligated. For further discussion, see Champoux and Sullivan 2006.

5. 1 U.S.C. § 104: Numbering of sections.

6. See also Li et al. 2015, which provides a thorough overview of the evolution of the *United States Code*, both as law and as a unique language comparable to computer science language.

7. While the *Code* is very inclusive it does have some notable limitations: it does not include private laws and appropriations; "specific" legislation, such as the naming of post offices; or programs that are created and authorized for less than one year in duration.

8. See Section 327 (Office of the Legislative Counsel 1995).

9. Our sources for identifying these programs include a list from the Balanced Budget Act of 1997 as well as other programs identified in the *Federal Account Symbols and Titles (FAST) Book*, the Catalog of Federal Domestic Assistance website, various Congressional Research Service reports, and the Budget Appendix made available on the White House website. Special thanks to Molly Reynolds for generously providing us with the primary list of mandatory programs used to identify them in our data.

10. These are programs that (1) are not demonstration or pilot programs, (2) have been expired eight or more years, and (3) are not simple authorizations.

11. Section numbers vary somewhat over time as new sections are added and others are removed (or omitted).

12. "Amended" was defined by the OLRC, and we understand this to mean that the wording of the section was changed in any fashion by congressional statute.

13. Creating this measure requires summarizing expiration activity across the two sessions of a congressional term. Accordingly, we consider congressional activity occurring in either year of the term as occurring during the same period. For example, if an expiration occurs in the first year of a term—say, in 1995—but the reauthorization is not enacted until the following year (1996), we consider this activity to have occurred in the 104th Congress. For our purposes, such an example would be considered an "on time" reauthorization. If the difference between the expiration and reauthorization stretches across two years but those years are sessions of two distinct congressional terms (e.g., 1996, the second term of the 104th Congress, and 1997, the first term of the 105th Congress), that would constitute a "late" reauthorization.

14. Renewals also include those sections that contain expirations that were currently and previously repealed.

15. Thanks to Sarah Binder for providing these data.

Chapter Thirteen

The authors thank participants at the 2018 State of Congressional Capacity Conference, the 2018 American Political Science Association Conference, the 2018 Association for Public Policy Analysis and Management Conference, Emory University, University of Kentucky, and New York University, as well as Chris Den Hartog, Lee Drutman, Vlad Kogan, Tim LaPira, Tony Madonna, and anonymous reviewers for thoughtful comments. Thanks also to the "Congress and

Its Experts" undergraduate research lab at the University of Michigan (see Crosson, n.d.-a) and research assistants at James Madison University for their excellent work assembling and cleaning the staff experience data. Crosson thanks the University of Michigan Library for its Data Purchase Grant. The authors also thank the Madison Initiative of the William and Flora Hewlett Foundation, the Democracy Fund, Vanderbilt University, and the Frank Batten School at the University of Virginia for continuing support of the Center for Effective Lawmaking (www.the lawmakers.org).

1. Maintaining these types of close relations with the district is correlated with increased electoral fortunes (Romero 2006) and with more favorable constituent views toward their elected representatives (Serra 1994).

2. Over our time period, the LES ranges from 0.0 to 18.7, with a median value of 0.5 and a long rightward tail.

3. The lawmaking benefits of committee staff are likewise important and worthy of further study; see chapter 7 in this volume on this topic.

4. See Crosson, n.d.-b, for greater detail.

5. Because the staff data are available annually, we average the two years' totals to calculate this variable's values within a given Congress.

6. An additional departure from McCrain's measure derives from our means for addressing the left-censored nature of the data. That is, while McCrain uses the natural log of staff experience as his dependent variable, we simply drop the first two Congresses from our analysis (therefore beginning the analysis in the 105th Congress), as experience measurements in those first two Congresses are artificially low.

7. Staff data are available from the 103rd through 113th Congresses. However, as noted previously, we drop observations from the 103rd and 104th Congresses to limit measurement error of the independent variable of interest.

8. In table 13.3 and subsequent tables, "other controls" include the following: whether the legislator is a member of the majority party; the member's seniority (number of terms served in the House); whether the legislator is a majority leader; whether the legislator is a minority leader; whether the legislator is a committee chair; whether the legislator is a subcommittee chair; whether the legislator serves on one of the House's so-called power committees; the absolute distance between the legislator's ideological score (DW-NOMINATE) and that of the median member of the House; the size of the legislator's home state's House delegation; the vote share won in the legislator's last election, and the square thereof.

9. Specifically, the average *Total Legislative Staff Experience* for committee chairs is 13.7 years, with a standard deviation of 7.52 years. The relevant calculation for impact on LES is, therefore, the relevant regression coefficients multiplied by this standard deviation: $(-0.0006 + 0.134) \times (7.52) \approx 1.003$.

10. We do not employ legislator fixed effects in the models in tables 13.4 and 13.5, due to the limited number of terms examined. Rather, the reported results are the estimates of linear regression models, with standard errors clustered by legislator, where appropriate.

11. Freshmen have an average LES of 0.611 over the period examined here. The relevant LES calculation is therefore $(0.0131) \times (5) / 0.611 \approx 10.7$ percent. The 95 percent confidence interval around this estimate ranges from just above 0 percent to 21 percent.

12. Table 13.5 shows the results of combining all lawmakers in their first through fourth terms together into a single analysis, and interacting the *Total Legislative Staff Experience* variable with *Seniority*. Consistent with the separate models and figure 13.1, the benefits of additional staff

experience are felt for low-seniority members but diminish quickly thereafter (shown by the negative coefficient on the interaction term).

13. The relevant LES calculation is $(0.0336) \times (5) / 1.00 \approx 16.8$ percent. The 95 percent confidence interval around this estimate ranges from 5 percent to 29 percent.

14. The relevant LES calculation is $(0.0223) \times (5) / 0.818 \approx 13.6$ percent. The 95 percent confidence interval around this estimate ranges from 3 percent to 24 percent.

15. The figure is based on the empirical models discussed in the chapter.

Chapter Fourteen

1. This aligns with the "pluralist adhocracy" regime type described in chapter 2 in this volume.

2. An online appendix with information on the data and measures used in this study, as well as the interviews, can be found at https://dataverse.harvard.edu/dataverse/congressionalcapacity/.

3. These effects are estimated using multilevel mixed-effects logistic regression models that calculate random effects parameters for each Congress and for the policy area addressed by each new law. The full analyses are in the online appendix. The analyses also include a control for whether or not a law was an appropriations measure.

4. Noting the difficulty of campaigning on bipartisan compromises that required each side to get only half a loaf, Frank once conceived of the tongue-in-cheek campaign slogan, "Things would have sucked worse without me!" (Calmes 2009).

5. Interviewees were promised anonymity and thus are each identified in subsequent note references simply as "Staffer." Each interviewee is identified only by the date of the interview, and further by a number in parentheses if we interviewed multiple people on that day. Further information on the interviews is in the online appendix.

6. The senior staff interviews conducted for the CCS project were focused primarily on questions of congressional staff levels and roles. The interviews gave only limited attention to legislative processes and the shift from regular order to greater centralization. Even so, discussions of regular order did come up in some of the interviews, as will become evident in the text discussion. Like our interviewees, CCS participants also are identified only as "Staffer."

7. Staffer, December 4, 2017 (1).

8. Staffer, Congressional Capacity Interviews, docid_7.

9. Staffer, Congressional Capacity Interviews, docid_1.

10. Staffer, October 11, 2017 (1).

11. Staffer, Congressional Capacity Interviews, docid_24.

12. Staffer, Congressional Capacity Interviews, docid_1.

13. Staffer, Congressional Capacity Interviews, docid_1.

14. Staffer, October 17, 2016.

15. Staffer, December 5, 2017.

16. Staffer, October 11, 2017 (1).

17. Staffer, September 9, 2016.

18. Staffer, August 5, 2016.

19. Staffer, December 4, 2017 (4).

20. Staffer, August 2, 2016.

21. Staffer, December 4, 2017 (1).

22. Staffer, September 9, 2016.

23. Staffer, August 2, 2016.

24. Staffer, August 24, 2016.

25. Staffer, October 10, 2017 (2).

26. Staffer, October 11, 2017 (1).

27. Staffer, December 6, 2017 (2).

28. Staffer, December 5, 2017.

29. Staffer, December 4, 2017 (3).

30. Staffer, October 10, 2017 (1).

31. Staffer, December 4, 2017 (4).

32. Staffer, July 29, 2016.

33. Staffer, August 24, 2016.

34. Staffer, August 2, 2016.

35. Staffer, September 9, 2016.

36. Staffer, August 2, 2016.

37. Staffer, October 9, 2017.

38. Staffer, Congressional Capacity Interviews, docid_24.

39. Staffer, Congressional Capacity Interviews, docid_24.

40. Staffer, August 2, 2016.

41. Staffer, October 10, 2017 (2).

42. Staffer, August 2, 2016.

43. Staffer, September 9, 2016.

44. Staffer, August 24, 2016.

45. Staffer, Congressional Capacity Interviews, docid_2.

46. Staffer, September 9, 2016.

47. Staffer, August 24, 2016.

48. Staffer, August 24, 2016.

49. Staffer, October 10, 2017 (1).

50. Staffer, October 11, 2017 (3).

51. Staffer, Congressional Capacity Interviews, docid_22.

Chapter Fifteen

1. Replication files available in the Harvard Dataverse (https://doi.org/10.7910/DVN/I9 GCXV).

2. Partisan agenda setting is measured as the percentage of cosponsored bills with a House roll call vote that were partisan (less than 20 percent of the cosponsors from the party opposite the sponsor). Legislative success is the percent of House-passed bills that were enacted into law.

3. While inaction sometimes reflects party leaders' choice to pursue "messaging" bills (Lee 2016), frequent and persistent inaction across many issues risks damaging the party brand.

4. There were 327 staff who responded to the bipartisanship questions; nonresponse to other demographic measures reduces the N in subsequent regression results to 300.

5. PR-focused jobs included press secretary, communications director, and House press secretary. Since the survey was geared toward policy-focused staff, the number of PR-focused staff is relatively small. Results for all other variables in the model are similar if PR-focused staff are omitted from the analysis.

6. This variable is coded one for staffers in the Senate and zero otherwise. The zero category includes House staffers and five staffers in other categories (e.g., congressional delegation, joint committee).

7. Ideology is measured from staffer responses to five questions about agreement with various political statements about the role of government. This scale runs from -1 (liberal) to 1 (conservative), so ideological extremity is the absolute value of this measure, with higher values indicating greater extremity.

8. Respondents were asked how long they envisioned working in a position inside Congress, with response options of less than 1 year, 1–2 years, 3–5 years, 6–10 years, and more than 10 years.

9. Few institutional or demographic variables predict which staffers are more likely to focus on policy content. A logistic regression where the dependent variable is a focus on policy content and all independent variables from table 15.1 are included as regressors finds few significant effects. For communication with staff in one's own party, PR-focused staff are less likely to focus on policy content. For policy communication with staff in the other party, serving in a member's personal office (relative to committee) has a negative effect, staff tenure has a positive effect, and tenure squared has a negative effect.

Chapter Sixteen

1. Establishing a Joint Committee on the Organization of Congress, H. Con. Res. 18 § 2, 70th Cong., 1st Sess. (February 19, 1945).

2. "Executive Summary," in *Final Report of the House Members of the Joint Committee on the Organization of Congress*, 103rd Cong., 1st Sess. (Washington: GPO, 1993).

3. *Meeting of the Joint Committee on the Organization of Congress*, January 6, 1993, 103rd Cong., 1st Sess. (Washington: GPO, 1993).

4. "Executive Summary."

Chapter Seventeen

The authors would like to thank Michael Lynch, Thomas Hammond, Joel Sievert, and the Everett Dirksen Center for their support and assistance and Sarah Binder, Lee Drutman, Josh Huder, Tim LaPira, Frances Lee, Ruth Bloch Rubin, and other participants at the State of Congressional Capacity Conference for their helpful comments.

1. 88 Cong. Rec. H7697 (daily ed. October 1, 1942) (statement of Rep. Dirksen).

2. 24 Cong. Rec. H2476 (daily ed. March 2, 1893) (statement of Rep. Tillman).

3. Based on the *Congressional Record*, Senate clerks were not approved until 1884, after efforts failed by roll call votes once in 1878 and twice in 1882. House clerks were authorized during a lame-duck Congress in 1893 after failures in 1887, 1888, and 1891.

4. 113 Cong. Rec. 18165 (1967). An early example of a workload-based argument for staff resources occurred in 1893. Rep. Charles Jahleal Boatner (D-LA), argued for House clerks by suggesting "any member who concludes that he has been sent here by his constituents to consume most of his time in merely clerical work belittles the House and belittles the high office to which the people have called him" (24 Cong. Rec. H2477 [daily ed. March 2, 1893] [statement of Rep. Boatner]).

5. Opponents of staff expansion often complained about not getting recorded votes. For example, during debate over a resolution compensating committee clerks for work completed,

Rep. William Samford (D-AL) complained that it was "impossible" to get enough men to "call the yeas and nays" in many cases on these questions (7 Cong. Rec. H1879 [daily ed. June 6, 1877] [statement of Rep. Samford]).

6. Arguing in favor of the reforms, Rep. Tom Davis (R-VA) claimed they would "mean fewer staff, less taxpayer money expended on duplicative and unnecessary staff and office expenses, less bureaucracy, less gridlock, less special interest power, and more accountability to the voters" (141 Cong. Rec. H486 [daily ed. January 4, 1995] [statement of Rep. Davis]). Senate committee staff also fell by roughly a quarter (Reynolds 2017a, 2019).

7. The committee staff cuts passed 416–12, with the 12 no votes all coming from Democrats. Democrats did not reverse these staff cuts when they retook control of Congress in the 110th (2007–8) and 111th (2009–10) Congresses.

8. Lipinski, Bianco, and Work (2003) provide perhaps the only direct test, reporting that members who made positive statements about Congress received fewer votes in the 1994 election than their colleagues did.

9. An exception to the rule is leadership staff in both chambers, which have increased sharply since 1995 (Reynolds 2017a).

10. While arguing for consideration of public attitudes, Hibbing and Theiss-Morse (1995, 155) are skeptical that public support for Congress would move even after these reforms.

11. The survey was part of the 2014 Cooperative Congressional Election Study (CCES) conducted by YouGov online in two waves that year—in October and November. The sampling frame was American adults, and the sample size for these staff questions was 1,000. See also Madonna and Ostrander 2015.

12. Among our respondents, 32.87 percent selected "don't know." The distribution of antistaffing opinion was high among all ideological categories but is intuitively more pronounced in conservative respondents. When broken down across the ideological groups "liberal," "moderate," and "conservative," a substantial supermajority of the respondents in each group agree with the statement that there are too many staffers or assistants in Congress. However, the "conservative" category has the fewest number of those who disagreed or answered "don't know." These data show that the antistaffing bias exists across the political spectrum and is not isolated to those who seek smaller government.

13. When asked how the size of members of Congress' budget for congressional staff changed over the last twenty years, 187 (18.91 percent) selected "don't know." Of the remaining respondents, just 13 (or 1.62 percent) selected "decreased," 72 (7.28 percent) selected "stayed about the same," and 717 (89.4 percent) responded "increased."

14. Answers to this question varied drastically, from 0 to 1,000.

15. For example, while Republicans made staff cuts a central element of their campaign in 1994, they also focused on substantive issues such as gun control and welfare reform. It seems likely those substantive issues played a larger role in the success.

16. Members of both parties expressed this position in a series of essays edited by Crespin and Madonna (2016).

17. 88 Cong. Rec. H7700 (daily ed. October 1, 1942) (statement of Rep. Dirksen).

References

Aberbach, Joel D. 1987. "The Congressional Committee Intelligence System: Information, Oversight, and Change." *Congress and the Presidency* 14 (1): 51–76.

———. 1990. *Keeping a Watchful Eye: The Politics of Congressional Oversight*. Washington, DC: Brookings Institution Press.

Adler, E. Scott. 2002. *Why Congressional Reforms Fail: Reelection and the House Committee System*. Chicago: University of Chicago Press.

Adler, E. Scott, and John D. Wilkerson. 2012. *Congress and the Politics of Problem Solving*. New York: Cambridge University Press.

———. n.d.-a. "Codebooks and Crosswalks." Congressional Bills Project. Accessed August 11, 2019. http://www.congressionalbills.org/codebooks.html.

———. n.d.-b. Congressional Bills Project (website). Accessed August 11, 2019. http://www.congressionalbills.org/.

Aftergood, Steven. 2006. "More Turmoil at the Congressional Research Service." *Secrecy News* (blog), Federation of American Scientists. February 9. https://fas.org/blogs/secrecy/2006/02/more_turmoil_at_the_congressio/.

———. n.d. Congressional Research Service (CRS) Reports (website). Accessed August 12, 2019. https://fas.org/sgp/crs/.

Agri-Pulse. 2016. "Will the House Join the Senate in Passing a Bipartisan Energy Bill?" May 25. https://www.agri-pulse.com/articles/7031-will-the-house-join-the-senate-in-passing-a-bipartisan-energy-bill.

Aldrich, John H. 1995. *Why Parties? The Origin and Transformation of Political Parties in America*. Chicago: University of Chicago Press.

Aldrich, John H., and David W. Rohde. 1997–98. "The Transition to Republican Rule in the House: Implications for Theories of Congressional Politics." *Political Science Quarterly* 112, no. 4 (Winter): 541–69.

———. 2000a. "The Consequences of Party Organization in the House: The Role of the Majority and the Minority Parties in Conditional Party Government." In *Polarized Politics: Congress and the President in a Partisan Era*, edited by John R. Bond and Richard Fleisher, 31–72. Washington, DC: CQ Press.

———. 2000b. "The Republican Revolution and the House Appropriations Committee." *Journal of Politics* 61 (1): 1–33.

American Community Survey. n.d. "Estimates." United States Census Bureau. Accessed February 6, 2018. https://www.census.gov/topics/income-poverty/income.html.

Anderson, Sarah E., Daniel M. Butler, and Laurel Harbridge-Yong. 2020. *Rejecting Compromise: Legislators' Fear of Primary Voters.* New York: Cambridge University Press.

Anderson, Sarah E., and Jonathan Woon. 2014. "Delaying the Buck: Timing and Strategic Advantages in Executive–Legislative Bargaining over Appropriations." *Congress and the Presidency* 41:25–48.

APSA (American Political Science Association). 1950. "Toward a More Responsible Two-Party System: A Report of the Committee on Political Parties." *American Political Science Review* 44 (3): Supp.

Arendt, Hannah. 1958. *The Human Condition.* Chicago: University of Chicago Press.

Arnold, R. Douglas. 1979. *Congress and the Bureaucracy: A Theory of Influence.* New Haven, CT: Yale University Press.

———. 1990. *The Logic of Congressional Action.* New Haven, CT: Yale University Press.

Bach, Stanley, and Steven S. Smith. 1988. *Managing Uncertainty in the House of Representatives: Adaptation and Innovation in Special Rules.* Washington, DC: Brookings Institution Press.

Bachrach, Peter, and Morton S. Baratz. 1962. "Two Faces of Power." *American Political Science Review* 56, no. 4 (December 1): 947–52.

Baker, Ross K. 2015. *Is Bipartisanship Dead? A Report from the Senate.* Boulder, CO: Paradigm.

Barber, Michael, and Nolan McCarty. 2016. "Causes and Consequences of Polarization." In Mansbridge and Martin, *Political Negotiation*, 37–89.

Barkley, Frederick. 1942. "Proposes Congress Hire Owen Experts." *New York Times*, October 2.

Baumgartner, Frank R., and Bryan D. Jones. 1993. *Agendas and Instability in American Politics.* Chicago: University of Chicago Press.

———. 2015. *The Politics of Information: Problem Definition and the Course of Public Policy in America.* Chicago: University of Chicago Press.

Bawn, Kathleen. 1999. "Constructing 'Us': Ideology, Coalition Politics, and False Consciousness." *American Journal of Political Science* 43 (2): 303–34.

Bawn, Kathleen, Martin Cohen, David Karol, Seth Masket, Hans Noel, and John Zaller. 2012. "A Theory of Political Parties: Groups, Policy Demands and Nominations in American Politics." *Perspectives on Politics* 10, no. 3 (September): 571–97.

Bendix, William. 2016. "Bypassing Congressional Committees: Parties, Panel Rosters, and Deliberative Processes." *Legislative Studies Quarterly* 41 (3): 687–714.

Bensel, Richard. 2011. "Sectionalism and Congressional Development." In *The Oxford Handbook of the American Congress*, edited by Frances E. Lee, and Eric Schickler, 761–92. Oxford: Oxford University Press.

Bernhard, William, and Tracy Sulkin. 2018. *Legislative Style.* Chicago: University of Chicago Press.

Bernstein, Jonathan. 2015. "Why Are Republicans Still Bashing Congress?" *Bloomberg View*, April 15. https://www.bloomberg.com/opinion/articles/2015-04-15/why-are-republicans-still-bashing-congress-.

Berry, Christopher R., and Anthony Fowler. 2018. "Congressional Committees, Legislative Influence, and the Hegemony of Chairs." *Journal of Public Economics* 158 (2): 1–11.

BeShears, Elizabeth. 2015. "Happy Warrior: A Little-Known Alabamian Is Conservatives' Secret Weapon in DC." *Yellowhammer News*, January 20. http://yellowhammernews.com/politics-2/happy-warrior-a-little-known-alabamian-is-conservatives-secret-weapon-in-dc/.

Bessette, Joseph. 1994. *The Mild Voice of Reason: Deliberative Democracy and American National Government*. Chicago: University of Chicago Press.

Beth, Richard S., Valerie Heitshusen, Bill Heniff Jr., and Elizabeth Rybicki. 2009. "Leadership Tools for Managing the US Senate." Paper presented at the Annual Meeting of the American Political Science Association, Toronto, September 3–6.

Bhattacharya, Megha. 2017. "Congressional Pit Stop: How Legislative Dysfunction Deters Young Talent." LegBranch.org. August 3. https://www.legbranch.org/2017-8-2-congressional-pit-stop-how-legislative-dysfunction-deters-young-talent/.

Bibby, John F. 1966. "Committee Characteristics and Legislative Oversight of Administration." *Midwest Journal of Political Science* 10, no. 1 (February): 78–98.

Biggs, Jeffrey R., and Thomas S. Foley. 1999. *Honor in the House: Speaker Tom Foley*. Pullman: Washington State University.

Bimber, Bruce. 1996. *The Politics of Expertise in Congress: The Rise and Fall of the Office of Technology Assessment*. New York: State University of New York Press.

Binder, Sarah A. 1996. *Minority Rights, Majority Rule: Partisanship and the Development of Congress*. New York: Cambridge University Press.

———. 2003. *Stalemate: Causes and Consequences of Legislative Gridlock*. Washington, DC: Brookings Institution Press.

———. 2014. *Polarized We Govern?* Washington, DC: Center for Effective Public Management, Brookings Institution.

———. 2016. "Legislating in Polarized Times." In *Congress Reconsidered*, 11th ed., edited by Lawrence C. Dodd and Bruce I. Oppenheimer, 189–206. Washington, DC: CQ Press.

Binder, Sarah A., and Steven E. Smith. 1997. *Politics or Principle? Filibustering in the United States Senate*. Washington, DC: Brookings Institution Press.

Bipartisan Policy Center. 2014. *Governing in a Polarized America: A Bipartisan Blueprint to Strengthen Our Democracy*. Washington, DC: Bipartisan Policy Center.

———. n.d. "Healthy Congress Index." Accessed February 16, 2018. https://bipartisanpolicy.org/congress/?cldee=Ymh1ZG51dEBiaXBhcnRpc2FucG9saWN5Lm9yZw==&recipientid=contact-c831603db28fe61180c100155d47857d-7fa71afa794143d1818ac2124ec838d8.

Black, Duncan. 1958. *The Theory of Committees and Elections*. New York: Cambridge University Press.

Blackburn, Marsha. 2014. "332 Bills #StuckInTheSenate." Twitter, July 25, 11:39 a.m. https://twitter.com/MarshaBlackburn/status/492695577407541248.

Blair, Peter D. 2013. *Congress's Own Think Tank: Learning from the Legacy of the Office of Technology Assessment*. New York: Palgrave.

Blanes i Vidal, Jordi, Mirko Draca, and Christian Fons-Rosen. 2012. "Revolving Door Lobbyists." *American Economic Review* 102, no. 7 (December): 3731–48.

Bloch Rubin, Ruth. 2017. *Building the Bloc: Intraparty Organization in the US Congress*. New York: Cambridge University Press.

BLS (Bureau of Labor Statistics). 2019. "CPI Research Using Current Methods (CPI-U-RS)." Consumer Price Index. Last modified July 16. https://www.bls.gov/cpi/research-series/home.htm.

Bolling, Richard Walker. 1965. *House Out of Order*. New York: Dutton.

Bordewich, Fergus M. 2016. *The First Congress: How James Madison, George Washington, and a Group of Extraordinary Men Invented the Government*. New York: Simon and Schuster.

Bowman, Bridget. 2015. "Flat Funding Could Hurt Congressional Research Service." *Roll Call*, April 28.

Brady, David W. 1981. "Personnel Management in the House." In *The House at Work*, edited by Joseph Cooper and G. Calvin Mackenzie, 151–82. Austin: University of Texas Press.

Brady, David W., and Craig Volden. 2006. *Revolving Gridlock*. 2nd ed. Boulder, CO: Westview Press.

Brookings Institution. 2019. *Vital Statistics on Congress*. Last updated March 4. https://www.brookings.edu/multi-chapter-report/vital-statistics-on-congress/.

Browne, William P. 1990. "Organized Interests and Their Issue Niches: A Search for Pluralism in a Policy Domain." *Journal of Politics* 52, no. 2 (May 1): 477–509.

Brudnick, Ida A. 2009. *Members' Representational Allowance: History and Usage*. CRS Report R40962. Congressional Research Service. December 1. https://www.everycrsreport.com/files/20091201_R40962_39e52a233c07043a9f1f04a71b9f056cfb867109.pdf.

———. 2014. "Congressional Staffing: The Continuity of Change and Reform." In *The Evolving Congress*, by Committee on Rules and Administration, United States Senate, 145–62. S. Prt. 113-30, December. Washington, DC: GPO. https://www.govinfo.gov/content/pkg/CPRT-113SPRT89394/html/CPRT-113SPRT89394.htm.

———. 2016a. *Congressional Salaries and Allowance: In Brief*. CRS Report RL30064. Congressional Research Service. Published July 14, 2016; updated April 11, 2018. https://crsreports.congress.gov/product/pdf/RL/RL30064.

———. 2016b. *Legislative Branch: FY2016 Appropriations*. CRS Report R44029. Congressional Research Service. February 1. https://crsreports.congress.gov/product/pdf/R/R44029.

———. 2016c. *Senators' Official Personnel and Office Expense Account (SOPOEA): History and Usage*. CRS Report R44399. Congressional Research Service. Updated February 25. https://crsreports.congress.gov/product/pdf/R/R44399.

[———]. 2017. *Members' Representational Allowance: History and Usage*. CRS Report R40962. Congressional Research Service. Updated September 27. https://www.everycrsreport.com/files/20170927_R40962_68dcd9011a6251f50670f7d385d26e76cc3c96d4.pdf.

Burgat, Casey. 2017. "Among House Staff, Women Are Well Represented: Just Not in the Senior Positions." *Washington Post*, June 20.

Butler, Daniel M., and Eleanor Neff Powell. 2014. "Understanding the Party Brand: Experimental Evidence on the Role of Valence." *Journal of Politics* 76 (2): 492–505.

Cain, Bruce E., and Lee Drutman. 2014. "Congressional Staff and the Revolving Door: The Impact of Regulatory Change." *Election Law Journal: Rules, Politics, and Policy* 13 (1): 27–44.

Cain, Bruce, John Ferejohn, and Morris Fiorina. 1987. *The Personal Vote: Constituency Service and Electoral Independence*. Cambridge, MA: Harvard University Press.

Calmes, Jackie. 2009. "The Comedy Duo of Palin and Frank." *New York Times*, December 6.

Calvert, Randall L. 1995. "The Rational Choice Theory of Social Institutions: Cooperation, Coordination, and Communication." In *Modern Political Economy: Old Topics, New Directions*, edited by Jeffrey S. Banks and Eric A. Hanushek, 216–67. New York: Cambridge University Press.

Carpenter, Daniel. 2001. *The Forging of Bureaucratic Autonomy: Reputations, Networks, and Policy Innovation in Executive Agencies, 1862–1928*. Princeton, NJ: Princeton University Press.

———. 2005a. "The Evolution of National Bureaucracy in the United States." In *The Executive Branch*, edited by Joel D. Aberbach and Mark A. Peterson, 41–71. New York: Oxford University Press.

———. 2005b. *The Forging of Bureaucratic Autonomy, Reputations, Networks, and Policy Innovation in Executive Agencies, 1862–1928*. Princeton, NJ: Princeton University Press.

Carpenter, Daniel, and Keith Whittington. 2003. "Executive Power in American Political Development." *Perspectives on Politics* 1, no. 3 (September): 495–513.

Carter, Susan B., Scott Sigmund Gartner, Michael R. Haines, Alan L. Olmstead, Richard Sutch, and Gavin Wright. 2006. *Historical Statistics of the United States: Earliest Times to the Present.* Millennial edition. 5 vols. New York: Cambridge University Press.

CBO (Congressional Budget Office). 2015. *Congressional Budget Office, Unauthorized Appropriations and Expired Authorizations.* Report No. 49871. Washington, DC: CBO. January 15. https://www.cbo.gov/publication/49871.

———. 2016. *An Introduction to the Congressional Budget Office.* Washington, DC: CBO. July. https://www.cbo.gov/sites/default/files/cbofiles/attachments/2016-IntroToCBO.pdf.

Chambers, Simone. 2003. "Deliberative Democratic Theory." *Annual Review of Political Science* 6:307–26.

Champoux, Mark, and Dan Sullivan. 2006. "Authorizations and Appropriations: A Distinction without Difference?" Briefing paper, Federal Budget Policy Seminar, Harvard Law School, Cambridge, MA.

Chantrill, Christopher. n.d. "US Spending." US Government Spending (website). Accessed August 30, 2019. https://www.usgovernmentspending.com.

Chausow, Lara E., R. Eric Petersen, and Amber Hope Wilhelm. 2016a. *House Staff Levels in Member, Committee, Leadership, and Other Offices 1977–2016.* CRS Report R43947. Updated September 13. https://crsreports.congress.gov/product/pdf/R/R43947.

———. 2016b. *Senate Staff Levels in Member, Committee, Leadership, and Other Offices 1977–2016.* CRS Report R43946. Updated September 13. https://crsreports.congress.gov/product/pdf/R/R43946.

Chubb, John E., and Paul E. Peterson, eds. 1989. *Can the Government Govern?* Washington, DC: Brookings Institution Press.

Clarke, Andrew J. 2017. "Congressional Capacity and the Abolition of Legislative Service Organizations." Paper presented at the Annual Meeting of the Midwest Political Science Association, Chicago, April 6–9.

Committee on Appropriations, US House of Representatives. 2010. *Legislative Branch Appropriations for 2011: Part 1: Justification of the Budget Estimates.* Washington, DC: GPO. https://babel.hathitrust.org/cgi/pt?id=uc1.31210022612715&view=1up&seq=7.

Committee on House Administration, US House of Representatives. 2012. *A History of the Committee on House Administration, 1947–2012.* Washington, DC: GPO. https://www.govinfo.gov/content/pkg/CPRT-112HPRT72170/pdf/CPRT-112HPRT72170.pdf.

Comparative Agendas Project. n.d. "CAP Topics." Accessed August 6, 2019. http://www.comparativeagendas.net/pages/master-codebook.

Conde, James, and Michael Greve. 2015. "*Yakus* and the Administrative State." George Mason Legal Studies Research Paper No. LS 15-43, George Mason University, Fairfax, VA, December 3. https://papers.ssrn.com/sol3/Papers.cfm?abstract_id=2698833.

"Congress Cuts Legislative Funds." 1996. *CQ Almanac 1995*, 51st ed. Washington, DC: Congressional Quarterly, 11-61–11-65.

Congressional Hispanic Staff Association. 2010. *Unrepresented: A Blueprint for Solving the Diversity Crisis on Capitol Hill.* Washington, DC: Congressional Hispanic Staff Association, February. http://media.washingtonpost.com/wp-srv/politics/documents/diversity_on_the_hill_report.pdf.

Congressional Management Foundation. 2004. *2004 House Staff Employment Study.* Washington, DC: Congressional Management Foundation. http://www.congressfoundation.org/component/content/article/41.

———. 2005. *Communicating with Congress: How Capitol Hill Is Coping with the Surge in Citizen Advocacy.* Washington, DC: Congressional Management Foundation. http://www.con gressfoundation.org/storage/documents/CMF_Pubs/cwc_capitolhillcoping.pdf.

———. 2011. *Communicating with Congress: How Citizen Advocacy Is Changing Mail Operations on Capitol Hill.* Washington, DC: Congressional Management Foundation. http://www.congress foundation.org/projects/communicating-with-congress/how-citizen-advocacy-is-changing -mail-operations-on-capitol-hill.

———. n.d. "Senate Staff Employment Data: 1991–2001." Accessed August 5, 2019. http://www .congressfoundation.org/component/content/article/26.

Connelly, William, John Pitney, and Gary Schmitt, eds. 2017. *Is Congress Broken? The Virtues and Defects of Partisanship and Gridlock.* Washington, DC: Brookings Institution.

Cooper, Joseph. 1970. *Origins of the Standing Committees and the Development of the Modern House.* Houston, TX: Rice University Press.

Cooper, Joseph, and David W. Brady. 1981. "Institutional Context and Leadership Style: The House from Cannon to Rayburn." *American Political Science Review* 75 (2): 411–25.

Cox, Gary W., and Mathew D. McCubbins. 1993. *Legislative Leviathan: Party Government in the House.* New York: Cambridge University Press.

———. 2005. *Setting the Agenda: Responsible Party Government in the US House of Representatives.* New York: Cambridge University Press.

CQ Magazine. 2017. "Bad News for Cash-Strapped Congressional Staffers." June 19.

Crawford, Sue E. S., and Elinor Ostrom. 1995. "A Grammar of Institutions." *American Political Science Review* 89, no. 3 (September): 582–600.

Crespin, Michael H., and Anthony J. Madonna. 2016. "New Directions in Legislative Research: Lessons from Inside Congress." *PS: Political Science and Politics* 49 (3): 473–77.

Crespin, Michael H, David W. Rohde, and Ryan J. Vander Wielen. 2013. "Measuring Variations in Party Unity Voting: An Assessment of Agenda Effects." *Party Politics* 19 (3): 432–57.

Crosson, Jesse M. n.d.-a. "Collaborators and Research Assistants." Jesse M. Crosson (website). Accessed August 23, 2019. https://jessemcrosson.com/collaborators-and-research-assistants/.

———. n.d.-b. "Papers and Projects." Jesse M. Crosson (website). Accessed August 23, 2019. http://www.jessemcrosson.com/research.

Crosson, Jesse M., Zander Furnas, and Timothy LaPira. 2018. *Congress and Its Experts.* University of Michigan electronic data set.

CRS (Congressional Research Service). 1976. *Annual Report of the Congressional Research Service of the Library of Congress for Fiscal Year 1975.* Washington, DC: Congressional Research Service.

———. 2009. *The Budget Resolution and Spending Legislation.* CRS Report R40472. Washington, DC: CRS.

———. 2017. *CRS Annual Report: Fiscal Year 2016.* Washington, DC: CRS.

———. n.d. "Appropriations Status Table." Accessed September 25, 2019. https://crsreports.con gress.gov/AppropriationsStatusTable.

Curry, James M. 2015. *Legislating in the Dark: Information and Power in the House of Representatives.* Chicago: University of Chicago Press.

Curry, James, and Frances Lee. 2019a. "Congress at Work: Legislative Capacity and Entrepreneurship in the Contemporary Congress." In Lee and McCarty, *Can America Govern Itself?*, 181–219.

Curry, James M., and Frances E. Lee. 2019b. "Non-Party Government: Bipartisan Lawmaking and Party Power in Congress." *Perspectives on Politics* 17 (1): 47–65.

Cyert, Richard M., and James G. March. 1963. *A Behavioral Theory of the Firm*. Englewood Cliffs, NJ: Prentice-Hall.

Dahl, Robert Alan. 1961. *Who Governs? Democracy and Power in an American City*. New Haven, CT: Yale University Press.

Davidson, Roger H. 1990. "The Advent of the Modern Congress: The Legislative Reorganization Act of 1946." *Legislative Studies Quarterly* 15, no. 3 (August): 357–73.

Davidson, Roger H., and Walter Oleszek. 1977. *Congress against Itself*. Bloomington: Indiana University Press.

Davis, Tom, Martin Frost, and Richard E Cohen. 2014. *The Partisan Divide: Congress in Crisis*. Campbell, CA: Premiere.

Deering, Christopher J., and Steven S. Smith. 1997. *Committees in Congress*. 3rd ed. Washington, DC: CQ Press.

DeGregorio, Christine. 1988. "Professionals in Congress: An Analysis of Working Styles." *Legislative Studies Quarterly* 13 (November): 459–76.

———. 1995. "Staff Utilization in the US Congress: Committee Chairs and Senior Aides." *Polity* 28 (2): 261–75.

———. 1996. *Networks of Champions: Leadership, Access, and Advocacy in the US House of Representatives*. Ann Arbor: University of Michigan Press.

DeMuth, Christopher Sr. 2016. "Can the Administrative State Be Tamed?" *Journal of Legal Analysis* 8 (June): 121–90.

Den Hartog, Chris, and Nathan W. Monroe. 2011. *Agenda Setting in the US Senate: Costly Consideration and Majority Party Advantage*. New York: Cambridge University Press.

Dennison, Mike. 2012a. "Ad Watch: Ad against Rehberg Fudges on 'Voted for' Pay Raises Analysis." *Missoulian*, March 24.

———. 2012b. "Ad Watch: Rehberg Ad Accuses Tester of Peddling 'Baloney.'" *Billings Gazette*, September 23.

Desai, Saahil. 2018. "When Congress Paid Its Interns." *Washington Monthly*, January/February/March. https://washingtonmonthly.com/magazine/january-february-march-2018/when-congress-paid-its-interns/.

Desilver, Drew. 2017. "Congressional Productivity Is Up but Many New Laws Overturn Obama-era Rules." *FactTank* (blog), Pew Research Center. August 29. http://www.pewresearch.org/fact-tank/2017/08/29/115th-congress-productivity/.

Dickson, Cecil B. 1942. "Congress Let Power Slip, Dirksen Says." *Washington Post*, October 2.

Diermeier, Daniel, and Timothy J. Feddersen. 2000. "Information and Congressional Hearings." *American Journal of Political Science* 44, no. 1 (January): 51–65. https://doi.org/10.2307/2669292.

DiIulio, John. 2014. *Bring Back the Bureaucrats*. Philadelphia: Templeton Press.

Dodd, Lawrence C. 1977. "Congress and the Quest for Power." In *Congress Reconsidered*, edited by Lawrence C. Dodd and Bruce Oppenheimer. Washington, DC: CQ Press.

———. 1986. "The Cycles of Legislative Change: Building a Dynamic Theory." In *Political Science: The Science of Politics*, edited by H. F. Weisberg, 82–104. New York: Agathon Press.

———. 2012. Th*inking About Congress: Essays on Congressional Change*. New York: Routledge.

Drutman, Lee. 2015. *The Business of America Is Lobbying: How Corporations Became Politicized and Politics Became More Corporate*. New York: Oxford University Press.

———. 2016. *Political Dynamism: A New Approach to Making Government Work Again.* Washington, DC: New America.

———. 2017. "House Leadership Has Been Writing Bills behind Closed Doors for Years." *Vox*, March 3. https://www.vox.com/polyarchy/2017/3/3/14805112/house-bills-secretive-history.

Drutman, Lee, Alexander Furnas, Alexander Hertel-Fernandez, Kevin Kosar, and Timothy M. LaPira. 2017a. "2017 Congressional Capacity Staff Interviews." James Madison University. https://dataverse.harvard.edu/dataverse/congressionalcapacity/.

———. 2017b. 2017 Congressional Capacity Staff Survey, CCS_2017_1.3. James Madison University. https://dataverse.harvard.edu/dataverse/congressionalcapacity/.

Drutman, Lee, and Peter Hanson. 2019. "Does Regular Order Produce a More Deliberative Congress? Evidence from the Annual Appropriations Process." In Lee and McCarty, *Can America Govern Itself?*, 155–80.

Drutman, Lee, and Steven Teles. 2015a. "A New Agenda for Political Reform." *Washington Monthly*, March/April/May.

———. 2015b. "Why Congress Relies on Lobbyists Instead of Thinking for Itself." *Atlantic*, March 10. https://www.theatlantic.com/politics/archive/2015/03/when-congress-cant-think-for-itself-it-turns-to-lobbyists/387295/.

Dwyer, Paul, Lorraine Tong, David Huckabee, and Taeku Lee. 1996. *Legislative Branch Budget Authority, FY 1968–FY 1996.* CRS Report 96-201 GOV. Washington, DC. March 22.

Eagly, Alice H., and Linda L. Carli. 2003. "The Female Leadership Advantage: An Evaluation of the Evidence." *Leadership Quarterly* 14 (6): 807–34.

Edwards, George C., III, Andrew Barrett, and Jeffrey Peake. 1997. "The Legislative Impact of Divided Government." *American Journal of Political Science* 41, no. 2 (April): 545–63.

Eguia, Jon X., and Kenneth A. Shepsle. 2015. "Legislative Bargaining with Endogenous Rules." *Journal of Politics* 77, no. 4 (October): 1076–88.

Endicott, Gary. 2016. "Changes in Legislative Drafting and Procedure in the US Senate over the Last 30 Years." *Loophole: Journal of the Commonwealth Association of Legislative Counsel*, no. 2 (May): 23–28.

Epstein, David, and Sharyn O'Halloran. 1999. *Delegating Powers: A Transaction Cost Politics Approach to Policy Making under Separate Powers.* New York: Cambridge University Press.

Esterling, Kevin. 2018. "Constructing and Repairing our Bridges: Statistical Considerations When Placing Agents into Legislative Preference Space." Working paper, University of California–Riverside. March. https://www.researchgate.net/publication/322644908_Constructing_and_Repairing_our_Bridges_Statistical_Considerations_When_Placing_Agents_into_Legislative_Preference_Space.

Evans, C. Lawrence. 2018. *The Whips: Building Party Coalitions in Congress.* Ann Arbor: University of Michigan Press.

Evans, C. Lawrence, and Walter Oleszek. 1997. *Congress under Fire: Reform Politics and the Republican Majority.* Boston: Houghton Mifflin.

———. 1999. "The Strategic Context of Congressional Party Leadership." *Congress and the Presidency: A Journal of Capital Studies* 26 (1): 1–20.

———. 2001. "Message Politics and Senate Procedure." In *The Contentious Senate: Partisanship, Ideology, and the Myth of Cool Judgment*, edited by Colton C. Campbell and Nicol C. Rae, 107–28. Lanham, MD: Rowman and Littlefield.

Faler, Brian. 2017. "'Holy Crap': Experts Find Tax Plan Riddled with Glitches." *Politico*, December 6. http://www.politico.com/story/2017/12/06/tax-plan-glitches-mistakes-republicans-208049.

Federal Acquisition Institute. 2013. *FY 2012 Annual Report on the Federal Acquisition Workforce.* December 17. https://www.fai.gov/sites/default/files/FY%202012%20Annual%20Report%20 on%20the%20Federal%20Acquisition%20Workforce.pdf.

Federal Procurement Data System. 2017. *Top 100 Contractors Report, Fiscal Year 2016.* Washington, DC: Federal Procurement Data System.

Federation of American Scientists. n.d. "OTA Publications." Office of Technology Assessment Archive. https://ota.fas.org/otareports/.

Fenno, Richard F. 1962. "The House Appropriations Committee as a Political System: The Problem of Integration." *American Political Science Review* 56 (2): 310–24.

———. 1966. *The Power of the Purse: Appropriations Politics in Congress.* Boston: Little, Brown.

———. 1973. *Congressmen in Committees.* Boston: Little, Brown.

———. 1978. *Home Style: Representatives in Their Districts.* Boston: Little, Brown.

Finocchiaro, Charles J., and David W. Rohde. 2008. "War for the Floor: Partisan Theory and Agenda Control in the US House of Representatives." *Legislative Studies Quarterly* 33 (1): 35–61.

Fiorina, Morris P. 1989. *Congress: Keystone of the Washington Establishment.* 2nd ed. New Haven, CT: Yale University Press.

Fiorina, Morris P., Samuel Abrams, and Jeremy Pope. 2005. *Culture War? The Myth of a Polarized America.* New York: Pearson Longman.

Forgette, Richard. 2004. "Party Caucuses and Coordination: Assessing Caucus Activity and Party Effects." *Legislative Studies Quarterly* 29, no. 3 (August): 407–30.

Fort Collins Coloradan. 2010. "Local Briefs: Sheriff Plans Forum to Discuss Budget Concerns." July 30.

Fox, Harrison W., and Susan Webb Hammond. 1977. *Congressional Staffs: The Invisible Force in American Lawmaking.* New York: Free Press.

Fox, Richard, and Zoe Oxley. 2003. "Gender Stereotyping in State Executive Elections: Candidate Selection and Success." *Journal of Politics* 65 (3): 833–50.

Francis, Katherine, and Brittany Bramlett. 2017. "Precongressional Careers and Committees: The Impact of Congruence." *American Politics Research* 45 (5): 755–89.

Friedman, Sally, and Robert T. Nakamura. 1991. "The Representation of Women on US Senate Committee Staffs." *Legislative Studies Quarterly* 16, no. 3 (August): 407–27.

Fund, John. 2007. "Earmark Cover-up." *Wall Street Journal,* March 26.

Galloway, George B. 1946. *Congress at the Crossroads.* New York: Thomas Y. Crowell.

———. 1951. "The Operation of the Legislative Reorganization Act of 1946." *American Political Science Review* 45 (1): 41–68.

———. 1953. *The Legislative Process in Congress.* New York: Thomas Y. Crowell.

Galston, William A. 2010. *Can a Polarized System Be Healthy?* Issues in Governance Studies 34. Washington, DC: Brookings Institution.

Galvin, Daniel J. 2012. "The Transformation of Political Institutions: Investments in Institutional Resources and Gradual Change in the National Party Committees." *Studies in American Political Development* 26 (1): 50–70.

Gangitano, Alex. 2016. "The Sisterhood of the Capitol Hill Staffers." *Roll Call.* December 7. https://www.rollcall.com/hoh/the-sisterhood-of-the-capitol-hill-staffers.

GAO (Government Accountability Office). 2016. *Performance and Accountability Report: Fiscal Year 2016.* Report no. GAO-17-1SP. November 15. https://www.gao.gov/assets/690/681058 .pdf; see also https://www.gao.gov/products/GAO-17-1SP.

———. 2017. *Performance and Accountability Report: Fiscal Year 2017*. Washington, DC: Government Accountability Office. Report no. GAO-18-2sp. November 15. https://www.gao.gov/assets/690/688372.pdf.

———. n.d.-a. "Congressional Review Act." GAO. Accessed May 1, 2018. https://www.gao.gov/legal/other-legal-work/congressional-review-act.

———. n.d.-b. "GAO at a Glance." GAO. Accessed May 1, 2018. https://www.gao.gov/about/gglance.html.

———. n.d.-c. "The History of GAO: The Early Years." GAO. Accessed May 1, 2018. https://www.gao.gov/about/history/earlyyears.html.

Gelman, Jeremy, Gilad Wilkenfeld, and E. Scott Adler. 2015. "The Opportunistic President: How US Presidents Determine Their Legislative Programs." *Legislative Studies Quarterly* 40 (3): 363–90.

Gilligan, Thomas W., and Keith Krehbiel. 1990. "Organization of Informative Committees by a Rational Legislature." *American Journal of Political Science* 34 (2): 531–64.

Glassman, Matthew. 2012. "Congressional Leadership: A Resource Perspective." In *Party and Procedure in the United States Congress*, edited by Jacob R. Straus, 15–32. Lanham, MD: Rowman and Littlefield.

Glastris, Paul, and Haley S. Edwards. 2014. "The Big Lobotomy." *Washington Monthly*, June.

Goldschmidt, Kathy. 2017. *State of the Congress: Staff Perspectives on Institutional Capacity in the House and Senate*. Washington, DC: Congressional Management Foundation.

Graves, Zach, and Kevin R. Kosar. 2018. "Bring in the Nerds: Reviving the Office of Technology Assessment." *R Street Policy Study*, no. 128 (January): 1–11. R Street Institute. http://2o9ub0417c hl2lg6m43em6psi2i.wpengine.netdna-cdn.com/wp-content/uploads/2018/01/Final-128.pdf.

Green, Matthew, and Daniel Burns. 2010. "What Might Bring Regular Order Back to the House?" *PS: Political Science and Politics* 43 (2): 223–26.

Grimmer, Justin. 2013. *Representational Style in Congress: What Legislators Say and Why It Matters*. New York: Cambridge University Press.

Grodzins, Morton. 1966. *The American System: A New View of Government in the United States*. Chicago: Rand McNally.

Grose, Christian R., Maurice Mangum, and Christopher Martin. 2007. "Race, Political Empowerment and Constituency Service: Descriptive Representation and the Hiring of African American Congressional Staff." *Polity* 39, no. 4 (September): 449–78.

Gross, Bertram M. 1953. *The Legislative Struggle: A Study in Social Conflict*. New York: McGraw-Hill.

Gutmann, Amy, and Dennis F. Thompson. 1998. *Democracy and Disagreement*. Cambridge, MA: Harvard University Press.

Hacker, Jacob S. 2005. "Policy Drift: The Hidden Politics of US Welfare State Retrenchment." In *Beyond Continuity: Institutional Change in Advanced Economies*, edited by Wolfgang Streeck and Kathleen Thelen, 40–82. Oxford: Oxford University Press.

Hacker, Jacob S., Paul Pierson, and Kathleen Thelen. 2015. "Drift and Conversion: Hidden Faces of Institutional Change." In *Advances in Comparative-Historical Analysis*, edited by James Mahoney and Kathleen Thelen, 180–208. New York: Cambridge University Press.

Haeberle, Steven H. 1978. "The Institutionalization of the Subcommittee in the United States House of Representatives." *Journal of Politics* 40, no. 4 (November): 1054–65.

Hall, Keith. 2016. "Statement for the Record: CBO's Appropriation Request for Fiscal Year 2017." Congressional Budget Office. March 22. https://www.cbo.gov/system/files/2018-10/51372-bud getstatementfortherecord.pdf.

Hall, Richard L. 1993. "Participation, Abdication, and Representation in Congressional Committees." In *Congress Reconsidered*, 5th ed., edited by Lawrence C. Dodd and Bruce I. Oppenheimer. Washington, DC: CQ Press.

———. 1996. *Participation in Congress*. New Haven, CT: Yale University Press.

Hall, Richard L., and Alan V. Deardorff. 2006. "Lobbying as Legislative Subsidy." *American Political Science Review* 100, no. 1 (February): 69–84.

Hall, Thad E. 2004. *Authorizing Policy*. Columbus: Ohio State University Press.

Hansen, John Mark. 1991. *Gaining Access: Congress and the Farm Lobby, 1919–1981*. Chicago: University of Chicago Press.

Hanson, Peter. 2014a. "Abandoning the Regular Order: Majority Party Influence on Appropriations in the US Senate." *Political Research Quarterly* 67 (3): 519–32.

———. 2014b. *Too Weak to Govern: Majority Party Power and Appropriations in the US Senate*. New York: Cambridge University Press.

———. 2016. "The Endurance of Nonpartisanship in House Appropriations." In *Congress Reconsidered*, 11th ed., edited by Lawrence Dodd and Bruce Oppenheimer. Washington, DC: CQ Press.

———. 2017. "Ending the Omnibus: Restoring Regular Order in Congressional Appropriations." In Connelly, Pitney, and Schmitt, *Is Congress Broken?*, 175–88.

Harbridge, Laurel. 2015. *Is Bipartisanship Dead? Policy Agreement and Agenda-Setting in the House of Representatives*. New York: Cambridge University Press.

Harbridge-Yong, Laurel. 2019. "Replication Data for Congressional Capacity and Bipartisanship in Congress." Harvard Dataverse, V1, UNF:6:Kd/61WGBw+Wa8gg7Iqot6w== [fileUNF]. https://doi.org/10.7910/DVN/I9GCXV.

Heaney, Michael T. 2004. "Outside the Issue Niche: The Multidimensionality of Interest Group Identity." *American Politics Research* 32, no. 6 (November 1): 611–51.

Heclo, Hugh. 1978. "Issue Networks and the Executive Establishment." In *The New American Political System*, edited by Anthony King, 87–121. Washington, DC: American Enterprise Institute Press.

Heinz, John P., Edward O. Laumann, Robert L. Nelson, and Robert H. Salisbury. 1993. *The Hollow Core: Private Interests in National Policy Making*. Cambridge, MA: Harvard University Press.

Heitshusen, Valerie, and Garry Young. 2006. "Macropolitics and Changes in the US Code: Testing Competing Theories of Policy Production, 1874–1946." In *The Macropolitics of Congress*, edited by E. Scott Adler and John Lapinski, 129–50. Princeton, NJ: Princeton University Press.

Heniff, Bill, Jr. 2015. *Congressional Budget Resolutions: Historical Information*. CRS Report RL30297. Washington, DC: Congressional Research Service.

Hibbing, John R., and Elizabeth Theiss-Morse. 1995. *Congress as Public Enemy: Public Attitudes toward American Political Institutions*. Cambridge: Cambridge University Press.

Higgs, Robert. 1987. *Crisis and Leviathan*. New York: Oxford University Press.

Hofstadter, Richard. 1966. *Anti-Intellectualism in American Life*. New York: Vintage.

Hopkins, Daniel J. 2018. *The Increasingly United States: How and Why American Political Behavior Nationalized*. Chicago: University of Chicago Press.

House Republicans. 2014. "#StuckInTheSenate." August 5. http://www.gop.gov/media/stuckinthe senate/.

Howell, William, Scott Adler, Charles Cameron, and Charles Riemann. 2000. "Divided Government and the Legislative Productivity of Congress, 1945–94." *Legislative Studies Quarterly* 25, no. 2 (May): 285–312.

Howell, William, and Terry Moe. 2016. *Relic: How Our Constitution Undermines Effective Government—And Why We Need a More Powerful Presidency*. New York: Basic Books.

Huber, George P. 1991. "Organizational Learning: The Contributing Processes and the Literatures." *Organization Science* 2, no. 1 (February): 88–115.

Huber, John, and Charles R. Shipan. 2002. *Deliberate Discretion?* New York: Cambridge University Press.

Hudak, John. 2013. "Congress, the Affordable Care Act, and the Myth of the 'Exemption.'" *Brookings Blog*, Brookings Institution. October 4. https://www.brookings.edu/blog/fixgov/2013/10/04 /congress-the-affordable-care-act-and-the-myth-of-the-exemption/.

Huntsman, Jon, and Joe Manchin, eds. 2014. *No Labels: A Shared Vision for a Stronger America*. New York: Diversion Books.

Jenkins, Jeffery A. 1998. "Property Rights and the Emergence of Standing Committee Dominance in the Nineteenth-Century House." *Legislative Studies Quarterly* 23 (4): 493–519.

Jenkins, Jeffery A., and Charles Stewart III. 2018. "The Deinstitutionalization (?) of the House of Representatives: Reflections on Nelson Polsby's 'Institutionalization of the House of Representatives' at Fifty." *Studies in American Political Development* 32 (2): 166–87.

Jenkins-Smith, Hank C., Gilbert K. St. Clair, and Brian Woods. 1991. "Explaining Change in Policy Subsystems: Analysis of Coalition Stability and Defection over Time." *American Journal of Political Science* 35, no. 4 (November): 851–80.

Jensen, Jennifer M. 2011. "Explaining Congressional Staff Members' Decisions to Leave the Hill." *Congress and the Presidency* 38 (1): 39–59.

Jochim, Ashley E., and Bryan D. Jones. 2013. "Issue Politics in a Polarized Congress." *Political Research Quarterly* 66 (2): 352–69.

Johannes, John R., and John C. McAdams. 1981. "The Congressional Incumbency Effect: Is It Casework, Policy Compatibility, or Something Else? An Examination of the 1978 Election." *American Journal of Political Science* 25 (3): 512–42.

John, Richard R. 1998. *Spreading the News: The American Postal System from Franklin to Morse*. Cambridge, MA: Harvard University Press.

Joint Center for Political and Economic Studies. 2015. *Diversity among Top Senate Staff*. Washington, DC: Joint Center for Political and Economic Studies.

Jones, Bryan D. 1994. *Reconceiving Decision-Making in Democratic Politics: Attention, Choice, and Public Policy*. Chicago: University of Chicago Press.

———. 2001. *Politics and the Architecture of Choice: Bounded Rationality and Governance*. Chicago: University of Chicago Press.

Jones, Bryan D., Sean M. Theriault, and Michelle Whyman. 2019. *The Great Broadening: How the Vast Expansion of the Policymaking Agenda Transformed American Politics*. Chicago: University of Chicago Press.

Jones, Charles O. 1975. "Somebody Must Be Trusted: An Essay on Leadership of the US Congress." In *Congress in Change: Evolution and Reform*, edited by Norman J. Ornstein. New York: Praeger.

Jones, David R. 2010. "Partisan Polarization and Congressional Accountability in House Elections." *American Journal of Political Science* 54 (2): 323–37.

Joyce, Philip G. 2011. *The Congressional Budget Office: Honest Numbers, Power, and Policymaking*. Washington, DC: Georgetown University Press.

Kaiser, Frederick. 2008. *GAO: Government Accountability Office and General Accounting Office*. CRS Report RL30349. September 10. https://www.everycrsreport.com/reports/RL30349.html.

Kaiser, Robert G. 2013. *Act of Congress: How America's Essential Institution Works, and How It Doesn't*. New York: Alfred A. Knopf.

Kanwisher, Nancy. 1989. "Cognitive Heuristics and American Security Policy." *Journal of Conflict Resolution* 33 (4): 652–75.

Katzmann, Robert A. 1989. "The American Legislative Process as a Signal." *Journal of Public Policy* 9, no. 3 (July–September): 287–306.

Katznelson, Ira. 2014. *Fear Itself: The New Deal and the Origins of Our Time*. New York: Liveright.

Keiper, Adam. 2004–5. "Science and Congress." *New Atlantis*, no. 7 (Fall–Winter): 19–50. https://www.thenewatlantis.com/docLib/TNA07-Keiper.pdf.

Kelly, Sean Q. 1993. "Divided We Govern? A Reassessment." *Polity* 25 (3): 475–84.

Kiewiet, D. Roderick, and Mathew D. McCubbins. 1991. *The Logic of Delegation: Congressional Parties and the Appropriations Process*. Chicago: University of Chicago Press.

Kingdon, John W. 1984. *Agendas, Alternatives, and Public Policies*. New York: HarperCollins.

———. 1989. *Congressmen's Voting Decisions*. 3rd ed. Ann Arbor: University of Michigan Press.

Klein, Ezra. 2015. "Corporations Now Spend More Lobbying Congress than Taxpayers Spend Funding Congress." *Vox*, updated July 15. https://www.vox.com/2015/4/20/8455235/congress-lobbying-money-statistic.

Koger, Gregory. 2010. *Filibustering: A Political History of Obstruction in the House and Senate*. Chicago: University of Chicago Press.

Koger, Gregory, and Matthew J. Lebo. 2017. *Strategic Party Government: Why Winning Trumps Ideology*. Chicago: University of Chicago Press.

Kosar, Kevin R. 2015a. "How to Strengthen Congress." *National Affairs* (Fall): 48–61.

———. 2015b. "Where Taxpayers Pay ($100 Million a Year) but Interest Groups Benefit." *Washington Post*, November 10.

———. 2015c. "Why I Quit the Congressional Research Service." *Washington Monthly*, January/February.

———. 2018a. "The Atrophying of the Congressional Research Service's Role in Supporting Committee Oversight." *Wayne Law Review* 64 (1): 149–62.

———. 2018b. "The Struggle between Objectivity vs. Neutrality Continues at the Congressional Research Service." LegBranch.org, February 13. https://www.legbranch.org/2018-2-11-the-struggle-between-objectivity-vs-neutrality-continues-at-the-congressional-research-service/.

Kousser, Thad. 2005. *Term Limits and the Dismantling of State Legislative Professionalism*. New York: Cambridge University Press.

Kramer, Curtlyn. 2017. "Legislative Branch Staffing Down 45 Percent Since 1975." LegBranch.org. May 30. https://www.legbranch.org/2017-5-25-legislative-branch-staffing-down-45-percent-since-1975/.

Kramnick, Isaac, ed. 1987. *The Federalist Papers*. New York: Penguin Books.

Kravitz, Walter. 1990. "The Advent of the Modern Congress: The Legislative Reorganization Act of 1970." *Legislative Studies Quarterly* 15, no. 3 (August): 375–99.

Krehbiel, Keith. 1991. *Information and Legislative Organization*. Ann Arbor: University of Michigan Press.

———. 1998. *Pivotal Politics: A Theory of US Lawmaking*. Chicago: University of Chicago Press.

Krimmel, Katherine. 2017. "The Efficiencies and Pathologies of Special Interest Partisanship." *Studies in American Political Development* 31, no. 2 (October): 149–69.

Krutz, Glen. 2001. *Hitching a Ride: Omnibus Legislating in the US Congress*. Parliaments and Legislatures Series, edited by Samuel Patterson. Columbus: Ohio State University Press.

———. 2005. "Issues and Institutions: Winnowing in the US Congress." *American Journal of Political Science* 49 (2): 313–26.

Kuklinski, James H., and Norman L. Hurley. 1994. "On Hearing and Interpreting Political Messages: A Cautionary Tale of Citizen Cue-Taking." *Journal of Politics* 56, no. 3 (August): 729–51.

Kuklinski, James H., and Paul J. Quirk. 2000. "Reconsidering the Rational Public: Cognition, Heuristics and Public Opinion." In *Elements of Reason: Cognition, Choice, and the Bounds of Rationality*, edited by Arthur Lupia, Mathew McCubbins, and Samuel Popkin, 153–82. New York: Cambridge University Press.

Lambro, Donald. 1980. *Fat City: How Washington Wastes Your Money*. Washington, DC: Regnery.

LaPira, Timothy M., and Herschel F. Thomas III. 2014. "Revolving Door Lobbyists and Interest Representation." *Interest Groups and Advocacy* 3 (1): 4–29.

———. 2017. *Revolving Door Lobbying: Public Service, Private Influence, and the Unequal Representation of Interests*. Lawrence: University Press of Kansas.

Lau, Richard R., and David P. Redlawsk. 2001. "Advantages and Disadvantages of Using Cognitive Heuristics in Political Decision Making." *American Journal of Political Science* 45, no. 4 (October): 951–71.

Laumann, Edward O., and David Knoke. 1987. *The Organizational State: Social Choice in National Policy Domains*. Madison: University of Wisconsin Press.

Lawless, Jennifer L., Sean M. Theriault, and Samantha Guthrie. 2018. "Nice Girls? Sex, Collegiality, and Bipartisan Cooperation in the US Congress." *Journal of Politics* 80 (4): 1268–82.

Layman, Geoffrey C., and Thomas M. Carsey. 2002. "Party Polarization and 'Conflict Extension' in the American Electorate." *American Journal of Political Science* 46 (4): 786–802.

Lazarus, Jeffrey, and Amy McKay. 2012. "Consequences of the Revolving Door: Evaluating the Lobbying Success of Former Congressional Members and Staff." Paper presented at Annual Meeting of the Midwest Political Science Association, Chicago, April 12–15.

Lazarus, Jeffrey, Amy McKay, and Lindsey Herbel. 2016. "Who Walks through the Revolving Door? Examining the Lobbying Activity of Former Members of Congress." *Interest Groups and Advocacy* 5 (1): 82–100.

Leadership Directories. 1994–2008. *The Congressional Yellow Book*. Washington, DC: Leadership Connect.

Lee, Frances E. 2009. *Beyond Ideology: Politics, Principles, and Partisanship in the US Senate*. Chicago: University of Chicago Press.

———. 2015. "How Party Polarization Affects Governance." *Annual Review of Political Science* 18 (1): 261–82.

———. 2016. *Insecure Majorities: Congress and the Perpetual Campaign*. Chicago: University of Chicago Press.

Lee, Frances E., and Nolan McCarty, eds. 2019. *Can America Govern Itself?* New York: Cambridge University Press.

LegiStorm. n.d. "Congress by the Numbers: 115th Congress (2017–2019)." Accessed February 12, 2018. https://www.legistorm.com/congress_by_numbers/index/by/house/mode/age/term_id/62.html.

Lewallen, Jonathan. 2018. "Congressional Attention and Opportunity Structures: The Select Energy Independence and Global Warming Committee." *Review of Policy Research* 35 (1): 153–69.

Lewallen, Jonathan, Sean M. Theriault, and Bryan D. Jones. 2016. "Congressional Dysfunction: An Information Processing Perspective." *Regulation and Governance* 10 (2): 179–90.

Lewis, David. 2003. *Presidents and the Politics of Agency Design: Political Insulation in the United States Government Bureaucracy, 1946–1997*. Stanford, CA: Stanford University Press.

Li, William, Pablo Azar, David Larochelle, Phil Hill, and Andrew W. Lo. 2015. "Law Is Code: A Software Engineering Approach to Analyzing the United States Code." *Journal of Business and Technology Law* 10 (2): 297–374. https://digitalcommons.law.umaryland.edu/jbtl/vol10/iss2/6.

Liasson, Mara. 2001. "Conservative Advocate." NPR (website). May 25. https://www.npr.org/tem plates/story/story.php?storyId=1123439.

Library of Congress. 1986. *Annual Report of the Librarian of Congress for the Fiscal Year Ending September 30, 1985.* Washington, DC: Library of Congress. https://files.eric.ed.gov/fulltext /ED273292.pdf.

———. 2016. *Fiscal 2017 Budget Justification.* Washington, DC: Library of Congress. https://www .copyright.gov/about/budget/2016/loc-fy2017-budget-justification.pdf.

———. n.d. "History of the Library of Congress." Library of Congress (website). Accessed August 6, 2019. https://www.loc.gov/about/history-of-the-library/.

Lindblom, Charles Edward. 1965. *The Intelligence of Democracy: Decision Making through Mutual Adjustment.* New York: Free Press.

Lipinski, Daniel, William T. Bianco, and Ryan Work. 2003. "What Happens When House Members 'Run with Congress'? The Electoral Consequences of Institutional Loyalty." *Legislative Studies Quarterly* 28 (3): 413–29.

Loewenberg, Gerhard. 1971. "The Role of Parliaments in Modern Political Systems." In *British and French Parliaments in Comparative Perspective*, edited by Gerhard Loewenberg, 1–20. New Brunswick, NJ: Transaction Publishers.

Loomis, Burdett A. 1979. "The Congressional Office as Small (?) Business: New Members Set Up Shop." *Publius* 9, no. 3 (Summer): 35–55.

Lowi, Theodore J. 1979. *The End of Liberalism: The Second Republic of the United States.* Vol. 2. New York: Norton.

Maass, Arthur. 1983. *Congress and the Common Good.* New York: Basic Books.

Madison, James. 1999. "Federalist 48." In *Madison: Writings*, edited by Jack N. Rakove, 281–85. New York: Library of America.

Madonna, Anthony, and Ian Ostrander. 2015. "If Congress Keeps Cutting Its Staff, Who Is Writing Your Laws? You Won't Like the Answer." Monkey Cage (blog), *Washington Post.* August 20. https://www.washingtonpost.com/news/monkey-cage/wp/2015/08/20/if-congress-keeps -cutting-its-staff-who-is-writing-your-laws-you-wont-like-the-answer/.

Mair, Patrick, and Reinhold Hatzinger. 2007. "Extended Rasch Modeling: The eRm Package for the Application of IRT Models in R." *Journal of Statistical Software* 20, no. 9 (May): 1–20.

Maisel, Louis Sandy. 1981. "Congressional Information Sources." In *The House at Work*, edited by Joseph Cooper and G. Calvin Mackenzie, 247–74. Austin: University of Texas Press.

Malbin, Michael J. 1980. *Unelected Representatives: Congressional Staff and the Future of Representative Government.* New York: Basic Books.

Mann, Thomas, and Norman Ornstein. 1992. *Renewing Congress: A First Report.* Washington, DC: Brookings Institution.

———. 2006. *The Broken Branch: How Congress Is Failing America and How to Get It Back on Track.* New York: Oxford University Press.

———. 2012. *It's Even Worse Than It Looks: How the American Constitutional System Collided with the New Politics of Extremism.* New York: Basic Books.

Manning, Jennifer. 2018. *Membership of the 115th Congress: A Profile.* CRS Report 44762. Washington, DC: Congressional Research Service. Updated December 20. https://crsreports.con gress.gov/product/pdf/R/R44762.

Mansbridge, Jane J. 1980. *Beyond Adversary Democracy*. Chicago: University of Chicago Press.

———. 2003. "Rethinking Representation." *American Political Science Review* 97 (4): 515–28.

———. 2009. "A 'Selection Model' of Political Representation." *Journal of Political Philosophy* 17, no. 4 (December): 369–98.

Mansbridge, Jane J., and Cathie Jo Martin, eds. 2013. *Negotiating Agreement in Politics: Report of the Task Force on Negotiating Agreement in Politics*. Washington, DC: American Political Science Association.

———. 2016. *Political Negotiation: A Handbook*. Washington, DC: Brookings Institution.

Mashaw, Jerry L. 2012. *Creating the Administrative Constitution: The Lost One Hundred Years of American Administrative Law*. New Haven, CT: Yale University Press.

Maskell, Jack. 1998. *"Hatch Act" and Other Restrictions in Federal Law on Political Activities of Government Employees*. CRS Report 98-885A. Congressional Research Service. October 23. https://www.everycrsreport.com/reports/98-885.html.

Masters, G. N. 1982. "A Rasch Model for Partial Credit Scoring." *Psychometrika* 47, no. 2 (June): 149–74.

Matthews, Donald R. 1960. *US Senators and Their World*. Chapel Hill, NC: University of North Carolina Press.

Matthews, Donald R., and James Stimson. 1975. *Yeas and Nays: Normal Decision-Making in the US House of Representatives*. New York: John Wiley and Sons.

Mayer, Kenneth R., and David T. Canon. 1995. *The Dysfunctional Congress?* Boulder, CO: Westview Press.

Mayhew, David. R. 1974. *Congress: The Electoral Connection*. New Haven, CT: Yale University Press.

———. 1991. *Divided We Govern: Party Control, Lawmaking, and Investigations, 1946–1990*. New Haven, CT: Yale University Press.

———. 2000. *America's Congress: Actions in the Public Sphere, James Madison through Newt Gingrich*. New Haven, CT: Yale University Press.

McCarty, Nolan. 2016. "The Decline of Regular Order in Appropriations: Does It Matter?" In *Congress and Policy Making in the 21st Century*, edited by Jeffrey Jenkins and Eric Patashnik, 162–86. New York: Cambridge University Press.

McCarty, Nolan, Keith Poole, and Howard Rosenthal. 2006. *Polarized America: The Dance of Ideology and Unequal Riches*. Cambridge, MA: MIT Press.

McCrain, Joshua. 2018. "Revolving Door Lobbyists and the Value of Congressional Staff Connections." *Journal of Politics* 80, no. 4 (October): 1369–83.

McCubbins, Mathew D., Roger Noll, and Barry Weingast. 1987. "Structure and Process, Politics and Policy: Administrative Arrangements and the Political Control of Agencies." *Virginia Law Review* 75:431–82.

McCubbins, Mathew D., and Thomas Schwartz. 1984. "Congressional Oversight Overlooked: Police Patrol versus Fire Alarms." *American Journal of Political Science* 28 (1): 165–77.

McMorris Rodgers, Cathy. n.d. "Unauthorized Spending Accountability Act of 2019." Accessed August 22, 2019. https://mcmorris.house.gov/usaact/.

Miler, Kristina C. 2007. "The View from the Hill: Legislative Perceptions of Constituents." *Legislative Studies Quarterly* 33 (4): 597–628.

———. 2009. "The Limitations of Heuristics for Political Elites." *Political Psychology* 30 (6): 863–94.

———. 2010. *Constituency Representation in Congress: The View from Capitol Hill*. New York: Cambridge University Press.

Mills, Russell W., and Jennifer L. Selin. 2017. "Don't Sweat the Details! Enhancing Congressional Committee Expertise through the Use of Detailees." *Legislative Studies Quarterly* 42, no. 4 (May 15): 611–36.

Moe, Terry. 1989. "The Politics of Bureaucratic Structure." In Chubb and Peterson, *Can the Government Govern?*, 267–329.

Montgomery, Jacob M., and Brendan Nyhan. 2017. "The Effects of Congressional Staff Networks in the US House of Representatives." *Journal of Politics* 79 (3): 745–61.

Mucciaroni, Gary, and Paul J. Quirk. 2006. *Deliberative Choices: Debating Public Policy in Congress.* Annotated ed. Chicago: University of Chicago Press.

Murray, Stuart. 2012. *The Library: An Illustrated History.* New York: Skyhouse.

Neblo, Michael A., Kevin M. Esterling, and David M. J. Lazer. 2018. *Politics with the People: Building a Directly Representative Democracy.* New York: Cambridge University Press.

Newport, Frank, and Lydia Saad. 2016. "Congress' Harshest Critics Identify a Crisis of Influence." Washington, DC: Gallup. June 23. http://www.gallup.com/poll/193079/congress-harshest-crit ics-identify-crisis-influence.aspx.

Nichols, Tom. 2017. *The Death of Expertise: The Campaign against Established Knowledge and Why It Matters.* Oxford: Oxford University Press.

Office of Management and Budget. 2019a. "Historical Tables: Table 12.1—Summary Comparison of Total Outlays for Grants to State and Local Governments, 1940–2024." Accessed September 24, 2019. https://www.whitehouse.gov/wp-content/uploads/2019/03/hist12z1-fy2020.xlsx.

———. 2019b. "Historical Tables: Table 16.1—Total Executive Branch Civilian Full-Time Equivalent (FTE) Employees, 1981–2020." Accessed September 24, 2019. https://www.whitehouse .gov/wp-content/uploads/2019/03/hist16z1-fy2020.xlsx.

Office of Technology Assessment. 1989. *Cost and Effectiveness of Cholesterol Screening in the Elderly.* Washington, DC: Office of Technology Assessment, Congress of the United States, April. https://www.princeton.edu/~ota/disk1/1989/8911/8911.PDF.

———. 1996. *Annual Report to the Congress: Fiscal Year 1995.* Washington, DC: Office of Technology Assessment, Congress of the United States, March. http://ota.fas.org/reports/9600.pdf.

Office of the Legislative Counsel, US House of Representatives. 1995. *House Legislative Counsel's Manual on Drafting Style.* Washington, DC: Government Printing Office, November. http:// legcounsel.house.gov/HOLC/Drafting_Legislation/draftstyle.pdf.

Ornstein, Norman J., Thomas E. Mann, Michael J. Malbin, Andrew Rugg. 2013. *Vital Statistics on Congress: Data on the US Congress—A Joint Effort from Brookings and the American Enterprise Institute.* 4th ed. Washington, DC: American Enterprise Institute and Brookings Institution.

Paine, Albert Bigelow. 1912. *Mark Twain, A Biography: The Personal and Literary Life of Samuel Langhorne Clemens.* Vol. 2. New York: HarperCollins.

Paris, Celia. 2017. "Breaking Down Bipartisanship: When and Why Citizens React to Cooperation across Party Lines." *Public Opinion Quarterly* 81 (2): 473–94.

Parrillo, Nicholas R. 2015. *Against the Profit Motive: The Salary Revolution in American Government, 1780–1940.* New Haven, CT: Yale University Press.

Pearson, Kathryn. 2015. *Party Discipline in the US House of Representatives.* Ann Arbor: University of Michigan Press.

Pertschuk, Michael. 2017. *When the Senate Worked for Us: The Invisible Role of Staffers in Countering Corporate Lobbies.* Nashville, TN: Vanderbilt University Press.

Petersen, R. Eric, and Lara E. Chausow. 2016a. *Staff Pay Levels for Selected Positions in House Member Offices, 2001–2015.* CRS Report R44323. Congressional Research Service. Published

November 9, 2016; updated June 11, 2019, by R. Eric Petersen and Raymond T. Williams. https://crsreports.congress.gov/product/pdf/R/R44323.

———. 2016b. *Staff Pay Levels for Selected Positions in Senators' Offices, FY2001–FY2015.* CRS Report R44324. Congressional Research Service. Published November 9, 2016; updated June 11, 2019, by R. Eric Petersen and Raymond T. Williams. https://crsreports.congress.gov /product/pdf/R/R44324.

Petersen, R. Eric, Sarah J. Eckman, and Lara E. Chausow. 2016. *Congressional Staff: CRS Products on Size, Pay, and Job Tenure.* CRS Report R44688. Congressional Research Service. Updated November 14. https://crsreports.congress.gov/product/pdf/R/R44688.

Petersen, R. Eric, Parker H. Reynolds, and Amber Hope Wilhelm. 2010. *House of Representatives and Staff Levels in Member, Committee, Leadership, and Other Offices, 1977–2010.* CRS Report R41366. Washington, DC: Congressional Research Service.

Pierson, Paul. 2004. *Politics in Time: History, Institutions, and Social Analysis.* Princeton, NJ: Princeton University Press.

Pitkin, Hanna F. 1967. *The Concept of Representation.* Berkeley: University of California Press.

Polsby, Nelson W. 1963. *Community Power and Political Theory.* Vol. 7. New Haven, CT: Yale University Press.

———. 1968. "The Institutionalization of the US House of Representatives." *American Political Science Review* 62 (1): 144–68.

———. 1969. "Policy Analysis and Congress." *Public Policy* 18 (1): 61–74.

———. 1975. "Legislatures." In *Handbook of Political Science,* edited by Nelson W. Polsby and Fred I. Greenstein. Reading, MA: Addison-Wesley.

———. 2004. *How Congress Evolves: Social Bases of Institutional Change.* Oxford: Oxford University Press.

Poole, Keith T. 2006. *Ideology and Congress: A Political Economic History of Roll Call Voting.* 2nd ed. New Brunswick, NJ: Transaction Publishers.

Poole, Keith T., and Howard Rosenthal. 1997. *Congress: A Political-Economic History of Roll Call Voting.* New York: Oxford University Press.

Porter, H. Owen. 1974. "Legislative Experts and Outsiders: the Two-Step Flow of Communication." *Journal of Politics* 36, no. 3 (August): 703–30. https://doi.org/10.2307/2129252.

Posner, Eric, and Adrian Vermeule. 2010. *The Executive Unbound: After the Madisonian Republic.* New York: Oxford University Press.

Powell, G. Bingham. 2000. *Elections as Instruments of Democracy: Majoritarian and Proportional Visions.* New Haven, CT: Yale University Press.

Price, David E. 1971. "Professionals and 'Entrepreneurs': Staff Orientations and Policymaking on Three Senate Committees." *Journal of Politics* 33, no. 2 (May): 316–36.

———. 1972. *Who Makes the Laws?* Cambridge, MA: Schenkman.

Quirk, Paul J. 2005. "Deliberation and Decision Making." In *The Legislative Branch,* edited by Sarah A. Binder and Paul J. Quirk, 314–48. New York: Oxford University Press.

Radford, Gail. 2013. *The Rise of Public Authority: Statebuilding and Economic Development in Twentieth-Century America.* Chicago: University of Chicago Press.

Reich, David. 2016. "Proposals to Address 'Unauthorized Appropriations' Would Likely Do More Harm Than Good." Center on Budget and Policy Priorities. August 31. https://www.cbpp .org/research/federal-budget/proposals-to-address-unauthorized-appropriations-would -likely-do-more-harm#ftn10.

Relyea, Harold C. 2010. "Across the Hill: The Congressional Research Service and Providing Research for Congress—A Retrospective on Origins." *Government Information Quarterly* 27 (4): 414–22.

———. 2012a. "Across the Hill: The Congressional Research Service and Providing Research for Congress—A Retrospective on Personal Experience." *Government Information Quarterly* 29 (2): 275–80.

———. 2012b. "Across the Hill: The Congressional Research Service and Providing Research for Congress—Considering the Future." *Government Information Quarterly* 29 (3): 424–28.

Reynolds, Molly E. 2017a. "Congressional Staff and Operating Expenses." In *Vital Statistics on Congress*. Washington, DC: Brookings Institution. https://www.brookings.edu/wp-content/uploads/2017/01/vitalstats_ch5_full.pdf.

———. 2017b. *Exceptions to the Rule: The Politics of Filibuster Limitations in the US Senate*. Washington, DC: Brookings Institution Press.

———. 2019. "Congressional Committee Data." In *Vital Statistics on Congress*. Washington, DC: Brookings Institution. Updated March 4. https://www.brookings.edu/wp-content/uploads/2017/01/vitalstats_ch4_full.pdf.

Rhodes, Richard. 1987. *The Making of the Atomic Bomb*. New York: Simon and Schuster. Kindle.

Rich, Andrew. 2005. Th*ink Tanks, Public Policy, and the Politics of Expertise*. New York: Cambridge University Press.

Riddick, Floyd, and Alan S. Frumin. 1992. *Riddick's Senate Procedure*. Washington, DC: US Government Printing Office.

Riker, William H. 1962. *The Theory of Political Coalitions*. New Haven, CT: Yale University Press.

———. 1980. "Implications from the Disequilibrium of Majority Rule for the Study of Institutions." *American Political Science Review* 74:432–46.

———. 1982. *Liberalism against Populism: A Confrontation between the Theory of Democracy and the Theory of Social Choice*. San Francisco: W. H. Freeman.

———. 1986. *The Art of Political Manipulation*. New Haven, CT: Yale University Press.

Ripley, Randall B. 1969. *Power in the Senate*. New York: St. Martin's Press.

Rogers, Lindsay. 1941. "The Staffing of Congress." *Political Science Quarterly* 56, no. 1 (March): 1–22.

Rohde, David W. 1991. *Parties and Leaders in the Postreform House*. Chicago: University of Chicago Press.

Rohde, David W., and John Aldrich. 2010. "Consequences of Electoral and Institutional Change: The Evaluation of Conditional Party Government in the US House of Representatives." In *New Directions in American Political Parties*, edited by Jeffrey M. Stonecash. New York: Routledge.

Romero, David W. 2006. "What They Do Does Matter: Incumbent Resource Allocations and the Individual House Vote." *Political Behavior* 28 (3): 241–58.

Romzek, Barbara S., and Jennifer Utter. 1997. "Congressional Legislative Staff: Political Professionals or Clerks?" *American Journal of Political Science* 41 (4): 1251–79.

Roosevelt, Franklin D. 1933. Inaugural Address. American Presidency Project, UC Santa Barbara. March 4. https://www.presidency.ucsb.edu/documents/inaugural-address-8.

———. 1939. "Proclamation 2352, Proclaiming a National Emergency in Connection with the Observance, Safeguarding, and Enforcement of Neutrality and the Strengthening of the National Defense Within the Limits of Peace-Time Authorizations." American Presidency

Project, UC Santa Barbara. September 8. https://www.presidency.ucsb.edu/documents/pro
clamation-2352-proclaiming-national-emergency-connection-with-the-observance.

———. 1941. "Proclamation 2487, Proclaiming That an Unlimited National Emergency Con-
fronts This Country, Which Requires That Its Military, Naval Air and Civilian Defenses Be
Put on the Basis of Readiness to Repel Any and All Acts or Threats of Aggression Directed
Toward Any Part of the Western Hemisphere." American Presidency Project, UC Santa
Barbara. May 27. https://www.presidency.ucsb.edu/documents/proclamation-2487-proclaiming
-that-unlimited-national-emergency-confronts-this-country.

———. 1942. "Message to Congress on Stabilizing the Economy." American Presidency Project, UC Santa Barbara. September 7. https://www.presidency.ucsb.edu/documents/message
-congress-stabilizing-the-economy.

Rosenbloom, David H. 2000. *Building a Legislative-Centered Public Administration: Congress
and the Administrative State, 1946–1999.* Tuscaloosa: University of Alabama Press.

Rowberg, Richard. 2016. "How Did the Reports of OTA, the Congressional Research Service,
and the National Academies Differ?" LegBranch.org. November 15. https://www.legbranch
.org/2016-11-14-how-did-the-reports-of-ota-the-congressional-research-service-and-the
-national-academies-differ/.

R Street Institute and Demand Progress. 2017. "Letter to House on CBO Amendments." July 26.
https://s3.amazonaws.com/demandprogress/letters/2017-07-26-Letter-to-House-on-CBO
-amendments.pdf.

Rubin, Edward. 2005. *Beyond Camelot: Rethinking Politics and Law for the Modern State.* Princeton, NJ: Princeton University Press.

Rubin, Richard. 2017. "A Bill Without a Hearing?" WSJ.com (*Wall Street Journal*), November 13.
http://www.wsj.com/livecoverage/tax-bill-2017/card/1510607902.

Sabatier, Paul, and David Whiteman. 1985. "Legislative Decision Making and Substantive Policy
Information: Models of Information Flow." *Legislative Studies Quarterly* 10 (3): 395–421.

Salisbury, Robert H., and Kenneth A. Shepsle. 1981a. "Congressional Staff Turnover and the
Ties-That-Bind." *American Political Science Review* 75 (2): 381–96.

———. 1981b. "US Congressman as Enterprise." *Legislative Studies Quarterly* 6, no. 4 (November 1):
559–76.

Saturno, James, Jessica Tollestrup, and Megan Lynch. 2016. *The Congressional Appropriations Process: An Introduction.* CRS Report R42388. Washington, DC: Congressional Research Service.

Schick, Allen. 1975. "The Battle of the Budget." *Proceedings of the Academy of Political Science*
32 (1): 51–70.

———. 1980. *Congress and Money: Budgeting, Spending and Taxing.* Washington, DC: Urban
Institute Press.

———. 2007. *The Federal Budget: Politics, Policy and Process.* 3rd ed. Washington, DC: Brookings Institution Press.

Schickler, Eric. 2000. "Institutional Change in the House of Representatives, 1867–1998: A Test
of Partisan and Ideological Power Balance Models." *American Political Science Review* 94,
no. 2 (June): 269–88.

———. 2001. *Disjointed Pluralism: Institutional Innovation and the Development of the US Congress.* Princeton, NJ: Princeton University Press.

Schlozman, Kay Lehman, Sidney Verba, and Henry E. Brady. 2012. *The Unheavenly Chorus: Unequal Political Voice and the Broken Promise of American Democracy.* Princeton, NJ: Princeton University Press.

Schuman, Daniel. 2010. *Keeping Congress Competent: Staff Pay, Turnover, and What it Means for Democracy.* Washington, DC: Sunlight Foundation, December 21. https://sunlightfoundation .com/wp-content/uploads/2016/11/Staff-Pay-Blogpost.pdf.

Schwin, Beth. 1992. "Cox Blasts Government Waste but Spends Big Bucks." States News Service, November 5.

Seelye, Katherine Q. 1994. "GOP Decides to Halt Money to 28 Caucuses." *New York Times*, December 7.

Serra, George. 1994. "What's in It for Me? The Impact of Congressional Casework on Incumbent Evaluation." *American Politics Quarterly* 22 (4): 403–20.

Shapiro, Ira. 2018. *Broken: Can the Senate Save Itself and the Country?* Lanham, MD: Rowman and Littlefield.

Shepherd, Katie. 2016. "Part-Time Jobs and Thrift: How Unpaid Interns in D.C. Get By." *New York Times*, July 5. https://www.nytimes.com/2016/07/06/us/part-time-jobs-and-thrift-how -unpaid-interns-in-dc-get-by.html.

Shepsle, Kenneth A. 1988. "Representation and Governance: The Great Legislative Trade-off." *Political Science Quarterly* 103 (3): 461–84.

———. 1989. "The Changing Textbook Congress." In Chubb and Peterson, *Can the Government Govern?*, 338–51.

Shepsle, Kenneth, and Mark Bonchek. 1997. *Analyzing Politics: Rationality, Behavior, and Institutions.* New York: W. W. Norton.

Shepsle, Kenneth A., Robert P. Van Houweling, Samuel J. Abrams, and Peter C. Hanson. 2009. "The Senate Electoral Cycle and Bicameral Appropriations Politics." *American Journal of Political Science* 53 (2): 343–59.

Simon, Herbert A., and Allen Newell. 1964. "Information Processing in Computer and Man." *American Scientist* 52, no. 3 (September): 281–300.

Sinclair, Barbara. 1983. *Majority Leadership in the United States House.* Baltimore: Johns Hopkins University Press.

———. 1989. *The Transformation of the US Senate.* Baltimore: Johns Hopkins University Press.

———. 1990. "Congressional Leadership: A Review Essay and a Research Agenda." In *Leading Congress: New Styles, New Strategies*, edited by John J. Kornacki. Washington, DC: CQ Press.

———. 1995. *Legislators, Leaders, and Lawmaking: The US House of Representatives in the Postreform Era.* Baltimore: Johns Hopkins University Press.

———. 1998. *Legislators, Leaders, and Lawmaking: The US House of Representatives in the Postreform Era.* Baltimore: Johns Hopkins University Press.

———. 2003. "The Dream Fulfilled? Party Development in Congress, 1950–2000." In *Responsible Partisanship? The Evolution of American Political Parties since 1950*, edited by John C. Green and Paul S. Herrnson, 121–40. Lawrence: University of Kansas Press.

———. 2007. *Unorthodox Lawmaking: New Legislative Processes in the US Congress.* 3rd ed. Washington, DC: CQ Press.

———. 2008. "Spoiling the Sausages? How a Polarized Congress Deliberates and Legislates." In *Red and Blue Nation? Consequences and Correction of America's Polarized Politics*, edited by Pietro S. Nivola and David Brady, 55–87. Washington, DC: Brookings Institution Press.

———. 2016. *Unorthodox Lawmaking: New Legislative Processes in the US Congress.* 5th ed. Washington, DC: Sage CQ Press.

Skocpol, Theda. 1995. *Protecting Soldiers and Mothers: The Political Origins of Social Policy in the United States.* Cambridge, MA: Harvard University Press.

Skowronek, Stephen. 1982. *The Politics Presidents Make: Leadership from John Adams to Bill Clinton*. Rev. ed. Cambridge, MA: Belknap Press of Harvard University Press.

Smith, Steven S. 1989. *Call to Order: Floor Politics in the House and Senate*. Washington, DC: Brookings Institution Press.

———. 2007. *Party Influence in Congress*. New York: Cambridge University Press.

———. 2014. *The Senate Syndrome: The Evolution of Procedural Warfare in the Modern US Senate*. Norman: University of Oklahoma Press.

Smith, Steven S., and Christopher J. Deering. 1984. *Committees in Congress*. Washington, DC: CQ Press.

Smith, Steven S., and Hong Min Park. 2013. "Americans' Attitudes about the Senate Filibuster." *American Politics Research* 41 (5): 735–60.

Starr, Paul. 2011. *Remedy and Reaction: The Peculiar American Struggle over American Health Care Reform*. New Haven, CT: Yale University Press.

Stathis, Stephen W. 2014. "CRS at 100: A History." In *CRS at 100: The Congressional Research Service*, 9–43. Washington, DC: Congressional Research Service. https://archive.org/details /CRSAt100Booklet072014.

Stein, Harry, and Ethan Gurwitz. 2015. "Congress Makes Itself Dysfunctional with Legislative Branch Cuts." Center for American Progress, June 15. https://www.americanprogress.org /issues/economy/news/2015/06/15/114975/congress-makes-itself-dysfunctional-with-leg islative-branch-cuts/.

Stid, Daniel. 2017. "Two Pathways for Congressional Reform." In Connelly, Pitney, and Schmitt, *Is Congress Broken?*, 11–36.

Stimson, James A. 2015. *Tides of Consent: How Public Opinion Shapes American Politics*. New York: Cambridge University Press.

Stokes, Donald E. 1963. "Spatial Models of Party Competition." *American Political Science Review* 57 (2): 368–77.

Stone, Deborah A. 1997. *Policy Paradox: The Art of Political Decision Making*. New York: W. W. Norton.

Strand, Mark, and Tim Lang. 2017. "Fixing the Authorization Process: Restoring Checks and Balances." Congressional Institute. October 19. https://www.conginst.org/2017/10/19/fixing -the-authorization-process-restoring-checks-and-balances/.

Sunstein, Cass R. 2006. *Infotopia: How Many Minds Produce Knowledge*. New York: Oxford University Press.

Swift, Elaine K. 2002. *The Making of an American Senate: Reconstitutive Change in Congress, 1787–1841*. Ann Arbor: University of Michigan Press.

Tapper, Jake. 2016. "Zombies among Us: Government Programs Live Past 'Expiration Date.'" Originally aired February 19, on *The Lead with Jake Tapper*. CNN. Video, 2:59. http://www.cnn.com /videos/tv/2016/02/19/america-debt-crisis-zombie-government-programs-tapper-dnt.cnn.

Taylor, Steven L., Matthew Soberg Shugart, Arend Lijphart, and Bernard Grofman. 2014. *A Different Democracy: American Government in a 31-Country Perspective*. New Haven, CT: Yale University Press.

Tetlock, Philip E. 2005. *Expert Political Judgment: How Good Is It? How Can We Know?* Princeton, NJ: Princeton University Press.

Theriault, Sean M. 2008. *Party Polarization in Congress*. Cambridge: Cambridge University Press.

———. 2013. *The Gingrich Senators: The Roots of Partisan Warfare in Congress*. New York: Oxford University Press.

Theriault, Sean M., and Jonathan Lewallen. 2012. "Congressional Parties and the Policy Process." In *The Parties Respond*, 5th ed., edited by Mark D. Brewer and L. Sandy Maisel. Boulder, CO: Westview Press.

Tiefer, Charles. 2016. *The Polarized Congress: The Post-Traditional Procedure of Its Current Struggles*. Lanham, MD: University Press of America.

Tollestrup, Jessica, and Brian Yeh. 2014. *Authorization of Appropriations: Procedural and Legal Issues*. CRS Report R42098. Washington, DC: Congressional Research Service.

Trask, Roger R. 1991. *GAO History, 1921–1991*. Report No. OP-3-HP. Washington, DC: Government Accounting Office.

Tress, Will. 2009. "Lost Laws: What We Can't Find in the United States Code." *Golden Gate University Law Review* 40 (2): 129.

Truman, David B. 1951. *The Governmental Process; Political Interests and Public Opinion*. New York: Knopf.

Turner, Michael. 2012. "Turner Returns over 11% of Office Budget to US Treasury." January 25. News release. https://turner.house.gov/media-center/press-releases/turner-returns-over-11-of-office-budget-to-us-treasury.

Tversky, Amos, and Daniel Kahneman. 1974. "Judgment under Uncertainty: Heuristics and Biases." *Science* 185, no. 4157 (September 27): 1124–31.

Urbinati, Nadia. 2006. *Representative Democracy: Principles and Genealogy*. Chicago: University of Chicago Press.

US Bureau of Economic Analysis. 2019a. "Gross Domestic Product: Implicit Price Deflator [GDPDEF]." Accessed September 24 via FRED, Federal Reserve Bank of St. Louis database. https://fred.stlouisfed.org/series/GDPDEF.

———. 2019b. "Population [B230RC0A052NBEA]." Accessed September 24 via FRED, Federal Reserve Bank of St. Louis database. https://fred.stlouisfed.org/series/B230RC0A052NBEA.

US House of Representatives. 2018. "Statement of Disbursements." Data for 2001–17, as compiled by and downloaded by LegiStorm, accessed March 2018. https://www.house.gov/the-house-explained/open-government/statement-of-disbursements.

US Senate. 2007. "Rule XX: Questions of Order." In *Standing Rules of the Senate*. Washington, DC: Government Printing Office.

Vera, Carlos. 2017. "Memo to Jason Chaffetz: These Are the Congressional Workers Who Actually Need a Stipend." *Washington Post*, July 7. https://www.washingtonpost.com/opinions/memo-to-jason-chaffetz-these-are-the-congressional-workers-who-actually-need-a-stipend/2017/07/07/2093c776-619b-11e7-8adc-fea80e32bf47_story.html.

Vincent, Carol Hardy. 1997. *House Committee Staff and Funding*. CRS Report 97-148 GOV. Washington, DC. May 30.

Vinik, Danny. 2016. "Meet Your Unauthorized Federal Government." *Politico*, February 3. https://www.politico.com/agenda/story/2016/02/government-agencies-programs-unauthorized-000036-000037.

Volden, Craig, and Alan E. Wiseman. 2014. *Legislative Effectiveness in the United States Congress: The Lawmakers*. New York: Cambridge University Press.

———. 2016. "Are Bipartisan Lawmakers More Effective?" Nashville, TN: Center for the Study of Democratic Institutions.

———. 2018. "Legislative Effectiveness in the United States Senate." *Journal of Politics* 80 (2): 731–35.

Wallach, Philip. 2018. "Congress Indispensable." *National Affairs* 34 (Winter): 19–32.

Wallison, Ethan. 2001. "House Staffers Getting Big Salary Increases." *Roll Call*, January 4.

Wallner, James I. 2013. *The Death of Deliberation: Partisanship and Polarization in the United States Senate*. New York: Lexington Books.

———. 2017. "Intraparty Caucus Formation in the US Congress." In *Party and Procedure in the United States Congress*, 2nd ed., edited by Jacob R. Straus and Matthew E. Glassman, 261–78. Lanham, MD: Rowman and Littlefield.

Warren, Mark E., and Jane Mansbridge. 2016. "Deliberative Negotiations." In Mansbridge and Martin, *Political Negotiation*, 141–96.

Washington Post. 1886. "The Latest Salary Grab." July 10.

Wawro, Gregory J. 2000. *Legislative Entrepreneurship in the US House of Representatives*. Ann Arbor: University of Michigan Press.

Wawro, Gregory J., and Eric Schickler. 2006. *Filibuster: Obstruction and Lawmaking in the US Senate*. Princeton, NJ: Princeton University Press.

Weisman, Jonathan. 2012. "Nonpartisan Tax Report Withdrawn After GOP Protest." *New York Times*, November 1.

Werner, Erica. 2018. "Congress's Special Committee to Fix the Broken Budget Process Has Broken Down." *Washington Post*, November 29. https://www.washingtonpost.com/business/econ omy/congresss-special-committee-to-fix-the-broken-budget-process-has-broken-down /2018/11/29/51768f50-f424-11e8-aeea-b85fd44449f5_story.html.

White, Joseph. 1989. "The Functions and Power of the House Appropriations Committee." PhD diss., University of California–Berkeley.

Whiteman, David. 1995. *Communication in Congress: Members, Staff, and the Search for Information*. Lawrence: University of Kansas Press.

Whittington, Keith. 1999. *Constitutional Construction: Divided Powers and Constitutional Meaning*. Cambridge, MA: Harvard University Press.

Whyman, Michelle. 2017. "What Is a Productive Congress?" Paper presented at the Midwest Political Science Association Annual Conference, Chicago, April 6–9.

Wildavsky, Aaron. 1979. *The Politics of the Budgetary Process*. 3rd ed. Boston: Little, Brown.

Wilson, Woodrow. (1885) 1981. *Congressional Government: A Study in American Politics*. Baltimore: Johns Hopkins University Press.

Wolak, Jennifer. 2017. "Support for Compromise in Principle and in Practice." Paper presented at the Annual Meeting of the American Political Science Association, San Francisco, August 31–September 3.

Wolfensberger, Donald R. 2013. "A Brief History of Congressional Reform Efforts." Washington, DC: Bipartisan Policy Center and Woodrow Wilson Center. https://www.wilsoncenter.org /sites/default/files/brief_history_congressional_reform_efforts.pdf.

Wong, Scott. 2012. "Frugal Senators Return Office Funds." *Politico*, January 20.

Woon, Jonathan, and Sarah Anderson. 2012. "Political Bargaining and the Timing of Congressional Appropriations." *Legislative Studies Quarterly* 37 (4): 409–36.

Wyatt, Alexandra M. 2018. "Memorandum to Congressional Research Service and the Library of Congress." January 12. https://www.legbranch.org/app/uploads/2018/02/2018-01-12-Hayden -Mazanec-Letter.pdf.

Zelizer, Julian E. 2004. *On Capitol Hill: The Struggle to Reform Congress and Its Consequences, 1948–2000*. New York: Cambridge University Press.

———. 2006. *On Capitol Hill: The Struggle to Reform Congress and its Consequences, 1948–2000*. New York: Cambridge University Press.

———. 2015. "When Liberals Were Organized." *American Prospect*, January 22.

Contributors

E. SCOTT ADLER is dean of the Graduate School and professor of political science at the University of Colorado–Boulder. His current research uses theoretical models of legislative organization to examine congressional agenda setting and committee power. He is the author of two books and the coeditor of *The Macropolitics of Congress* (Princeton University Press, 2006). Adler received his PhD from Columbia University.

RYAN W. BELL is a graduate student in the Department of Politics at Princeton University, specializing in American politics and quantitative methods after having completed his BA in political science and mathematics. His primary research interests are in political behavior, identity, and attitudes generally, and the effects of political alienation on participation more specifically.

RUTH BLOCH RUBIN is assistant professor at the University of Chicago and studies legislative institutions, political parties, and American political development. Her current work explores impacts of political party divisions on Congress. She is also researching Congress's provision of health services to American Indians in the early nineteenth century. She was previously a Robert Wood Johnson Scholar in Health Policy Research at Harvard. Bloch Rubin received her PhD from the University of California–Berkeley.

CASEY BURGAT is a senior governance fellow at the R Street Institute, where he researches and writes about congressional capacity and ways to make the first branch of government work better. He received his PhD from the University of Maryland–College Park, where his dissertation focused on the impacts of congressional staff.

JESSE M. CROSSON is visiting research scholar at Princeton University's Center for the Study of Democratic Politics and assistant professor of political science at Trinity University in San Antonio, Texas. He received his PhD from the University of

Michigan in 2019 and studies how electoral competition, lobbying, and legislative resources influence policy change and gridlock in American legislatures.

JAMES M. CURRY is associate professor of political science at the University of Utah. He is author of *Legislating in the Dark* (University of Chicago Press, 2015) and recipient of the 2016 Alan Rosenthal Prize. His research has appeared in the *Journal of Politics*, *Legislative Studies Quarterly*, *Perspectives on Politics*, and other journals. He received his PhD from the University of Maryland in 2011 and previously worked in the Capitol Hill offices of Rep. Daniel Lipinski (D-IL) and the House Appropriations Committee.

LEE DRUTMAN is a senior fellow in the Political Reform program at New America. He is the author of *Breaking the Two-Party Doom Loop: The Case for Multiparty Democracy in America* (Oxford University Press, 2020) and *The Business of America is Lobbying* (Oxford University Press, 2015). He is the recipient of the 2016 Robert A. Dahl Award.

ALEXANDER C. FURNAS is a PhD candidate in political science at the University of Michigan in American politics and quantitative methods. He specializes in the role of information and expertise in the US Congress. His dissertation examines how Congress uses private information from outside organizations in the policymaking process. He is a coprincipal investigator of both the 2017 and 2019 Congressional Capacity Surveys.

PETER HANSON is associate professor of political science at Grinnell College and the author of *Too Weak to Govern: Majority Party Power and Appropriations in the US Senate* (Cambridge University Press, 2014). He is a specialist on Congress and the politics of the federal budget. He was a staff member for Senate Democratic Leader Tom Daschle from 1996 to 2002. He received his PhD from the University of California–Berkeley.

LAUREL HARBRIDGE-YONG is associate professor in the Department of Political Science and faculty fellow at the Institute for Policy Research at Northwestern University. Her research focuses on partisan conflict and the lack of compromise in American politics. She is the author of *Is Bipartisanship Dead?* (Cambridge University Press, 2015) and articles in the *American Journal of Political Science*, *Legislative Studies Quarterly*, and *Political Behavior*, among others. She received her PhD from Stanford University.

ALEXANDER HERTEL-FERNANDEZ is an assistant professor of international and public affairs at Columbia University, where he studies American political economy. He is the author most recently of *State Capture: How Conservative Activists, Big Businesses, and Wealthy Donors Reshaped the American States—and the Nation* (Oxford University Press, 2019).

CHARLES HUNT is an assistant professor of political science at Boise State University. His primary areas of study include congressional elections, representation, and partisanship. He received his PhD from the University of Maryland.

BRYAN D. JONES is a professor in the Department of Government at the University of Texas–Austin and codirects the Policy Agendas Project. His research interests center on the study of public policy processes, American governing institutions, and the connection between human decision making and organizational behavior. Jones has also held professorships at the University of Washington, Texas A&M University, Wayne State University, and the University of Houston. He is author or coauthor of five books.

KEVIN R. KOSAR is a resident scholar at the American Enterprise Institute and a cofounder of the nonpartisan Legislative Branch Capacity Working Group. Previously, he was a vice president at the R Street Institute and a researcher at the Congressional Research Service. He studies Congress, legislative branch support agencies, and American governance institutions. He received his PhD from New York University.

STEFANI R. LANGEHENNIG received her PhD at the University of Colorado–Boulder studying American politics and political methodology. Her research focuses on institutions, policymaking, and congressional organization.

TIMOTHY M. LAPIRA is professor of political science at James Madison University in Virginia and faculty affiliate at the Center for Effective Lawmaking. In 2019, he served as the American Political Science Association Public Service Fellow detailed to the United States House Select Committee on the Modernization of Congress. His expertise is on Congress and its staff, interest groups, and lobbying. He is coauthor of *Revolving Door Lobbying: Public Service, Private Influence, and the Unequal Representation of Interests* (University Press of Kansas, 2017). He is principal investigator of the 2017 and 2019 Congressional Capacity Surveys. LaPira received his PhD from Rutgers.

FRANCES E. LEE is professor of politics and public affairs at Princeton University. She is author of *Insecure Majorities: Congress and the Perpetual Campaign* (University of Chicago Press, 2016) and *Beyond Ideology: Politics, Principles, and Partisanship in the US Senate* (University of Chicago Press, 2009) and coauthor of *Sizing Up the Senate: The Unequal Consequences of Equal Representation* (University of Chicago Press, 1999). Lee received her PhD from Vanderbilt University.

JONATHAN LEWALLEN is assistant professor of political science at the University of Tampa. His research focuses on the policy process and agenda setting in US political institutions and has appeared in journals including the *Review of Policy Research* and *Presidential Studies Quarterly*. He is working on a book that explains the decline in congressional lawmaking as a committee-driven phenomenon. Lewallen received his PhD from the University of Texas–Austin.

GEOFFREY M. LORENZ is assistant professor of Political Science at the University of Nebraska–Lincoln and a faculty affiliate of the Center for Effective Lawmaking.

His expertise is in interest group influence and legislative behavior in the US Congress. His research has been published in the *Journal of Politics* and *Interest Groups and Advocacy*. He received his PhD from the University of Michigan.

ANTHONY MADONNA is an associate professor of political science at the University of Georgia. His research interests include American political institutions and development, with an emphasis on US Congressional politics and procedure. His work has appeared in such journals as the *American Journal of Political Science*, the *Journal of Politics*, and *Legislative Studies Quarterly*. He received his PhD from Washington University in St. Louis.

KRISTINA C. MILER is an associate professor in the Department of Government and Politics at the University of Maryland. She is the author of *Poor Representation: Congress and the Politics of Poverty* (Cambridge University Press, 2018), which received the APSA Woodrow Wilson Award, and *Constituency Representation in Congress: The View from Capitol Hill* (Cambridge University Press, 2011), which received the APSA Alan Rosenthal Prize. Her research focuses on political representation in the US Congress. She received her PhD from the University of Michigan.

IAN OSTRANDER is assistant professor in the Department of Political Science at Michigan State University. His research interests concern American political institutions, with a particular emphasis on the US presidency, Congress, bureaucracy, and the interaction of all three. His work has appeared in such journals as the *American Journal of Political Science*, *Legislative Studies Quarterly*, and *Presidential Studies Quarterly*. He received his PhD from Washington University in St. Louis.

MOLLY E. REYNOLDS is a Brookings Governance Studies senior fellow. Her book *Exceptions to the Rule* (Brookings Institution Press, 2017) explores the creation, use, and consequences of the budget reconciliation process and other procedures that prevent Senate filibusters. Her research focuses on Congress, how rules and procedures affect domestic policy, the congressional budget process, and the consequences of partisanship. She also supervises the maintenance of the Brooking Institution's *Vital Statistics on Congress*. Reynolds received her PhD from the University of Michigan.

SEAN M. THERIAULT is a Distinguished Professor in the Department of Government at the University of Texas–Austin. He has published three books on Congress, dealing with party polarization, competition, and public attention. He has also published numerous journal articles on subjects ranging from presidential rhetoric to congressional careers and the Louisiana Purchase to the Pendleton Act of 1883. Theriault received his PhD from Stanford University.

CRAIG VOLDEN is professor of public policy and politics at the University of Virginia, with appointments in the Frank Batten School of Leadership and Public Policy and the Woodrow Wilson Department of Politics. He is codirector of the Center for Effective Lawmaking. He studies legislative politics and the interaction among political institutions, with a focus on what policy choices arise from legislative–executive relations and from American federalism. He received his PhD from Stanford University.

PHILIP A. WALLACH is a senior fellow in governance at the R Street Institute. In 2019, he was fellow at the United States House Select Committee on the Modernization of Congress. He researches the American separation of powers with a focus on the relationship between Congress and the administrative state. He was previously a senior fellow in governance studies at the Brookings Institution, where he authored *To the Edge: Legality, Legitimacy, and the Responses to the 2008 Financial Crisis* (2015).

JAMES WALLNER is a senior fellow at the R Street Institute, where he researches and writes about the theory and practice of democratic politics with an emphasis on Congress, political parties, and the policy process. He is also a professorial lecturer in the Department of Government at American University and a fellow at its Center for Congressional and Presidential Studies.

ALAN E. WISEMAN is chair of the Department of Political Science at Vanderbilt University, where he is the Cornelius Vanderbilt Professor of Political Economy, the Joe B. Wyatt Distinguished University Professor, and professor of political science and law. He is codirector of the Center for Effective Lawmaking. His research interests focus on legislative politics, regulation and bureaucratic policymaking, and business–government relations. He received his PhD from Stanford University.

Index

Page numbers in italics refer to illustrations and tables.

doing communications work, 37; recent data for, 279n6

Lee, Frances E., 7, 37, 157, 242

Legislative Branch Capacity Working Group, 2–3

legislative branch support agencies: and balance of power in two chambers and between branches of government, 129; downsizing and fear of political retribution, 136–41; employees of, 128; frequency of staffer use of vs. other government agencies and perceived trustworthiness for budget and health care issues, 136, 137; FY 2016 output, 135–36, 136; increase in responsibilities without necessary resources, 46–48, 48; role of increasing legislative capacity and reducing legislators' dependency on lobbyists, 128–29; staff head counts, 1976–2015, 137, 138; staffing and funding levels, 1980–2016, 42–46, 49, 135. See also Congressional Budget Office (CBO); Congressional Research Service (CRS); Government Accountability Office (GAO); Office of Technology Assessment (OTA)

"legislative cartels," theory of, 168

Legislative Drafting Office, 260

legislative procedure. See Appropriations Committee and appropriation process; authorization; committees/committee system; Senate, amendment process

legislative productivity: assessments of, 192–93; and bipartisanship, 239, 240, 251; effects on party and institutional approval, 242. See also Appropriations Committee and appropriation process; congressional staff experience, and legislator effectiveness; reauthorization

Legislative Reference Service, 260

Legislative Reorganization Act of 1946, 22, 32, 34, 64, 130–31, 260, 268, 280n3, 286n33

Legislative Reorganization Act of 1970, 34, 141, 182, 262, 264

Legislative Reorganization Act of 1978, 65

legislative service organizations, 266

LegiStorm, personnel compensation database, 119, 211, 281nn5–6

Lend-Lease Act of 1941, 62

Lewallen, Jonathan, 6

Library of Congress, 130, 284n2

Lincoln, Abraham, assassination of, 55

Lloyd-LaFollette Act of 1912, 58

lobbyists: congressional dependence on expertise of, 11, 32, 268, 269; and increased powers of special interests, 234

Lockheed Martin, 68

logrolling, 21, 235

Lorenz, Geoffrey, 6

Louisiana Purchase, 53

Lynch, Loretta, 180

Madison, James, 53, 179, 284n5, 287n2 (ch. 10)

Madonna, Anthony, 7, 293n16

Maloney, Francis, 259

Mansbridge, Jane, 157

Mansfield, Mike, 4

"marble cake" federalism, 68

Markey, Betsy, 40

Mayhew, David, catalog of historic statutes, 192–93

McCarthy hearings, 17

McCarty, Nolan, 151

McConnell, Mitch, 172, 173, 287n13

McCormack, John, 260

McCrain, Joshua, 209–10, 289n6

McCubbins, Mathew D., 168

"messaging bills," 243, 291n3

Michel, Bob, 4

Mikulski, Barbara, 180

Miler, Kristina, 6, 283n1

Monroney, Mike, 64, 259, 261

Montgomery, Jacob, 209

Murkowski, Lisa, 242

National Emergencies Act of 1976, 66

nationalization, of American politics, 32

National Labor Relations Board, 59

National Recovery Administration, 62

National School Lunch Act, 201

National Science Foundation, 194

New America, 2

New Deal: agencies with independent policy authority, 61–62; and increased role of presidency, 31–32; and parochial patronage regime, 22

New York Times, 77, 193, 204

9/11 attacks, 267

Nixon, Richard, 66, 263

Norquist, Grover, 51

Northrop Grumman, 68

"nuclear option," 161, 172, 287n13

Nyhan, Brendan, 209

Obama, Barack, 69

Obey Commission (1976–77), 34

Office of Law Revision Counsel (OLRC), 197, 198, 288n12

Office of Management and Budget (founded as Bureau of the Budget), 131, 260

Office of Price Administration, 63

Office of Technology Assessment (OTA), 128, 285n20; defunded in 1995, 43, 134, 270; justifications for creation of, 132–33; and questions about the feasibility of the Strategic Defense Initiative (SDI) missile defense system ("Star Wars"), 138

Office of the Clerk of the House of Representatives, 284n2